Better Homes and Gardens®

T·R·E·A·S·U·R·Y
OF
COUNTRY
CRAFTS AND FOODS

BETTER HOMES AND GARDENS® BOOKS

Editor: Gerald M. Knox
Art Director: Ernest Shelton
Managing Editor: David A. Kirchner

Crafts Editor: Nancy Lindemeyer
Crafts Books Editor: Joan Cravens
Associate Crafts Books Editors: Debra Felton, Laura Holtorf,
James A. Williams

Food and Nutrition Editor: Doris Eby
Department Head—Cook Books: Sharyl Heiken
Senior Food Editor: Elizabeth Woolever
Senior Associate Food Editors: Sandra Granseth,
Rosemary C. Hutchinson
Associate Food Editors: Jill Burmeister, Julia Malloy,
Linda Henry, Alethea Sparks, Marcia Stanley, Diane Yanney
Recipe Development Editor: Marion Viall
Test Kitchen Director: Sharon Stilwell
Test Kitchen Home Economists: Jean Brekke, Kay Cargill,
Marilyn Cornelius, Maryellyn Krantz, Marge Steenson

Associate Art Director (Managing): Randall Yontz
Associate Art Directors (Creative): Linda Ford, Neoma Alt West
Copy and Production Editors: Nancy Nowiszewski,
Lamont Olson, Mary Helen Schiltz, David A. Walsh
Assistant Art Directors: Faith Berven, Harijs Priekulis
Graphic Designers: Mike Burns, Alisann Dixon, Mike Eagleton,
Lynda Haupert, Deb Miner, Lyne Neymeyer,
D. Greg Thompson

Editor in Chief: Neil Kuehnl
Group Editorial Services Director: Duane Gregg

General Manager: Fred Stines
Director of Publishing: Robert B. Nelson
Director of Retail Marketing: Jamie Martin
Director of Direct Marketing: Arthur Heydendael

Treasury of Country Crafts and Foods
Crafts Editor: Ann Levine
Food Editor: Rosemary C. Hutchinson
Copy and Production Editor: Lamont Olson
Graphic Designer: Faith Berven

Our seal assures you that every recipe in
Treasury of Country Crafts and Foods is endorsed by
the Better Homes and Gardens Test Kitchen. Each recipe is
tested for family appeal, practicality, and deliciousness.

TREASURY OF COUNTRY CRAFTS AND FOODS

CONTENTS

We Americans are heirs to a history of crafts and stitchery that remains uniquely our own. It developed from many cultures and was brought to our shores by immigrants who shared their native skills.

From this medley of crafts grew a style we've come to call "American country." To salute the generations who contributed to our craft heritage, here and on the next 10 pages are traditional country crafts that look as charming today as they did in days gone by. Instructions for the projects begin on page 49.

This white-on-white embroidered tablecloth (also called "whitework") is reminiscent of the lacy look of days gone by. Worked in satin and outline stitches, it gives this room the warmth and feeling of a country inn. Once you master the basic needle-and-thread techniques, you can apply them to almost anything, including linen blouses such as the ones shown here. Some of these embroidered designs are padded to highlight certain motifs. Instructions for these projects begin on page 65.

A handmade coverlet such as this can be highly personal and richly prized. It conjures up images of old-world crafters who make something beautiful from the simplest materials. This craft originated in the mountains of Appalachia, and it is just as easy to create this coverlet today as it was in the days of our forebears. All you do is work French knots into a graceful design using cotton string and unbleached muslin. When finished, the coverlet makes a family heirloom to pass on to future generations. The complete instructions begin on page 127.

Practical materials and enduring designs combine to make this appliquéd prairie rug an attractive addition to any home. Handmade with felt appliqués on felt backgrounds, the designs are stitched in place by machine, a convenient change from pioneer days when garments and home accessories were stitched by hand. The five different designs make a striking pattern portfolio. When finished, the 15 squares are arranged in rows to make a 37x64-inch rug in nature's glorious colors. Use leftover felt to stitch matching pillows if desired. The complete instructions begin on page 157.

ull of warmth and old-time comfort, this true lovers' knot quilt is an example of the pioneer adage, "waste not, want not." It uses bits and pieces of blue and white fabrics like those culled from the sewing baskets of colonial women. This pattern, a variation of the nine-patch, is an example of American quilting, a folk art that is part of our national history. Each quilt block consists of square and rectangular shapes pieced together with straight seams that even an inexperienced quilter can master. The quilt blocks are then stitched together using 4-inch borders. Instructions begin on page 97.

E ver since the colonists learned to plant corn, Americans have been keenly interested in food and cooking. The recipes shown here and on the next few pages are examples of our culinary heritage. Take *Homemade Granola* for example. This classic began as an out-of-hand snack. Now it is used in an assortment of recipes such as *Granola Casserole Bread, Stuffed Cabbage Rolls, Granola-Rice Stuffing* for Cornish hens, and *Granola Ripple Cake*. (See the index for all recipe pages.)

S ome of the oldest country recipes are those developed by the early settlers in New England. They took the unfamiliar ingredients they found in the New World and worked them into their favorite Old World dishes. The result is what we call Yankee cooking. A few examples of this cuisine are pictured here: the crumb-topped *Fish-Wine Bisque, New England Clam Chowder*, hot cider, *Tourtiere*, and *Yankee Corn Sticks*. (See index for recipe pages.)

Each ethnic group that came to America added its dishes to our cooking heritage. Some of the best are holiday desserts. The Austrians gave us *Salaburger Nockerl* (front left), lemon meringues baked in butter. *Regal Plum Pudding* (front center) is an English recipe served with *Fluffy Hard Sauce*. Many European countries claim *Holiday Rice Pudding* (front right) but the *Currant-Raspberry Sauce* makes it uniquely American. The Scots serve *Scotch Black Bun* (back left) on New Year's Eve. *Cassata* (back right) is a rich Italian cake. (See the index for recipe pages.)

COUNTRY CRAFTS TO DECORATE THE HOME

Handmades for Every Room in Your House

hen you examine our craft heritage, it's hard to imagine where we would be without what is considered the most traditional of American folk arts—quilting. In this instance we have updated this age-old technique to avoid the time-consuming piecing step and to emphasize the quilt pattern template designs. The projects shown here and on pages 24 and 25 are all worked on muslin fabric using a simple backstitch, creating a striking variation of rustic old-time quilts. Although these projects aren't worked in typical pieced patterns, they still maintain the warmth and charm of American country quilts through the use of ever-popular quilting templates. To stitch the template designs, select embroidery floss in rich jewel-tone colors; then choose from a wide range of projects for all around your house, including the quilt and cornice shown here. For more on this new-style quilting technique, please turn the page.

When our pioneer ancestors decided to create a quilt, they knew it would involve long hours of cutting and piecing. Not anymore. For quilting that is fast, easy on the budget, and simple to learn, you can't beat the projects shown here. These new-style quilting projects involve just one basic embroidery stitch and several of your favorite quilt pattern templates. By teaming these two things together, you can fashion a whole roomful of delightful stitcheries.

The "heartfelt" apron (top right) is bordered with strips of fabric and then attached to a skirt in a coordinated print. The pillow and chair cushion (bottom right) prove that you can do as much or as little stitching as you'd like, using a small floral motif or an entire quilting design. The handy tote and dresser-top box (opposite) are worked in traditional heart, feather, and fan designs that appear on countless old-fashioned quilts.

Using a backstitch to embroider these projects (instead of quilting stitches) eliminates lots of time and adds to the overall effect of the designs. For instructions, see page 30.

All of the projects shown here should be worked in an embroidery hoop or on a quilting frame to avoid distortion. Stitch the designs with two hands, one on top of the fabric and one below. To change the size of the quilt (pages 22-23), increase or decrease the total number of quilt blocks or alter the width of the border strips.

Nothing says country quite like the stenciled designs shown here. And you'll find that very little artistic talent is required to transform wood, glass, and fabric into stenciled beauties.

To give an everyday window (top right) a design with an etched-glass look, cut a stencil from stencil paper using an old-fashioned quilting pattern for your design. Tape the stencil to the glass and dip a stencil brush into a small amount of high gloss enamel paint (keep the brush fairly dry at all times). Hold the brush perpendicular to the stencil and use an up-and-down motion to paint the design.

Treat a wooden kitchen table like this one (bottom right) to a refreshing face-lift by applying a coat of sealer/filler/stain to the sanded surface. Tape any stencil design (we used American primitive motifs) to the tabletop and add artist's oil paints to the remaining stain. Wrap your finger in a clean, soft cloth and rub the tinted stain into the stenciled design with your finger. Let the stencils dry and apply a coat of clear polyurethane.

The colorful heirloom quilt (opposite) looks like an intricate appliquéd project but the designs are actually stenciled to the fabric. For instructions, see page 33.

When cutting a stencil, make sure your cutting tool is sharp enough to ensure clean edges. Keep the stencil as close to the stenciling surface as possible in order to achieve crisp, clear designs. (Use your free hand to press down the edges of the stencil.) Lift the stencil carefully after you've finished painting and let the paint dry.

There's nothing quite as inviting as a country table at mealtime, especially when it's set with do-it-yourself dishes and linens like these. To design a set of dishes for your own breakfast table, start with pre-molded dishes from a ceramic shop, paint the landscape designs on each piece, and add a clear glaze finish. You can fire the pieces at a local ceramic studio for a small fee.

To create the cloud designs that drift across the dishes, make "stencils" from round adhesive-backed labels (available at stationery and art stores), then outline the white shapes with black overglazing.

For matching table accessories, play up the rural designs with a machine-appliquéd round tablecloth complete with a panoramic view. Start with a king-size bed sheet to simplify piecing the tablecloth. Then top the finished cloth with a layer of crisp blue gingham.

Finish the pastoral look with sunburst napkins, cloud place mats, and a quilted tea cozy. For instructions, see page 34.

Although you may be equipped to handle most of the steps to create these dishes at home, you may choose to work with a local ceramist. There are many ceramic studios across the country that can provide instructions, tools, materials, and tips. These studios are also able to fire your work for a nominal fee.

QUILTING PROJECTS
pages 22-25

General Instructions

Enlarge the patterns shown here and trace them onto muslin using a water-

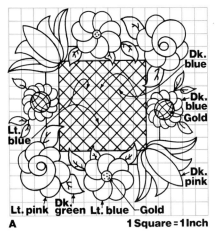

B   1 Square = 1 Inch

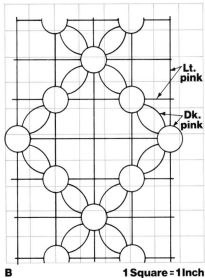

A   1 Square = 1 Inch

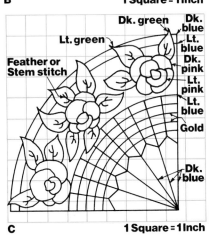

C   1 Square = 1 Inch

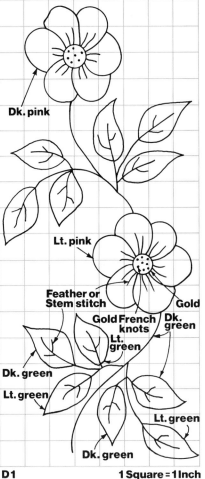

D 1   1 Square = 1 Inch

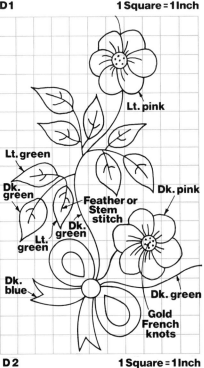

D 2   1 Square = 1 Inch

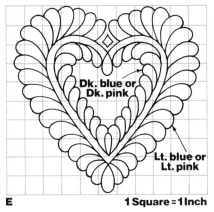

E   1 Square = 1 Inch

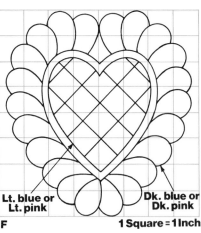

F   1 Square = 1 Inch

erasable pen. Place a layer of batting between muslin and batiste backing fabric; baste pieces together.

Mount your fabric in an embroidery hoop; work the quilting design in back-stitches, using 6 strands of floss. (For stitch diagrams, see the glossary on page 374.) Stitch through all 3 layers of the fabric.

To add French knots to the centers of the flowers, use 6 strands of gold floss; stitch through the top layer of fabric only. Work stem-stitch or feath-erstitch veins in some leaves, using 3 strands of green floss; work through top layer of fabric.

Quilt, pages 22-23

Finished size is 78x78 inches.

Materials: 3½ yards *each* of muslin and batiste; 4½ yards of floral backing fabric; 2½ yards of coordinated striped fabric (for the border strips); 80x80-inches of quilt batting; 2 skeins *each* of embroidery floss in light and dark pink, light and dark blue, light and dark green, and gold; water-erasable marking pen; a large embroidery hoop; crewel embroidery needles.

Instructions: Preshrink all fabric. Read the instructions thoroughly before cutting the fabric.

Enlarge patterns A, B, C, D1, and D2. Cut 20½-inch squares of muslin, batiste, and batting for the center quilt block; trace a 16½-inch square in center of muslin block. Trace pattern A, centered, on muslin.

Layer the 3 pieces, placing batting between muslin and batiste; baste the pieces together. Place the fabric in an embroidery hoop and work the design in backstitches.

Cut four 15x20½-inch rectangles *each* of muslin, batiste, and batting; trace an 11x16½-inch rectangle in the center of muslin pieces. Trace pattern B, centered, onto muslin rectangles, repeating the pattern until each rectangle is completely filled within the 11x16½-inch lines. Layer and baste the muslin, batiste, and batting as described for the center square (to make 4 rectangles). Place the fabric in the hoop. Work the designs in backstitches.

Cut four 15-inch squares *each* of muslin, batiste, and batting. Trace an 11-inch square in center of each muslin piece; trace pattern C, centered, onto muslin squares. Layer pieces as described for center square; baste pieces together. Place fabric in hoop and work the design in backstitches.

Assemble the 9 quilt blocks as follows: Trim the *batting* ¼ inch around all of the quilted pieces (do not trim fabric beyond the marked lines); fold under muslin edges ¼ inch all around and whipstitch the 9 blocks together, arranging blocks as shown in the photograph. (Fans in the 4 corner pieces should face outward.) Turn the quilt over; repeat for batiste edges.

Cut 4-inch-wide strips of striped fabric for dividing strips; fold long edges under ¼ inch. Center these strips between each block (over the seams) and stitch them in place.

Cut two 13¼x49½-inch strips of muslin for the side borders and two 13¼x78-inch muslin strips for top and bottom borders. For each piece of muslin, cut matching pieces of batiste and batting. Layer and baste pieces as described for center square (above). Trace pattern D1 on side borders, beginning

in the center and working out toward ends. Leave the lower 3½ inches of each side border (parallel to long edge) free; leave the final 6 inches of the repeat pattern untraced. (Leaves at the ends of each side border extend over onto top and bottom borders after corners are joined.) Work the side borders in backstitches.

Trace quilting designs onto top and bottom borders, assemble borders as described for center square, and work designs in backstitches. End top and bottom borders with the bow pattern (D2) in corners.

Sew borders to quilt as described for joining blocks.

Sketch a set of 5 leaves extending on each end of side borders over the seam onto top and bottom borders. Work leaves in backstitches.

Stitch strips of striped fabric between quilt borders and center section of quilt, turning raw edges under and centering strips over seams.

Cut and piece a matching-size piece of floral fabric for the backing fabric and baste it to the quilt top. Quilt around each block and down the center of each dividing strip.

To bind the edges of the quilt, cut and piece 7½-inch-wide lengths of striped fabric. Fold raw edges under ¼ inch; stitch binding to front of quilt. Next, fold strip to the back of the quilt and stitch the binding in place, turning raw edges under.

Cornice, pages 22-23

Instructions: Enlarge patterns D1 and D2. Cut a piece of foam-core board (available in art stores) to fit desired window. Place the foam-core board atop muslin; cut muslin 3 inches larger all around. Cut batiste and batting to match muslin.

Trace floral border patterns (D1 and D2), centered, onto muslin. Layer the 3 fabric pieces; baste. Work the designs in backstitches.

Stretch fabric over the foam-core backing, clip corners, and glue fabric to back of foam-core board.

Cut another piece of muslin slightly smaller than the cornice piece; glue it to the back of the foam-core board, or whipstitch it to fabric already in place, turning edges under.

Apron, page 24

Materials: 11-inch squares of muslin, batiste, and quilt batting; 2 yards of coordinated striped fabric for borders and waistband; 1 skein *each* of light and dark blue *or* light and dark pink embroidery floss; embroidery hoop; crewel embroidery needle; water-erasable marking pen.

Instructions: Enlarge pattern F (opposite). Trace the design, centered, onto the muslin square. Layer fabric pieces, placing batting between muslin and batiste; baste together diagonally, from top to bottom, and side to side.

Work the design in backstitches, then back the quilted design with a matching-size piece of floral fabric.

To bind the 2 sides and the top edge of the design, cut 4-inch-wide strips of striped fabric and turn the edges under ¼ inch. Fold the strips in half and sew 1 edge of the binding to the front of the design, mitering the corners. Turn the binding to back of the design and sew the other edge in place.

Cut two 3x32-inch pieces of striped fabric for the waistband; then cut and piece a 30x72-inch piece of floral fabric for the apron skirt. Hem the short sides of the skirt and gather 1 long edge to fit the front waistband piece. Center the skirt along the top edge of the waistband (right sides facing) and pin it in place.

Pin the unbound edge of the quilted bib to the top of the waistband (centered), with raw edges even. (The right side of the bib should face the wrong side of the waistband.) Fold under the raw edges of the back waistband strip; baste it to the wrong side of the apron front.

Sew the waistband pieces together, catching bottom of quilted bodice and top of gathered skirt in stitching. Pull up the waistband front and back to hide raw edges; topstitch along top fold. Add snaps to the ends of the waistband.

Cut and stitch two 1½-inch-wide striped shoulder straps; sew them to the bodice. Add snaps to secure straps to back of waistband.

Hem the skirt to desired length.

Tote Bag, page 25

Materials: Two 14-inch squares of quilt batting; one 14-inch square *each*
(Continued)

of muslin and batiste; three 14-inch squares of floral fabric; ½ yard of floral fabric (for lining); ¼ yard coordinated striped fabric for sides of tote; pieces of fabric for trim and handles; 1 skein *each* of light and dark blue *or* light and dark pink embroidery floss; embroidery hoop; a water-erasable marking pen; embroidery needle.

Instructions: Enlarge pattern E on page 30; mark a 10½-inch square in the center of the muslin square, then trace the design, centered, onto the muslin. Layer the muslin, batiste, and batting, and baste the pieces together from top to bottom and side to side. Work the design in backstitches.

Frame design with narrow strips of fabric. Baste a 14-inch square of floral fabric to the back of the design. Layer a piece of batting between 2 pieces of floral fabric and sew pieces together for back of tote.

Cut and piece a 4x42-inch piece of striped fabric for the sides of the tote. Baste this piece to matching-size pieces of batting and floral lining fabric. Quilt the pieces along the fabric stripes.

With lining sides facing and using a ¼-inch seam, sew a boxing strip to the front of the tote along the 2 sides and bottom of the quilted design. Repeat for back of tote. Bind all raw edges with 1½-inch-wide bias strips.

Cut two 3x14-inch strips of fabric for handles. Fold each strip around a 1¼-

inch-wide piece of batting, turn raw edges under, and quilt handles lengthwise. Turn raw edges under at both ends of handles; sew the handles to edges of tote.

Fan Box, page 25

Materials: Pieces of heavy cardboard; fabric for covering and lining the box; 3x73 inches of blue grosgrain ribbon; masking tape; craft knife; fabric glue; straightedge ruler; pieces of muslin, batiste, and batting for the quilted fan design; 1 skein *each* of embroidery

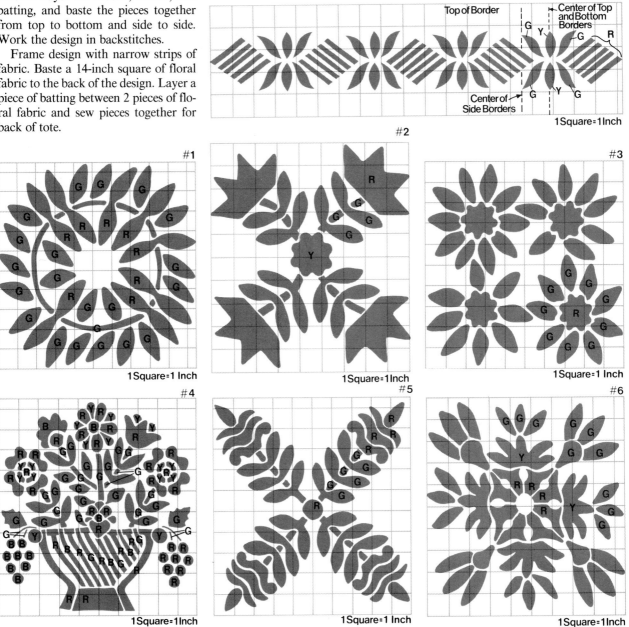

#2

Top of Border — Center of Top and Bottom Borders

Center of Side Borders

1 Square = 1 Inch

#1

1 Square = 1 Inch

#3

1 Square = 1 Inch

#4

1 Square = 1 Inch

#5

1 Square = 1 Inch

#6

1 Square = 1 Inch

floss in light and dark blue, light and dark pink, light and dark green, and gold; water-erasable marking pen; embroidery hoop or frame; crewel embroidery needle.

Instructions: Enlarge pattern C and transfer the design onto the center of the muslin. Layer the 3 fabric pieces, placing batting between muslin and batiste. Baste all the pieces together and work the design in backstitches. Cut 3 quarter-circles (each with a 9½-inch radius) for top, bottom, and top lining pieces of the box. Cut two 2½x9-inch strips of cardboard for the sides of the box and a 2½x15¼-inch strip for curved front side of the box.

Secure the sides to the bottom of the box with masking tape, reinforcing the corners with extra tape. Cover the inside and outside of the box with fabric, gluing it into place.

For the top of the box, stretch and glue the quilted design to a remaining quarter-circle of poster board. Trim excess batting and batiste; then pull muslin edges to the back of cardboard, gluing fabric in place.

For the ruffle, fold a 3-inch-wide strip of fabric in half lengthwise, press, and gather the raw edges. Glue the ruffle in place to the underside of the cardboard box top.

Cover the last quarter-circle of the cardboard with fabric; glue it to bottom of box top to conceal raw edges.

Weight the box top under several books to dry. Finish with gold trim and a small blue ribbon bow.

Pillows and Seat Cushions, page 24

Instructions: Any of the 7 quilting patterns can be made into pillows or seat cushions. We used pattern B to stitch the seat cushion on page 24.

Work the designs as described for the quilt blocks and "frame" them with strips of fabric if desired.

Back each pillow or seat cushion, then add a ruffle or cording and stuff with fiberfill or foam padding.

STENCILED QUILT
page 27

Each quilt block is made in a quilt-as-you-go fashion: Stencil a design on muslin; layer the stenciled square, batting, and backing fabric; baste and quilt the squares; then stitch the quilt together. Finished size: 72x82 inches.

Materials: 12¼ yards of muslin (45 inches wide); ½-inch-thick quilt batting; ecru quilting thread; 10 yards red piping (optional); fabric or acrylic paints in the following colors and amounts: 5 ounces red, 5 ounces green, 3 ounces yellow, and ¾ ounce blue; stencil paper; stencil brush; craft knife; stapler and staples; 14x14-inch piece of fiberboard; spray adhesive or white glue.

Instructions: To cut stencils, enlarge the patterns (opposite); transfer to paper to use as master patterns.

Glue master patterns to a sheet of cardboard. For block motifs, center a 12-inch square of stencil paper over the pattern. Cut away pattern (shaded areas on diagrams) using a craft knife. Center border on a 6x18-inch piece of stencil paper; cut away pattern areas.

For best results, cut separate stencil for each color of paint. For example, stencils for the red and green wreath design (pattern 1) would include separate stencils for red leaves and green leaves. Label each stencil with the appropriate color.

To prepare the fabric, preshrink and iron all the muslin. Cut sixty 12¾x12¾-inch muslin squares, 30 for stenciled fronts and 30 for backs. For the border, cut 2 muslin strips 13x68 inches and 2 strips 13x92 inches. Press border strips in half lengthwise, wrong sides facing.

Cut quilt batting into thirty 12-inch squares, two 6x64-inch and two 6x88-inch batting strips for the border.

To stencil the designs, first staple a fabric square to a piece of fiberboard. Carefully position staples within the ⅜-inch seam allowance to avoid visible holes once blocks are joined. Slip typing paper under the muslin before stenciling to absorb any paint that bleeds through the fabric. Center the stencil over the muslin square; pin each stencil corner to secure it.

Practice stenciling on fabric scraps. Pour a small amount of paint onto a plate. *Lightly* dip the brush into the paint (always begin with a dry stencil brush). Then dab the brush on newspaper to remove excess paint.

Holding the brush perpendicular to the work surface and using an up-and-down motion, gently dab the paint onto the fabric.

Over large areas begin stenciling the outside of the design and work toward the center. Paint light colors first, then darker colors. After stenciling a color, let paint dry before moving to the next color.

Once you've mastered this technique, stencil each of the 6 designs onto 5 blocks, for a total of 30 blocks.

To stencil the top and bottom borders (the shorter of the border pieces), mark the center of each strip (crosswise) with a row of pins. Unfold the strips and staple them to the fiberboard. Stenciling should be done on the top half of the strip, above the fold. Match the center line of the stencil to the row of pins; align bottom edge of stencil with pressed fold.

Pin the design in place; stencil. When you've reached the edge of the fiberboard, remove the fabric, reposition it, and continue working. Stencil to one end of the strip and then to the other end, finishing with a diamond on each end. There will be 13 flowers and 14 diamonds on each top and bottom border strip. (There will be 4 inches of extra fabric at each end of each strip.)

The side borders, unlike the top and bottom borders, are not symmetrical. Therefore, to make stenciling easier, lay the side border strips on the floor with folded edges to left and right, just as they will appear on the finished quilt. Label each strip (right or left side border); also mark the top (narrow) edge that will be sewn to the narrow edge of the top border design. Next, fold each strip in half crosswise and mark the center with pins.

Begin stenciling on the left side border. Position the fabric on the fiberboard, and match the center line on the pattern to the row of pins just as for the top and bottom border. Stencil toward the end marked "top" until there are 10 diamonds; end with the tenth diamond. Then stencil to the opposite end, until there are 10 flowers; end with a flower. There will be 19 flowers and 19 diamonds on the strip; the excess fabric will be turned under when the quilt is assembled.

(Continued)

33

To stencil the right side border, repeat this procedure, *except turn the stencil around,* so the side of the stencil marked "top" rests on the fold of the muslin. (This reverses the design.)

When the paint is completely dry, set the color by pressing the fabric with a warm iron. (Cover the stenciled fabric with a press cloth.)

To quilt each block, sandwich batting between a stenciled top square and a plain (unpainted) backing square. Pin the layers together and baste diagonally between the corners (making an X) and around the edges to prevent puckering. Using a quilting needle and thread, make small running stitches around each stenciled shape. Repeat this process for each block.

To quilt the border, insert the batting strips inside the folded border fabric. Pin and baste the layers together; quilt as for the blocks. *Do not quilt the last 2 motifs on the ends of each of the side borders.* These are quilted after the top is assembled.

Assemble the quilt by stitching blocks together into 6 rows of 5 blocks each, as follows:

Row 1: patterns 6, 3, 6, 3, 6.
Row 2: patterns 5, 2, 5, 2, 5.
Row 3: patterns 4, 1, 4, 1, 4.
Row 4: patterns 3, 6, 3, 6, 3.
Row 5: patterns 2, 5, 2, 5, 2.
Row 6: patterns 1, 4, 1, 4, 1.

To join blocks, pin 1 block to the adjacent one, with right sides of stenciled blocks facing. Pin backing and batting on each block out of the way; stitch the 2 front blocks together (3/8-inch seam). Finger-press.

To finish the back seam, open up the 2 blocks and place them facedown. If necessary, trim some of the batting to avoid a bulky seam.

Then, turn under the seam allowance of the backing on 1 block and blindstitch it along the seam line on the back of the second block, covering the raw edges. Adjust the seam allowance to 1/4 inch if necessary to keep seams straight.

Continue joining blocks until you have 6 rows.

To join rows, use the same procedure as for joining blocks. When all of the rows are stitched together, remove all of the basting threads except those that are along the outer edges of the blocks where the borders will be sewn.

To attach piping, align raw edges of blocks with raw piping edge on the blocks' front sides. Using a 1/4-inch seam, sew together across top and bottom quilt edge. Then sew piping to quilt sides, crossing over the piping on the top and bottom of the quilt.

To attach borders, repeat process for joining blocks, *except* whipstitch the batting to the seam before blindstitching the backing pieces together. Secure the top and bottom borders in place first, trimming away the fabric that extends past the block assembly. Attach the side borders to the sides of the quilt, including the narrow ends of the top and bottom borders.

Cut away excess batting within the side borders; carefully whipstitch the batting to the seam on the reverse side of the quilt.

Before blindstitching the border back to the quilt back, turn under top and bottom raw edges of side border, and square up the side borders to the top and bottom borders. Blindstitch the border backing to the quilt; quilt the remaining motifs on the ends of each side border.

Cleaning instructions: For best results, have painted fabric items dry-cleaned by a reputable firm.

DISHES AND LINENS
pages 28-29

Ceramic Dinnerware
Materials: Greenware (the name for unfired clay forms) for pieces of dinnerware (see the note below); opaque underglazes in the following colors: fern green, lettuce green, neptune green, field mouse gray, red, lobster red, mandarin orange, marigold yellow, canary yellow, bright blue, oyster white; cleaning tool; scrubber; silk sponge; assorted brushes; typing paper; gray graphite paper; compass; clear glaze; black china paint (overglaze); round adhesive-backed labels in various sizes.

Note: **Read all labels carefully, and store and use supplies properly.** First decide on the style of dinnerware you'd like to use. We chose Arnel's Danish Modern pattern. You may either pur-

chase molds and pour the liquefied clay (called "slip") into molds yourself, or a ceramic studio will do the casting for you using its molds.

After the clay has dried, it becomes "leather-hard" and is removed from the mold to dry further. The pieces are called "greenware" at this stage. Greenware is *extremely* fragile, so take care when working with it.

Use the cleaning tool to remove any seam marks and imperfections in the greenware. Hold the tool diagonally; clean both inside and outside surfaces. Use the scrubber to smooth away the seam lines and edges. Finally, wipe greenware with a damp sponge to remove clay dust.

Enlarge the dinnerware pattern shown opposite and transfer it to pieces of typing paper for master patterns. Refer to the photographs on pages 28-29 for designs and below for specific how-to instructions.

Adapt the size and arrangement of the motifs to your own dinnerware.

To transfer the pattern, position graphite paper over the greenware, then cover the paper with the master pattern. Tape pattern in place and trace over the design with a pencil. Mark the rim and circumference of each plate with a compass and pencil.

Color Key:
1—Fern green
2—Lettuce green
3—Neptune green
4—Field mouse gray
5—Red
6—Lobster red
7—Mandarin orange
8—Marigold yellow
9—Canary yellow

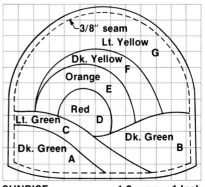

SUNRISE TEA COZY   **1 Square = 1 Inch**

10—Bright blue

11—Oyster white

For pieces with clouds, apply a series of round adhesive labels. For each cloud, begin with a large circle near the center of the cloud; add smaller circles around the edges, overlapping edges. Areas around the labels will later be underglazed blue; areas beneath labels will remain white.

Decorating begins with the underglazes. Brush on the underglazes starting with the background and ending with the foreground. Use assorted green colors for the tree clusters in the background. For larger areas, sponge on the underglaze. Apply all underglaze colors *except* red, lobster red, mandarin orange, and marigold yellow at this time. (These colors are applied *after* the first firing.) Apply 3 coats of underglaze to all color areas *except* in the blue areas, which should receive 4 coats. Be careful to layer them exactly

(Continued)

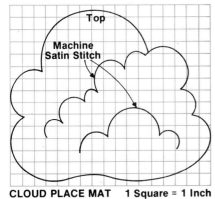

NAPKIN   1 Square = 1 Inch

CLOUD PLACE MAT   1 Square = 1 Inch

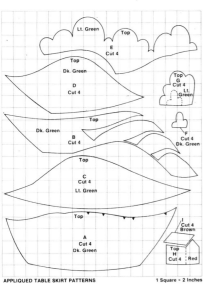

APPLIQUED TABLE SKIRT PATTERNS   1 Square = 2 Inches

1 SQUARE = ½ INCH

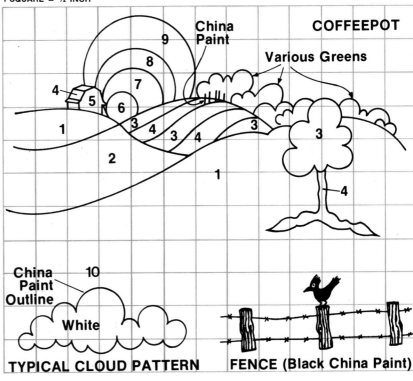

TYPICAL CLOUD PATTERN   **FENCE (Black China Paint)**

PLACEMENT DIAGRAM
APPLIQUED TABLE SKIRT

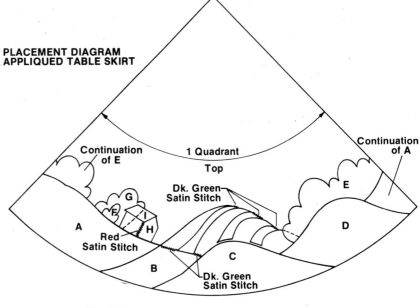

35

and smoothly to achieve crisp edges. Allow all glazes to dry *thoroughly* between coats.

The specific directions for decorating each piece follow:

Coffeepot and teapot: Bands of blue (with clouds) and green (with hills, tree, etc.) encircle the top and bottom of the pots. Each band conforms to the shape of the pot.

To transfer the designs to the pots, first mask the bottom ½ inch (above the bottom lip edge) on the coffeepot, or the bottom ¼ inch on the teapot, using masking tape. These areas will remain white.

Next, on the back of the coffeepot, use masking tape to edge a 3-inch-wide band (green). Sketch the 3-inch band in place on the front side of the pot, using a pencil.

On the back of the teapot, use masking tape to mark a 1½-inch-wide band. Continue the band across the front of the teapot, using a pencil to mark the lines. Then overlap a landscape pattern on the front green band.

For the blue bands, mask the first ½ inch below the top of the coffeepot and the first ¼ inch below the top of the teapot, using masking tape. Mask the coffeepot band so it is 1¾ inches wide; the teapot band is 1 inch wide.

Apply round labels for clouds on top bands of both pots; paint bands blue. Transfer hills, sun, and other design elements to front of pot along top of band line (sketch in pencil); paint, following general directions and the color key.

Sketch a tree (using the tree in the landscape as a guide) in the center of the green band on the back of each pot (opposite the landscape on the front); then paint. Paint the tops of the lid handles blue.

After second firing, draw in fence motif using black china paint.

(If necessary, adjust the scale or position of the landscape elements to fit ceramic pieces.)

Sugar bowl: Mask ¼ inch around top and bottom (above the protruding edge) of bowl, using tape; these edges will be white. Apply labels for clouds; paint blue. Paint lid handles blue.

Cream pitcher: Position the 1-inch-wide blue band ½ inch down from the top edge of the pitcher. Apply labels for clouds; paint. Position the 1⅜-inch-

wide green band ½ inch above the bottom protruding edge; paint. Add fence and bird after second firing.

Salt and pepper shakers: Position the ¾-inch-wide blue band ½ inch below the top. Apply labels for the clouds; paint. Position the 1¼-inch-wide green band ⅜ inch above the bottom edge; paint.

Coffee mug: Position the 1-inch-wide blue band ⅜ inch below the top edge of the mug. Apply labels for clouds; paint. Position the 1¼-inch-wide green band ½ inch from the bottom; paint. China-paint fence and bird on green band.

Dinner plate: Measure rim and center circumference; mark with large compass. Position the 1½-inch-wide blue band from the rim toward the center of the plate. Leave a ½-inch-wide white space; paint the remaining area green. Freehand-paint a single tree in the center of the plate.

Salad plate: Position a 1½-inch-wide green band from the rim to the center of the plate. Leave the center white, with a single tree in the center.

Teacup: Position blue area ¼ inch from top and bottom edges of cup. Apply labels for clouds; paint.

Saucer: Paint a green band from rim to raised cup lip. Leave center white.

Serving pieces: Apply labels for the clouds; paint all remaining areas blue.

All pieces: Leave the undersides of all pieces white (unglazed).

Gently peel off adhesive-backed labels while the last coat of blue underglaze is still damp.

The greenware is now ready for the first kiln firing. Ask the kiln operator to fire the greenware to "cone 04 bisque" to resist chipping. The pieces will be white on all unglazed areas after bisque firing.

Apply the red, lobster red, mandarin orange, and the marigold yellow glazes to areas indicated (sunburst and barn). Apply 3 coats, allowing the underglaze to dry thoroughly between coats. When pieces are completely dry, apply 2 to 3 coats of clear glaze to the entire piece. The bisque (fired greenware) is now ready for the second firing (cone 06 glaze firing).

After the second firing, use the black china paint and a fine brush to accent

the designs, painting in outlines and details on clouds, trees, and barn. Vary the width of the brushstrokes at will, but use the paint sparingly. Paint the picket fence and bird on the upright pieces; add a bird in flight to the serving pieces. Then fire the pieces to cone 018, the third and final firing.

Table Linens

Instructions follow for the round gingham tablecloth (66 inches in diameter), cloud place mat (14x16¾ inches), tea cozy (10x11½ inches), napkins (14x14 inches), and appliquéd table skirt. The table skirt will cover a 36-inch-diameter, 30-inch-high round table. All fabric requirements are for 44/45-inch-wide fabric.

Materials for all projects: Size 70 sewing machine needle; typing paper; even-feed attachment for sewing machine (optional); brown paper; tissue paper; machine embroidery threads in colors that match fabrics. (For yardage requirements, see the individual instructions below.)

Note on machine appliqué: For machine appliqué, satin-stitch at a medium to wide setting. Prewash all the fabric; first cut out appliqué pieces, then iron in place onto the background fabric using fusible webbing.

When appliquéing, slip a piece of typing paper under the background fabric to prevent puckering. Carefully tear it away after stitching.

Gingham Tablecloth

Materials: 4 yards of blue gingham; white thread.

Instructions: Cut gingham into two 2-yard lengths; cut one of the pieces in half lengthwise. Piece the 3 lengths together with the widest length in the center, then trim fabric into a 72-inch square. Save fabric scraps to use in the tea cozy.

Fold the cloth into quarters. Tie a string to a pencil and cut the string to 33 inches. Using a thumbtack to hold the string end in place, draw a quarter-circle arc. Cut through all 4 layers of fabric along this arc.

Turn under raw edges ¼ inch twice, making a double hem; stitch.

Cloud Place Mat

Materials (for one): ½ yard of white fabric cut into two 18x19-inch pieces; ½ yard of polyester fleece cut into one 18x19-inch piece.

Instructions: Enlarge the pattern (page 35) and transfer to a piece of tissue paper for the master pattern.

Trace the pattern outline onto one white fabric rectangle. *Lightly* pencil in the lines inside the cloud shape using a hard lead pencil.

Place the polyester fleece between the 2 white fabric pieces and pin or baste the 3 layers together.

Using white machine embroidery thread, satin-stitch along the inner cloud lines first, then around the entire outline of the place mat. (Pad the edge of the place mat by stitching over white embroidery floss or pearl cotton if desired.) Cut away excess fabric close to the outer satin stitches.

Appliquéd Table Skirt

Materials: 1 yellow king-size flat sheet; 2 yards of light green fabric; 3⅓ yards of dark green fabric; scraps of red and brown fabric; 5 yards of fusible webbing; dark green, red, and brown machine embroidery thread.

Instructions: *Note:* To make a skirt for a table that is a different size, adjust the dimensions of the appliqué pieces *or* alter the number of pieces in the design by subtracting some elements or adding others.

Enlarge the pattern pieces (page 35); transfer to tissue paper for your master patterns.

Cut four of *each* pattern from fabric colors indicated *without* adding seam allowances. Cut pieces of fusible webbing to match pattern pieces. Cut king-size sheet into a 97-inch-diameter circle. To do this, cut a 97-inch square from the sheet and fold the square into quarters. Tie a string to a pencil and cut the string to 48½ inches. Mark and cut the circle the same as for gingham tablecloth (opposite).

Mark the circle into quarters, using basting stitches, and spread the circle on the floor. Position and pin one set of pattern pieces A through I onto the quarter circle. Follow the diagram on page 35 for proper placement of the pieces. Overlap the pieces slightly, trimming if necessary. Repeat with the remaining three quadrants.

Cut 4 sets of pieces A through I from fusible webbing to match fabric pieces. Slip webbing under pattern pieces and re-pin in place. With the circle on the floor, iron all pieces to secure. Repeat

until all pattern pieces are fused to the background fabric, moving the ironing surface as necessary. When all pieces are secured, move circle to an ironing board and press on the wrong side of the sheet.

Machine-appliqué the pieces to the background fabric by machine satin-stitching around the perimeter of each pattern piece. Stop all machine satin-stitching ⅜ inch from the bottom edge of the skirt to prevent unnecessary bulk in the hem.

To hem, fold the edge under ¼ inch, then an additional ¼ inch and machine-stitch along the fold.

Napkins

Materials (for two): Two 10½-inch squares of white fabric; two 16-inch squares of dark yellow fabric; scraps of dark yellow, orange, and red fabric; eight 1x12-inch strips of blue fabric; scraps of fusible webbing; machine embroidery thread.

Instructions: Enlarge the corner pattern (page 35) and transfer it to tissue paper for the master pattern. Cut corresponding fabric pieces *without* adding seam allowances.

Position the pattern pieces in one corner of a white fabric square, and secure the pieces with fusible webbing. Machine satin-stitch each fabric piece, using matching machine embroidery thread.

With right sides facing, sew a blue fabric strip along each side of the white square, using a ¼-inch seam and mitering the corners.

Center this appliquéd and bordered square atop a 16-inch yellow square and baste in place. Turn up the edges of the yellow square ¼ inch; press. Fold the edges over again so they overlap the blue strips ¼ inch to form the double-thick yellow border. Miter the corners and blindstitch the miters closed. Machine-stitch the yellow edge to the blue strip, sewing close to the folded edge of the yellow border.

Tea Cozy

Materials: Scraps of dark and light yellow, orange, red, and dark and light green fabrics; 15x15 inches of muslin; 15x15 inches of dark yellow fabric; two 15-inch squares of blue gingham; 15x15 inches of polyester fleece; ½ yard of

fusible webbing; two 15-inch squares of quilt batting; 1 yard of purchased yellow piping; and machine embroidery thread.

Instructions: Enlarge sunrise pattern (page 34) and transfer it to a piece of brown paper to serve as the master pattern. Carefully trace and cut the sunburst pattern pieces A through G from tissue paper.

Trace the tea cozy outline onto a 15-inch muslin square. Cut pattern pieces A through G from proper fabric colors *without* adding seam allowances. Position in place on muslin. Secure pattern pieces to muslin, using fusible webbing.

Place the muslin square atop the polyester fleece square, and machine satin-stitch around each of the pattern pieces.

Place the appliquéd square on top of the batting square. Using a running stitch, sew through all the layers following the shape of each appliqué piece. Machine-stitch a length of yellow piping along the seam line on the curved edge of the tea cozy front, except leave the bottom, straight edge without piping.

For the back, trace the cozy outline onto the square of dark yellow fabric. Place this over the second quilt batting square. Channel-quilt the back at intervals of 1¼ inches and machine-stitch around the penciled outline.

To assemble, pin the appliquéd front to the quilted back, right sides facing. To join, use the penciled, stitched outline on the back as a guide, but machine-stitch ⅜ *inch* inside this line. Leave the bottom edge open; clip the curves and trim seam.

For the lining, trace the tea cozy outline onto one of the 15-inch gingham squares. Place the squares on top of each other, right sides facing. Using a ½-inch seam, stitch along the sides only, leaving the bottom edge open and the top of the curve open. Trim and grade the seams.

With right sides facing, sew the bottom of the lining to the bottom of the cozy in a ⅜-inch seam. Pull the cozy through the opening in the top of the lining; blindstitch the lining opening to close it. Push the lining up into the cozy. Pin or baste layers together. Then tack the lining in place at several points to keep it from slipping out.

COUNTRY CRAFTS TO DECORATE YOUR HOME

Accessories: A Little Bit Country

aking the time to add accessories to one or two of your favorite rooms can mean the difference between a house and a home sweet home. Just a few handcrafted accessories like the ones on these six pages can turn your house into a special place and give it a personality all its own. The crocheted accessories shown here add a touch of country to any room. They are fine examples of Irish crochet, a historic craft that emerged in the mid-19th century as a cottage craft industry. From these humble beginnings, Irish crochet developed into an art that is still being practiced today. The small, round antique doily shown here provided inspiration for the large, oval doily, a modern-day version of yesterday's laces using today's threads. Typical of Irish crochet are delicate rosettes and sawtooth patterns worked in small picots. Instructions for the oval doily and curtain panel begin on page 44.

Mix-and-match accessories such as these fit into almost any country-style decorating scheme. You just pick a color and paint or dye wicker baskets, chairs, almost anything.

To dye small items such as these baskets (right) immerse them in a tub or sink filled with a household dye solution. Soak the baskets for about 15 minutes or until you reach the desired color. For a large piece like the rocking chair (opposite), wet the wicker with water; then apply the dye solution with a large sponge. (Use a large plastic drop cloth to minimize the mess.)

Allow dyed items to "set" 10 minutes, then rinse with cold water.

Use spray paint in a base color plus several complementary colors to make these spatter-painted baskets (opposite). Spray the baskets with a base coat and let dry, then add mists and speckles of paint to the baskets using the remaining three or four colors. For an overall mist, spray the paint lightly from a distance. For a speckled effect, apply light, steady pressure to the spray valve to "catch" it at the point just before it releases a full spray of paint.

Unlike fabric, wicker is approximately the same color wet as it is dry. Wicker takes dye best if it has a dull surface, so sand your wicker items lightly if the surfaces seem too slick. Follow instructions on the package when mixing the dye solutions. Be sure to rinse all dyed items in cold water to "set" the colors.

For the spatter-painting, it is best to use baskets woven from flat strips. Use rubber gloves and work in a well-ventilated area.

The imaginative projects that are shown here have a fresh country flavor that blends easily with almost any home furnishings. Whether your crafting skills tend toward fabric or wood, you'll delight in this trio of ideas.

Machine-appliqué a scenic country landscape to the front of plain muslin curtains (left) using a handful of leftover calico fabrics. Secure the pattern pieces to the curtain panels using fusible webbing, then stitch around the raw edges of the appliqués for a finished look.

Our pioneer forebears knew the value of scrap fabrics and put them to use whenever possible. We've done the same thing with this glad rag lampshade (opposite), which is a wire lampshade base wrapped with strips of fabric remnants.

Pennsylvania Dutch motifs turn these everyday kitchen tools (opposite) into something special, and all it takes is an easy-to-use electric woodburning tool. Transfer the designs to selected wooden utensils using carbon paper and burn the designs into the wood.

The how-to instructions for these projects begin on page 44.

One of the nicest things about woodburned utensils (above) is that once the designs have been burned into the wood, they are there to stay. Before you begin your designs, practice on pieces of scrap wood and experiment with a variety of attachments and tips.

IRISH CROCHET
pages 38-39

See page 373 for crochet abbreviations.
Oval Doily, pages 38-39
Finished size is 15x26 inches.

Materials: Clark's "Big Ball" three-cord mercerized cotton, size 50: 1 ball white; sizes 13 and 14 steel crochet hooks; 15x25 inches white linen.

Instructions: *Rosette motif* (make 8): Beg at center with larger hook, ch 6; join with sl st to form ring. *Rnd 1:* Ch 6, (dc in ring, ch 3) 8 times; join to 3rd ch of ch-6—9 sps. *Rnd 2:* Ch 1, * in next sp make sc, 5 dc, and sc. Rep from * around; join to first sc—9 petals. *Rnd 3:* Ch 1, * holding petals forward sc in back of work bet last petal and next petal, ch 5. Rep from * around; join to first sc.

Rnd 4: Ch 1, * in next lp make sc, 9 dc, and sc. Rep from * around; join to first sc. *Rnd 5:* Making ch 7 instead of ch 5, work as for Rnd 3. *Rnd 6:* Ch 1, * in next lp make sc, 11 dc, and sc. Rep from * around; join to first sc. *Rnd 7:* Sl st in first 3 dc; * (ch 7, sc in 5th ch from *hook for picot) twice; ch 2*—picot lp made; sk next 5 dc, sl st in next dc, make a picot lp, sl st in 3rd dc of next petal. Rep from * around, ending with sl st in 3rd sl st made at beg of rnd. *Rnd 8:* Sl st to center bet next 2 picots, ch 1, sc in same sp, make a picot lp, * sc in ch-2 sp bet next 2 picots, make a picot lp. Rep from * around; join to first sc.

Rnd 9: Sl st to tip of next picot, ch 1, sc in same picot, ch 3, * sc in next picot, ch 3. Rep from * around; join to first sc. Fasten off.

Preparing the doily: Preshrink and press linen. Cut a 13½x24-inch oval from paper to serve as master pattern. Trace around pattern on fabric; machine-stitch along this line. Cut oval from fabric just outside of machine stitching; make a rolled hem. *Edging: Rnd 1:* With right side of oval facing, and with lp on smaller hook, *insert hook through fabric 3/16 inch in from finished edge, yo and draw up a lp through fabric, yo and draw through two lps on hook*—sc made. Continue around work, making 8 sc per inch evenly spaced—238 sc. *Rnd 2:* Ch 4, dc in joining, * ch 2, sk next sc, in next st work dc, ch 1, dc—V-st made.* Rep from

* around, ending with ch 2; join with sl st in 3rd ch of beg ch-4. *Rnd 3:* Ch 6, sl st in 3rd ch from hook for picot, ch 4, sl st in 3rd ch from hook for picot, ch 1, dc in ch-1 sp of next V-st, * ch 3, sl st in 3rd ch from hook for picot, ch 4, sl st in 3rd ch from hook for picot, ch 1, dc in ch-1 sp of next V-st. Rep from * around, ending last rep with ch 1, join in 3rd ch of beg ch-6. *Rnd 4:* * (Ch 4, sl st in 3rd ch from hook) 3 times; sc in next dc. Rep from * around, ending with sl st in joining of Rnd 3—238 picot lps.

Points: Row 1: Sl st to sp bet first and 2nd picot of first lp, * ch 3, sl st in 3rd ch from hook, (ch 4, sl st in 3rd ch from hook) twice; sc bet first and 2nd picots of next lp *. Rep bet *s 7 times more—8 lps. *Row 2:* Turn, sl st to sp bet 2nd and 3rd picots of first lp; rep bet *s of Row 1 seven times—7 lps. Turn. Rep Rows 1 and 2, working one less lp each row until 1 lp rem. Fasten off. ** With right side facing, join thread in ch-sp bet first and 2nd picot of next free lp of Rnd 4; work as for First Point. Rep from ** around—34 points.

Setting rosettes into fabric: Space all 8 motifs evenly along edge of doily, ¾ inch from hem. Cut a hole in the fabric ½ inch in diameter smaller than the rosettes. Clip curves and make a rolled hem in each cutout. Whipstitch rosettes in place.

LACE EDGING AND CURTAIN
pages 38-39

Edging repeat is 2 inches wide.
Materials: Clark's "Big Ball" mercerized cotton, size 50; size 14 steel crochet hook; purchased or custom-made curtain panels.

Instructions: Decide which edge of panel is to receive lace. Trim panel to a measurement divisible by 2; hem.

Edging: Row 1: With right side of panel facing and with lp on hook, insert hook through fabric at right-hand corner 3/16 inch in from the finished edge, yo hook and draw lp through fabric and up to edge, yo and through 2 lps on hook. Continue across edge, making 8 sc per inch evenly spaced. *Row 2:* Ch 4,

turn, dc in same sc as ch-4, * ch 2, sk next sc, in next sc work dc, ch 1, dc—V-st made. Rep from * across. (*Note:* Ch 4 at beg counts as 1 dc and ch 1.) *Row 3:* Ch 6, turn, sl st in 3rd ch from hook for picot, ch 4, sl st in 3rd ch from hook for picot, ch 1, dc in ch-1 sp of V-st, * ch 3, sl st in 3rd ch from hook for picot, ch 4, sl st in 3rd ch from hook for picot, ch 1, dc in ch-1 sp of next V-st. Rep from * across. *Row 4:* Turn, * (ch 4, sl st in 3rd ch from hook) 3 times; sc in next dc. Rep from * across.

Points: Row 1: Turn, sl st up to ch bet 2nd and 3rd picot, * ch 3, sl st in 3rd ch from hook, ch 4, sl st in 3rd ch from hook twice, sc bet 2nd and 3rd picots of next picot lp *. Rep bet *s 7 times more. *Row 2:* Turn, sl st to sp bet first and 2nd picots. Rep bet *s of Row 1 seven times—7 lps. Rep Rows 1 and 2, making one less lp on each row until one lp rem. Fasten off. **

From right side, join thread in ch-1 bet 2nd and 3rd picots of next free lp of Row 4; work same as for First Point. Rep from ** across.

LANDSCAPE COUNTRY CURTAINS
page 42

On ecru fabric, mark curtain panels to fit window. Pattern below fits 45x45-inch curtains. Adjust field, sky to fit. Cut pattern pieces from tissue paper.

Referring to the color photograph on page 42, or using scraps of fabric to match your decor, cut the fabric pieces

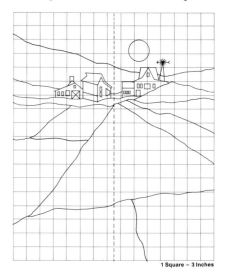

1 Square = 3 Inches

without adding the seam allowances. Baste fabric to the curtain panel. Machine zigzag stitch around each piece with black thread. Embroider windmill with black embroidery floss. Line curtains; attach rings for hanging.

GLAD RAG SHADE
page 43

Tear 44-inch-wide fabric (in assorted prints) into 2½- to 3-inch-wide strips. Purchase or salvage a metal lampshade frame that has an uneven number of spokes. Conceal top and bottom hoops by folding a fabric strip in half lengthwise; wrap hoops spirally with fabric, placing a folded edge over a raw edge.

Beginning at the bottom of the shade base, wrap one end of a long strip of fabric around a spoke. Using sewing thread to match fabric, tack securely in place.

Weave the strip over and under the spokes, wrapping strip around each spoke as you work. Tuck under raw edges of the strip to hide frayed edges. Join a new strip on the bias when necessary. Continue weaving, crushing the strips together (see photograph). Slipstitch end to last spoke wrapped.

Make tiny stitches between rows to hold strips. Complete wiring.

WOODBURNED ACCESSORIES
page 43

Enlarge the Pennsylvania Dutch woodburning patterns (right), or design your own simple motifs. Transfer them to kitchen utensils with carbon paper or dressmaker's carbon.

Position small motifs on the backs of spoons or below fork tines. Larger motifs are for recipe boxes, bread boxes, or the backs of cutting boards. Position the small horizontal motifs around the rims of wooden bowls.

Following the manufacturer's directions, practice woodburning on pieces of scrap lumber until you can control the thickness of the lines and make graceful curves. (Some woodburning tool sets include attachments that vary the nature of the burned line. Experiment with these attachments so that

you can incorporate various types of lines into your work.) When you have mastered the technique, burn designs into the backs of the utensils.

(Continued)

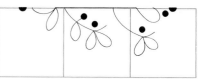

1 Square = 1 Inch

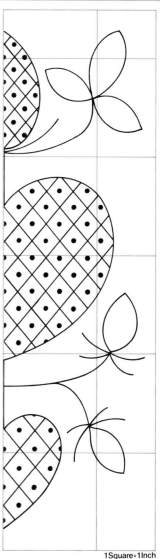

1 Square = 1 Inch

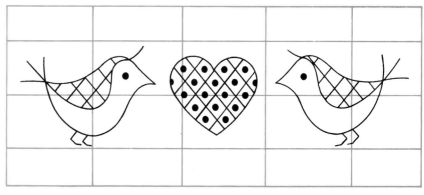

45

CHEVRON TABLECLOTH
page 3

Tablecloth measures about 50 inches across center from point to point. See page 373 for crochet abbreviations.

Materials: J & P Coats "Knit-Cro-Sheen" mercerized cotton: 11 balls no. 42 cream, 4 balls no. 4-A medium blue, and 4 balls no. 43 dark yellow; size 7 steel crochet hook.

Directions: Begin at center using cream, ch 8; sl st to form ring. *Rnd 1:* Ch 4, (dc in ring, ch 1) 15 times; join to 3rd ch of ch-4. *Rnd 2:* Ch 6, (dc in next dc, ch 3) 15 times; join to 3rd ch of ch-6. *Rnd 3:* Sl st in next sp, ch 3, make 3 dc in same sp, * ch 1, make 4 dc in next sp. Rep from * around, ending with ch 1; join to top of ch-3. *Rnd 4:* Sl st in last ch-1 sp made, ch 8, * sk next 4 dc, dc in next ch-1 sp, ch 5. Rep from * around; join to 3rd ch of ch-8. *Rnd 5:* Sl st in next sp, ch 3, make 5 dc in same sp, ch 1, * make 6 dc in next sp, ch 1. Rep from * around; join to top of ch-3. *Rnd 6:* Sl st in last sp made, ch 10, sk next 6 dc, * dc in next ch-1 sp, ch 7. Rep from * around; join to 3rd ch of ch-10. *Rnd 7:* Sl st in next sp, ch 3, make 7 dc in same sp, ch 1, * 8 dc in next sp, ch 1. Rep from * around; join to top of ch-3. *Rnd 8:* Sl st in last ch-1 sp made, sc in same place, * ch 9, sc in next ch-1 sp. Rep from * around, ending with ch-9; join to first sc. *Rnd 9:* Ch 1, sl st in joining, * ch 9, sl st in next sc. Rep from * around, ending with ch 9; join to first sl st. *Rnd 10:* Sl st in next 2 ch, ch 3, working over lps of last 2 rnds, thread over, insert hook under first lp of last 2 rnds and complete a dc; in same place make dc, ch 3, and dc; ch 3, * working over next lp of last 2 rnds, make 3 dc, ch 3, and 3 dc in lp as before; ch 3. Rep from * around; join to top of ch-3. *Rnd 11:* Sl st in next 2 dc, ch 3; in next sp make 3 dc, ch 3, and 3 dc; dc in next dc, ch 1, sc in next sp, ch 1, * sk next 2 dc, dc in next dc; in next sp make 3 dc, ch 3, and 3 dc; dc in next dc, ch 1, sc in next sp, ch 1. Rep from * around; join to top of ch-3. *Rnd 12:* Sl st in next 2 dc, ch 3, dc in next dc, * in next sp make 3 dc, ch 3, and 3 dc; dc in next 2 dc, ch 3; sk next 2 ch-1 sps and following 2 dc; dc in next 2 dc. Rep from * around, ending with ch 3; join to top of ch-3.

Rnd 13: Sl st in next 2 dc, ch 3, dc in each dc to next ch-3 sp, * in next sp make 3 dc, ch 3, and 3 dc; dc in each dc to within last 2 dc of same grp, ch 2, sc in next ch-3 sp, ch 2, sk next 2 dc on next grp, dc in each dc to next ch-3 sp. Rep from * around, ending with ch 2; join to top of ch-3. *Rnd 14:* Sl st in next 2 dc, ch 3, dc in each dc to next ch-3 sp, * in sp make 3 dc, ch 3, and 3 dc; dc in each dc to last 2 dc of same grp, ch 3; sk next 2 ch-2 sps and following 2 dc; dc in each dc to next ch-3 sp. Rep from * around, ending with ch-3; join to top of ch-3. Last 2 rnds form pat. *Rnds 15-17:* Work in pat. At end of Rnd 17 fasten off cream. *Rnd 18:* Sk first 2 dc on first grp, attach blue to next dc, ch 3, complete rnd in pat. *Always change color this way.* Continuing in pat, work 5 more rnds with blue; now work 6 rnds each of cream, yellow, cream, blue, cream, yellow, and cream. Fasten off. *Border—Rnd 1:* With right side facing, attach blue to any ch-3 sp; *ch 4, dc in same sp*—starting V st made; * ch 3, sk next 2 dc; in next dc make dc, ch 1, and dc—V st made; (ch 3, sk next 5 dc, V st in next dc) 9 times; sk last dc of this grp and first dc of next grp, V st in next dc, (ch 3, sk next 5 dc, V st in next dc) 9 times; ch 3, sk next 2 dc, V st in next ch-3 sp. Rep from * around, ending with ch 3; join to 3rd ch of ch-4. *Rnd 2:* Sl st in sp of first V st; *ch 4, dc in same sp*—starting V st over V st made; * (ch 2, sc in next sp, ch 2; *in ch-1 sp of next V st make dc, ch 1 and dc—V st over made*) 10 times; V st over next V st; (ch 2, sc in next ch-3 sp, ch 2, V st over next V st) 10 times. Rep from * around, ending with ch 2; join to 3rd ch of ch-4. Fasten off blue. *Rnd 3:* Attach cream to sp of first V st; make a starting V st, * (ch 3, V st over next V st) 9 times; ch 3, dc in next V st, ch 1, dc in following V st, (ch 3, V st over next V st) 10 times. Rep from * around, ending with ch 3; join to 3rd ch of ch-4. *Rnd 4:* Sl st in sp of first V st, ch 3; (in same sp make dc; *ch 4, sl st in 4th ch from hook—picot made*) 3 times; dc in same sp, * (ch 2, sc

1 Square = 1 Inch

in next ch-3 sp, ch 2; in sp of next V st make dc, picot, and dc) 9 times; ch 2, sc in next ch-1 sp, ch 2; (in next V st make dc, picot, and dc; ch 2, sc in next ch-3 sp, ch 2) 9 times; in sp of next V st make 2 dc and (picot, dc) 3 times. Rep from * around, ending with ch 2; join to top of ch-3. Fasten off.

BLUE AND WHITE CERAMICS
page 3

Materials: Unfired ceramic greenware bowl, cup, saucer, plate, and teapot; small sponge; greenware cleaning tools; blue glaze pencils; graphite.

Directions: Unless you have access to a kiln, you should work with a local ceramic studio to complete these projects. Greenware and glazes are sold at ceramic studios, and they will be able to fire your projects for a nominal fee. They also will provide you with lessons and instructions if you haven't worked with ceramics before.

Select the greenware pieces you like. If the studio does not have a particular piece on hand, the personnel can order molds for you and pour them. Handle greenware *very* carefully; it is extremely fragile.

Working with a cleaning tool and damp sponge, clean greenware pieces, removing seams and labels. (For best results, work over a sink.)

Have the greenware fired to bisque. Plan the geometric design on paper first, using the pattern (opposite) as a guide. (The pattern shown is for one quarter of a dinner plate, but it can be adapted to fit many other ceramic pieces.) Divide circular and spherical pieces into bands; fill remaining areas with flowers and geometric shapes.

Transfer the design to the bisque pieces using graphite paper and a *very sharp* lead pencil. As you work, check periodically to see that the design is transferring. If the pencil becomes dull while you are tracing the design, re-sharpen it. Color each area with glaze pencil. (Graphite burns away during firing.) Use enough pressure on the pencils to make a solid coat of glaze. Blow dust from pencils periodically.

Have pieces fired again at a bisque firing to set the glaze pencil designs.

Apply two coats of clear glaze to pieces according to manufacturer's directions. Have pieces fired to glaze.

ANTIQUE DOORSTOPS
page 3

Materials: ¾x6x24 inches pine; jigsaw; sandpaper; acrylic paints.

Directions: Enlarge patterns for the figures (below) and transfer them to wood. Cut around the outlines of the figures with a jigsaw. For each figure, also cut a wedge-shaped stop 1½ inches wide by 4 inches long.

Sand the pieces and give each one a base coat of gesso or white acrylic paint. When dry, sand the painted surfaces lightly until smooth. Transfer design details to the fronts of each piece using carbon paper.

Paint clothing and features for each of the figures with acrylic paints. Varnish when dry if desired. When wedge-shaped stops are dry, nail and glue them to the backs.

Right Foot

1 Square=1 Inch

DRESDEN PLATE QUILT
page 3

Materials: 12 yards of 45-inch-wide white or off-white fabric; assorted fabric scraps (see note below); 81x97 inches of quilt batting; thread.

Directions: *Note:* Our 79x97-inch quilt is composed of twenty 17-inch-square blocks. Each plate design has 19 wedges in it.

To determine the amount of fabric needed for wedges, plan to cut 18 plate wedges from ¼ yard of fabric, or 28 wedges from ⅓ yard. To make a quilt the same size as the one shown, cut 380 plate wedges and 117 print border wedges.

Enlarge the pattern (below) and transfer it to brown paper for a master pattern. Without adding seam allowances, trace the wedge pattern onto cardboard, sandpaper, or a plastic lid (to use as a template) and cut it out, keeping edges straight.

Before cutting the pieces for the entire quilt, cut and piece a sample block: Cut out 19 wedges from different fabrics by tracing the pattern onto fabric for each wedge. Space pattern pieces at least ½ inch apart to allow for ¼-inch seams. Trace and cut out pieces with straight grain of fabric running down center of wedge.

(Continued)

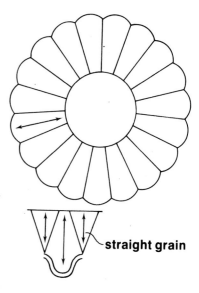

straight grain

Piece together the wedges by hand or machine, using ¼-inch seams, except leave ¼ inch of the seam unsewn at each end of each wedge so the inner and outer edges of the plate can be turned easily when the design is appliquéd to the square block. Press all the seams carefully to one side.

When the plate design is assembled, carefully pin and baste a ¼-inch hem along both the inner and outer edges of the circle. Press.

Cut a 17½ x 17½-inch background block from white fabric. Center the plate motif on the block, checking its position against the master pattern. Pin and baste the design into place.

To appliqué, whipstitch the inner edge first, then the outer edge, making sure that the pattern lies flat and smooth. If it does not sit correctly on the block, adjust the seams between the pieces or alter the pattern for the wedge. Make a record of any changes you make in the pattern.

When the sample block is satisfactory, cut wedges for the remaining 19 blocks and piece and appliqué them to the background blocks.

To assemble the quilt top, stitch four blocks together into a row, using ¼-inch seams. Make five rows, then stitch the rows together.

To make the border for the quilt, cut 109 white triangles and 117 print border wedges. Except in the corners of the quilt, piece wedges and triangles alternately as shown in the photograph.

To make the corners, piece three of the border wedges together. With the right sides facing, sew the border to the edge of the quilt in a ¼-inch seam. Press the seam allowance to one side. To make the binding, cut and piece 1-inch-wide white bias strips until they measure 13 yards. Set aside.

To assemble the quilt, first cut and piece backing fabric to size. Next, lay out backing fabric, wrong side up. Top with batting, then the quilt top. Pin and baste all layers together. After basting, quilt in patterns of your choice.

Bind the edges of the quilt with white bias strips: With right sides together, sew the binding strip to the front of the quilt in a ¼-inch seam. Clip curves and corners; fold the strip in half. Turn under the remaining raw edge; sew binding to quilt back.

CORN HUSK DOLLS
page 3

See page 333 for a list of the materials needed and complete how-to instructions for the dolls.

WOODBURNED DUCK DECOYS
page 3

See page 342 for complete how-to instructions for duck decoys.

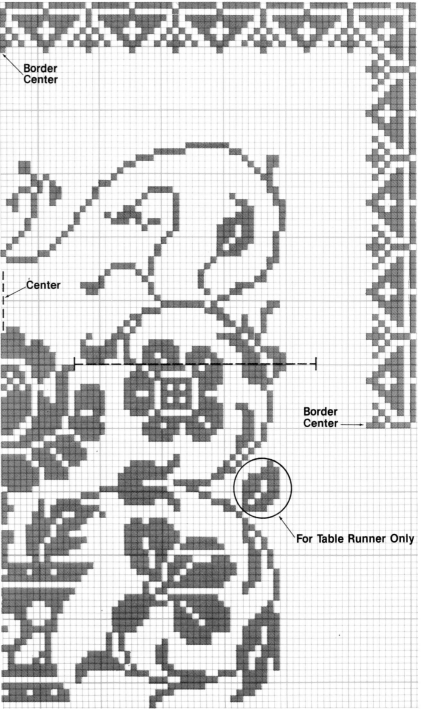

Border Center

Center

Border Center

For Table Runner Only

1 Square = 1 Stitch

FLORAL PILLOW
page 6

Finished size is of the pillow is approximately 13 square inches.

1 Square = 1 Cross-Stitch

Center →

center

Materials: One 20-inch square of #10-mesh needlepoint canvas; blue and white 3-ply yarn; tapestry needle; stretcher frame; staple gun; graph paper; ½ yard of backing fabric; cording; fiberfill or pillow form.

Instructions: Transfer the diagram (opposite) onto graph paper, eliminating the circled leaf area. Flop the design to complete the center motif and half of the border design. Flop the border design once again to complete the pattern.

Tape raw edges of the canvas and staple canvas onto stretcher frame.

Locate center of design and center of canvas; begin stitching blue pattern here using continental stitches.

Fill in the background with white yarn worked in basket-weave stitches. Add several rows of white outside the blue border if desired. Eliminate distortion by blocking.

Cut out backing, adding ½ inch for seam allowances. Sew cording to pillow top. With right sides together, stitch pillow front to back, leaving an opening for turning. Turn to right side, stuff with fiberfill or a pillow form, and slip-stitch the opening closed.

CROSS-STITCH TABLE RUNNER
page 6

Finished size is approximately 15x40 inches.

Materials: ½ yard white hardanger fabric; blue embroidery floss; embroidery needle and hoop; graph paper.

Instructions: Transfer the center motif for the needlepoint pillow (opposite) onto graph paper, excluding the border and eliminating the area above the dashed line. Transfer the design (left) to the center motif, matching cross-stitches along dashed lines. (The cross-stitches overlap.) Flop the image *(Continued)* to complete the center motif. Flop once again to complete the pattern.

A portion of the border is indicated on the table runner diagram. Extend border design to desired length and width, squaring corners as indicated on needlepoint pillow diagram.

Mark the center of the design. Locate the center of the fabric and mark it with a pin or a tailor's tack worked in regular sewing thread. Starting in the center of the fabric, count over three threads for each square on the graph; begin stitching at cross-stitch marked with an arrow (see diagram).

Work all of the cross-stitches over three threads.

When the embroidery is finished, steam press it on the wrong side, then cut excess fabric from around the finished piece, allowing ½-inch margin. Sew rolled hem.

EMBROIDERED GINGHAM TABLECLOTH
pages 6-7

Finished size is about 50x50 inches.

Materials: 1¼ yards (44/45 inches wide) gingham; #3 white pearl cotton thread; needle; embroidery hoop; 5 yards each of 1-, 2-, and 4-inch-wide white eyelet trim; dressmaker's carbon.

Instructions: Enlarge the diagram (below) and flop the image to complete the pattern.

Draw a 42-inch square, centered, on gingham fabric. Using dressmaker's carbon, transfer the design to one or more corners of cloth. Position it 1½

inches above edge of square. Mount the fabric in an embroidery hoop. Stitch French knots in flower center. Work stems in outline stitches; use satin stitches for leaves and petals.

When embroidery is finished, press, then cut out square on the marked line. Sew a rolled hem.

Finally, sew eyelet lace trim into place, positioning the widest trim on the bottom and the narrowest on the top next to the gingham.

PAINTED WOODEN BOWL AND PLATES
pages 6-7

Materials: 12-inch-diameter wooden bowl and plates; midnight blue and white acrylic paints; #10 flat artist's paintbrush; a liner brush; sandpaper; dressmaker's carbon or graphite paper.

Instructions: Trace the full-size diagram shown on page 49 onto brown wrapping paper. (The diagram equals $\frac{1}{6}$ of pattern.) Flop the image twice for half of the pattern. Flop the half image once more to complete the design.

Sand pieces, then paint with two coats of white acrylic paint. Sand lightly between coats and again after the second coat is dry.

Transfer the pattern onto the wooden bowl and plates using dressmaker's carbon or graphite paper.

With midnight blue paint, side load a #10 flat brush and make tulips and comma strokes around the border and center design on ALL shaded areas of the pattern.

Paint dark lines and commas using liner brush. Make dots with handle of the brush dipped into paint.

FRENCH KNOT DOILY
page 7

Finished size is 11 inches in diameter.

Materials: ½ yard of finely woven white fabric; #5 white and #5 blue variegated pearl cotton floss; embroidery hoop and needle; dressmaker's carbon paper.

Instructions: Enlarge doily pattern (opposite); flop the image twice to complete the pattern. Transfer the pattern to fabric with dressmaker's carbon.

Do not cut out the doily until the embroidery is completed. For best results, mount the fabric in an embroidery hoop before stitching.

With variegated blue thread, work the stems in outline stitches and the leaves and petals in satin stitches.

To enhance the appearance of the finished doily, pad the areas to be worked in satin stitches with rows of outline stitches or running stitches; work satin stitches over padding.

Fill the embroidered band with clusters of French knots worked in white pearl cotton. Do not embroider the center of the doily.

Iron the finished embroidery on the wrong side using a damp press cloth between the fabric and the iron.

Carefully cut out the doily along the edge indicated on the pattern. Work closely spaced buttonhole stitches all around to stabilize the edge.

Center→

1 Square = 1 Inch

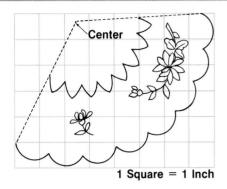

Center

1 Square = 1 Inch

BUTTERFLY TEA TOWEL
page 7

Finished size is 17x26 inches.

Materials: ¾ yard of blue linen (or similar fabric) for the towel; scrap of lightweight white fabric for the butterfly appliqué; 1 skein each of six-strand embroidery floss in the following colors: pink, gold, yellow, brown, green, and black; embroidery hoop and needle; white double-fold bias tape; light-colored dressmaker's carbon paper.

Instructions: Cut the blue linen fabric into a piece that measures 17½x-26½ inches. Bind the raw edges with white bias tape.

Enlarge the diagram (below) onto brown wrapping paper, flopping the image to complete the pattern.

Transfer the pattern onto the tea towel using dressmaker's carbon paper. (Refer to the photograph on page 7 for placement of the design.)

Center

1 Square = 1 Inch

Using the pattern once again, transfer the outline of the butterfly onto white fabric. Cut out the shape, adding ¼ inch for seam allowances. Turn under the raw edges and baste. Then baste the butterfly to the tea towel.

Use four strands of floss for all embroidery. Outline the butterfly wings with black buttonhole stitches first. Then remove the basting stitches.

Work gold running stitches for the antennae. Satin-stitch the upper portion of the butterfly body and outline-stitch the lower portion of the body with yellow floss.

Work yellow French knots in the centers of the flowers. Work the remaining dots on the pattern in gold French knots.

Stitch leaves and identical shapes on the butterfly wings with green lazy daisy stitches. Work pink straight stitches for large flower petals.

Trim the upper wings with brown straight stitches.

EMBROIDERED SHUTTERS
pages 6-7

Finished size of the screen inset is 5½x21 inches.

Materials: Hardware cloth (available at lumberyards) with 8 squares per inch; Belding Lily's Sugar 'n' Cream cotton yarn in white, cream, and 2 shades of blue (or a suitable substitute); large tapestry needle; window shutters; staple gun; masking tape, wire cutters; graph paper; colored pencils.

Instructions: To make the embroidery easier to work, transfer the design (right) onto graph paper using colored pencils. Flop the motif once to complete the top half and once again to complete the entire pattern.

Cut wire screens to fit window panel openings. Tape all of the raw edges so they are not sharp or scratchy.

Locate the center of the screen and the center of the design; begin stitching here and work toward the edges. Work the design with long, vertical stitches (like satin stitches) covering the back and front of the screen. Carefully conceal loose threads by weaving in and out of stitched areas on the back.

Sand window shutters smooth; varnish if desired. Assemble the window panels. Staple screens into place.

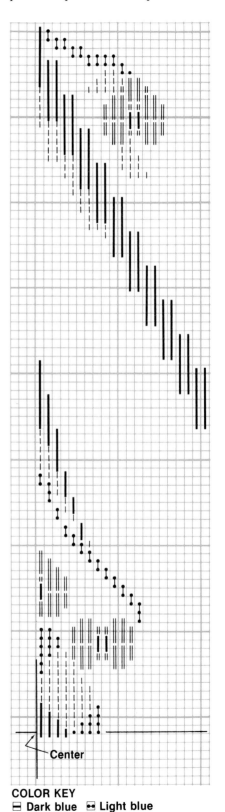

Center

COLOR KEY
⊟ **Dark blue** ⊞ **Light blue**
⊡ **White** ☰ **Cream**

51

COUNTRY CRAFTS TO DECORATE YOUR HOME

Country Elegance

ountry elegance is a delightfully fresh concept. It reflects a sense of restraint and simplicity rather than extravagance and opulence. It also means dressing up your rustic country crafts with a few lacy treasures from yesteryear. By teaming your country-best with heirloom lace, antique doilies, and other fancy finery, you can lend a slight touch of elegance to any country dwelling. Here's a perfect example of what we mean by country elegance: exquisite handmade doilies side by side with your Sunday-best country accessories. We give instructions for five of the doilies shown here—two embroidered, two crocheted, and one cutwork. These doilies can be reproduced exactly as shown or you can adapt some of the patterns and designs to other needlework projects. Either way, you'll be creating needlework treasures that will be prized by future generations. For the instructions, see pages 60, 61, and 62.

Although reminiscent of the Victorian era, these lovely old-fashioned collages are at home with country surroundings as well.

To create framed beauties like the ones shown above, select a fabric or printed paper for your background. Arrange pieces of ribbon and lace on top of the background, adding paper doilies, floral appliqués, antique greeting cards, or decoupage cutouts. Glue all the pieces in place with clear-drying glue and cover each collage with glass. Frame your collage as desired.

For pressed-flower pictures such as these (opposite), pick small, thin-centered flowers. Press the flowers in a thick book, covering the printed pages with blotting paper. (Do not overlap flowers.) Leave several empty pages between the pages with flowers.

Close and weight the book and place it in a warm, dry place for about one week while the flowers dry. When flowers are dry, store them in shallow, covered boxes.

To compose a pressed-flower picture, cover a piece of cardboard or foam-core board with an attractive background fabric or paper. Use tweezers to arrange the flowers on the background, starting with the tallest flower and gradually filling in the design.

Next, secure each of the flowers to the background by applying a dot of quick-drying white glue to each piece with a toothpick.

Use an antique frame to add to the old-fashioned look of these pictures. Look in your favorite antique stores, at auctions, and at flea markets for a frame about the size of your picture. If necessary, you can mat the picture to make it fit the frame you choose.

Hang your picture away from direct sunlight to protect the flowers from fading.

Gather flowers at midday after the dew has dried and when the flowers are in full bloom. When you choose flowers, keep in mind that they become quite fragile when dried, and that their colors often change or fade.

For a touch of simple elegance, dress up your tables with these two imaginative tabletop ideas. The tea cozy doll (left) stands about 17 inches tall and is made entirely of fabric with an extra layer of quilt batting under the skirt to keep your tea piping hot.

The richly embroidered table runner (opposite) is worked in a variety of textured stitches using pearl cotton thread on even-weave linen. Stitch the flower basket design at both ends of the runner and add a few simple design elements between the two motifs. Finish the raw edges of the linen with purchased braid or trim. The large weblike flowers are worked in a variation of whipped spider-web stitch to create a raised, spiral effect.

Instructions for these projects begin on page 62.

Stuff the tea cozy doll's head firmly with bits of polyester fiberfill to emphasize its shape and dimension. Then, embroider the facial features with one or two strands of floss and color the cheeks with powdered rouge. All you need to complete the doll are some small-scale print fabrics, muslin, batting, and lace trims.

S hed some light on the subject of custom-made lampshades and make a visible improvement in your country furnishings with these lace lighting ideas. You can transform wire lampshade frames into something special using just a little fabric and lace.

The lampshades work up quickly and easily. Best of all, you can achieve this elegant look at a relatively low cost, especially if you look for lace doilies at garage sales and secondhand stores. To help keep costs even lower, use up bits and pieces of leftover fabric from your sewing basket instead of buying additional fabric from the store. To trim your lampshades, use lace edging, braid, or decorative trim.

The secret to making these lampshades is to wrap the wire frames with seam binding and then cover each section between wire spokes with fabric that is pulled taut. To create a special color scheme, you can dye your lace with fabric dyes. For instructions, see page 64.

Although the lampshade above is strictly for inspiration, you can create something similar by using pieces of Irish crochet and following the instructions for the trio of lampshades pictured at left.

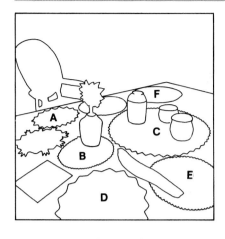

and pad-stitch the scalloped border with double-running stitches.

Work the rose petals and leaves in long-and-short stitches, using the pale green for the lower part of the leaves (closest to the stems) and pale pink for the tips. Work wide stems in medium green outline stitches. Shade petals as indicated on the pattern.

Work scallops around the edge of the doily in small, closely spaced ecru buttonhole stitches. Use outline stitches for the flourish at the base of each scallop motif.

To finish, trim excess fabric beyond buttonhole stitching; press wrong side of doily on padded ironing board.

SILK ROSE EMBROIDERED DOILY (A)
pages 52-53

Materials: 15x15 inches of handkerchief linen or other finely woven, lightweight white fabric; silk or cotton embroidery floss in dark, medium and light red, very pale pink, medium and very pale green, and ecru; very fine embroidery needles; dressmaker's carbon paper, water-erasable needlework marking pen, or transfer pencil.

Instructions: Enlarge the pattern (below right) and transfer it, centered, to the fabric using carbon, pencil, or pen. If desired, mount the fabric in an embroidery hoop.

Color Key:
1—dark red
2—medium red
3—light red
4—medium green
5—pale green
6—pale pink

Use one strand of floss throughout. To give the design dimension, outline and pad-stitch portions of the large rose and one of the loose rose petals, as indicated on the pattern.

To pad these areas, first outline each section with small backstitches. Next, work rows of double running stitches back and forth across the area until it is completely filled. Then embroider satin stitches over the running stitches, between but not over the outline stitches that surround the shape. If you are embroidering with silk floss, use a white cotton floss for the pad-stitching; otherwise, pad-stitch with thread that closely matches the final color. Also outline

MULTICOLORED FLOWER DOILY (B)
pages 52-53

Materials: 12x12 inches of white handkerchief linen or other finely woven fabric; cotton embroidery floss in

medium yellow-green, light and medium blue, light and medium pink, light and medium yellow, and lavender; embroidery needles; 30 inches of ⅝-inch-wide lace edging.

Instructions: Enlarge the pattern (opposite), and transfer it, centered, to the fabric. For best results, mount the fabric in an embroidery hoop before stitching.

Use two strands of cotton floss for the embroidery. Outline and pad-stitch the pink center flower and lavender flowers in the garland before you begin final stitching, following directions for the rose doily.

Outline yellow circles and pad them by working a double cross-stitch in the center of each.

Use satin stitches for the large flowers and yellow circles. (Work half of the circles in light yellow, half in medium yellow.) Work the center blue circle and green stems of the garland in outline stitches; leaves are single chain stitches. Work small dots in the center

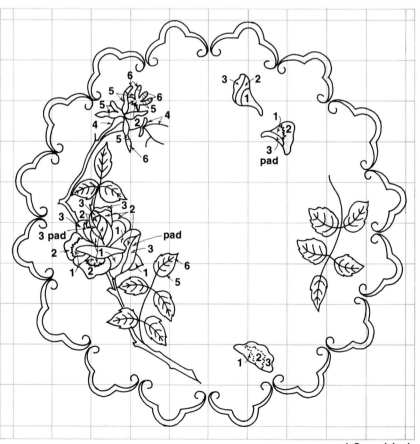

1 Sq. = 1 inch

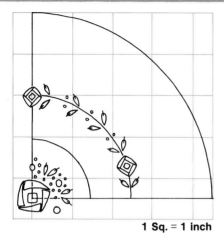

circle with French knots in shades of blue. Small dots along garland are pairs of French knots worked in pink, lavender, and blue. Press the finished embroidery on the wrong side.

Trim the fabric to an 8½-inch circle, make a narrow rolled hem around the edge, and attach lace edging.

CUTWORK DOILY (C)
page 53

Materials: 24x24 inches of finely woven white linen or cotton; white cotton embroidery floss; embroidery needles; small, sharp-pointed scissors; embroidery hoop or frame.

Instructions: The pattern at right is for one-third of the doily design. Enlarge the pattern to size, rotating it to complete the circular design.

Transfer the pattern to fabric, stretch the fabric in an embroidery hoop, and embroider the doily before cutting it out. Use one strand of floss throughout.

Work the stems in outline stitches. Outline all remaining areas, including eyelets and scallops around the outer edge, with small backstitches.

Pad-stitch all areas except the eyelets (which will be cut out) with short running stitches worked back and forth inside the backstitched outlines. Lay the padding stitches close together, then work satin stitches over padding stitches and outlines of each shape.

To work the eyelets, first cut out the centers of the circles with small, sharp scissors. Bind the raw edges of the circles with closely spaced overcast stitches worked over the backstitch outlines.

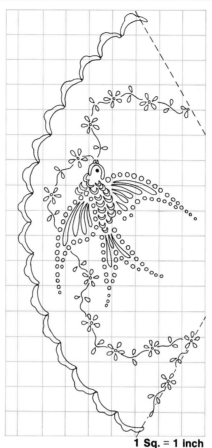

To work the border scallops, embroider closely spaced buttonhole stitches over the padding and outline stitches.

When the entire edge is stitched, use small, sharp scissors to carefully trim excess fabric from beyond the scallops. Block the doily by dampening it and pinning to a padded board to dry; this also shrinks the fabric slightly, so any frayed edges draw up into the embroidered areas.

DOILY WITH CROCHETED EDGING (D)
pages 52-53

Approximately 11 inches in diameter.

Materials: Clark's "Big Ball" Mercerized Cotton, Size 40: 1 ball of #1 white; size 11 steel crochet hook; small piece of linen fabric (approximately 5½ inches square).

Border is worked in 3 sections: *Center section:* Ch 6, dc in first ch, ch 3; over the bar of dc just made make 7 dc, ch 2 and dc—mark the right side of this dc-group to be used later; ch 3, turn; * over the ch-2 loop just made make 7 dc, ch 3 and dc; ch 3, turn. Rep from * until there are 48 dc-groups with right side showing and 47 dc-groups with wrong side showing; make 6 dc over the ch-2 loop just made, being careful not to twist dc-groups, sl st in first ch of starting ch-6, then sl st in next 2 ch of same ch-6, then sl st in last ch-2 loop used. Fasten off. *Inner section: Rnd 1:* With wrong side of free dc-groups facing, attach thread to top of ch-3 of any dc-group, ch 1, sc in same place, * ch 5, sc in top of ch-3 of next dc-group. Rep from * around. Join to first sc. *Rnd 2:* Ch 5, dc in first loop, ch 3, * dc in next sc, ch 2, dc in next loop, ch 3. Rep from * around. Join to 3rd ch of ch-5. *Rnd 3:* Sl st in next sp, ch 5, * dc in next sp, ch 2. Rep from * around. Join to 3rd ch of ch-5. Fasten off. *Outer section: Rnd 1:* With right side of marked dc-group facing, attach thread to top ch-3; ch 1, sc in same place, * ch 7, sc in top of ch-3 of next right side facing dc-group. Rep from * around, end with ch 5, hdc in first sc to form last loop—48 loops. *Rnd 2:* Ch 5, * in next loop make (dc, ch 2) twice and dc; ch 2, in following loop make (dc, ch 2) three times and dc; ch 2, in next loop make (dc, ch 2) twice and dc, ch 2. Rep from * around. Join to 3rd ch of ch-5—160 sps. *Rnd 3:* Sl st in first sp, ch 3, 2 dc in same sp, 2 dc in next sp, * (3 dc in next sp, 2 dc in each of next 2 sps) twice; (3 dc in next sp, 2 dc in next sp) twice. Rep from * to last 2 sps, 3 dc in next sp, 2 dc in last sp. Join to top of ch-3. *Rnd 4:* Ch 1, sc in joining; sc in next 9 dc, * ch 3, skip next 3 dc; *in next dc make dc, ch 3 and dc—V st made;* ch 3, skip next 3 dc, sc in next 17 dc. Rep from * around, end with sc in last 7 dc. Join to first sc. *Rnd 5:* Ch 1, sc in joining; sc in next 8 sc, * ch 3, dc in next sp, ch 2, *V st in sp of next V st—V st over V st made;* ch 2, dc in next sp, ch 3, skip next sc, sc in next 15 sc. Rep from * around, end with ch 3, skip next sc, sc in last 6 sc. Join as before. *Rnd 6:* Ch 1, sc in joining; sc in next 7 sc, * ch 3, (dc in next sp, ch 2) twice, V st over V st, (ch 2, dc in next sp) twice, ch 3, skip next sc, sc in next 13 sc. Rep from * around, end with ch

(Continued)

3, skip next sc, sc in last 5 sc. Join. *Rnd 7:* Ch 1, sc in joining, sc in next 6 sc, * ch 3, (dc in next sp, ch 2) 3 times, V st over V st, (ch 2, dc in next sp) 3 times, ch 3, skip next sc, sc in next 11 sc. Rep from * around, end with ch 3, skip next sc, sc in last 4 sc. Join. *Rnd 8:* Ch 1, sc in joining; sc in next 5 sc, * ch 3, (dc in next sp, ch 2) 4 times, V st over V st, (ch 2, dc in next sp) 4 times, ch 3, skip next sc, sc in next 9 sc. Rep from * around, end with ch 3, skip next sc, sc in last 3 sc. Join. *Rnd 9:* Ch 1, sc in joining; sc in next 4 sc, * ch 3, (dc in next sp, ch 2) 5 times, V st over V st, (ch 2, dc in next sp) 5 times, ch 3, skip next sc, sc in next 7 sc. Rep from * around, end with ch 3, skip next sc, sc in last 2 sc. Join. *Rnd 10:* Ch 1, sc in joining, sc in next 3 sc, * ch 3, (dc in next sp, ch 2) 6 times, V st over V st, (ch 2, dc in next sp) 6 times, ch 3, skip next sc, sc in next 5 sc. Rep from * around, end with ch 3, skip next sc, sc in last sc. Join. *Rnd 11:* Ch 1, sc in joining; sc in next 2 sc, * ch 3 (dc in next sp, ch 2) 7 times, V st over V st, (ch 2, dc in next sp) 7 times, ch 3, skip next sc, sc in next 3 sc. Rep from * around, end last repeat with dc in last sp, dc in first sc. *Rnd 12:* Ch 1, sc over bar of last dc made, * sc in next sp, (in next sp make sc, ch 5 and sc) 15 times; sc in next sp. Rep from * around. Join. Fasten off.

Cut a circular piece of fabric for the center that is ¼ inch larger all around than center opening of crocheted piece. Machine-stitch fabric close to edge, then appliqué inner edge of crocheted piece over the edge of the fabric. Block.

CROCHETED DOILY (E)
page 53

About 10½ inches in diameter.

Materials: J & P Coats "Big Ball" Mercerized Cotton, Size 40: 1 ball of #1 white; size 12 steel crochet hook.

Instructions: Starting at center, ch 8. Join with sl st to form a ring. *Rnd 1:* Ch 3, make 26 dc in ring. Join to top of ch-3—27 dc, counting ch-3 as 1 dc. *Rnd 2:* Ch 6, skip next 2 dc, (dc in next dc, ch 3, skip next 2 dc) 8 times. Join to 3rd ch of ch-6—9 loops. *Rnd 3:* Ch 3, 7 dc in next loop, (dc in next dc, 7 dc in next loop) 8 times. Join to top of ch-3. *Rnd 4:* Ch 1, sc in joining, (ch 9, skip 7 dc, sc

in next dc) 8 times; ch 4, dtr in first sc to form last loop—9 loops. *Rnd 5:* Ch 1, 6 sc in loop just formed, 11 sc in each of next 8 loops, 5 sc in first loop used. Join to first sc. *Rnd 6:* Ch 1, sc in joining, ch 10, skip 10 sc, (sc in next sc, ch 10, skip 10 sc) 8 times. Join to first sc. *Rnd 7:* Ch 3, 13 dc in next loop, (dc in next sc, 13 dc in next loop) 8 times. Join to top of ch-3. *Rnd 8:* Ch 1, sc in joining, ch 7, skip next 6 dc, * sc in next dc, ch 7, skip next 6 dc. Rep from * around. Join to first sc—18 loops. *Rnd 9:* Ch 1, make 9 sc in each loop around. Join to first sc. *Rnd 10:* Sl st in next 3 sc, in next sc make sl st, ch 1 and sc, * ch 7, skip next 8 sc, sc in next sc. Rep from * around, end with ch 7. Join to first sc. *Rnd 11:* Rep Rnd 9. *Rnd 12:* Making ch 8 instead of ch 7, work as for Rnd 10. *Rnd 13:* Ch 1, make 11 sc in each loop around. Join to first sc. *Rnd 14:* Sl st next 4 sc; in next sc make sl st, ch 1 and sc, * ch 9, skip next 10 sc, sc in next sc. Rep from * around, end with ch 9. Join to first sc. *Rnd 15:* Ch 3, make 11 dc in first loop, * dc in next sc, 11 dc in next loop. Rep from * around. Join to top of ch 3. *Rnd 16:* Ch 4, skip next 2 dc, * dc in next dc, (ch 1, skip 1 dc, dc in next dc) 3 times; ch 1, skip 2 dc, dc in next dc, ch 1, skip next 2 dc. Rep from * around, end with ch 1, skip last 2 dc, join to 3rd ch of ch-4—90 sps. *Rnds 17-18:* Sl st in first sp, ch 5, * dc in next sp, ch 2. Rep from * around. Join to 3rd ch of ch-5. *Rnd 19:* Ch 3, 2 dc in first sp, dc in next dc, ch 2, * dc in next dc, 2 dc in next sp, dc in next dc, ch 2. Rep from * around. Join to top of ch-3. *Rnd 20:* Ch 5, * skip next 2 dc, dc in next dc, 2 dc in next sp, dc in next dc, ch 2. Rep from * around, end with 2 dc in last sp. Join to 3rd ch of ch-5. *Rnd 21:* Ch 3, 2 dc in first sp, dc in next dc, ch 2, * skip next 2 dc, dc in next dc, 2 dc in next sp, dc in next dc, ch 2. Rep from * around. Join to top of ch-3. *Rnd 22:* Ch 3, dc in next 3 dc, 4 dc in next sp, * dc in next 4 dc, 4 dc in next sp. Rep from * around. Join to top of ch-3. *Rnd 23:* Ch 3, dc in next dc and in each dc around. Join to top of ch-3. *Rnd 24:* Ch 4, skip next dc, * dc in next dc, ch 1, skip next dc. Rep from * around. Join to 3rd ch of ch-4. *Rnd 25:* Ch 4, * dc in next sp, ch 1. Rep from * around. Join

to 3rd ch of ch-4. *Rnds 26-28:* Rep Rnd 17. *Rnd 29:* Sl st in first sp, ch 3, in same sp make dc, ch 2 and 2 dc, ch 5, * skip next 3 sps; *in next sp make 2 dc, ch 2 and 2 dc—shell made;* ch 5. Rep from * around. Join to top of ch-3. *Rnd 30:* Sl st in next dc and in next ch-2 sp, ch 3, in same sp make dc, ch 2 and 2 dc, ch 4, * make shell in sp of next shell, ch 4. Rep from * around. Join to top of ch-3. *Rnd 31:* Sl st in next dc and in next ch-2, ch 3, in same sp make dc, ch 2, and 2 dc; * ch 3, insert hook under next loop of last 2 rnds and complete an sc, ch 3, shell in sp of next shell. Rep from * around, end with ch 3. Join as before. *Rnd 32:* Sl st in next dc, in next ch-2 sp make sl st, ch 1 and sc; ch 9, * sc in sp of next shell, ch 9. Rep from * around. Join to first sc. *Rnd 33:* Rep Rnd 15. *Rnd 34:* Ch 5, skip next 2 dc, * dc in next dc, ch 2, skip next 2 dc. Rep from * around. Join to 3rd ch of ch-5. *Rnds 35-36:* Rep Rnds 29 and 30. *Rnd 37:* Ch 1, sc in next dc, * ch 5, sc in next ch-2 sp, ch 5, sc in same sp, ch 5, sc in next dc, ch 3, insert hook under next loop of last 2 rnds and complete an sc, ch 3, skip next dc, sc in next dc. Rep from * around, end ch 5. Join to first sc. Fasten off. Starch lightly and press.

TEA COZY DOLL
page 56

Finished size is 17 inches high.

Materials: ½-inch-thick quilt batting; ¼ pound of fiberfill; ¾ yard muslin; ⅔ yard striped fabric; ½ yard print fabric that coordinates with striped fabric; 9-inch square of dotted swiss fabric for hankie; ½ skein tapestry or sport-weight yarn; embroidery floss; lace and ribbon trims; white glue.

Instructions: For the cozy, cut one 20x32-inch rectangle from the muslin and one from the batting.

Fold the muslin in half lengthwise. Lightly mark quilting lines with pencil as follows: Draw one horizontal line two inches from the folded edge. Mark vertical lines, spaced at 2-inch intervals, at right angles to this line to the raw edge. Unfold muslin and place atop batting; baste together.

Refold the cozy with the batting sides together. Machine-quilt along all lines. Roll the ends of the cozy together to form a 10-inch-high tube. Blind-stitch short ends of tube together, then machine-quilt along the seam.

For casing, cut one 2½x32-inch muslin strip; sew short ends together. With right sides together, sew strip to top of cozy. Fold in half (turning under raw edge) and slip-stitch to inside of the cozy. Run a gathering thread through the casing.

Enlarge the head pattern (right), and transfer it to brown paper. Cut two pattern pieces from muslin, adding ½-inch seam allowances. Place right sides together and stitch around, leaving an opening at top of head and at base of neck. Trim seams, clip curves, and turn right side out. Run gathering thread around top of head opening and pull closed; secure thread. Stuff head and neck firmly.

Transfer the facial features (right), onto the face. Embroider face, using one strand of floss for eyelashes and two strands for remaining features. Color cheeks with powdered rouge.

For bodice, cut one 7½x14½-inch rectangle from print fabric. With the right sides together, sew a ¼-inch seam along the short edge. Turn under raw edges at top and bottom; stitch. Run gathering thread around top and bottom edges. Turn to right side.

Insert neck into top of bodice. Pull thread taut around neck; slip-stitch neck to bodice.

Stuff bodice firmly; pull gathering thread at bottom and secure thread.

Gather cozy to fit around bottom of bodice; pin in place. Sew to bodice.

Enlarge the arm pattern; transfer it to brown paper. Cut four pattern pieces from the muslin, adding a ½-inch seam allowance. Stitch around, leaving open at top; trim seams. Turn right side out. Stuff arms to within 1¾ inches of top edge. (This makes arms easier to position.) Turn raw edges under; slip-stitch arms to bodice.

For hair, cut a 6x12-inch cardboard rectangle. Wrap the yarn lengthwise around cardboard until it is completely full. *Do not cut yarn loops.* Slip yarn off cardboard; center the bundle of yarn lengthwise across a vertical 2x5-inch muslin strip. Sew yarn to strip. Trim muslin ¼ inch from stitching.

Glue strip down center of head. Grasp looped ends on either side and

twist toward face into chignon; slip-stitch into place.

For bottom skirt, cut one 13x45-inch rectangle from striped fabric. Cut an 11x45-inch rectangle from print fabric for top skirt. With right sides together stitch short sides, leaving a three-inch opening at top for placket. Turn up hem on top skirt; add trim.

Slip top skirt over bottom skirt, matching placket openings. Run a row of gathering threads around top edge and pull it to fit waistline 3 inches below neckline; secure gathers and remove from bodice.

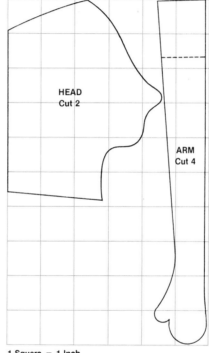

HEAD
Cut 2

ARM
Cut 4

1 Square = 1 Inch

For waistband, cut a 2-inch-wide printed strip long enough to encircle the waist, plus 1 inch. With right sides together, stitch waistband to skirt. Fold in half to inside, turn raw edges, and stitch in place.

For skirt bow, cut a 4½x24-inch print rectangle. Fold in half with right sides together; stitch, leaving an opening for turning. Trim; turn to right side and stitch opening closed. Tie into bow; tack to waistband.

For sleeves, cut two striped rectangles, each 11x15 inches. With right sides together, stitch short sides. Turn under raw edges at top and bottom and stitch. Run gathering thread along top edge. Gather sleeve to fit around arm; secure thread. Slip sleeve over arm and stitch in place.

Run gathering thread through bottom edge. Pull thread to fit wrist and secure in place. Add trim to neckline.

Cut edges of hankie with pinking shears. Fold into square, gather, and stitch into position in left hand. Sew hands to body. Trim hair with bow.

EMBROIDERED TABLE RUNNER
page 57

Approximate size: 16x43½ inches.
Materials: ½ yard of white even-weave linen; 1 skein each of pearl cotton thread in the following colors: blue, green, black, white, yellow, rose, and pink; embroidery hoop; 3½ yards of braid or trim for edging; dressmaker's carbon paper; tracing wheel.

Instructions: The pattern on page 64 is for one-half of the entire design. Enlarge the pattern and repeat it for the remaining half of the design.

Cut a 17x44½-inch piece of linen and stitch a rolled hem along the raw edges of the fabric. (If desired, cut a scalloped or curved edge along the two short ends.) Finish the edges with a row of decorative trim.

Transfer the embroidery pattern to the fabric using light-colored dressmaker's carbon paper. Place the fabric in an embroidery hoop and begin working the design, referring to the stitch glossary on page 374. (Refer to the photograph for color details.)

(Continued)

63

FOLD

1 Square = 2 Inches

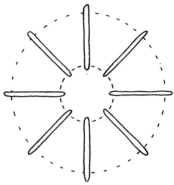

Diagram A

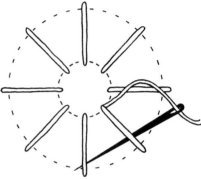

Diagram B

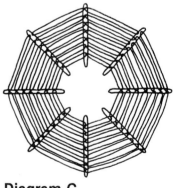

Diagram C

Work black stems, blue basket, and blue lattice in outline stitches; work blue basket handle and large green leaves in satin stitches. Small green leaves are lazy daisy stitches; small flowers are French knots.

To work large flowers, stitch a foundation as shown in diagram A (above right), making black "spokes" that extend from flower centers. Bring working thread up at start of one of the spokes; lay it back over thread to right (diagram B) so needle is inserted under that thread as well as under spoke to left. When needle is pulled through, working thread should be between next pair of spokes to left. Repeat this procedure, carrying needle *under* spoke to right of working thread and from right to left *under* spoke on left of working thread. Work until loops are formed along entire length of all spokes and flower is filled in (diagram C). Work French knots in center of flowers.

LACE LAMPSHADES
pages 58-59

Materials (for all lampshades): Metal lampshade frames in desired shapes and sizes; enough muslin or printed fabric to cover shades; seam binding to wrap metal frames; liquid fabric dye; glue; spray adhesive; needle and thread; straight pins; lace trims and edgings.

Instructions: *For small lampshade,* wrap entire frame tightly with a single layer of seam binding; this provides a base for attaching fabric cover.

Select a doily whose radius extends 2 or more inches beyond the height of the lampshade. Color doily and fabric with fabric dyes; dry and press.

Draw a pattern for each section of shade on paper; trace pattern onto dyed fabric on the *bias* the required number of times, adding 1 inch all around for seam allowances. Cut out the pattern.

Stretch one pattern piece over section of frame, pulling fabric taut and securing to frame with pins pushed into the seam binding. The fabric *must* lie smoothly on frame. Whipstitch fabric to frame, remove pins, and trim fabric close to stitching. Repeat process to cover each section of frame.

Stretch the doily over the frame; pull it taut and pin into place. Tack around top edge of frame; cut out center of doily, allowing ½-inch seam margin. Turn under raw edge; glue to inside of shade. Glue lace trim or ribbon to top and bottom of frame.

For green lampshade: Make as directed above, eliminating doily. Glue narrow lace trim over seams. Slip-stitch dyed crocheted edging to lower edge of shade. Add edging around the top.

For printed fabric lampshade: Make same as small shade using printed fabric. If fabric is not sufficiently opaque, cover frame with muslin first.

Cover seams with narrow trim; glue in place. Cut appliqué motifs from bridal lace fabric; daub cut edges with glue to prevent fraying. When dry, position appliqués on shade and secure them with spray adhesive or dabs of glue.

To make multilayered ruffle, cut a strip of 3-inch-wide fabric twice the circumference of lower edge of shade. Turn under ¼ inch on one raw edge; press and stitch. Baste 2½-inch-wide lace along raw edge of strip. Next, sew a strip of narrow preruffled eyelet to underside of hem. Gather top (raw) edge of ruffle, and slip-stitch ruffle to bottom of shade. Cover seam with ¼-inch trim.

Center

1 Square = 1 Inch

WHITE EMBROIDERED TABLECLOTH
pages 8-9

Finished size is approximately 60 inches in diameter.

Materials: 1¾ yards (60-inch-wide) of white fabric or a purchased tablecloth; white embroidery floss; embroidery hoop and needle; 3-inch-wide lace as follows: 4 yards for insert, 5⅔ yards for tablecloth edging.

Instructions: Enlarge the diagram (above) onto brown paper. Flop the image to complete half of the design. Then flop the image once again to complete the pattern.

Cut out a 60-inch circle from fabric. (To do this, fold fabric in quarters and mark the 30-inch radius of the circle with a string tied to a pencil; cut along marked line.) Stitch a rolled hem.

Transfer the pattern to the center of cloth using dressmaker's carbon paper in a light color. Or, trace the design (with the fabric laid atop the pattern) with a water-erasable pen.

For best results, stretch the fabric in an embroidery hoop before stitching. Using three strands of floss, outline-stitch the stems and satin-stitch all other shapes. If desired, pad flower petals and leaves with closely spaced rows of running stitches before satin stitching.

When the embroidery is finished, cut inset lace into four 35-inch lengths. (This allows for a ½-inch overlap at the longest edge and a wider overlap at the shortest edge for mitering corners.)

Place the wrong side of the lace facing the right side of the tablecloth in a square border around the completed embroidery. (See photograph on page 9.) Hand- or machine-stitch the lace to the cloth along both sides, mitering corners.

Carefully cut out fabric from behind the lace, close to stitching lines.

Next, transfer daisy motifs to the bottom of the skirt, scattering the motifs as desired. Embroider as directed above.

Stitch lace edging to the hem of the tablecloth.

If desired, trim a set of napkins with one or more daisy motifs and narrow lace edging, to match the tablecloth.

COUNTRY CRAFTS TO DECORATE YOUR HOME

Build-It-Yourself Furniture

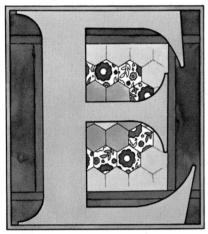

asy-to-build American primitives like these have become fixtures in homes all across the country. Their clean and simple lines make them perfect examples of the spirit that originated with our colonial ancestors. The reproduction pieces shown here are constructed of pine, making them just as utilitarian today as when they were first introduced. Although modest in design, these pieces earn their merit by combining timeless, inherent beauty with function and practicality. For added ambience, chain-stitch the hex symbol throw and pillows pictured here with the settle and Pennsylvania Dutch chair. The cross-stitch sampler (near the colonial hutch) works up fast and easy and provides inspiring words to live by. Our quick-and-easy version of the traditional Grandmother's flower garden quilt (opposite) saves time by eliminating many of the hexagon-shaped pieces. How-to instructions for these projects begin on page 72.

Thanks to a practical approach to design, these two hardworking pieces of furniture are at home in a large rambling farmhouse, in a small house in the city, or wherever else you choose to hang your hat.

To add some country flavor to your own special place, build this modern-day adaptation of an old-fashioned porch swing (right). Begin by cutting two 47-inch 2x12s for the seat and placing them side by side. Screw two lengths of 1x6 across the underside to join the two pieces. Drill the ends of the seat for arm support dowels, with a 1-inch dowel on each end and four 5/8-inch dowels between. Cut a 22-inch 2x4 for each arm; then drill a 1-inch hole in each end to accommodate the hanging chains. Drill holes in the seat and in the underside of the arms; then cut dowels to 8½ inches and glue them in place.

Cut a 43-inch 2x4 for the back. Cut two 12-inch 1x6s for the center panel and add a heart cutout as shown. Cut eight 5/8-inch dowels 14 inches long for the back. Drill the seat and the underside of the back for dowels. (Angle holes in the seat at 20 degrees; there are several electric drill attachments available to simplify this.) Secure the panel in place with 3/8-inch dowel joints. Glue the dowels in place.

Attach 4 eyebolts in the corners of the seat. Next, thread four 48-inch lengths of chain from the bolts through the holes in the arms. At-

tach a length of chain where these meet with S-hooks and hang the swing from ceiling joists.

For the old-time cabinet (opposite), cut two 13½x69-inch sides, one 13½x37½-inch bottom, and one 14x40-inch top from ¾-inch plywood. Glue and nail the pieces together. Then glue and nail a 1x4 to the front of the cabinet and measure the opening.

For the doors, cut enough 62½-inch lengths of beaded ceiling strips to fit across half of the opening; secure them together with 3 lengths of bevel-cut 1x3s. Repeat for the

other door and hinge the doors to the unit. Sand all edges and surfaces, and finish as desired.

For a professional wood finish, sand your project until it is smooth before applying the first coat of stain or varnish. Let it dry for 48 hours and sand again. Continue sanding and finishing until you have applied the last coat. Then let the piece dry about two weeks and buff with fine steel wool.

Decorative painting on furniture is as much a part of American style as the homey, primitive pieces built by our forebears. In early times, fine craftsmen and traveling artists alike were skilled in adding color and pattern to simply designed chairs, benches, and chests such as those shown here. The result was a blend of function and folk art that you can re-create today with carving tools, a woodburner, and acrylic paints.

Fanciful Jacobean-style garlands, inspired by old-world floral designs, adorn these pieces. To make your own lively country accents, start with unfinished furniture. On the rocker and chest use carving tools to outline each flower, leaf, and stem. Paint the motifs with artist's acrylics, then trim every shape with a thin outline of dark brown paint.

Embellish the back of a traditional deacon's bench with woodburned flowers, using different tips on the woodburner to texture parts of the design. Finish with a touch of color on the motifs.

Before you begin woodburning on furniture, practice on scrap lumber. Woodburning tools come equipped with several tips, including a chisel tip for broad lines and a pointed tip for narrow ones. Try them out, then select the textures most suited to your design.

PENNSYLVANIA DUTCH CHAIR
page 66

Finished size is 42 inches high.

Instructions: From 1-inch lumber, cut a 9x42-inch back upright. Draw a 6-inch-diameter circle at the top, then draw a horizontal line 5 inches below top. Center a 2-inch-diameter circle on midpoint of 6-inch circle. Cut out small

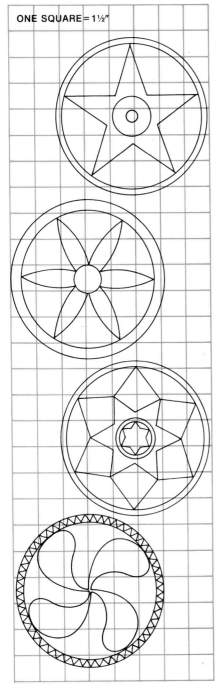

ONE SQUARE = 1½"

circle with jigsaw. Draw a 3x10-inch rectangle, centered, at base of upright. Cut it out to form two "legs."

Cut two 3x14-inch front legs. Cut and shape a 4x12-inch stretcher to span front legs under seat. Glue and screw stretcher to center of legs. Cut and assemble a 17x18-inch seat from two lengths of 1-inch pine. Round corners; cut a ¾x9-inch notch along back edge of seat to receive upright. Cut a 12x4-inch stretcher to span space between upright and front stretcher between legs. Secure front-to-back stretcher to upright and to stretcher assembly between front legs. Secure seat. Sand, stain, and finish.

HEX-SYMBOL THROW AND PILLOWS
pages 66-67

Finished size is 48x72 inches.

Instructions: Hem 48x72 inches of white wool. Enlarge patterns (left) to 9 inches in diameter; transfer to throw edges with dressmaker's carbon.

Embroider the designs in closely spaced rows of chain stitches using wool yarns in colors of your choice (also see the photograph for color suggestions). Trim the edges of the throw with jumbo rickrack tacked into place.

For pillows, transfer four 6-inch-diameter designs to 15-inch-square pillow covers, or 15-inch-diameter designs to the same size pillow covers.

SETTLE WITH STORAGE
pages 66-67

Finished size is 48x36x26 inches.

Instructions: Refer to the diagram (opposite). Cut sides from #2 common pine. Join shaped sides with spline joints. Cut pieces for the bottom and hinged seat. Make radius cuts along top header of seat back; cut six pieces for the back and boards for settle bottom.

To assemble, join seat back pieces to header. Construct a box for storage, and install a center support (see diagram). Secure sides to box and back assembly to side. Hinge seat to box. Sand, stain, and finish.

COLONIAL HUTCH
pages 66-67

Finished size is 36x72x22½ inches.

Instructions: *Note:* To join all side, top, and door pieces, use spline joints. Center a ⅛-inch-wide and ½-inch-deep dado along the edge of each piece, keeping dado ends 1 inch from board ends. Cut a 1-inch strip of ⅛-inch hardboard that is 2 inches shorter than the lumber. Glue strip in place; clamp.

Cut all pieces from #2 common pine. Refer to diagram (opposite) and cut 72-inch uprights to length. Make radius cuts for the shaped sides. Join to shorter uprights to form sides.

Piece lumber to form back. Add top header radius cuts. Build lower cabinet assembly; secure to uprights. Add the doors and shelves. Rout a ¼-inch-wide groove along the upper shelves; secure shelves to uprights. Sand, stain, and finish. Add porcelain door pulls. To hold doors closed, add a length of 1x2, screwed to upright between doors.

CROSS-STITCH SAMPLER
page 67

Finished size is about 16x20 inches.

Materials: ¾ yard of even-weave cotton or linen; embroidery floss in the following amounts (in yards) and colors: 2 yellow, 22 gold, 13 pink, 8 fuchsia, 10 red, 15 light blue, 4 dark blue, 22 light green, 17 dark green, 8 beige, 10 light brown, and 22 dark brown; embroidery hoop and needle; frame.

Instructions: Find and mark the center of the fabric and the center of the chart on page 74. Begin stitching in the center and work toward the edges.

Embroider the design in cross-stitches, using 3 strands of floss. On hardanger cloth (22 threads per inch) each cross-stitch should cover 2 threads. If your fabric has a different ratio of threads per inch, make each stitch over a greater or lesser number of threads.

To finish, lay the sampler facedown on a clean, padded surface and press lightly on the wrong side, using a damp cloth. Center it on a piece of heavy cardboard padded with a layer of quilt batting. Frame it as desired.

PINE BED
page 67

Instructions: (Headboard and footboard fit a standard size double bed. Adjust width to fit your own bed.)

Refer to the diagram (below) and cut the horizontal and shaped pieces. Join pieces using spline joints.

Cut the headboard and footboard uprights from 1¼x2-inch lengths of lumber. Round the tops as shown in the diagram; join the horizontal pieces to the uprights. Cut and assemble the supports for the box spring as shown. Sand, stain, and finish.

Set headboard and footboard upright. Screw rails to uprights; secure slats to rails.

QUICK FLOWER-GARDEN QUILT
page 67

Instructions: To make the quilt, use a hexagon pattern that is 2 inches across at its widest point. Add ¼-inch seam margins, then cut and piece two rounds of "petals" for each block: six hexagons in a solid color fabric and 12 in a print fabric. (See the photograph for reference.)

Appliqué the pieced hexagon "garden" to a 15-inch-square, solid-color background block. (The background fabric forms the center.) Make as many blocks as desired; the number of blocks determines quilt size.

Join blocks with 2-inch-wide sashing strips (add seam allowances before cutting). When top is pieced, sandwich batting between top and backing fabric cut to size; outline quilt along all seams.

(Continued)

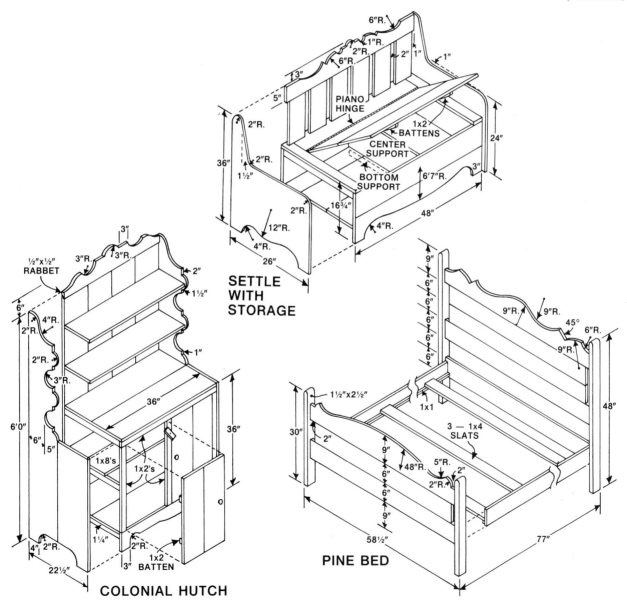

SETTLE WITH STORAGE

COLONIAL HUTCH

PINE BED

73

COLOR KEY

⊙ Yellow	⊟ Pink	◳ Red	■ Dk. Blue	⧄ Dk. Green	◱ Lt. Brown
⊡ Gold	◣ Fuchsia	◿ Lt. Blue	⚫ Lt. Green	⊡ Beige	⊠ Dk. Brown

74

DECORATIVE PAINTING ON FURNITURE
pages 70-71

Materials: Unfinished furniture. *For all pieces:* Sandpaper; dressmaker's carbon paper; polyurethane finish; acrylic paints in colors of your choice. *For deacon's bench:* Woodburning tool; antique maple stain. *For rocker:* Antique maple stain; blue matte finish latex paint; curved gouger (wood carving tool); Tuffilm spray. *For chest:* Same as for rocker except eliminate stain.

Instructions: Sand pieces smooth.

The diagram on page 76 is a full-size pattern for use on all three pieces. Trace the pattern onto tissue paper, attaching the sections at lines A-B and C-D. Flop the design to complete the pattern. *Adjust the length of the pattern to fit your furniture by adding or eliminating motifs.*

Enlarge the chest top pattern (below) onto brown paper. Flop the image to complete the design.

For the deacon's bench: Transfer pattern to furniture using dressmaker's carbon. Woodburn the design. Next, stain the piece using antique maple finish. With thinned acrylic paints, paint the design in the colors of your choice. When dry, coat with polyurethane.

For the rocker: Stain the entire piece with antique stain. When dry, paint the upper back, arms, and rings around the rungs with blue paint (see photograph).

Transfer the pattern to the back of the rocker using dressmaker's carbon.

Using elements from the basic design, add flower motifs to arms if desired.

With a curved gouger, gouge out the outline of the design.

Paint the flowers and leaves with acrylic paints. Then outline all parts of the design with dark brown paint. When dry, set the painted designs with Tuffilm spray. Finally, spray the entire chair with clear polyurethane.

For the chest: Paint the chest blue. Transfer patterns onto chest top and front. Gouge the outline of the design using the curved gouger. (Practice on scrap lumber before you begin working on the furniture.) Then paint the design in colors of your choice. Set the painted areas with Tuffilm spray and finish with clear polyurethane.

(Continued)

◄Center

TRUNK — TOP

1 Square = 1 Inch

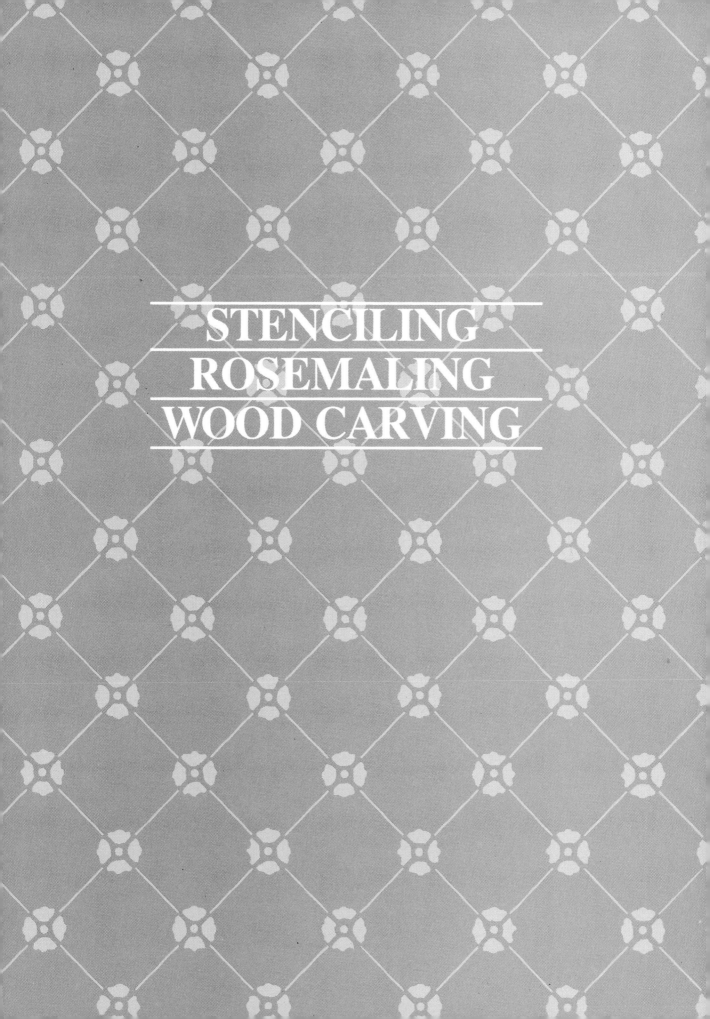

STENCILING
ROSEMALING
WOOD CARVING

STENCILING

If you are interested in designing and making your own stencils, two major steps are involved: cutting the stencil and stenciling the design onto a surface.

When you cut a stencil, it usually works best to use commercial stencil paper. However, you can also experiment with acetate, architect's linen, or tagboard.

To begin cutting your design, tape your pattern to the stencil paper and cut around the design with a craft knife or single-edge razor blade. (Be sure to allow for stencil "bridges," which are the ⅛-inch-wide sections between the cutout shapes that hold the design together and give the stencil extra strength.) It is important to keep your cutting tool sharp to get clean edges.

Holding the knife perpendicular to the stencil paper, make one stroke for each stencil cut, moving the knife toward you.

To stencil your design, use blunt-end, stiff-bristle stencil brushes in a range of sizes. If you want to experiment with other stencil applicators, try sponges, paint rollers, or water-color brushes.

Because acrylic paints dry quickly and are waterproof, they are a popular stencil medium. However, you also can use fabric dyes, pens, oil paints, or spray paints.

To begin stenciling, dip your brush into paint and remove excess paint by tapping the brush up and down on newspaper. (Be sure your brush remains fairly dry.) Hold the brush perpendicular to the stencil and use an up-and-down motion to apply paint. Keep the stencil as close to the surface as possible to ensure a crisp, clear design. Use your free hand to press down the edges of the stencil.

Lift the stencil carefully after you have finished painting; let dry.

1) Using carbon or graphite paper, trace the pattern onto stencil paper. Cut out the design using a sharp craft knife. To prevent tears and fraying, begin cutting in the center and work toward the edges, rotating the stencil paper as needed. Read the stenciling information at left before you start. Refer to books on stenciling and to the photograph (opposite) for design ideas.

2) Tape the stencil to an unfinished wooden container such as the box shown here. (Only raw wood is suitable for this project because wax and dyes must soak into the wood.)

Hold the stencil in place, dip a stencil brush into neutral-colored shoe polish paste, and apply the polish to the stencil. (Shoe polish has a wax base and resists water-soluble dyes.)

3) Gently remove the stencil and let the wax dry thoroughly.

Mix two parts liquid dye to one part cold water and wipe the dye onto the wood with a paper towel. (The shoe polish will resist the dye on the stenciled areas.)

Remove any beads of dye on the waxed area with a clean paper towel and let dry.

4) Pour a thin coat of turpentine over the waxed area and let it soak into the shoe polish for several minutes. Scrub the stenciled areas with a small brush until the polish is removed. Wipe away the turpentine with paper towels and let the wood dry thoroughly.

Apply a coat of non-water-base polyurethane, shellac, or varnish.

ROSEMALING

Rosemaling is a form of decorative flower painting that developed in rural areas of Norway during the late eighteenth century. Then as now, the hand-painted designs were used to embellish home furnishings and accessories. They were especially popular for wooden tables and chairs, storage trunks, and ceilings and walls.

Virtually every shade of every color was used at some time by rosemaling artists in Norway. Grayish blues, blue-greens, dull reds, and red-oranges often covered the design backgrounds. Medium greens, reds, whites, yellows, and shades of blue formed the basic designs. Yellow ochre was (and still is) a popular color for outlining.

There are five basic rosemaling brush strokes, including the C and reverse C (or parentheses strokes), the S curve, the O (or circle stroke), the straight line, and the dot. Practice these strokes until you can manipulate the brush skillfully. When you can, you'll be ready to begin your first rosemaling project, such as the wooden plate (right).

1) Repair the plate by filling holes, scratches, and nicks with wood filler. Sand well. Apply a coat of wood sealer and paint the plate with semigloss oil-base paint.

Sketch your rosemaling design onto plain brown wrapping paper and tape the pattern to the plate with a piece of carbon or graphite paper beneath it. Trace the main areas of the design onto the plate (you can fill in details later using the pattern as a guide).

2) Mix artist's oil paints on a foil-covered palette. Then add a mixture of four parts linseed oil and one part turpentine until the paint is a creamy consistency.

Use the five brush stroke techniques to paint the designs. Never start in the middle of a stroke. If you must refill your brush with paint in the middle of a stroke, start again at the beginning position.

Use one brush for each paint color. If you are a novice, work with only two or three colors of paint on a single project and proceed to more colors as you gain experience.

Don't expect each brush stroke to be identical. Slight variations in the hand-painted designs will add charm to the project.

As you paint, steady the plate by holding it with your free hand.

3) After painting the main part of your design, go back and fill in details such as dots and shadings, being careful not to let the paint dry in the brushes. (If you wish to duplicate the colors shown above, use olive green, muted red, gold, and muted white.)

After completing the design, let the paint dry thoroughly and wipe off tracing lines, smudges, and fingerprints. Apply a coat of varnish using a wide, soft-bristle brush. Apply the varnish with as few strokes as possible to get an even coat.

After the varnish is dry, rub it down with pumice and water to dull the finish, if desired.

WOOD CARVING

1) Begin carving a wooden duck decoy by tracing the basic shapes onto a double thickness of basswood, sugar pine, or white cedar (available at lumberyards by special order). The body pieces are then cut out with a band saw. (Body pieces are cut in halves, hollowed out, and then rejoined.) The head and body are treated as individual pieces.

2) Temporarily join the top and bottom halves of the duck with wood screws and secure the pieces in a vise. Careful honing with a drawknife will further delineate the exact shape of the decoy. At this point, use reference books to recreate a particular species. Separate the top and bottom halves of the body before the next step.

3) Because competition-quality decoys must float in perfect balance, the top and bottom portions of the duck are hollowed out before the halves are permanently joined. Use a chisel and mallet to roughly gouge out the areas, and try to keep the "walls" an even thickness all around. Later a keel is added to ensure that the finished decoy will float upright.

Balky tools can take the joy out of any craft, so keep your knives, chisels, and gouges sharp. When a tool dulls, remove any nicks or burrs, using a file if necessary. Restore the cutting edge to its original angle by stroking it carefully across a whetstone lubricated with a few drops of honing oil.

4) The next step in duck decoy carving is to hand carve feathers and other features to create realistic detail. Individual feathers are painstakingly carved out of the body of the decoy with a small knife. The head (which has not yet been attached to the body) is carved separately and then glued into place. Refer to wildlife photographs to reproduce feathering.

5) After the body has been decoratively carved, add fine lines of intricate feathering detail by using a woodburning tool (available at art supply stores). After all feathering and other details are added, seal the duck decoy with waterproof materials, then paint it. Consult reference books for accuracy. Better yet, visit a game bird sanctuary for lifelike details.

Patchwork and Quilting

Traditional Pieced Patterns

uthentic country quilts like the ones shown on the next 10 pages have become part of American history. They are valued for the stories they tell of long-ago quilters who frugally saved bits and pieces of fabric to create beautiful bedcovers for their pioneer families. American quilts are also appreciated for their artistic quality, a creative blend of piecing and stitching different fabrics together to make a kaleidoscope of colors and patterns. The wild goose chase quilt shown here is an example of both the history and artistry of quiltmaking at its best. The pattern is a two-patch design in which the pieced four-square blocks are sewn together in lengthwise strips, then joined together with long narrow strips of triangles. The finished quilt measures 70x80 inches but can be adjusted by changing the number and the length of the pieced strips. For the instructions, turn to page 94.

In years gone by, young girls learned the art of patchwork by stitching quilts for their marriage chests. After mastering simple patterns made up mostly of squares and rectangles, they moved on to the challenging task of piecing triangles, diamonds, and other shapes with bias edges into warm coverlets for their future homes.

Enhance your quilting skills and your home by making the colorful quilt at right or the intricately pieced design opposite.

The pyramid quilt (right) is 88 inches square. It is made by cutting assorted fabrics into triangles and stitching the pieces into rows, alternating the direction of the pyramids as you piece the quilt top.

The spectacular blazing star quilt (opposite) is an elaborate rendition of the traditional star-pattern quilts. To make each medallion, start in the center of the circle with an eight-point star. Work the remaining design in rounds, adding rows of rectangles and triangles. The quilt shown measures 96x96 inches. It contains nine 24-inch-square star motifs and three-inch-wide borders around the outside edges.

Keep in mind that it's what you do with your quilt top after it's pieced that makes it a real work of art. It is important to select a quilting design that is compatible with your patchwork pattern. To make sure the two designs are compatible, draw a portion of your quilting design on tracing paper and place it on top of the quilt. Study the quilting design to make sure it will augment rather than detract from the finished quilt.

There are several attractive and popular ways of quilting. Outline quilting, probably the most common, is worked in running stitches that are placed ⅛ to ¼ inch on either side of the seam lines (so each patchwork piece is outlined).

In diagonal quilting, the diagonal lines are stitched at regular intervals across the quilt top. Stitching in the opposite direction as well results in a diamond pattern.

For a shell pattern, sew quilting stitches in curved lines or scallops.

Although patchwork is an excellent way to use up fabric scraps, it requires years of saving and collecting to develop a really well-rounded scrap bag. If you can't get the look you want with scraps, buy one or two new fabrics that will work well with your pattern and color scheme.

This charming rendition of the traditional square-in-square pattern (above) is worked in 2½-inch squares of fabric for a classic patchwork look. The brightly colored squares are placed against a subtle polka dot background and arranged to form designs in the center and corners.

The postage-stamp quilt (opposite) is so named because of its tiny, stamp-size patches. You can create your own version of this pattern by concentrating on an original color scheme and arranging your fabric pieces according to color. (We placed print fabrics in the center of each motif and solid-color fabrics around the outer edges.)

Before you begin cutting, make sure your scissors are sharp and lay the fabric on a large, flat surface. Cut the pieces individually and sort them according to color and shape.

There are many wonderfully decorative ways to use quilts other than in the traditional manner as bed coverlets. Pretty up a kitchen with one, as we did above. Or cut up worn or damaged quilts and make them into curtains, pillows, fashions—even stuffed toys.

Mastering the old-fashioned chimney sweep (or courthouse square) quilt pattern (above) is easy because it's a simple mix of squares and rectangles. To enhance the patchwork, stitch some elaborate quilting designs such as those at right if you wish.

Star quilt patterns open up a whole galaxy of design possibilities, as evidenced by the quilts shown here (opposite). The prairie star quilt (at left in the photo) and the rolling star quilt (at right) are two all-time favorites.

Heirloom quilting patterns like the one shown at left are reminiscent of the time and care women took when they stitched old-time country quilts.

Known as the grandmother's fan pattern, this authentic vintage quilt creates a parasol-like effect by stitching anything-goes fabrics into large round shapes. Our quilt measures 72x72 inches but you can make your quilt larger or smaller simply by changing the number of fan motifs.

To store old country quilts, cover a long cardboard tube with muslin and roll your quilt loosely around it. Hang the tube in a dry, well-ventilated area away from extreme temperatures or direct sunlight and cover the quilt loosely with a bedsheet (or any lightweight fabric).

If rolled storage is impractical, fold your quilt and place it in a roomy fabric bag. (Do not seal the end of the bag.) Air and refold your quilt at least once a year, padding the folds with several layers of tissue paper.

Instructions for the quilt shown here are on page 96.

Handmade quilts like this grandmother's fan pattern are sought-after items in fine arts and antique markets across the country. To maintain the value (and beauty) of your quilt, always treat it with tender loving care when cleaning or storing it.

TRADITIONAL PIECED PATTERNS

General quilting instructions: How-to directions follow for stitching and assembling the tops of the quilts shown on the preceding pages.

When your quilt top is complete, mark the quilting motifs of your choice (for example, wreaths, feather patterns, or shells). Then assemble the layers as follows: Place backing fabric wrong side up on a flat surface, cover backing fabric with a layer of quilt batting, then add the quilt top, right side up.

Pin and baste the layers together, starting in the center of the quilt and working toward the corners and sides.

Place fabric in a quilting frame or hoop and begin quilting. Take small running stitches, using a short, sharp needle and glazed or waxed thread.

Bind the raw edges of the quilt with narrow bias strips sewn to the edges. Or, fold the edge of the backing fabric over the edge of the quilt top, turn under the seam allowance, and hem it to the face of the quilt.

WILD GOOSE CHASE
pages 84-85

Finished size is about 70x80 inches.

Materials: A variety of cotton fabrics (44/45 inches wide) equivalent to 2½ yards for squares, 2 yards for larger triangles, and 2¾ yards for smaller triangles; 4⅔ yards of backing fabric; 70x80 inches of quilt batting; thread.

Instructions: Enlarge one triangle, one square, and one-half triangle in the pattern below and make into templates, adding ¼ inch margins for seams. Cut shapes from fabric.

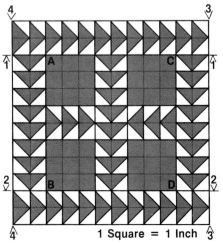

1 Square = 1 Inch

Assemble sections marked 1-2 on the diagram. Stitch squares A-B together with a short triangular section between. Then sew one section 1-2 to one section A-B. Repeat 13 times until you have completed a strip the width of the coverlet; then add an additional triangular section to the end of the A-B section.

Stitch section 3-4, sewing triangles and half triangles together until the strip measures the width of the coverlet. Make nine strips.

To assemble the top, sew pieced strips together, alternating a narrow one with a wider one (see photo).

Finish according to the general instructions, then bind the raw edges with bias strips.

PYRAMID QUILT
page 86

Finished size is about 88x88 inches.

Materials: Cotton print fabric scraps for pyramids (see note below); 36-inch-wide cotton fabric—2¼ yards rust print and 2½ yards brown print; 5 yards (44-inch-wide) fabric for backing; thread; quilt batting.

Instructions: *Note:* To make this quilt you will need to cut 480 pyramids and 30 half-pyramids from assorted print fabrics. One-half yard of 44-inch-wide fabric yields 54 pyramids. Also note that after cutting border strips, remaining brown and rust print fabric can be cut into pyramids. Purchase fabric accordingly.

Use ¼-inch seams throughout.

Enlarge pattern (above right) and make into template adding ¼-inch seam allowances. (Dotted line indicates cutting line for half-pyramids.) Cut pyramids and half-pyramids from desired fabrics.

Choose a pleasing color sequence for pyramids and stitch into rows using the diagram as a guide. Each row consists of 32 pyramids and 2 half-pyramids. Make 15 rows. Stitch rows together.

For borders, cut two 5½x66½-inch strips and two 5½x76½-inch strips from rust fabric. Stitch short strips to side edges of quilt top. Then, stitch long strips along top and bottom edges. Cut

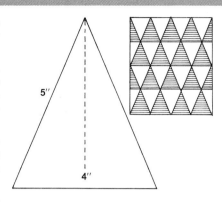

two 6½x76½-inch strips and two 6½x88½-inch strips from brown fabric. Stitch to rust borders in same manner as above. Finish quilt according to the general instructions. Piece fabric for the quilt backing if necessary.

BLAZING STAR QUILT
page 87

Finished size is about 96x96 inches.

Materials: 44-inch-wide fabric in the following amounts (in yards) and colors: 3½ dark brown print, 3½ medium blue print, 3¼ white with brown dots, 3 rust print, 2¼ brown floral, 1 navy print, ½ beige print, ½ red print, and 6 backing fabric; quilt batting; thread.

Instructions: Enlarge pattern pieces A-H in diagram (below); add ¼-inch seam allowances and make patterns into templates.

For each block, cut pieces A and B from red print, C and G from polka dot fabric, F from dark brown print, and H from blue print. Cut 8 D pieces from beige print and 8 from brown floral. Cut 8 E pieces from navy print and 8 from rust print. Make 9 blocks.

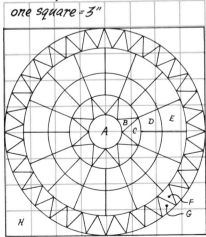

one square = 3"

To assemble blocks, work in rounds from center (A); stitch H pieces in place last. For D and E rounds, alternate color of pieces. Also, alternate placement of darker colored pieces on each round so beige print falls below navy print and brown floral falls below rust print (see diagram). Stitch blocks together into 3 rows of 3 blocks each.

For borders, cut two 3½x72½-inch strips and two 3½x78½-inch strips from brown floral. Sew shorter strips to sides of quilt top. Sew remaining strips to top and bottom edges.

Cut two 3½x78½-inch strips and two 3½x84½-inch strips from blue print, two 3½x84½-inch strips and two 3½x90½-inch strips from rust print, and two 3½x90½-inch strips and two 3½x96½-inch strips from brown print. Sew strips to quilt in same manner as above in following color sequence: blue, rust, and brown. Finish quilt according to general instructions.

SQUARE-IN-SQUARE QUILT
page 88

Finished size is about 98x98 inches.

Materials: 4¾ yards brown polka dot fabric; 6 yards backing fabric; ⅞ yard blue print fabric; assorted print fabric scraps; thread.

Instructions: Cut 948 squares from assorted print fabrics, 448 from polka dot fabric, and 124 from blue. All squares are 2½x2½ inches, including the seam allowance.

Following the diagram below and beginning with the bottom row, stitch squares into rows. Use ¼-inch seams

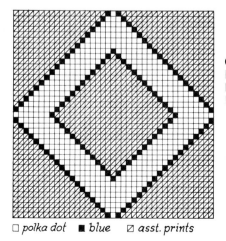

□ polka dot ■ blue ☒ asst. prints

throughout. When first two rows are completed, sew them together. Then, sew squares for third row; sew third row to second row. Continue in this manner until the quilt top is assembled.

For borders, cut two 10½x78½-inch strips and two 10½x98½-inch strips from polka dot fabric. Stitch shorter strips to sides and longer strips to top and bottom of the quilt top. Finish according to general instructions.

POSTAGE-STAMP QUILT
page 89

Materials: Cotton fabric scraps in prints and solid colors; quilt batting.

Instructions: Our design is pieced from 1½-inch squares (including the seam allowance). Just cut your scrap bag fabrics into squares and hand- or machine-stitch them together using ¼-inch seams. Follow our diamond diagram or create your own geometric pattern.

The diamond design consists of a central diamond made from print fabric scraps surrounded by diamonds of solid-color squares. The center square in each diamond is black, as are the squares of the diamond "points."

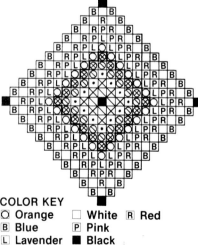

COLOR KEY
◯ Orange   ☐ White   ℝ Red
ⓑ Blue   ℙ Pink
ⓛ Lavender   ■ Black

Each diamond measures approximately 11½x11½ inches. Stich just one diamond at a time, making enough to create the desired-size quilt top. (Notice in the photograph that the black squares are a connecting point between

the diamonds. So when piecing diamonds, make half with black squares at the "points" and half without.) Piece triangles (half-diamonds) to fill edges of quilt top in order to "square up" quilt. Finish according to general instructions (opposite).

PRAIRIE STAR QUILT
page 91

Finished size is about 78x78 inches.

Materials: Cotton fabrics (44/45 inches wide) in the following amounts and colors; 2¼ yards red, 3 yards white, 1¼ yards each of pink, green, and yellow; 4⅔ yards backing fabric; 78-inch-square quilt batting.

Instructions: Enlarge square, triangle, diamond in pattern below; make templates (add ¼-inch seam margins) from cardboard or plastic lids.

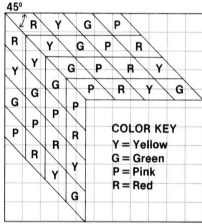

COLOR KEY
Y = Yellow
G = Green
P = Pink
R = Red

1 Square = 1 Inch

Cut out pieces, placing the 90-degree angles on straight grain of fabric.

Piece diamonds, two triangles, and squares together as shown, to make ¼ of the block. Complete block to make one prairie star. (Stitch a sample block first to check accuracy of your pattern.) Make a total of 9 star blocks for the quilt center.

For borders, cut two 2-inch-wide strips the length of the shorter sides from white fabric, allowing ¼ inch for seams; sew in place. Cut two more strips for long sides; sew to top. Repeat for middle band of red and outer band of white.

Finish the quilt according to general instructions.

(Continued)

TRADITIONAL PIECED PATTERNS

ROLLING STAR QUILT
page 91

Finished size is about 66x83 inches.

Materials: (Fabrics are 44/45 inches wide.) 3¾ yards each of white and blue fabrics; 4¾ yards of fabric for backing; 66x83 inches of quilt batting; thread.

Instructions: Enlarge the pattern, below. Add ¼-inch seam allowances and cut templates from cardboard or plastic for a diamond, square, and one large and one small triangle.

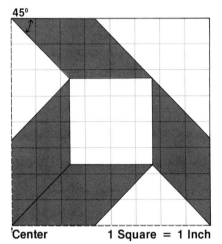

45°

Center   1 Square = 1 Inch

Cut shapes from fabric, placing 90-degree angles with grain of fabric.

Refer to diagram to assemble quilt pieces. Make four of these, then stitch them together to make one quilt block. Twelve of these make up the top.

For the first of three border bands, cut two 3½-inch-wide white strips the length of the top. (Add ¼-inch seam allowances.) Stitch to sides. Cut two 3½-inch-wide strips the length of the remaining sides and sew to top.

Repeat for the middle 2¾-inch-wide blue band and for the outer three-inch-wide white band to finish top.

Complete quilt according to general instructions on page 94.

CHIMNEY-SWEEP QUILT
page 90

Finished size is about 76x76 inches.

Materials: Cotton small-print fabric (44/45 inches wide) equivalent to 2 yards; 4¼ yards peach print fabric; 2¼ yards pink print fabric; 4½ yards fabric

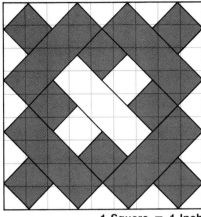

1 Square = 1 Inch

for the backing; 76-inch-square quilt batting; thread.

Instructions: Enlarge the pattern (above). Make templates (add ¼-inch seam allowance) for a square, rectangle, and triangle, and for a 9-inch-square block and a triangle measuring half of the 9-inch square, folded on the bias. Cut shapes from fabric, placing 90-degree angles on straight grain.

Cut 16 nine-inch-square blocks from peach fabric. Assemble the quilt blocks (25 total) using the diagram as a guide.

Alternate a pieced block with a plain block, sewing them together in a diamond pattern. Refer to photograph. Piece large triangles between the outside blocks to make straight edge.

For first of four border bands, cut two 1¾-inch-wide strips from pink print the length of one side. (Add seam allowances.) Stitch to either side. Cut two more 3¾-inch-wide strips the length of the remaining sides and sew to quilt top.

Repeat for remaining three bands, cutting two strips 1½ inches wide from peach, pink, and again from peach fabric. Finish quilt according to general instructions.

GRANDMOTHER'S FAN QUILT
pages 92-93

Finished size is about 72x72 inches.

Materials: 2 yards of 44-inch-wide white cotton fabric; assorted prints for the fan pieces; 4 yards of 44-inch-wide

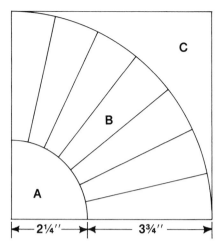

2¼"   3¾"

lavender cotton fabric for the backing; thread; quilt batting.

Instructions: The quilt consists of thirty-six circular motifs, each 12 inches in diameter. Each motif consists of four fan motifs shown in diagram above. Enlarge pieces A, B, and C to size, add ¼-inch seam allowances, and make into templates. Cut 1 piece A from a dark colored print, 7 pieces B from various prints, and 1 piece C from white fabric for each fan motif.

Stitch each fan motif separately. Then, stitch four fan motifs into a circular motif. Make 36 circular motifs. Assemble quilt top into 6 rows, each with 6 motifs. Finish according to general instructions.

TRUE LOVER'S KNOT QUILT
pages 14-15

Finished size is about 85x85 inches.

Materials: (Fabrics are 44/45 inches wide.) 3¼ yards each of blue print and

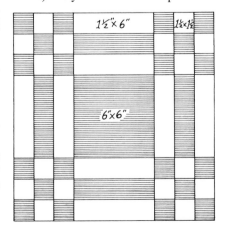

1½"x 6"   1½"x1½"

6"x 6"

white fabric; quilt batting; 5 yards of fabric for quilt back; thread.

Instructions: Enlarge the diagram (opposite below), add ¼-inch seam margins to the pattern pieces, and cut pieces from correct-color fabric. Use ¼-inch seams throughout.

Piece block as shown in diagram. (Shading represents blue, white represents white fabric.) Make 16 blocks.

Cut twelve 4½x15½-inch strips from the white fabric. For each horizontal row, join four blocks and three strips, starting and ending with a block. Cut three 4½x72½-inch strips from white fabric and stitch alternate rows of blocks and strips.

For side borders, cut four 3x72½-inch strips from white fabric and two 2x72½-inch strips from blue. Stitch a white strip to each side of assembled quilt blocks. Then, stitch blue strips to white strips and finish with white strips along blue strips.

For top and bottom borders, cut four 3x85½-inch white strips and two 2x85½-inch blue strips. Stitch them in place in same color sequence as the side border strips. Finish according to general instructions.

CARING FOR HANDMADE QUILTS

Whether your handmade quilt is a collector's item or a treasured family keepsake, it deserves special handling and care. Here are some tips for cleaning and storing all types of handmade quilts.

Identifying quilt fabrics: If your quilt needs cleaning, first identify its fabrics. Cotton and linen, derived from plant fibers, require different handling than wool and silk, made from animal fibers.

Most antique quilts are cotton, wool, or a combination of cotton and wool. You can usually identify fabric by its feel, or you can use the "burn test." Snip a thread of cloth from the quilt and light the thread in an ashtray. Cotton burns quickly and smells like charred paper; wool smolders and gives off a strong odor.

The cotton/wool test won't work for crazy quilts because they're made from a combination of silk, velvet, and wool,

which makes them difficult to clean. For advice on the care of crazy quilts, ask a textile expert.

Cleaning wool quilts: Quilts that contain any wool must be cleaned as if they were all wool. Although old wool quilts can be washed safely, a careful dry cleaning may be easier and safer.

Use a reputable cleaner who does his/her own work. Ask that a fresh supply of dry cleaning solvent be used, and emphasize that the quilt is not to be pressed after dry cleaning.

Cleaning cotton quilts: Before cleaning a cotton quilt, test the dyed areas of the fabric for colorfastness. Mix one teaspoon of fine-washable cold-water detergent in a quart of soft water. Place two or three drops of this solution on a patch of cloth. Wait about five seconds, then press the moist area between several white tissues and check for traces of dye. Rinse the fabric with clear water and blot with a clean towel.

If each fabric is colorfast, it is safe to wash the quilt. If one color bleeds, consult a textile expert before washing.

For extra protection during washing, make a "bag" of white nylon net that is eight to nine inches wider and longer than your quilt. Leave one end open and insert the quilt. Stitch the end closed and sew a large X from opposite corners through all three layers. If your quilt is dusty, vacuum it through the nylon bag before washing.

To hand-wash your cotton quilt, run lukewarm water into a clean bathtub. If the water is hard, add 1½ tablespoons of water softener for every three gallons of water. Soak the quilt for about one hour, then drain.

Refill the tub, adding 1½ tablespoons of fine-washable cold-water detergent per gallon of softened water. Soak the quilt for about 30 minutes, gently moving the fabric up and down. Drain and repeat two or three times until the water is clear.

Gently rinse the quilt in lukewarm softened water and drain. Repeat this procedure until all soap is removed. For the final rinse, omit the water softener and rinse in clear water.

Press water from the quilt without wringing or squeezing. Blot quilt with towels to remove excess moisture.

To dry, hang your quilt in the shade over three or four parallel clotheslines on a dry, slightly breezy day.

If your quilt is new, sturdy, or not very valuable, you might try machine washing. (Never machine-wash an old or valued quilt.) Sew the quilt into a white nylon mesh bag; fill the machine with lukewarm, softened water. Add 1½ teaspoons of fine-washable cold-water detergent per gallon of water. Let the quilt soak for 30 to 40 minutes, then set the machine on a gentle cycle and let the quilt agitate for about three minutes. Drain and repeat until dirt is removed. Rinse the quilt in cool water, then machine-dry on a gentle cycle or hang it on the line.

Removing stains: If the quilt has spots or stains, ask an expert for advice on removing them. They may need special treatment, since untreated stains on cloth undergo chemical changes.

Mending your quilt: If you plan to sell your quilt someday, don't try to mend it. Collectors often prefer items in their original condition; alterations may lower your final selling price.

However, if you plan to keep your quilt for future generations, apply new binding to worn edges and mend any holes. If the holes fall in the pattern area, there are two ways to repair them.

One way is to appliqué over the hole with cotton thread that is a close color match to the original cloth. Or, you can appliqué over the hole with fine transparent nylon thread in a blending tone. The cotton thread will duplicate the original color now, but may not later because it fades differently than the older cloth surrounding it. The nylon, even though it doesn't match the old fabric, is inconspicuous and keeps the damage from spreading.

Storing quilts: To avoid creases and dust, cover a wooden dowel that is 5 inches longer than the quilt with muslin. Roll the quilt loosely onto the dowel. Hang it in a dark, well-ventilated storage area, avoiding extreme dampness or heat. Cover it with muslin.

If roll storage is impractical, folding and bagging the quilt is the alternative. Air and refold your quilt four times a year, padding the folds with tissue paper. Wrap the quilt lightly in a piece of fabric. If the quilt contains wool, add one cup of moth crystals; seal tightly.

Patchwork and Quilting

Appliquéd Quilts

ppliquéd quilts like those on the next three pages are fine examples of fabric art. Using fabric the way an artist uses paint, you can create masterpieces of color and design. Vibrant colors make these quilts anything but pallid, and the workmanship and design are superbly blended. The exuberant orange basket quilt shown here is a delightful takeoff on the traditional tulip basket pattern. Simply substitute round oranges for the more complicated flower shapes. To make this quilt, appliqué each orange basket motif (we used 20 in all) to 9½-inch squares of off-white fabric. Assemble the quilt by alternating plain squares with basket squares and add a border of orange and off-white triangles along the edges. For complete how-to instructions, see page 102.

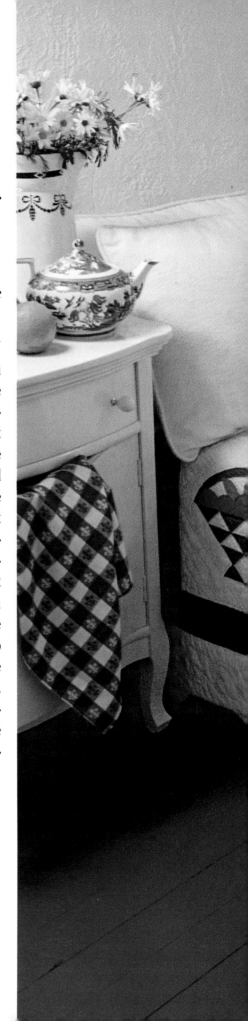

Appliquéd Quilts

Springtime pastels and three sprightly designs adorn these lovingly hand-rendered appliquéd quilts. The butterfly quilt (above left) is worked in a variety of print fabrics and then embroidered with black floss. If you wish, you can alternate the direction of the butterflies to give a feeling of movement. A scroll-type quilting pattern within the peach-colored borders helps finish the overall design.

The twin-size tulip quilt (above right) combines vivid colors with soft pastels in each floral cluster. Although the tulip is a common old-time pattern loved by quilters everywhere, this quilt receives a refreshing new treatment with its bold, graphic images. If you look carefully, you can see how the de-sign of the hand-stitched quilting mimics the tulip appliqués. Scallop-like quilting adorns the outer edges of the quilt.

The ribbons and flowers quilt (opposite) is a graceful example of using delicate appliqués on a pure white background. The colors and shapes work in close harmony to produce a rich garland of ribbons and flowers in the center panel, and floral bouquets in the corners and along the border panels.

A pattern for accomplished quilters, this design will enable you to show off your stitchery skills. After the quilt is assembled (the finished size is 80x95 inches), embellish the background with an all-over diamond quilting pattern. Then bind the edges with blue bias strips.

A pair of sharp scissors or shears is a must for cutting appliqués and keeping the fabric edges from fraying. Embroidery scissors can be handy for cutting small shapes and clipping seam allowances along curves. Stainless steel pins and needles are also helpful when you work with fabric appliqués. Cotton or polyester thread usually is used for most appliqué projects.

APPLIQUÉ BASICS

Before you begin any of the appliquéd quilts shown on pages 98 through 101, read this general information.

The first step in appliqué is to select a design. If you are a beginner, choose a design with straight lines or gradual curves, and one with a relatively small number of predominantly large or medium-size pieces.

Next, decide on the technique you will use to secure the appliqué to the background fabric. While it is possible to glue fabrics or fuse them with iron-on webbings, sewing by hand or machine is more secure and usually more practical. Choose fabrics that are easy to sew and you will have made a good start.

Selecting and Preparing Fabrics

Choose your fabric on the basis of the technique you will use (hand or machine appliqué), care requirements of the article you are making (will it be washed?), and compatibility of the fabrics you want to use together.

Felt is a good fabric for appliqué because it works well with either hand or machine stitching. Because felt is not woven, it will not ravel so you never need to turn under the edges. It does fade, however, and most felt must be dry-cleaned.

For hand appliqué in which you will turn under the edges of the pattern pieces before stitching, choose supple, light- to medium-weight fabrics that are easy to manipulate. One hundred percent cottons (or cotton blends) such as broadcloth, gingham, denim, and sailcloth and lightweight wools are suitable. Some knits work well, but if a knit is very stretchy, back it with a scrap of cotton or iron-on interfacing to stabilize it.

For machine appliqués you can select from most weights, including upholstery fabrics. Some lightweight fabrics have enough body to sew well. Others, however, need interfacing to stitch well by machine.

Depending on the effect you are seeking, you will find interesting textures for machine work in velveteen, corduroy, peau de soie, and even vinyl, leather, and felt.

The basic test for appliqué fabric is this: How easily does a needle slip through the fabric? Wool, wool felt, and cotton broadcloth all sew easily. However, the fine percales, such as those found in sheets, are sometimes difficult to stitch because they are closely woven with a high number of threads per inch.

Next, how easily does a fabric ravel? Loosely woven fabrics ravel easily, making them hard to stitch by hand. One hundred percent cottons tend to ravel less than blends, making them favorites among quilters.

Evaluate each fabric by itself and in combination with others. For most projects, you will want to use fabrics of about the same weight, care requirements, and durability.

When buying fabrics, start with the background color. It is easier to develop a whole scheme once you have selected the major color.

Before cutting pattern pieces, preshrink fabrics; straighten the grains.

Making Appliqué Patterns

After choosing a design for appliqué, enlarge the pattern on a large sheet of paper. This is your master pattern.

Make a second pattern to cut apart for the individual design elements. To keep track of the pieces, number or letter corresponding shapes on the cutting pattern and the master pattern. On large projects, jot down the total number of pieces to cut for each shape on the master.

For each shape to be used often in the overall design, make a sandpaper, cardboard, or plastic template that can be traced around many times. For other pieces, make heavy paper patterns. Do not add seam allowances to pattern pieces.

Cutting Pattern Pieces

When laying out patterns for cutting, position large appliqués so the straight grain of the fabric runs the same direction on both the appliqué and the background fabric. This prevents puckering and stretching of the appliqué during the stitching or after washing. (The lengthwise grain runs parallel to the selvage of the fabric; the crosswise grain runs at right angles to the selvage.)

With fabric faceup, lay out pattern pieces, leaving *at least* ½ to 1 inch between them to allow for seams.

Trace patterns with a sharp pencil. *The pencil line represents the stitching or folding line, not the cutting line.* Unless directions for your project specify otherwise, cut pieces ¼ inch beyond the penciled outline.

If raw edges of appliqué pieces begin to ravel, touch the edges with a dot of white glue. When dry, the glue will be clear and the edge will hold securely.

Sometimes you will need to interface a piece. For machine appliqué, use iron-on interfacing on lightweight fabrics to prevent puckering. Also, if one piece of a pattern will partially cover another and the lower fabric is visible through the upper one, interface the top piece to hide the shadow or cut away the lower fabric after stitching.

For hand appliqué, cut interfacing without seam allowances. For machine appliqué, cut it the same size as the pattern piece.

Appliquéing by Hand

The first step in hand appliqué is to turn under seam allowances on pattern pieces. If you desire, machine-stitch along the seam line (¼ inch from raw edges). Clip the seam allowance to the stay-stitching on curves and corners so turned edges lie flat and smooth. Next, baste along the fold of each piece or turn raw edges under as you stitch them to the background.

Sometimes two or more shapes are layered together onto the background. A flower petal, for example, may overlap a stem. Do not turn under the seam allowance on the lower shape where it will be covered by the upper shape. Instead, clip the seam allowance and tuck the raw edge under the overlap.

Pin and baste the appliqués in place on the background fabric. Then you are ready to stitch.

Most hand appliqué is based on a variation of a running stitch. The traditional appliqué stitch is the *whipstitch*. For this stitch, bring the needle up through the appliqué ⅛ to $\frac{1}{16}$ inch from the edge and reinsert it into the background at the edge of the appliqué, making a small diagonal stitch. Bring the needle up again through the background and the appliqué and continue stitching.

With whipstitching, the edge of the appliqué will be held flat and secure against the background fabric.

The *backstitch* is similar to the whipstitch in that it makes a flat edge and is very secure.

With the *blind stitch,* the stitches are almost invisible. Bring the needle through the fold of the seam allowance and pick up a thread or two of background fabric at that point. Then pick up a thread or two along the fold of the appliqué. Repeat around the appliqué shape, making stitches about ¼ inch apart. This stitch is secure and gives the edge of the appliqué a soft, puffy look.

The running stitch is often used in hand appliqué. Weave the needle in and out close to the folded edge of the appliqué, taking tiny stitches. When worked in embroidery thread, this stitch is very decorative.

Much appliqué stitching will occur along straight edges or curves and will present no problems. *On inside curves and corners,* however, snip the seam allowance so it can be turned smoothly. Then stitch as you would a straight edge, taking a tiny whipstitch where needed to prevent fraying.

To make an outside corner, first stitch one edge up to the hem allowance. Then, using the needle, turn the hem of the second edge under and continue stitching. *To make a pointed edge,* stitch one edge first. Then, using the needle, turn under the second edge. Make a tiny whipstitch at the tip to keep the corner from fraying. Then stitch along the second edge.

Machine Appliqué

Most machine appliqué is done on a zigzag machine, although successful projects also can be completed on a straight-stitching machine.

For a straight-stitch machine, cut appliqué pieces with a ¼-inch seam allowance. Stitch along the seam line and clip curves as needed. Press seam allowance under and pin the appliqué piece to the background fabric. Machine-stitch around all edges ⅛ inch from the fold.

To make the almost "traditional" machine satin stitch, cut all pieces, allowing at least ½ inch for seams on all sides. Pin appliqué pieces in position on background fabric and hand-baste if desired.

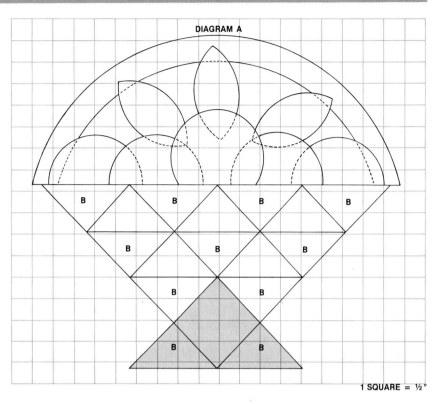

DIAGRAM A

1 SQUARE = ½"

DIAGRAM B

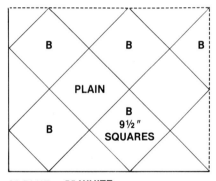

PLAIN

B
9½"
SQUARES

3" BLUE   5" WHITE

Next, machine-baste. With a short, straight stitch and matching thread, machine-stitch on marked lines. Or set the machine for medium-wide, medium-long zigzag stitches (10 to 12 stitches per inch) and zigzag-baste the appliqué in place. Trim excess fabric beyond the stitching with a small, sharp scissors.

To finish, set the machine for a zigzag satin stitch and zigzag over the basting on the appliqué pieces, covering the raw edges.

When the design requires stitching a sharp corner, zigzag up to the corner and leave the needle in the fabric at the outside of the line of stitches. Then lift the presser foot and pivot the fabric. Lower the presser foot and start your stitching so the first stitch goes toward the inside of the design, overlapping the stitch just made.

BASKET OF ORANGES QUILT
pages 98-99

Finished size is 82x69 inches, excluding the border.

Materials: Cotton fabric (44/45 inches wide) in the following colors and amounts: 4¾ yards cream, 2⅔ yards blue, 1¼ yards green, ⅔ yard orange; 4⅔ yards of backing fabric; quilt batting; thread.

Instructions: From cream fabric, cut thirty-two 9½-inch squares (add ¼-inch seam allowances to all dimensions), 14 right triangles that measure 9½ inches along their longest sides, and four right triangles that measure 9½ inches along their shortest sides. (The large triangles are half the size of the squares and the small triangles are equal to a quarter of the squares.)

(Continued)

103

Enlarge the orange basket pattern, page 103; cut out 11 blue triangles for one basket, adding ¼ inch all around for turning under raw edges. Hand- or machine-appliqué triangles to square in position shown so corners of square are at top and bottom.

Cut blue arcs for basket handles, orange circles for fruit, and green leaves. Appliqué in place as shown in pattern. Make 20 basket squares.

To assemble the top, alternate an appliquéd square with a plain fabric square. (See diagram for placement.) Fill in sides with larger triangles, and piece four small triangles in corners.

Stitch a 3-inch-wide border of blue around the perimeter of the cream pieces. Add a 5-inch-wide cream border around the blue border. Miter corners on all border pieces.

For sawtooth border, enlarge the triangle border pattern. Plan 19 triangles along each long edge and 15 along each short edge; alternate orange and cream.

Cut two pattern pieces for each triangle, adding seam allowances; with right sides together, seam the two short sides. Turn and press.

Fold edges of pieced top under, and baste triangles to underside. Baste quilt top to batting and backing fabric and quilt as desired.

BUTTERFLY QUILT
page 100

Finished size is about 81x90 inches.

Materials: Printed fabric (44/45 inches wide) equivalent to 2 yards; 4 yards white fabric; 3 yards peach fabric; 81x90 inches of quilt batting; 5 yards fabric for backing; quilt thread; black embroidery floss.

Instructions: Enlarge the pattern (above right). Make templates for the butterfly and the square, adding ¼ inch seam allowances.

Cut the shapes from fabric. Transfer the butterfly pattern to each white square; appliqué butterflies in place.

Using two strands of floss, work French knots for the eyes, outline stitches on the antennae, running stitches along the dotted lines, and blanket stitches on the butterfly. The long and short dotted lines are for quilting when layers are basted together.

1 Square = 1 Inch

Sew together two strips of three butterflies each to make center panel.

Cut two 4¼-inch-wide bands from peach fabric the length of the center panel. Sew to either side. Cut two more bands the width of the center panel and sew in place.

Assemble two strips of three butterflies; stitch them to either side of the quilt. Sew two strips of six butterflies to the length (see photo).

Cut peach border strips in the same manner as before; attach to quilt top.

Sew two individual strips of six butterflies to either end of the width. Sew two strips of nine butterflies and attach to either side of the length.

Cut outer peach border and sew to quilt as instructed above to complete the quilt top. Finish according to the general instructions on page 94.

TULIP QUILT
page 100

Finished size is about 58x83 inches.

Materials: Colorful fabrics equivalent to ¾ yard (44/45 inches wide); 1 yard green fabric; 4½ yards white fabric; 4¾ yards fabric for the backing; 58x83 inches of quilt batting; thread.

Instructions: Enlarge the tulip pattern (above right), and flop the image to complete the block motif. Make templates from cardboard or plastic for the tulip shapes, triangle (half of triangle is indicated on the diagram), and square block, adding ¼-inch seam allowances.

Carefully cut tulip shapes from fabric. Cut 41 squares, 16 triangles, and

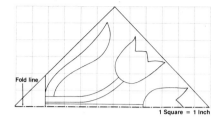

1 Square = 1 Inch

four half triangles for corners from the white fabric.

Transfer the tulip pattern to 25 of the white squares. Appliqué the tulip motifs in place.

Alternate an appliquéd block with a plain block, piecing them in a diamond pattern (see photo). Sew triangles in place along the outside edge.

Cut two 4-inch-wide bands from white fabric the width of the quilt. Sew in place. Cut two more bands the length of the quilt and sew in place to complete quilt top.

Finish according to the general instructions on page 94.

FLORAL RIBBON QUILT
page 101

Finished size is about 80x95 inches.

Materials: 8 yards (44/45 inches wide) white fabric for quilt top; 5½ yards of white fabric for backing; fabric scraps for flower and ribbon appliqués; 80x95 inches of quilt batting; 10 yards blue bias tape; quilting thread in appropriate colors.

Instructions: Enlarge the pattern (opposite). Cut squares and rectangles from white fabric for quilt top, adding ¼-inch seam allowances.

Transfer the appliqué lines to each white section. Make templates for the appliqués.

Carefully cut appliqués from fabric scraps (add seam allowances). Turn under raw edges ¼ inch, press, and sew to quilt top sections.

To assemble top, sew center panels together; stitch a floral border to two sides of center. Sew squares to ends of remaining floral borders and stitch to remaining sides of center. Repeat process to attach outer tulip borders, completing the quilt top.

Finish according to the general instructions on page 94. Bind raw edges with a blue bias strip.

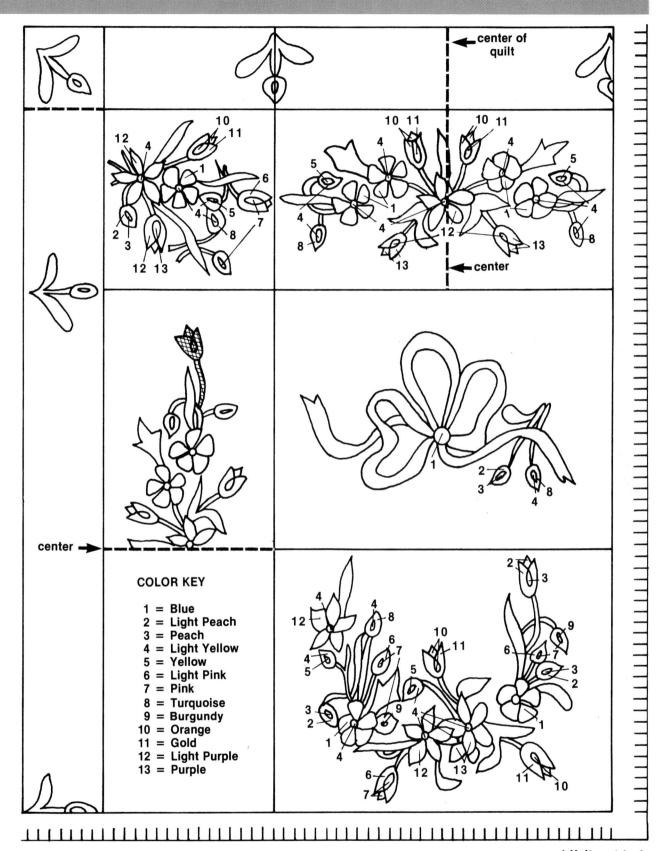

center of quilt

center

center

COLOR KEY

1 = Blue
2 = Light Peach
3 = Peach
4 = Light Yellow
5 = Yellow
6 = Light Pink
7 = Pink
8 = Turquoise
9 = Burgundy
10 = Orange
11 = Gold
12 = Light Purple
13 = Purple

1 Unit = 1 Inch

105

PATCHWORK AND QUILTING

Amish Quilts

Rich with heritage and tradition, the Amish-style quilts shown here and on the following pages are masterpieces of color and design. Because Amish women limited their creative sewing to functional items only, they always paid special attention to colors and patterns when preparing to make a quilt. It was not uncommon for these women to reuse fabric from clothing. The Amish people dressed only in solid colors, so they had a wide range of fabric colors to choose from when making a quilt. The simple star pattern shown here is made from eight prequilted diamond pieces that are stitched together. The star is then appliquéd to a background, and a border of random length strips is added. (To save steps and time, use prequilted furniture mover's blankets just as we did to make this quilt.) The instructions begin on page 110.

T he quiet Amish life-style has produced a wealth of quilts that are beautiful in their simplicity. Here are five patterns that are typical of the geometric shapes and robust colors.

A single-star quilt bordered by the familiar "bars" pattern and a nine-patch quilt are shown above. The center-diamond quilt (right) is a bold, graphic image. Colorful stars on a black background adorn the crib quilt, and rows of dark and light squares play against each other on the intricately stitched quilt (opposite). Complete instructions begin on page 110.

Although some of the quilt patterns shown here have been popular in many parts of the country for generations, they take on a dramatic quality when worked in the traditional Amish colors. Even a well-known star pattern like the design in the crib quilt (opposite) looks remarkably different because of its imaginative display of intense colors.

AMISH STAR QUILT
page 107

Materials: Prequilted furniture mover's blanket (available at most art supply stores); 1½ yards each of deep red and light red 45-inch-wide prequilted fabric; ½ yard each of red and purple prequilted fabric.

Instructions: Make a template for the diamond shape by cutting a 13x30-inch paper rectangle. Fold the rectangle in half crosswise and in half again lengthwise, then unfold. Draw lines from the ends of the vertical folded lines to the ends of the horizontal lines, forming a diamond. Use a protractor to make sure the angles on your diamond are 45 degrees and 135 degrees. Adjust the pattern, if necessary, and cut out the diamond. (Diamond shape includes ½-inch seam allowance.)

Using this pattern, cut four diamonds each of deep red and light red prequilted fabric. Cut the remaining fabric in 5½-inch-wide strips. (This includes the half-yard pieces of red and purple fabric.)

Piece diamonds, interchanging colors as you stitch. Use ½-inch seams and carefully position points at center. Press seams open; press remaining raw edges under ½ inch. Hand-sew the star to the center of the mover's blanket.

Patch the strips together end to end in random lengths. Press the raw edges of the strip under ½ inch. Cut the strip in four sections to fit around the star; pin in place. Cut away excess fabric and machine-stitch sections in place.

STAR AND BARS QUILT
page 108

Finished size is about 74x79 inches.

Materials: 44/45-inch-wide cotton fabric in the following amounts and colors: ¼ yard each of pink, gray, ecru, and beige; ⅓ yard sky blue; ⅔ yard each of red and gold; 1 yard brown; 2¼ yards navy blue; 4¼ yards backing fabric; 74x79 inches polyester batting; 8⅔ yards seam binding; quilting thread.

Instructions: Enlarge the pattern (right). With a ruler, pencil, and protractor, draw the shapes onto fabric, adding ¼ inch for seams. Make sure all

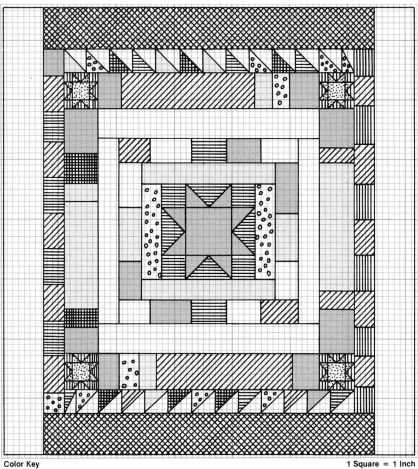

Color Key

▨ Pink	☰ Beige
▢ Red	▧ Gray
☐ Gold	▨ Brown
☐ Navy Blue	▨ Evergreen
▦ Sky Blue	▥ White

1 Square = 1 Inch

right angles measure 90 degrees. Place right angles with grain of fabric.

Cut out shapes; assemble according to diagram. Beginning with star motif, attach shorter bands on sides first, and attach longer bands next for the length. Continue until top is completed.

To finish the quilt, follow the general instructions on page 94.

NINE-PATCH QUILT
page 108

Finished size is about 71x80 inches.

Materials: 44/45-inch-wide cotton fabric in the following amounts and colors: 5⅓ yards black, 1 yard dark blue; ½ yard dark green; 4 yards backing fabric; 71x80 inches of quilt batting;

8½ yards seam binding; thread.

Instructions: Using a ruler and pencil, draw the following shapes onto tracing paper: one 1-inch square, one 3-inch square, two 9-inch squares.

On one of the 9-inch squares, draw an "X" from corner to corner on the diagonal. Cut the square in half along one diagonal line for triangle pattern (A). Cut the remaining triangle in half on the line for the corner triangle (B). Make templates from cardboard or plastic lids.

Adding ¼-inch seam allowances, cut 500 one-inch squares from dark blue fabric. From black fabric, cut 400 one-inch squares, 12 nine-inch squares, 14 triangles (A), four corner triangles (B), two 6x54-inch bands, and two 6x77¼-inch bands.

Cut and piece 1½-inch-wide strips from green fabric until two strips measure 51 inches each and two strips measure 65¼ inches each. (Note: Cut all bands slightly longer than measure-

110

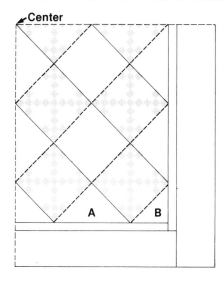

Center

A   B

ments if desired, since piecing may not be precise.) Be sure to place 90-degree angles with the grain of the fabric.

To assemble each of the checkerboard blocks, refer to the diagram (above). Make 20 blocks.

Before assembling the quilt, you may wish to complete the diagram by flopping the image once to create half of the quilt, then once again to complete it.

To assemble the quilt, start at the corner triangle (B), and begin assembling the checkerboard blocks, plain blocks, and triangles in diagonal rows. Sew diagonal bands together to complete the quilt center.

Stitch the 1½-inch green bands and the 6-inch border pieces in place.

See the general directions on page 94 for finishing instructions.

DIAMOND QUILT
page 108

Materials: One double-size moving blanket, available at art supply stores; 44/45-inch-wide prequilted fabric in the following amounts and colors: 2¼ yards red, 1 yard dark green, 2 yards yellow; red hem facing.

Instructions: Cut a 23-inch square of red quilted fabric, two 36-inch squares of yellow, four 7x56-inch strips of red, and four 7x34-inch strips of green fabric. Cut the yellow squares in half diagonally to make four triangles.

Machine stitch the pieces together in the following sequence: green strips to red square, yellow triangles to green

strips, and red strips around the outside. Use ½-inch seam allowances.

Press seams open and raw edges under around perimeter of appliqué panel; center the panel atop the moving blanket and hand-sew in place. Trim the quilt border with red hem facing.

AMISH CRIB QUILT
page 109

Finished size is about 36x55 inches.

Materials: Scraps of 44-inch-wide solid-color fabrics (except black) equivalent to ½ yard; 2⅜ yards black fabric; ¼ yard colored fabric for inner border; 1⅝ yards backing fabric; 36x55 inches quilt batting; 5½ yards bias tape; quilting thread.

Instructions: The diagram (below) is for one half of the quilt. Transfer the drawing to graph paper, flopping it to complete the design. Assign a color to each unshaded piece in the diagram. All shaded pieces are cut from black fabric. Make templates and cut pieces from fabric as follows, *adding ¼-inch seam allowances.*

From colored fabric:
A. 15 squares, each 2¼x2¼ inches
B. 120 triangles 2¼x1⅝x1⅝ inches
From black fabric:
C. 60 squares, each 2¼x2¼ inches
D. 120 triangles 2¼x1⅝x1⅝ inches
E. 8 squares, each 6¾x6¾ inches

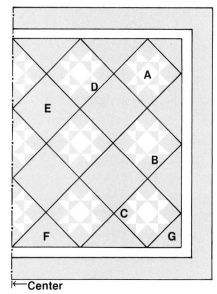

Center

F. 12 triangles 6¾x6¾x9½ inches
G. 4 triangles 6¾x4¾x4¾ inches

Assemble 15 patterned blocks; stitch to plain blocks and triangles using the diagram as a guide.

For the inner border, cut and piece two strips each 1¾ inches wide (plus seam allowances) the length of one side; sew in place. Cut two more strips the length of the remaining sides and sew to the quilt top. Repeat for the outer border, cutting the strips 3½ inches wide, plus seam allowances.

Quilt according to directions on page 94. Bind edges with bias tape.

DARK-AND-LIGHT-SQUARES QUILT
page 109

Finished quilt is 70x85½ inches.

Materials: 44/45-inch-wide solid, somber-color fabrics equivalent to 4 yards (the quilt shown is done in light blue, medium blue, rust, gray, black, dark green, rose, beige, and gold); ½ yard of fabric for inner border; 1¼ yards for outer border; 4 yards for backing; 70x85½ inches quilt batting; quilting thread; 9 yards of bias tape.

Instructions: Make templates for a 5½-inch square; a triangle measuring half the square, folded on the diagonal; and a triangle measuring one-fourth the square. Add ¼-inch seam allowances on all sides of all pieces.

From different fabrics, cut 126 squares, 32 large triangles, and 2 small triangles. Stitch squares together into 3 rows of 14 squares, and 2 rows each of 2, 4, 6, 8, 10, and 12 squares.

Lay rows side by side on the diagonal to make a rectangular quilt. Sew rows together, filling in with large triangles at the ends. The small triangles are for the ends of the rows in two opposite corners of the quilt. Refer to photograph as you assemble quilt top.

For the inner border, piece two strips each 1¾ inches wide (plus seam allowances) the length of one side; sew in place. Cut two more strips the length of the remaining sides; sew in place. Repeat for outer border, cutting strips 5 inches wide, plus seam allowances.

Quilt according to the general instructions on page 94. Bind the edges with bias tape.

STITCHERY AND NEEDLECRAFTS
Embroidery

titchery crafts have been favorites of crafters everywhere for many years, and this collection of embroidery and needlecraft projects is certain to delight all country artisans. On these eight pages we feature a range of stitches and techniques to adorn everything from bedcovers to table toppers. The key to success is careful execution of the stitches, which is the secret to all beautiful embroidery. The projects shown here are brimming with design possibilities: 26 letters and four fancy borders that can be used countless ways. The sampler shows all of the motifs; work every one or choose your favorites. We used monograms and initials to bedeck the pillow and pillowcases shown here. Floral borders adorn the sheets and picture frame. Size these designs large or small to embellish everything from a wool blanket to a delicate handkerchief. Instructions for these projects begin on page 120.

Yesterday's accessories add warmth and charm to today's homes, and these doilies and tablecloths from our past are reminiscent of days gone by.

Enhance your table with this field-of-daisies tablecloth (above). The center of each daisy is worked in a cluster of bullion knots. A splash of blue paint inside the ring of the design helps emphasize the embroidered flowers.

The stitcheries at right combine embroidered designs with antique lace and crocheted edgings. The doilies are spin-offs of the tablecloth using portions of the same fruit designs. To achieve the variegated shading, combine several colors of floss.

The doily (opposite) is made special by its embroidered bird design and its crocheted grapes and grape leaves edging.

To apply color to the fabric for the daisy cloth (opposite), use a liquid fabric dye. Follow the package instructions when you mix the dye and use a paintbrush to apply dye to the fabric. Press the fabric with a warm iron to "set" the dye.

There is a sense of quality and craftsmanship inherent in a great many country crafts, and this appreciation of time-honored craft techniques fosters a special attitude toward country-style living. Using and enjoying handmade crafts like these in your home creates a sense of family heritage because many traditional embroidery designs have been worked for generations and will continue to survive the test of time.

The flower basket stitchery at right is unusual because the embroidered designs determine the shape of the cloth. Place a flower basket design in each corner of your fabric, then cut away the fabric so the basket designs extend beyond the perimeter of your basic shape. Use French knots, outline stitches, and running stitches to work the designs, then add a delicate picot-like edging. If you wish, stitch a monogram onto the cloth to personalize the project.

A fresh addition to any tablecloth is this pert teapot appliqué, which is embellished with fanciful stitchery. Use black embroidery floss to outline the teapot in buttonhole stitches. Then stitch the teapot handle and the flower branch in running stitches. For extra color and texture, add clusters of French knots for flowers. The leaves are worked in lazy daisy stitches, a simple variation of the chain stitch. To finish the edges of the fabric, add decorative trim.

Make an entire set of coordinated table accessories using this basic teapot design. Size each of them according to use—for napkins, place mats, coasters, etc.

As with many craft designs, these motifs can be used to embellish other home crafts besides table linens. For example, you might stitch them on curtains, hot pads, a tea cozy, or a toaster cover. Or paint your favorite design onto a wooden tray.

The how-to instructions begin on page 125. For information on embroidery stitches, see the stitch glossary on page 374.

Concentric circles of French knots, worked closely together with two shades of floss, form the flowers on the teapot tablecloth (opposite page). Add French knots in darker shades for the centers of the flowers.

Scatter a wreath of prairie flower and field flower designs across the top of this 62x62-inch cloth and stitch the designs in place using satin stitches, outline stitches, French knots, and other basic techniques. The beauty of this project is in the combination of red poppies, blue cornflowers, and golden wheat. The variety of colors and stitches provides a welcome challenge to embroiderers of all ages and abilities.

If you're not quite ready for such a large project, try making a set of embroidered napkins like those opposite. The napkins are adorned with small floral bouquets. The basic design for each bouquet is taken from the motifs in the tablecloth.

Consider outlining and padding portions of your design with additional stitches for neat, crisp edges and lovely rounded surfaces. Outlining and padding take a little extra time, but they help highlight important design elements.

To finish the tablecloth and napkins, add a row of hemstitching around the outside edges.

Be sure to work your embroidery designs in colorfast threads. If the thread isn't colorfast, soak it for a few minutes in cool water to remove color residue. To wash an embroidery, use a gentle detergent made for hand washing. Rinse well and dry flat away from direct sunlight.

ALPHABET SAMPLER
pages 112-113

Finished size is 23x25 inches.

Materials: 28x36 inches of heavy linen or wool broadcloth fabric; embroidery hoop; crewel needles; embroidery scissors; ruler; tracing paper; pencil; fine-tip permanent marker (or dressmaker's carbon paper).

Plus: Columbia Minerva needlepoint and crewel yarn (20-yard skeins) or a similar substitute in these amounts and colors: 2 skeins each of 511 Pecan (brownish green) and 754 Light Medium Blue; 1 skein each of 447 Mustard, 968 Summer Orange (medium orange), 827 Cerise, R60 Medium Dark Red, 580 Yellow Lime (light yellow), 545 Avocado, 527 Moss Green, 742 True Blue (dark royal blue), 611 Gypsy Blue (medium lavender blue), and 621 Aster (light lavender blue).

For fabric frame use artist's stretchers (28x30 inches), ½ yard each of medium blue print and light blue print fabric, 1 yard of quilt batting, 7 yards of pink piping or braid, and a staple gun.

Instructions: Enlarge the patterns (opposite) to size and make a full-size (23x25 inches) drawing of the alphabet with the border designs (right) on the tracing paper. Neatly print name and date to fit inside the lower right corner.

Use either of the following methods to transfer the design to the fabric: One method is to pin the drawing to the wrong side of fabric and hold both paper and fabric over a light box or tape to a clean window and lightly trace design onto the fabric with the fine-tip permanent marker. The other method is to pin the drawing to the right side of the fabric, insert dressmaker's carbon between the fabric and pattern, and use a pencil (rather than a tracing wheel) to transfer the design to the fabric. (Note: For all lazy daisy stitch flowers, transfer only a dot to represent the center of the flower. Do not trace petal loops.)

When working the sampler, use the yarn as single strands except when working the alphabet letters. To do them, use two strands of 754.

Color and stitch details are listed below in working order.

Alphabet Squares:
ABCs: Fill in with satin stitches (754); outline with stem stitches (742).

Stems and block division lines: Stem or outline stitches (511).

Division line flowers: 5-petal lazy daisy stitches (447).

Flower centers: French knots (580).

Leaves (streamers and realistic shapes): Satin stitches (545).

Leaves (abstract shapes—heart, star, trumpet): Satin stitches (527).

Grapes (clusters on stems): French knots (621).

Flowers: 5-petal lazy daisy stitches (use 447, R60, 968, and 827).

Name and date: Backstitches (742).

Narrow Inner Border:
Leaves: Satin (545).

Stems: Backstitch (511).

Grapes: French knot (621).

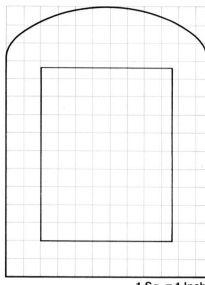

1 Sq. = 1 Inch

1 Sq. = 1 Inch

Flowers: 3-petal lazy daisy (611).

Middle Border:
Double scroll line: Backstitch (754).

Single scroll line: Backstitch (511).

Leaves: Satin (545).

Flowers: 4-petal lazy daisy (827).

Flower centers: French knot (580).

Outer Border:
Double scroll line: Backstitch (742).

Stems (single scroll line): Backstitch (511).

Grapes: French knot (621).

Leaves (realistic): Satin (545).

Leaves (abstract): Satin (527).

Flowers (leave centers unworked): Start at center top; work clockwise repeating 827, 447, 968, and R60.

Blocking: Block the finished sampler by laying it facedown on a towel, dampening it, then pressing well.

Framing: To finish the sampler as shown, frame it with fabric as follows:

(Continued)

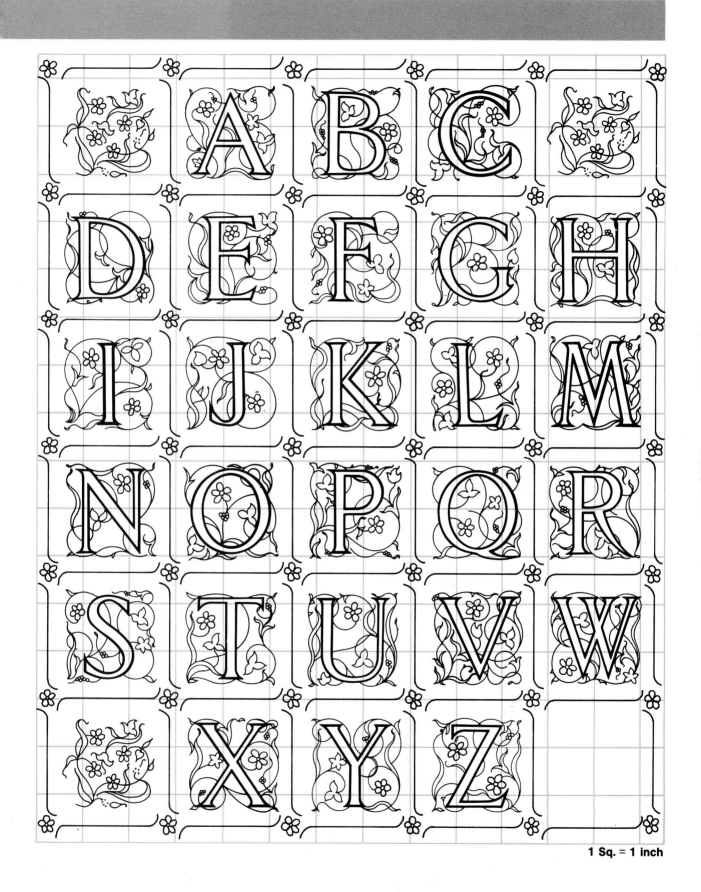

1 Sq. = 1 inch

121

strip of coral piping, a 1-inch-wide strip of light blue fabric, a second strip of piping, and a 3-inch border of medium blue print fabric. Carefully miter corners of fabric strips. Pad and quilt the fabric frame area, then stretch the entire sampler around a set of 28x30-inch artist stretchers and staple in place.

EMBROIDERED SHEETS AND PILLOWCASES
pages 112-113

Materials: Purchased or handmade pillowcases and sheets (linens may be solid or printed, but they must have white borders); eyelet lace to trim sheets and cases (optional); D.M.C. cotton embroidery floss in the following colors: purple (208), brown (830), pale yellow (745), yellow green (906), olive (3347), red (350), gold (972), light blue (334), orange (922), pink (718), dark blue (824).

Instructions: For pillowcases, trace an initial or initials from the sampler on page 121 onto the center of the hem. On each side, draw a section from the outer border of the sampler (we used only the center or inner part from the top of the sampler). Embroider, using the same stitches and colors as on the sampler, but using 3 strands of floss instead of the crewel yarn.

For the sheet, first find and mark the center of the sheet heading. Enlarge the side sections of the outermost sampler border to size and trace them onto the sheet heading, spacing them about 1½ inches on either side of the center. Embroider, using the same stitches and colors as for the sampler, but use 3 strands of floss instead of crewel yarn.

With both the sheet and the pillowcases, use whatever color you prefer for the large flowers.

When embroidery is finished, machine-stitch bands of contrasting piping and white eyelet to the edge of the sheet and pillowcase hems if desired.

EMBROIDERED PICTURE FRAME
page 113

Materials (For an 8x10-inch picture): Small skeins of Columbia Miner-va needlepoint and crewel yarn in the following colors: 827 Cerise, 545 Avocado, 527 Moss Green, 742 Gypsy Blue; 1½ yards of off-white China silk, silk taffeta, or similar fabric; 1 yard white cotton flannel for lining; ½ yard green silky fabric; 1½ yards piping cord; 1½ yards of 1½-inch-wide ruffled eyelet (optional); 14x16 inches of batting; art foam board; fabric glue.

Instructions: Enlarge the frame pattern on page 120 and trace onto tracing paper. For the embroidery pattern, trace off the narrow inner border from the set of sampler patterns on page 120. Arrange the pattern so there are three repeats of the design across the top and bottom of the frame opening and four repeats along the sides. End with the double leaves at the corners (as shown on the corners of the sampler). Note that the grapes of the border face the outside edges of the frame.

Position border so that it falls approximately ¾ inch from inside edge of frame. At center top of frame, draw in one of the large bouquets of flowers from middle border row of sampler.

With a hard lead pencil, trace the design only (not the frame lines) onto a piece of silk cut 2 inches larger all around than the frame. Do not cut out center of frame yet. Mark only the centers of flowers, not each petal. Cut a piece of flannel the same size and baste the two pieces of fabric together in rows on either side of the embroidery design.

Using an embroidery hoop and a very sharp needle, work the pattern in single strands of yarn as follows:

Stems: Stem stitch (527).
Grapes: French knots (742).
Leaves: Satin (545).
Flowers: Lazy daisy stitches (827) with French knot centers (742).

Press finished embroidery gently on wrong side.

Cut two pieces of art foam for the frame—one with the hole in the center cut out, and the second piece without the hole (for backing). Cover the frame with a layer of batting; pull excess to back and glue in place. Next, pin and stretch completed embroidery over the padded frame. Clip fabric into the corners, trim excess, and glue overlap to the back of the frame.

Cover the piping cord with 2-inch-wide bias strips of green silk and glue the piping to the inside of the frame. Next, glue in place a strip of ruffled eyelet as a "mat" for the picture. Cover backing piece of foam board with a layer of flannel and off-white silk; glue raw edges to wrong side of board, as for the front piece. Finish wrong sides of frame front and back with a piece of fabric glued in place to cover raw edges.

Cut three 1x9¾-inch braces from foam board, cover with off-white silk, and glue them to back of frame opening on bottom and sides so that they form an 8x10-inch support for the picture. Place glue on the three braces and lay the wrong side of the back piece on top, so that edges align with the front of the frame. Weight the frame with several books until glue dries.

Mirrors or glass and pictures can be inserted through top of frame. Attach a sawtooth hanger or cardboard easel to the back of the frame.

ROUND INITIAL PILLOW
page 113

Finished size is 16 inches in diameter, excluding the ruffle.

Materials: ½ yard of heavy linen or wool broadcloth; small skeins of Persian-type wool yarn in the colors listed for the sampler, plus 2 skeins of Zwicky silk floss in each of the following colors: pale lime (2038), soft green (2062), purple (2370), cerise (2216), and pale yellow (2017); embroidery transfer pen or hard lead pencil, embroidery hoop, needles, and tracing paper; 1⅓ yards each of 3-, 2-, and 1-inch-wide ruffled eyelet trim; 1⅓ yards of pink cording; fiberfill.

Instructions: Select any initial from the sampler and enlarge it to approximately 10 inches square on tracing paper. Then draw a circle about 15 inches in diameter around the letter. Around the circle, sketch the scrolly dividing vines from the sampler, spacing them about ½ inch apart. Place a dot for the center of a flower between each vine.

Details around each letter on the sampler vary slightly, so use the stitch, yarn and the color suggestions for the letter A (given on next page) as guides for the initial you have chosen. (Color numbers follow the stitch suggestions.) Use one ply of wool and three plies of silk.

Initial:

—diagonal laid work in both directions inside the initial (754).

—with upright cross-stitches tacking down the laid threads where they cross (742).

—outline with stem stitches (742).

Vine:

—stem stitch (511).

Three-pointed leaves:

—straight laid work inside (2062).

—couched down with (527).

—and outlined with stem stitches (527).

Loop leaf:

—staggered rows of running stitch inside the leaf, outlined with a backstitch (2062).

Trumpet leaf:

—seed stitch inside, then outlined in French knots (2062).

Grapes:

—satin stitch (2370).

Long leaves:

—chain stitch around the outside, then make zigzag stitches across the leaf by running needle under the chain from side to side on surface of the fabric; make a row of backstitches down the center of the zigzag (all in 2038).

Small leaves on vine:

—satin (2038).

Larger flower(s):

—long and short satin stitch (2216) on outer half of each petal, and (2017) on inner half of each petal.

—ring of French knots in the center (2017).

Border flower(s):

—five petals of lazy daisy stitch (2216).

—French knot in center (2017).

Border vine:

—stem stitch (2335).

To finish pillow, press embroidery gently on the wrong side, facedown on a terry towel. Add several layers of eyelet ruffles ½ inch outside embroidered border. Hand-sew pink cording to seam between eyelet ruffles and embroidered pillow top. Back pillow and stuff.

FIELD OF DAISIES TABLECLOTH
page 114

Finished size is 32 inches in diameter.

Materials: 1 yard ecru linen; #3 pearl cotton floss in the following colors: yellow, orange, rust, white, light and dark blue; blue liquid fabric dye; 3 yards of 2½-inch-wide lace edging; embroidery needle and hoop.

Instructions: Enlarge pattern (below), adding ½ inch for seam allowances. Rotate daisy pattern to the right four times to complete the design.

Transfer design to fabric. Do not cut out until embroidery is finished.

Paint light blue liquid dye on area between daisies, following package instructions. Let dry.

Work satin stitches with white pearl cotton floss on petals. Outline stitch around petals with dark blue thread. Satin stitch centers on small daisies using yellow, orange, and rust floss. Fill large daisy centers with bullion knots or French knots. Work parallel lines of running stitch on painted blue area, alternating rows of light and dark blue floss. Press, hem, and trim with lace.

FRUIT LUNCHEON CLOTH AND DOILIES
pages 114–115

Materials: 1⅓ yards of ecru linen; pearl cotton floss in a variety of colors and shades; embroidery hoop; embroidery needle; purchased or antique lace edgings; dressmaker's carbon paper.

Instructions: Draw a 10-inch-diameter circle onto paper for each doily, and a 33-inch-diameter circle for the cloth.

(Continued)

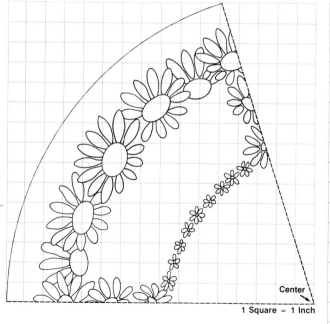

Center
1 Square = 1 Inch

CENTER

1 Square = 1 Inch

Mark a grid on the circles and enlarge the patterns (below).

Transfer patterns onto fabric using dressmaker's carbon. Do not cut them out until embroidery is completed.

Tape raw edges to prevent fraying. Mount fabric in a hoop. Keep fabric taut while stitching.

Use pearl cotton floss (or six-strand embroidery floss) for stitching.

For lemon doily: Embroider lemons using outline stitches worked close together, long and short stitches, or satin stitches. Use 2 or 3 shades of yellow pearl cotton to fill area. Satin-stitch leaves in 2 shades of green and light brown. Stitch the stems with closely spaced outline stitches in leaf colors (shades of yellow-green, blue-green, yellow, rust).

For grape leaf doily: Fill grapes using 4 shades of purple on three of the clusters. Work one cluster in light green, pink, and lavender. Use satin stitches, outline stitches worked close together, or long and short stitches on the grapes. Work the leaves and stems in 4 shades of green, using outline stitches worked close together to fill in large areas. Grape tendrils are worked with outline stitches in dark green.

For plum doily: Stitch plums with two shades of purple and pink using satin stitches or long and short stitches. Leaves are worked in the same stitches using gold, orange, and 3 shades of green. Use outline stitches to embroider stems with leaf colors.

To embroider the luncheon tablecloth: Numerous pearl cotton floss colors are used to stitch the luncheon tablecloth. For best results when several shades of the same color are used for embroidering, select shades that provide contrast.

1 Square = 1 Inch

1 Square = 1 Inch

1 Square = 1 Inch

The entire piece may be worked with satin stitches, long and short stitches, or outline stitches worked close together, whichever you prefer. Grape tendrils, leaf veins, and cherry stems are stitched with outline stitches in green, purple, rust, or gold.

The grapes are worked in shades of purple or light green, the cherries in shades of red, and the grapefruit in shades of yellow.

Use warm and cool shades of green to embroider leaves. Add highlights of yellow, rust, purple, or brown for interest. Use similar coloring on the stems.

The pomegranates are stitched with light green centers with purple or gold seeds inside, and with pinks or deep yellows for the outer areas.

Refer to the photograph for color selection and placement.

Press the finished piece using a damp cloth and a moderately hot iron.

To finish the tablecloth and doilies: Cut out the circles adding ½ inch for seam allowances. Sew a narrow double-fold hem around the border; stitch purchased lace trims in place. Or, arrange lace appliqués along the edge, slip-stitch in place, and cut out fabric that shows through the open lacework.

BIRD DOILY WITH GRAPE EDGING
page 115

Materials: ⅓ yard ecru fabric; embroidery floss or pearl cotton in gold, black, and 4 shades of rose; embroidery needle and hoop. *For edging:* Clark's "Big Ball" 3-cord mercerized cotton, size 10 (200-yard balls); 4 balls 61 ecru; size 8 steel crochet hook.

Instructions: Draw an 8-inch-diameter circle on paper. Enlarge the bird pattern (right) onto circle; transfer to fabric. Do not cut out until the stitching is completed.

Tape raw edges of fabric to prevent fraying. For best results, place fabric in an embroidery hoop and keep it taut while stitching.

Using three strands of floss or pearl cotton, fill in the bird motif in rows of outline stitches worked close together. Use gold floss for beak, shaded areas, and to outline areas of wings and body marked on the pattern. Use black floss

for the eye. Stitch the body in shades of rose, using the photo as a color guide.

Cut out circular shape, adding ½ inch for seams. Hem and press.

Edging: Make five leaves and five grape clusters.

Leaf section (make 3): Ch 20. *Row 1:* Sc in 2nd ch from hook, sc in next 17 ch; in last ch make sc, ch 3, and sc; then working along opposite side of beg ch, sc in next 16 sc; do not work over rem sts. Ch 1; turn. *Rows 2-10:* Sc in *back* lp of each sc to next ch-3 lp; in lp make sc, ch 3, and sc; then sc in *back* lp of each sc to last 2 sc; do not work over last 2 sc. Ch 1; turn. *Row 11:* Sc in each sc to ch-3 lp, sl st in lp. Fasten off. With the ch-3 lp of each section meeting at lower center, sew corresponding edges of the 3 sections together to form leaf.

Grape cluster (make 21)—*Rnd 1:* Beg at center, ch 2; make 5 sc in 2nd ch from hook. *Rnd 2:* Make 2 sc in each sc around. *Rnd 3:* (Sc in next sc, 2 sc in next sc) 5 times. *Rnd 4:* (Sc in next 2 sc, 2 sc in next sc) 5 times—20 sc. *Rnd 5:* (Sc in next 3 sc, sk next sc) 5 times; sl st in next sc. Fasten off.

Alternating clusters of grapes and leaves, sew together as shown below.

Rnd 1: With right side facing, attach thread to lower center of any leaf, ch 1, sc in same place as joining, * ch 27, sk next 8 sc on same leaf, sl st in next sc, make 8 sc over last 8 ch of the ch-27 for extension; ch 17, sl st in center of outer free edge on end grape on Row 6 of next cluster; make 8 sc *over* last 8 ch of the ch-17; ch 9, sl st in center of outer free edge of end grape on Row 7 of cluster; ch 8, sl st bet center 2 grapes on Row 6 of same cluster, ch 8, sl st in center of outer free edge of end grape on Row 7 of cluster, ch 17, sl st in center of outer free edge of end grape on Row 6 of cluster, make 8 sc *over* last 8 ch of the ch-17; ch 17, sk next 8 sc on following leaf, sl st in next sc on same leaf, make 8 sc *over* last 8 ch of the ch-17; ch 19, sl st in center of same leaf. Rep from * around. Join to first sc.

Rnd 2: Ch 1, sc in each *free* ch st of Rnd 1. Join to first sc. Break off.

Rnd 3: Ch 10, sl st in the 10th sc following joining; make 10 sc *over* the ch-10, sl st in last ch, mark this st, * (ch 19, sl st in sc opposite next extension, sc

over last 10 ch of the ch-19) twice; ch 19, sl st in the sc in line with next attached grape, make 10 sc *over* last 10 ch of ch-19, ch 10, sl st in the sc opposite next attached grape, make 10 sc over last 10 ch; (ch 19, sl st in sc opposite next extension, sc over last 10 ch of ch-19) twice; ch 19, sk next 9 sc of previous rnd, sl st in next sc, make 10 sc *over* last 10 ch of ch-19, sk next 18 sc on previous rnd, sl st in next sc, make 10 sc *over* last 10 ch. Rep from * around, ending with 10 sc over last 10 ch of ch-19. Join to marked st.

Rnd 4: Rep Rnd 2. *Rnd 5:* Ch 1, sc in each sc around. Join. Fasten off. Sew edging to doily.

FLOWER BASKET TABLECLOTH
page 116

Materials: 1 yard ecru linen; #3 pearl cotton floss in burgundy, rose, light blue, green, black, white, orange; 3¾ yards 1-inch-wide lace edging; embroidery hoop and needle.

(Continued)

1 Square = 1 Inch

—ROW 7

—ROW 6

125

Instructions: Enlarge the pattern on page 123, adding ½-inch seam allowances. Transfer design to fabric. Do not cut it out until embroidery is finished. Mount fabric in an embroidery hoop.

Outline stitch around the flower petals and centers with black floss on the outside, white on the inside. Work rows of alternating running stitches inside each flower—pink on the outside petals, red on the inside petals. Stitch gold French knots in the flower centers.

Work green outline stitches around leaves. Fill with rows of alternating running stitches in the same color.

Outline basket by couching gold lines of floss with black "pinning" stitches. Reverse the color sequence on the vertical lines inside the basket. Work cross-stitches with blue floss. Stitch remaining lines with alternating gold and black straight stitches.

Press finished piece. Hem, then trim with purchased or antique lace.

1 skein 6-strand embroidery floss in these colors: medium blue, light blue, medium rose, light rose, gold, yellow, medium green; scraps of medium-blue fabric; 4 yards purchased lace trim.

Instructions: Preshrink fabric; mark for 33-inch-square finished size. Enlarge the teapot pattern (below left); transfer the design diagonally to each corner (see photograph for reference).

Cut four teapot shapes (omitting handles) from blue fabric, adding ¼-inch seam allowances. Fold edges under; baste. Sew in place with buttonhole stitches using black floss. Add running stitch details; embroider the handle and branches with running stitches.

For flowers, stitch around circles using the lighter shades of blue, yellow, and rose. Work French knots as close together as possible. Fill centers with French knots in darker shades.

Work leaves in lazy daisy stitches, adding a short stitch of gold within the leaf centers. Finish the edges of the

cloth, then add lace trim, gathering and easing lace at the corners.

To clean this cloth and other embroidered cloths, it's best to wash by hand. Use a commercially made detergent for hand washing and wash according to package directions. Rinse thoroughly and dry away from heat and light. Or have delicate embroideries and laces professionally dry cleaned.

COUNTRY FLOWERS
CLOTH AND NAPKINS
pages 118-119

Finished tablecloth is approximately 62 inches square; napkins are 17 inches square.

Materials: Purchased tablecloth or fabric for a 62x62-inch cloth (wreath measures approximately 40 inches in diameter); six purchased napkins or 1¾ yards (44/45 inches wide) of linen; 6-strand embroidery floss in pink, cor-

TEAPOT LUNCHEON
CLOTH
page 117

Finished size is 33 inches square.
Materials: 1 yard linen or other white fabric (allow for shrinkage); 3 skeins black 6-strand embroidery floss;

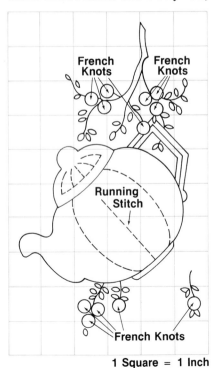

French Knots

French Knots

Running Stitch

French Knots

1 Square = 1 Inch

CENTER

Position this flower in center of each side

———— Double row of knots

- - - - Single row of Knots

1 Square = 2 Inches

al, red, burgundy, gold, white, black, and three shades each of blue, yellow, olive, yellow-green, blue-green; embroidery hoop and needle; tracing paper; dressmaker's carbon.

Instructions (*for napkins*): Cut out six 18-inch squares from linen. Hem.

Enlarge the napkin diagrams (right); transfer one motif to corner of each napkin using dressmaker's carbon paper (use each motif twice).

Stretch the fabric in an embroidery hoop to keep it taut. Use 2 strands of floss for all embroidery.

Embroider the designs in simple stitches—satin, long-and-short, chain stitches, French knots, etc. Refer to the photograph for colors.

To make the tablecloth: Hem the cloth. Enlarge the diagram (below); trace complete design onto cloth. Embroider, using 2 strands of floss; refer to the photograph for colors.

For the tablecloth border: Outline-stitch a black line 1½ inches above the hemmed edge. Satin-stitch a green ⅜-inch square in the four corners; outline stitch with black floss. At 2-inch intervals, satin-stitch a green ¾x⅞-inch box with a $^3/_{16}$x¼-inch box in the center top of each larger box. Outline with black floss. Adjust the distance of the intervals at the corners. Work a second black line ½ inch inside the first one.

CAROLINA COVERLET
pages 10-11

Materials: Muslin sheet; white cotton knitting yarn; fringe; large-eyed needle.

Instructions: Lay sheet on bed; mark center of top. Draw an octagon in sheet center 7 inches across to contain the center flower motif (see photograph). Draw circles 13 and 28 inches in diameter for wreath motifs.

Enlarge the pattern (opposite) for corners; position leaf and tulip shapes on wreaths and entire motif in corners as shown in photograph. Draw free-hand a seven-petaled flower in the center octagon.

Work the design in French knots. Space knots and rows ¼ inch apart along guidelines. Repeat a portion of the corner motif along the top of the spread if desired. Sew fringe to three edges of the coverlet.

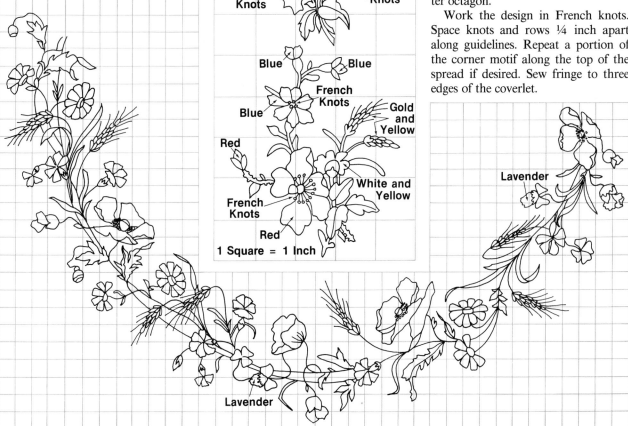

1 Square = 1 Inch

STITCHERY AND NEEDLECRAFTS

Cross-Stitch

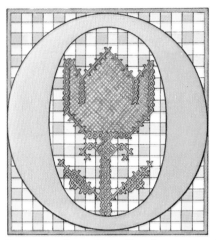

ne simple stitch yields all of the lively springtime floral designs shown here. It's the cross-stitch, an amazingly versatile part of every embroiderer's stitch repertoire. We have made stitching these designs even easier by working them on gingham fabric. All you need to do is plot your design on gingham, using the checks as a size guide for each stitch you make. Using gingham fabric in assorted colors and sizes creates a wealth of project possibilities, including the tablecloths, aprons, tea towel, and pillow shown here. The 16x16-inch pillow (in the chair at right in the photograph) displays all nine of the cross-stitch designs. Use as many of these designs as you wish to stitch the other projects, combining several different patterns into one project for a one-of-a-kind design. Instructions for these projects begin on page 134.

Block your finished sampler on a blocking board made of ½-inch-thick plywood that you have covered with gingham fabric. Sprinkle your sampler with water and pin it to the blocking board, using the gingham checks to align the edges. Let the sampler dry thoroughly, then press it lightly with a warm iron.

A book on country crafts just wouldn't be complete without a cross-stitch sampler or two. The cross-stitch sampler, a truly American folk art, originated as a teaching tool for pioneer schoolgirls who were taught to read and sew at a very young age. Although the samplers shown here are modern-day versions of traditional designs, they were inspired by authentic sampler designs of yore.

Help recall the memories of your wedding day by stitching this marriage sampler (opposite), a beautiful way to commemorate such an occasion. This project makes an especially meaningful family heirloom when handed down from generation to generation.

The entire project is worked in cross-stitches. Except for the personal information (names and date) and the alphabet, the design is symmetrical, which makes the pattern easier to work.

Declare a special fondness for your own abode—whether it be log cabin or ranch, farmhouse or apartment—by stitching this charming "home sweet home" design (left). Those three little words can mean so much when worked into such a striking design.

Instructions for these projects begin on page 137.

Work these old-fashioned cross-stitch designs and rekindle the do-it-yourself spirit of the past. Handmade projects like these are the beginnings of a down-home country look. For finishing touches, you can add other accessories, such as a pair of antique gloves or an old country quilt, that help show off your crafting skills.

The projects above are terrific for novice stitchers because they don't require much time or money. Embroider the picture frame with running, half-cross, and cross-stitches on perforated paper for a new twist. The pincushion (which you can work in needlepoint as shown or in cross-stitch) is a slight variation of the traditional wedding ring pillow (above) stitched on satin and edged with lace trim.

Make the 25x25-inch pillow (right) with even-weave linen, using embroidery floss in pastel colors to stitch the floral bouquets.

Instructions for these projects begin on page 138.

CROSS-STITCH ON GINGHAM
pages 128-129

General instructions: Cross-stitching on gingham is an easy technique to learn because the gingham check forms the boundary for each stitch you make.

When purchasing gingham, look for good quality woven gingham so that the checks are square and align with the grain of the fabric.

Use sharp embroidery needles and embroidery floss or pearl cotton.

Begin by securing the fabric in an embroidery hoop. Then make cross-stitches, following the stitch diagram on page 375. Make sure all stitches slant in the same direction.

Specific directions and patterns for completing the items shown on pages 128 and 129 follow.

Pillow
Finished size is 16 inches square.

Materials: ½ yard of ⅛-inch-check peach gingham; 2 skeins of embroidery floss in dark blue, light blue, yellow, dark orange, light orange, medium green; 3 yards eyelet lace; 16x16-inch pillow form.

Instructions: Cut an 18-inch square of gingham and mount it in a hoop. Beginning 3 inches in from any corner, work cross-stitch border motifs (opposite) according to pattern and color key. Use 3 strands of floss throughout.

Counting the squares carefully, work inner borders and squares that frame each motif. Work cross-stitch motifs within each square last. Press lightly and trim to 17x17 inches. Baste gathered eyelet around edges.

Cut 17x17 inches of gingham for pillow back. With right sides facing, sew back to front in a ½-inch seam. Leave one side open. Turn, press, and insert pillow form; stitch opening closed.

Square Tablecloth
Finished sizes will cover a 34-inch-square, 27-inch-tall card table.

Materials: 3⅔ yards of ¼-inch-check turquoise blue gingham; 3 yards of 1-inch-check turquoise gingham; 4 yards of ¼-inch-check pink gingham; 1½ yards of ¼-inch-check lavender gingham; #3 pearl cotton and cotton floss in colors and amounts specified for each layer; lace or eyelet ruffle.

Instructions: *Turquoise cloth (bottom layer)*—(This tablecloth is not embroidered.) For center of cloth, piece a 66-inch square of ¼-inch-check gingham. Cut strips 11 inches wide out of 1-inch check gingham for the 428-inch-long ruffle (includes ½-inch seam allowance). Piece ruffle, gather, and sew to center cloth. Add lace or eyelet ruffle trim if you wish.

Pink cloth (middle layer): Use 5 skeins of cotton floss in each of the following colors: green, light blue, dark blue, and rose.

Piece gingham to form a 64-inch square. Refer to patterns #2 and #6 of the pillow pattern. Substitute *rose* for light orange in pattern #2, *blue* for light orange in pattern #6, *purple* for yellow and dark orange in both patterns #2 and #6, and retain greens.

Using 2 strands of floss, work patterns #2 and #6 alternately around outside edge of cloth about 2 inches above the hem. Leave about 2 inches of space between motifs. Press, hem and stitch. Add lace or eyelet ruffle.

Lavender cloth (top layer): Use skeins of #3 pearl cotton in the following colors and amounts: 3 purple, 3 white, 3 rose, 2 pink, and 2 green.

Cut a 44-inch square of lavender gingham. Find the exact center of the cloth by counting squares, and work pattern #5. Substitute *white* for yellow and dark orange, *rose* for light blue, *pink* for dark blue; retain greens.

Work the border pattern, outlining squares as for the pillow. (Do not fill squares with motifs yet.) Substitute *rose* for light blue, *white* for yellow, and *purple* for dark blue.

Next, in each corner square, work pattern #7. Substitute *purple* for dark blue, *white* for yellow and dark orange, *pink* for light blue; retain greens. In addition, substitute *rose* for light blue flower motif to achieve a color balance.

For remaining four squares, work pattern #8, turning the motif a quarter turn each time so that the bottom of the flowerpot is closest to the edge of the cloth. Substitute *purple* for yellow, *rose* for dark orange, and *pink* for light orange and dark blue. Retain greens.

Press, turn up hem, and stitch. Add lace or eyelet ruffle if desired.

Round Tablecloth
Finished sizes will cover a 30-inch-diameter, 29-inch-tall round table.

Materials: 6 yards of 1-inch-check orange gingham; 4½ yards of ¼-inch-check yellow gingham; 1½ yards of ¼-inch-check green gingham; #3 pearl cotton in colors and amounts listed below; lace or eyelet ruffle (optional).

Instructions: *Orange cloth (bottom layer)*—(This tablecloth is not embroidered.) Piece a 70-inch-diameter round cloth. From remaining fabric, cut 8-inch-wide strips. Piece strips together, gather, and stitch to perimeter of cloth. Add lace or eyelet ruffle if desired.

Yellow cloth (middle layer): Use 5 skeins each of red, blue, and green #3 pearl cotton.

Cut and piece a 54-inch-diameter round cloth. From remaining fabric, cut 8-inch-wide strips. Piece them together to form a ruffle strip. Embroider the ruffle before gathering and stitching it to the round cloth.

Work a row of pattern #4 centered between raw edges across ruffle. Space motifs 5 inches apart. For the first motif, substitute *red* for light orange, and *blue* for dark orange. For the next motif, substitute *blue* for light orange, and *red* for dark orange. Retain greens as shown. Work the motifs alternately in these color combinations. Press.

Gather the ruffle, sew it to the circle (½-inch seam), and add lace or eyelet ruffle if desired.

Green cloth (top layer): Use skeins of #3 pearl cotton in the following colors and amounts: 4 white, 2 green, 2 yellow, and 1 brown. Cut a 44-inch square from green gingham.

Work five rows of border pattern evenly spaced across both length and width of cloth, counting carefully so intersections will align. Substitute *yellow* for light blue, and *brown* for yellow. Retain greens. On second and fourth rows, work one solid row of white cross-stitches on each side of border. Do this across both the length and width of cloth. Press. Roll hem, stitch, and add lace or eyelet ruffle.

Aprons
Purchase a commercial pattern for an apron or a pinafore and use ¼-inch-check gingham. Work the cross-stitch motifs of your choice along hem, pockets, bib, and waistband.

Embroider pattern pieces before assembling apron or pinafore. Mark the pieces (including all seam lines) on fabric using dressmaker's carbon paper. Mount the fabric in a hoop and stitch. When embroidery is finished, cut out pattern pieces and assemble according to pattern instructions.

Tea Towel

Using dressmaker's carbon paper (in a color just dark enough to see) or a hard lead pencil, mark a piece of ⅛-inch-check gingham so that after embroidering and hemming, the finished tea towel will be 12x27 inches. Do not cut out towel yet.

Mount fabric in a hoop and work pillow border pattern around edges. Plan 3 squares along narrow ends; fill in with 3 motifs (we used #1, #3, #9) from pillow pattern with 3 strands of embroidery floss. Cut out towel, hem and add lace or eyelet ruffle to the ends.

(Continued)

COLOR KEY

⊠ **Dark Blue**	⧄ **Yellow**	● **Dark Orange**
⊡ **Light Blue**	◤ **Green**	⊡ **Light Orange**

10 Squares = 1 Inch

135

CROSS-STITCH

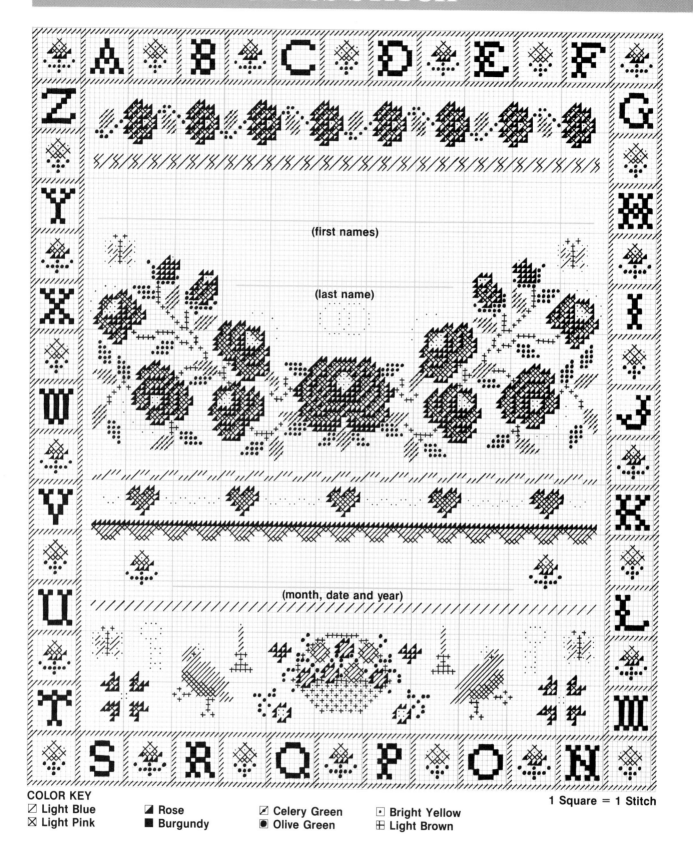

(first names)

(last name)

(month, date and year)

COLOR KEY

☑ Light Blue	◤ Rose	◪ Celery Green	⊡ Bright Yellow
⊠ Light Pink	■ Burgundy	⬤ Olive Green	⊞ Light Brown

1 Square = 1 Stitch

CROSS-STITCH WEDDING SAMPLER
page 130

Materials: 18x20 inches of 22-count even-weave linen; embroidery floss in light blue, light pink, rose, burgundy, celery, olive green, bright yellow, light brown; embroidery hoop and needle; masking tape; frame.

Instructions: Graph the names and date for the sampler on graph paper, following the alphabet and numbers (below). Position the words carefully on your sampler so each line is centered. (The names and date are worked in burgundy.) Bind the edges of the fabric with masking tape to prevent raveling. Locate the center of the fabric and the center of the design and begin stitching, following the pattern shown opposite. Keep the fabric taut in your embroidery hoop for best results.

Using three strands of embroidery floss throughout, work every cross-stitch over two threads of fabric.

When stitching is complete, block the fabric by pressing it lightly with a warm iron and a clean, damp towel. Center the sampler on a piece of mat board, leaving a 1-inch border around the design. Frame as desired.

HOME SWEET HOME SAMPLER
pages 130-131

Finished size is about 13x21 inches.

Materials: 15x22 inches of #14 off-white Aida cloth; embroidery floss in these colors: light and dark blue, light and dark pink, light and dark green, brown, and gold; embroidery hoop; needle; colored pencils; graph paper; masking tape.

Instructions: Using the pencils and graph paper, complete the chart (below). Flop the floral motif to the right side and graph. Flop entire motif above saying and graph. Complete lettering; motif to right of "Sweet" indicates the placement for "Home."

Bind edges of fabric with tape. Begin in centers of fabric and chart.

(Continued)

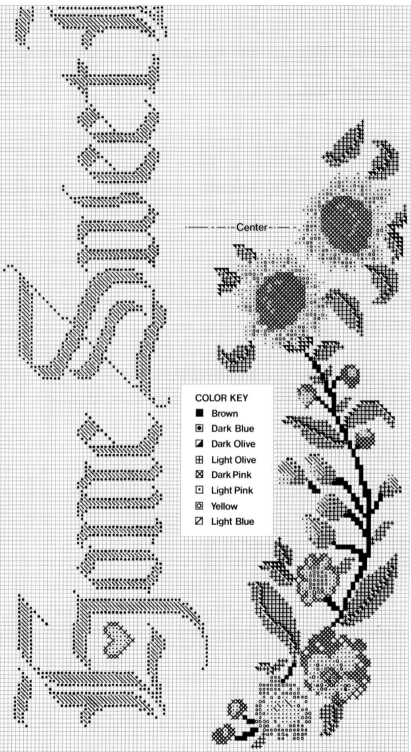

COLOR KEY

- ■ Brown
- ⊙ Dark Blue
- ◪ Dark Olive
- ⊞ Light Olive
- ⊠ Dark Pink
- ⊡ Light Pink
- ◎ Yellow
- ◩ Light Blue

1 Square = 1 Stitch

1 Square = 1 Stitch

137

Place fabric in hoop. Use two strands for working cross-stitches over one thread of the Aida cloth.

Block finished piece by pressing with a damp towel. Center sampler on a piece of mat board cut to size.

PERFORATED PAPER PICTURE FRAME
page 132

Finished size is 5x6½ inches.

Materials: Perforated paper (available in local craft shops, or write to Astor Place, Ltd., 239 Main Avenue, Stirling, NJ 07980); embroidery floss in the colors listed on diagram; tapestry needle; graph paper; colored pencils; 5x6½-inch piece of illustration board.

Instructions: Transfer design (below) onto graph paper with pencils. Complete it by flopping the image.

Begin stitching in upper right corner of design and 1 or 2 inches inside edge of paper. Use 6 strands of floss. Work half-cross stitches, running stitches, and cross-stitches as noted on diagram.

Cut out center along cutting line. Trim embroidered frame to size.

Center picture on illustration board; top with stitchery. Frame as desired.

NEEDLEPOINT PINCUSHION
page 132

Finished size is 4x4 inches.

Materials: 6x6 inches #15-count canvas; 3-ply yarn in the colors listed on diagram; backing fabric; covered piping; tapestry needle; fiberfill; graph paper; colored pencils; masking tape.

Instructions: Transfer design (below) onto graph paper with pencils. Complete design by flopping image.

Tape raw edges of of canvas. Use 2 strands of yarn; work in continental stitches.

Work 3 extra rows of needlepoint around the outside of the design to make finishing easier; block.

Sew piping to needlepoint. With right sides together, stitch backing fabric to needlepoint, leaving an opening. Turn, stuff, sew opening.

CROSS-STITCH BRIDAL PILLOW
page 132

Finished size is 8 inches square.

Materials: ⅓ yard each ecru and pink satin; 1 yard each ecru lace and pink trim; embroidery floss in colors noted at right below; embroidery hoop; embroidery needle; fiberfill; graph paper; colored pencils; dressmaker's carbon paper.

Instructions: Transfer the design (below) to graph paper using colored pencils and flopping the image as necessary to complete the pattern. Then, using dressmaker's carbon paper, transfer the design, centered, to the ecru fabric. Mount the fabric in a hoop and embroider using 3 strands of floss.

When embroidery is finished, trim excess fabric, allowing a 1½-inch margin all around. Cut pink backing fabric to match front. Trim front with lace along seam line (½ inch). Sew back to front; turn and stuff. Add pink trim.

CROSS-STITCH PILLOW
page 133

Materials: 30x30 inches of white #40-count even-weave linen; 6-strand embroidery floss in the colors noted on the chart (opposite); needle; fiberfill; white backing fabric.

Instructions: Before you begin, stay-stitch the edges of the fabric to prevent fraying. Then mark the center of the linen by working one light green cross-stitch. Following the chart and counting stitches carefully, begin working one corner of the design as shown.

Note: If you wish, transfer the chart to graph paper using colored pencils to represent each of the colors. Tape enough

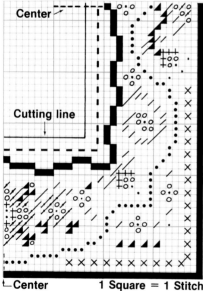

Center

Cutting line

└─Center   1 Square = 1 Stitch

COLOR KEY
- ☑ Peach
- ■ Dark blue
- ⊙ Light blue
- ⊞ Burgundy
- ⊠ Burgundy cross-stitch
- ⊘ Rose
- ◩ Dark green
- ☑ Celery green
- ⊡ Yellow
- ⊟ Rose running stitch

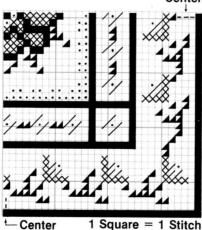

Center

└─Center   1 Square = 1 Stitch

COLOR KEY
- ■ Burgundy
- ⊠ Rose
- ⊡ Yellow
- ☑ Rust
- ◩ Olive

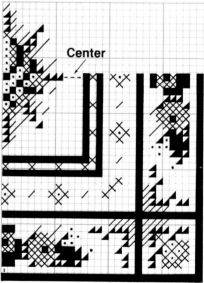

Center

└─Center   1 Square = 1 Stitch

COLOR KEY
- ■ Bright pink
- ⊠ Light pink
- ⊡ Yellow
- ◩ Dark green
- ☑ Light green

138

pieces of paper together to graph the entire design before you begin stitching.

Work each of the cross-stitches over 4 threads of fabric and use 2 strands of floss throughout. Stretch fabric in a hoop and maintain even tension while working so stitches will be uniform and consistent.

Stitch one section of color at a time. When you have completed the chart (one corner of the design), reverse and repeat the pattern three more times to complete the design.

To complete the pillow, cut a piece of backing fabric to match the pillow front. With right sides facing, stitch the two pieces together, leaving at least 1 inch of fabric between the design and the seam. Leave a 12-inch opening in one side and carefully turn the pillow right side out. Press lightly, stuff, and slip-stitch the opening closed. Or, if desired, sew a zipper into the seam so the cover can be removed for cleaning.

1 SQUARE = 1 STITCH   **TOP**

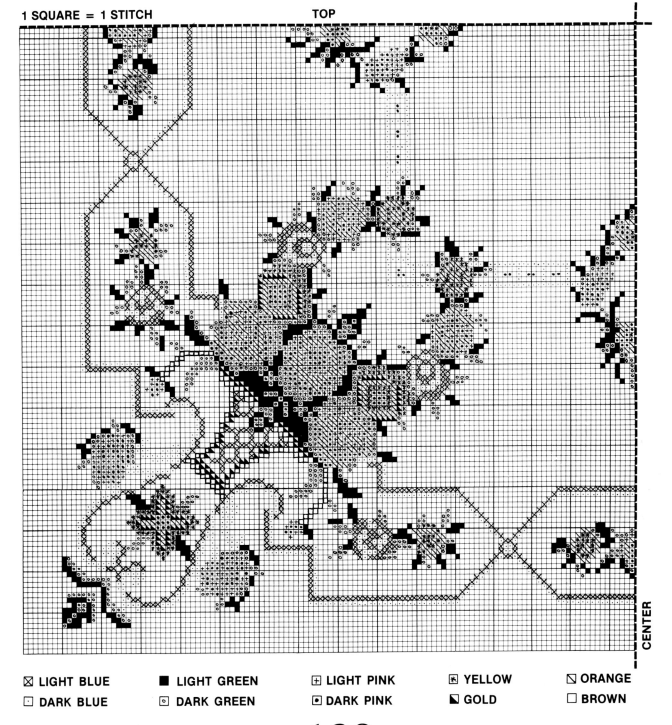

⊠ LIGHT BLUE	■ LIGHT GREEN	⊞ LIGHT PINK	✳ YELLOW	◩ ORANGE
☐ DARK BLUE	⊡ DARK GREEN	⊡ DARK PINK	◨ GOLD	☐ BROWN

139

STITCHERY AND NEEDLECRAFTS

Needlepoint

or country-fresh blossoms all through the year, stitch these needlepoint flowers in a kaleidoscope of colors and patterns. Elegant one-of-a-kind bouquets like this one will delight needlepoint buffs and flower fanciers alike. Each of the individually worked canvas petals is covered with easy bargello-type stitches. The petals are then grouped together with quick-stitched leaves and yarn-wrapped wire stems to form graceful blossoms that rival nature's own. After you've stitched a gardenful of flowers, use them for bridal bouquets, tabletop arrangements, or forever-fresh nosegays. Or you may wish to stitch just one elegant iris to grace your favorite bud vase. Experiment with color combinations for subtle gradations (it's a great way to use up bits and pieces of leftover yarns), or stitch the flowers in white with light green stems and leaves. See page 144 for the instructions.

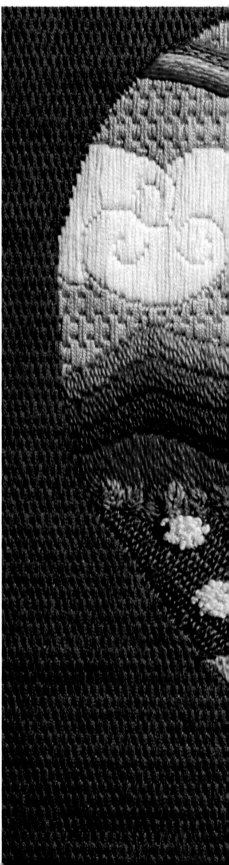

Out of America's heartland comes this spirited summertime scene with its mix-and-match approach to color, texture, and design. The dozens of fanciful stitches necessary to complete this 12x12-inch picture make it a delight for needlepointers. The design is worked on 22-count canvas and has enough country appeal to inspire you to start stitching now.

As you study the shapes and design elements, you'll notice a variety of textured stitches, including Hungarian, leaf, and wave stitches (refer to the needlepoint stitch glossary on page 375 for instructions). Once you begin working the design, pay close attention to the use of threads. You can combine many different threads, including embroidery floss, pearl cotton, and wool yarn, for an unusual design.

Instructions begin on page 144.

Cut the needlepoint yarn into short pieces to keep it from looking worn and thin after being pulled through the canvas too often. Cut embroidery floss or pearl cotton into 36-inch strands. Cut wool strands about 18 inches long. Silk and metallic threads should be cut to even shorter lengths.

Needlepoint Canvas

Needlepoint canvas is sturdy, open-weave fabric that is used as a framework for the stitches that are worked into it. It is available in several weaves and a large number of widths, and it is sized according to the number of vertical threads per inch. The larger the number of threads per inch, the smaller the stitches will be.

Mono canvas is made with single threads woven together in a plain over-and-under weave so each mesh (the space between threads) is the same size. It is available in #10-, #12-, #14-, #16-, #18-, #20-, and #24-count sizes (threads per inch).

Penelope canvas is made with *double* threads. It is a strong canvas that can be used for regular stitches that cover the double threads (gros point) or for fine stitches worked into smaller spaces formed by double threads (petit point).

The most widely used penelope canvas is #10/20-count; the first mesh number indicates threads per inch for gros point and the second indicates threads per inch for petit point. It can also be found in #11/22-count and #12/24-count sizes, and is available in #3½-, #4-, #5-, and #7-count sizes for rugs and other quickpoint projects.

Interlock canvas is a locked-weave canvas also made with double threads. Warp threads are twisted between each pair of weft threads, making this canvas resistant to raveling and distortion from the pull of the stitches.

Because of the way they are woven, the threads of interlock canvas cannot be separated for petit point, but they are easy to see through and paint. Interlock canvas is available in sizes ranging from less than three to more than 50 threads per inch.

While canvas is available in linen, nylon, or plastic, the most widely used form is cotton because it is strong and retains its starched body well (linen canvas tends to become limp). Nylon and plastic canvases are durable, but plastic is best for projects that need to be stiff and flat or that have pieces that are cut and pieced together. Nylon is similar to plastic but more flexible.

Most canvases are white, but some ecru, tan, and peach shades also are available. Cotton and linen canvases are easily dyed.

Yarns and Threads

The sky is the limit when choosing yarns and threads for needlepoint, as long as you can thread the fiber you've selected through the eye of a needle. Don't hesitate to use wool, cotton, linen, and silk yarns, as well as metallic threads, macrame cords, ribbons, and even fabric strips for special effects.

Wool is the most popular yarn for traditional needlepoint, however. Of the many types available, *Persian wool* is the most widely used because it wears well, is easy to work with, and is available in more than 300 colors. Each strand of Persian wool is made of three plies loosely twisted together so they can be separated and used individually.

Nantucket wool, which comes in tightly twisted four-ply strands, is comparable to a two-ply strand of Persian wool. Long fibers give this yarn a texture similar to tapestry yarn.

Tapestry wool comes in four-ply strands. It is a strong, smooth yarn available in a wide variety of lot-dyed colors so you can be sure colors are consistent, which makes it an excellent yarn for stitching backgrounds.

Crewel wool, used for embroidery, is a fine yarn that is especially nice for petit point. It comes in one-, three-, and five-ply sizes.

When purchasing yarn, try to buy enough for the entire project so you can be sure colors match. (Dye lots often vary slightly, so you might not find an exact match if you buy more yarn later.) Also, look for colorfast yarns so you won't ruin a beautiful piece of handwork in the blocking stage.

If yarns are not colorfast, rinse out any dye residues by soaking them in lukewarm water while they are still wrapped in skeins. Let them dry thoroughly before you begin stitching.

Needles and Other Tools

For stitching needlepoint, use tapestry needles with blunt tips and large, elongated eyes. They'll help you avoid splitting the yarns or threads of the canvas and won't put undue stress on the yarn in the needle.

The needle should be large enough to hold the thread easily, but small enough to pass through the canvas mesh without distorting the threads.

Equipment needed in addition to needles includes scissors with sharp, narrow points for snipping out mistakes; an emery-stuffed pincushion for polishing needles; masking tape; and a yarn caddy if desired.

Frames

Many needlepointers mount their canvases in a frame for working, freeing both hands for stitching (with one hand atop the canvas and the other beneath it). This often results in a more even tension, which minimizes distortion of the canvas during stitching and reduces the need for blocking. Large projects are frequently worked more easily on a frame than in your lap.

There are several types of frames available. A scroll or slate frame is the most commonly used type because it is adjustable and available in several sizes. To use one, attach canvas to rollers at top and bottom and lace it to the sides. (Make sure the grain of the canvas is straight as you attach it to the frame.) The rollers turn the canvas so you can work the design one section at a time.

Mount the frame on a floor stand or prop it against a table to free your hands for stitching.

To make your own frame, assemble artist's stretcher strips into a frame at least one inch larger on all sides than the finished dimensions of your project. Carefully staple your canvas to the frame, making sure you keep the grain lines straight.

If you wish to work in your lap, don't fold the canvas because you may break the sizing. Instead, roll it around a cardboard tube (from paper towels or decorative wrapping paper) and secure the ends with paper clips.

Working the Stitches

Whether you are a beginning needlepointer or an experienced one learning a new stitch, keep scrap canvas handy to practice on. The time spent mastering a new stitch will be amply rewarded once you switch to your project canvas. The tension on the stitches will be more uniform once you have mastered the technique, and you will spend less time picking out inaccurate stitches.

To avoid splitting and damaging stitches already worked, whenever possible stitch "from empty to full." To do this, bring the needle up from the back of the canvas to the front in an empty mesh; then take it down, from front to back, in a mesh that already has another stitch in it—a full one.

As you stitch, maintain even tension on the thread from stitch to stitch and with every motion needed to make a single stitch. If you pull the yarn too tight, it will not cover the canvas completely. When worked too loose, yarn tends to snag easily. With uniform tension, the stitches look better and you'll be less likely to distort the canvas.

Finally, it's easiest to stitch a design with separate needles threaded with yarn in each color. When working with several needles, however, don't carry the yarn more than a few meshes across the back of the canvas.

Instead, weave thread through the backs of stitches already worked. Or weave the thread end into the back, clip it, and start fresh in the new location.

Blocking Needlepoint Canvas

After stitching your needlepoint, return the canvas to its original shape by blocking it on a firm, flat surface. A good blocking job eliminates the distortion that occurs from the tension and pull of the stitches.

If you've worked in basket-weave stitches, which greatly reduce distortion, you may need only to steam-press the back of the canvas to restore its original shape. A design worked entirely in continental stitches, however, may be very distorted and need two or three blockings before it returns to its original shape. Here is an explanation of the correct procedure for blocking your needlepoint canvases.

Sprinkle the canvas with water until the yarn feels damp (but not drenched) on both sides. Or, wet a clean towel, wring it out, and leave the canvas wrapped inside the damp towel for several hours or overnight.

Tack the damp needlepoint face-down to a blocking board made of clean, ½-inch plywood or pine boards. (Be sure to use rustproof thumbtacks or pushpins.)

Make sure the blocking board is larger than the needlepoint piece and has straight edges. To help line up the edges, cover the board with high-quality gingham fabric and use the checks as a guide for squaring canvas, or mark it with a 1-inch grid drawn with a *waterproof* marking pen.

When tacking the canvas to the board, start in the lower left-hand corner and gradually move down the two adjacent sides, placing the tacks 1 inch apart. Make sure the canvas is flush with the blocking board so the edges are straight. Then continue along the third and fourth sides, ending in the upper right-hand corner.

Pull the canvas taut as you go, making sure the edges are straight and aligned with the gingham checks or the 1-inch grid.

Sprinkle the canvas with water again and let it dry thoroughly (at least 24 hours) before removing it from the blocking board.

NEEDLEPOINT FLOWERS
pages 140-141

Materials: #12-count interlock canvas; 18-inch pieces of #24 florist's wire; 3-ply Persian wool yarn in five shades of one color for each flower and three shades of green for each leaf.

Instructions: *Note*—Directions for three of the flowers shown on pages 140-141 are given here. In the colorful bouquet the leaf stitch flower is used three times and is most visible next to the vase. The iris is the large purple flower pointing toward the left. The tulip is the six-petaled flower in the center of the bouquet.

Leaf stitch flower: Work the petals in leaf stitches, referring to the pattern on page 146. As you begin stitching, hold the yarn tail on the back of the canvas at the center line until it is caught in subsequent stitches.

Using 2-ply strands of yarn, stitch five petals and two leaves for each flower, referring to the patterns on page 146. Start at the top of each petal and complete one leaf stitch using the darkest shade of yarn. Work your way down the petal, going from dark to light shades and stitching one row at a time. Repeat this procedure for the leaves, stitching three short bar stitches through the center of each leaf to make the "veins."

Cut out each petal and leaf, following the dotted lines on the patterns. (Note that at least one canvas intersec-

tion beyond the stitching is left intact.) Using the darkest shades of yarn, work binding stitches around the edge of each petal and leaf.

To make stamens, cut five 3x16-mesh canvas strips and fold them in half lengthwise. Cut five pieces of florist's wire 1 inch longer than the mesh strips. Place the wires inside the folds and bend each wire around the top 2 meshes. With the dark shade of yarn, stitch in the top mesh from the inside out, tucking the yarn tail into the fold. Holding folded edges together, make five small loops in the top 2 meshes; place yarn inside fold and cut.

With light shade of yarn, stitch from inside out in mesh below tufts, tucking tail inside fold. Wrap yarn around the folded strip, covering canvas completely. Stop at least two meshes above lower edge, knot yarn, and cut, leaving ½-inch tail. On fifth stamen, instead of cutting yarn, stitch back through other four stamens and gather into a bundle. Wrap the yarn around the bundle several times and sew back and forth to secure. Twist exposed wire ends together with pliers.

To assemble each flower, insert florist's wire into the center back of each petal. Work the end of the wire around the edges, ending at bottom tip of petal. Then work wire through center of petal, ending at top leaf stitch. Bend wire back ¼ inch and work end under yarn. Repeat procedure for leaves, using 6-inch wires.

To sew petals together, use lightest shade of yarn and stitch through base of each petal from front to back, just inside edge; go over wire and return yarn to front side. Pull tight and stitch to stamen bundle. Repeat procedure for other four petals, aligning petal to stamen. Sew back and forth through bundle to secure. Make sure that the wires extend to tips of petals and that the petals face in; then twist wires together to form the stem.

Add several wires to the stem for strength and wrap dark green yarn around stem, anchoring yarn in a stamen bundle. Attach first leaf after 4 inches of stem are wrapped. Hold leaf in place (front side facing stem) and twist exposed wires around stem. Then stitch through the base of the leaf with *(Continued)*

145

wrapping yarn and continue for 2 more inches. Repeat this procedure for the second leaf. Cut stem to desired length and finish wrapping. Shape petals and leaves as desired by bending wires.

Iris: To make the iris, refer to the patterns for the petals and leaves (right). Pattern A represents the lower petals; pattern B represents top petals.

For pattern A (lower petals), begin stitching around outer edge of petals, using darkest shade of yarn. Reverse color order for pattern B. (Refer to photograph on page 141 if necessary.)

Complete bargello-type patterns for both petal pieces except do not stitch the shaded areas. Leave yarn ends long to work these areas later. Cut out petals, carefully following dotted lines.

Stitch two leaves, referring to the pattern. To finish leaves, refer to instructions for leaf stitch flower.

Using the center of the petals as pivot points, move the flap under and in line with shaded area. Tack in place with single strand of yarn, making tent stitches over several canvas intersections. Complete the bargello pattern, working through both canvas pieces. Bind the petal edges with the darkest shade of yarn and insert florist's wire (see instructions for leaf stitch flower).

To assemble the iris, insert florist's wires along diagonal lines (as shown on patterns), letting the excess wire hang from center points. Insert wires from the top piece through the center point of the bottom piece.

With petals in alternating positions, tack the centers together. Complete the stem as for leaf stitch flower, adding leaves as desired. Curve the top petals up and together and curve the lower petals down, as shown in the photograph on pages 140-141.

Tulip: Stitch six petals according to diagram (right), using 2-ply strands of yarn. Begin stitching with the darkest shade of yarn along the top edge of the petal as shown; continue working bargello-type stitches, going from dark to light shades. If necessary, add some trame stitches on the back side to help cover the canvas. Cut out the petals and bind the edges the same way as for the leaf stitch flower.

Stitch one leaf according to the diagram; for the second leaf, reverse the pattern. Finish according to the directions given for the leaf stitch flower.

For stamens, cut three 4-mesh canvas circles, working a binding stitch around edges in darkest yarn. Fill center of circles with French knots in lightest yarn. Anchor florist's wire under knots and complete stem of stamen as for leaf stitch flower.

To assemble flower, insert wire in petals and leaves, referring to instructions for leaf stitch flower. Gather stamens and attach 3 petals; add last 3 petals. Finish as for leaf stitch flower.

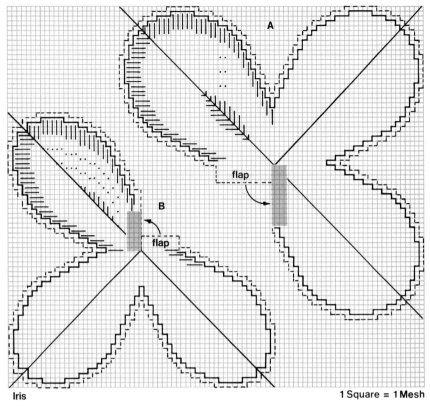

Iris   1 Square = 1 Mesh

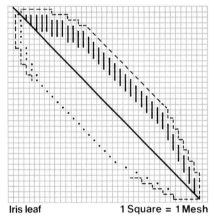

Iris leaf   1 Square = 1 Mesh

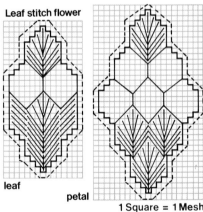

Leaf stitch flower

leaf   petal   1 Square = 1 Mesh

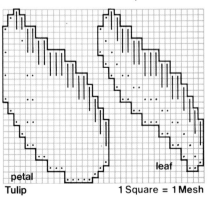

petal   leaf

Tulip   1 Square = 1 Mesh

146

HEART PICTURE
pages 142-143

Finished size of the design shown is 12x12 inches. To make a larger picture, use a needlepoint canvas with fewer squares per inch (such as 12- or 14-count canvas). Be sure to adjust the amount of canvas, thread, and other materials accordingly.

Materials: 16x16 inches of #22-count needlepoint canvas; 75 yards of dark blue embroidery floss for background; 20 yards of light blue embroidery floss for sky; small amounts of embroidery floss and Persian wool yarn in the colors listed in the color key (right); #22 tapestry needle; light-colored waterproof marking pen; black marking pen; masking tape; 12x12-inch artist's stretcher strips; 4½ feet of ½-inch-wide blue grosgrain ribbon for trim or picture frame; tracing paper; needlepoint frame.

Instructions: With a black marking pen, enlarge the pattern (right) onto tracing paper. (Or have the pattern enlarged photostatically at a photoduplication studio.)

Tape the pattern to your work surface. Then center the canvas over the pattern and secure it with masking tape. With a light-colored waterproof marking pen, transfer the design onto the canvas, using black outlines as a guide. Remove the canvas from the paper pattern and bind the edges with masking tape to prevent raveling while you work.

Mount the canvas in a needlepoint frame and begin working the background, stitching around the heart. Work the background in vertical brick stitches, using 6 strands of dark blue embroidery floss. (For diagrams of the stitches used, see the stitch glossary on page 375.)

Begin stitching the areas inside the heart, referring to the stitch and color keys (right). Work one section at a time, following the outlines on canvas.

When the heart is complete, block the canvas. Assemble stretcher strips to make a frame and mount the canvas in the frame, securing the edges in the back with staples or masking tape. Glue ½-inch-wide grosgrain ribbon around the edges or mount the finished picture in a frame.

Color key
A—light blue
B—medium blue
C—blue
D—dark blue
E—white
F—gray
G—yellow
H—red
I—orange
J—green
K—pink
L—coral
M—lavender
N—black
O—dark brown
P—golden brown
Q—tan
R—light olive green
S—medium olive green
T—dark olive green
U—light blue-green
V—medium blue-green
W—blue-green
X—dark blue-green
Y—forest green
Z—dark forest green

AA—light kelly green
BB—kelly green
CC—brown rust

Stitch key
1—vertical brick stitch
2—continental stitch
3—satin stitch
4—Parisian variation stitch
5—slanting Gobelin stitch
6—encroaching Gobelin stitch
7—wave stitch
8—Hungarian stitch
9—leaf stitch
10—fishbone leaf stitch
11—bullion stitch
12—French knot
13—outline stitch
14—lazy daisy stitch
* denotes embroidery floss

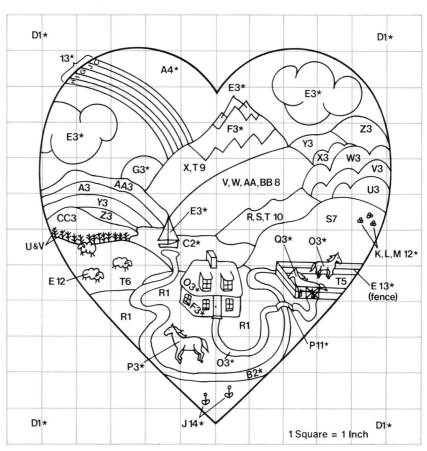

147

STITCHERY AND NEEDLECRAFTS

Rug Making

othing is as warm and cozy as a handmade rug, whether it is placed on a bare wood floor, in front of a fire, or under your dining room table. A rug that's crafted by hand, be it hooked, needlepointed, or braided, says "welcome" in a special way and adds big impact no matter where it is placed. This needlepoint rug is a delightful greeting to one and all, a sign of old-fashioned hospitality to those who see it. To make this 33x51-inch rug, work the design on 10-count canvas using shades of wool yarn. The wildflower and strawberry background is a repeat pattern designed to give the illusion of scattered flowers. The alphabet border is repeated four times to frame the overall design. For subtle shading, use two different colors of yarn to stitch the bunnies. For instructions, turn to page 154.

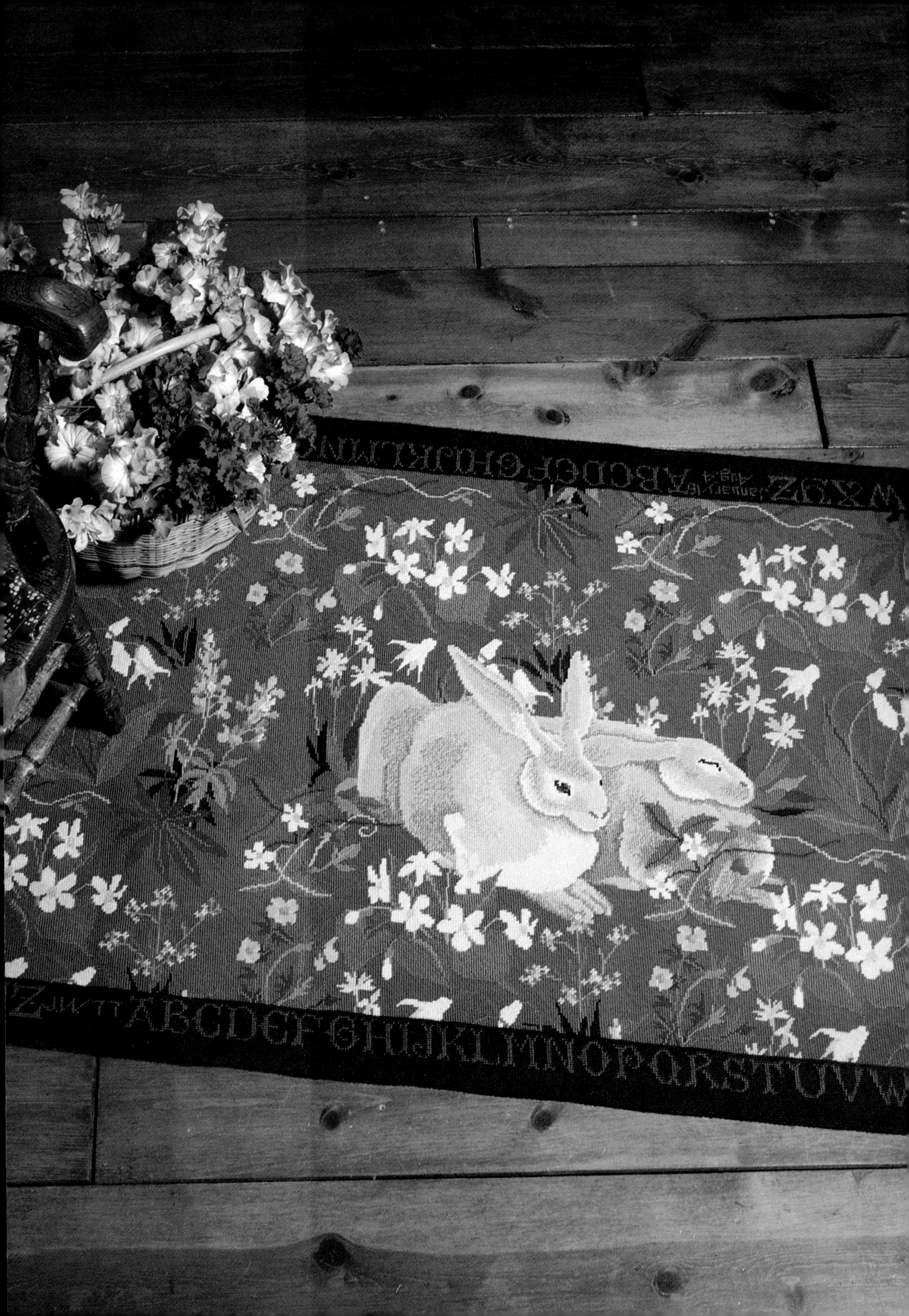
ABCDEFGHIJKLMNOPQRSTUVW

Create a down-home atmo-sphere by using only one smashing accessory like this 5x7-foot hooked rug, which is a contemporary version of an American folk art design. Originally called a "field of flags" design, the rug is updated with rich, vibrant colors of acrylic rug yarn.

Stretch a piece of burlap around a wooden frame and begin planning your design by sketching a grid of 5½-inch squares on the back of the burlap. Thread a punch needle tool (also called a rug hooking needle) with acrylic yarn and work a domino-like design inside each square of your grid. Surround two adjacent sides of the domino squares with stripes of primary and pastel colors.

By working your design from the back side, the pile will form on the front of the rug. Apply a coat of liquid latex to the back of the rug to achieve longer wear and to prevent slipping.

We used a crank-style punch needle to work our rug. To operate this particular needle, turn the handle eggbeater-style and "walk" the needle across the surface of the burlap.

You can achieve a striking color scheme by working an alternating pattern of dark and light squares. Highlight the dark squares with one or two stripes of light-colored yarn. Accent the light squares with several stripes of dark yarn.

To keep your hooked rug fresh, shake and air it frequently. To clean it, fill a tub with three inches of cold water and sprinkle laundry detergent on top. Lay the rug, pile side down, on top of the water and let it soak five minutes. Pound the rug with your hands to remove dust and dirt and rinse with cold water. Dry it on a flat surface.

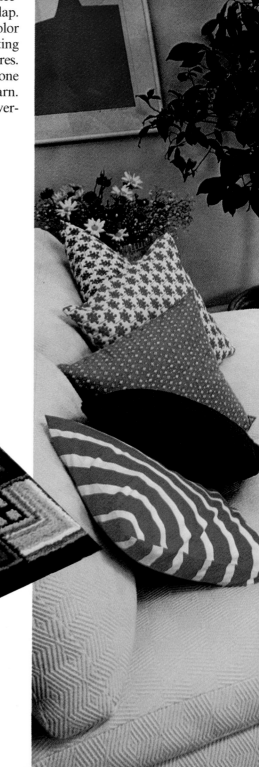

150

I f you want a friendly greeting inside your front door, make these stunning hooked rugs inspired by majestic North American landscapes and seascapes. They're a sign of country living at its best and proclaim a warm welcome to guests who visit your home. All three of these traditional rugs are worked on burlap backings in nature's softest colors.

The rug in the foreground is bordered by a graceful vine and dons a wild rose motif in the center. The rug at right features a single repeat pattern worked in several different colors. The rug at left is a pleasing arrangement of striped and floral motifs.

Use either strips of wool fabric (cut on the straight grain) or wool yarn to make these designs. This can be a chance to use random pieces of fabric and yarn from your sewing basket if you desire.

To finish these rugs, use rug binding around the edges.

If you've never worked with a rug hook before, you may wish to practice on a piece of burlap before you begin your project. As you work your project, make sure the burlap is tacked or stapled securely to a wooden frame.

WILDFLOWER RUG
Page 149

Materials: DMC 3-ply Persian wool yarn (Laine Divisible Floralia) in the following colors and amounts: *Wild-flowers*—130 yards of 7353; 10 yards each of 7342 and 7341; 125 yards of 7769; 50 yards of 7346; and 100 yards of Blanc. *Rabbits*—30 yards each of 7411, 7511, and 7415; 15 yards of 7715; and 16 yards of ecru. *Alphabet border*—155 yards of 7485; 450 yards of 7925; and 1050 yards of background color. The following colors will require one skein: 7428, 7564, 7257, 7896, 7709, 7895, 7800, 7799, 7302, 7666, 7155, 7304, 7153, 7106, 7850, 7204, 7133, 7192, 7579, 7745, 7434, 7168, 7499, 7618, and 7355.

Chart A

dark line indicates lower right corner of floral area→

Color Key: greens— 7353 7342 7341 7769 7346 7428 7564 ~ purples— 7257 7896 7709 7895
blues— 7800 7799 7302 7304   reds, pinks, oranges— 7666 7155 7153 7106 7850 7204 7133 7192
beige, yellows, browns — blanc 7597 7745 7434 7168 7485 7499   background color: 7295

Also, 1½ yards (36-inch-wide) #10 penelope or double-mesh canvas, tapestry needle, rug frame, masking tape, and an indelible marker.

Instructions: Using marker, mark alphabet border edge 4½ inches inside canvas edges; tape edges of canvas.

Chart A (opposite), for wildflowers works as a repeat pattern. Use outline indications for placement of repeats.

Begin stitching in lower right corner following color key. Work fragments of flowers as well as buttercups and white violets in continental and basket-weave stitches where applicable. After stitching strawberry plant, work rabbits (below). When rabbits are complete, fill in remaining flowers.

Following Chart C, work alphabet (using either continental or half-cross *(Continued)*

Chart B

Color Key: ■ *noir* ⊡ *ecru* ◪ *7411* ⊟ *7511* ◪ *7415* ◪ *7499* ⊞ *7618* ▣ *7192* ◪ *7355* ▬ *7925* **blends:** ◪ *1 strand 7715, 2 strands 7511*
◪ *1 strand 7715, 2 strands 7411* ▣ *1 strand each: 7411, 7511, 7715* ▭ *1 strand 7715, 2 strands 7415*
◪ *1 strand each: 7499, 7415, 7715* ▥ *1 strand 7415, 2 strands 7511* ◪ *1 strand 7415, 2 strands 7499*

Chart C

stitches) from lower right corner of rug. The farthest stitch of the A should be even with last row of floral background. Work the alphabet up the side and wrap it around the corner; refer to chart for spacing between letters and placement of letters around corners.

For second alphabet return to lower right corner; work backward (Z, Y, X, etc.) toward left. Farthest stitches of Z should be even with bottom of A from first alphabet. Work remaining two alphabets in same manner, using upper left corner of rug as starting point.

Use spaces between alphabets for signature or for personalizing the rug. Fill border with basket-weave stitches. Leave 1 inch of canvas unworked.

HOOKED FOLK ART RUG
pages 150-151

Finished size is 46x68 inches.

Materials: 56x78 inches of heavy-weight natural-colored burlap; about 130 ounces of acrylic worsted-weight rug yarn; rug hooking frame and needle; liquid latex for backing; a black *permanent* felt-tipped marker; 4x6-foot sheet of plywood; nails; paintbrush.

Instructions: To duplicate our rug, work stripes of every other square in dark colors with one or two light-colored accent stripes. Work remaining squares in pastels with dark accents.

Using *permanent* black felt-tipped pen, draw a grid of 5½-inch squares on burlap (center the block of squares). Rug shown is 12 squares long and eight squares wide. Draw a 1-inch border around the edge. Enlarge and transfer pattern (above right) to squares.

Secure a section of burlap to the rug frame, making sure grain lines are straight. The side facing you (with the pattern on it) will be *back* of rug.

Following the manufacturer's instructions, thread the rug hooking needle and adjust loop height to desired thickness. Changing yarn colors as necessary, hook outer stripes of squares first. Then, work four "dots" within smaller square. Finally, fill in area surrounding dots. Work border in black.

When all squares are filled, remove rug from frame. Hem the rug, then coat the underside with liquid latex to secure stitches and make rug skid-proof.

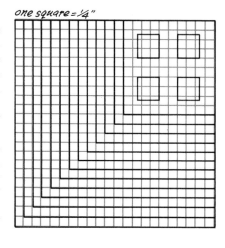

one square = ¼"

HOOKED FLORAL RUGS
pages 152-153

Materials: Burlap for backing; rug binding; rug hooking frame; woolen material for cutting strips or wool yarn; rug hook suitable for either cut-strip hooking or yarn hooking; thumbtacks or staples; waterproof felt marker.

General instructions: Begin by planning size of rug. For beginners, a rug no larger than 24 or 36 inches in either dimension is a good size. Draw the finished size on burlap. If you are working with cut wool strips, draw pattern on right side of burlap; if you use yarn, reverse pattern and work from wrong side of burlap.

Secure burlap to the frame with tacks or staples so that it is taut.

If you are working with wool strips, wash and dry all fabrics. With a razor blade, cut woolens *on the straight grain* into 12- to 15-inch-long strips each ⅛-inch wide. Follow manufacturer's instructions for using hook; work from right to left if you are right-handed. (If you have not worked with rug hooking before, practice on scrap burlap first.)

If you are working with yarn, thread the hollow-handle hook according to manufacturer's instructions. Work design elements first, then background areas. When all areas have been hooked,

1 Square = 1 Inch

clip off any too-long loops. Or, clip all loops to blend wool colors together.

To finish, trim burlap to within 1 inch of finished design. Double-fold edge under and slip-stitch in place. Cover hem with rug binding.

For the large (27x54-inch) rug in the foreground on pages 152-153, enlarge the half-pattern (opposite). Refer to the photograph for colors.

For the 18x30-inch rug (rear left, page 152), draw 6-inch squares on the burlap. Draw an X in alternate squares; work these lines and outlines of all squares in black. Hook rows of random colors connecting the crossed lines. Use wool scraps, alternating light and dark

1 Square = 1 Inch

shades. Position floral pattern (above) in remaining squares.

For the 25x36-inch rug (right rear) draw twenty-four 5½-inch squares on burlap; add a 1½-inch border. Enlarge the pattern (below) and work it in each square, alternating colors of flowers as desired. Work the border in green or any color you prefer.

1 Square = 1 Inch

FELT APPLIQUÉ RUG
pages 12-13

Finished size is 42x69 inches.

Materials: 54- to 60-inch-wide felt in the following colors and amounts (in yards): 5 brown, 2 rust, 1½ light olive green; ½ each of aqua, chartreuse, salmon pink, orange, yellow-orange, dark beige, and dark olive; ¼ each of pale beige, pale yellow (cream), and gold; thread; scissors; yardstick.

Instructions: Enlarge patterns (below and right). Cut flowers, leaves, and other shapes from felt, referring to photograph for colors. Cut three sets of each design, varying colors for each.

Cut fifteen 12-inch squares of rust-colored felt. Machine appliqué one set of patterns to each square. Pin appliquéd squares atop 47x74 inches of dark brown felt (3 blocks wide by 5 blocks deep). Leave a 4-inch outside border and 1½ inches between squares.

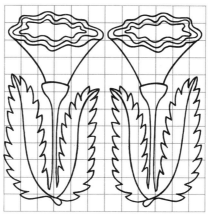

1 Square = 1 Inch

1 Square = 1 Inch

Cut dark brown felt 42x69 inches; center and pin to back of rug. Fold under edges of rug top 2½ inches all around, leaving a 1½-inch border on the outside edges. Miter corners; baste turned-under edges to backing. Zigzag edges of squares in place, being sure to catch backing fabric and folded-under borders as you stitch.

1 Square = 1 Inch

1 Square = 1 Inch

1 Square = 1 Inch

STITCHERY AND NEEDLECRAFTS

Special Stitchery Techniques

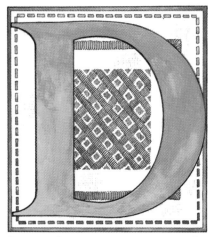

arning is a needle art that once was widely practiced by the pioneers. Out of necessity, women would learn various darning stitches to mend clothes for their families from one season to the next. From their frugality developed a new manner of stitching that was both artistic and practical. The efforts of these women so long ago inspired this darning sampler, a veritable anthology of the art of darning. The sampler lets you practice basic stitchery skills, which are decorative as well as functional, while making use of bits and pieces of embroidery floss. Each design is carefully counted and stitched using linen, twill, and damask darning stitches. The patterns are then displayed inside colorful running stitch borders. Instructions for this project begin on page 166. For more information on darning, refer to *Encyclopedia of Needlework* by Therese de Dillmont.

Tatting

If you think tatting is a dying art, think again. Just look at these dainty blossoms and this delicate table mat, both modern designs made from basic tatting techniques. Tatting was popular many years ago (around the turn of the century), and it is now enjoying a widespread revival.

Originally developed from seafaring knots used by fishermen and sailors, tatting eventually developed into a refined art form, as did bobbin lace, Battenburg lace, and many other lacemaking techniques. The knots used for tatting were originally designed for more functional purposes. Now, however, these knots are strictly ornamental.

The basic tatting knot is a double knot composed of two half-hitches, one the mirror image of the other. Both of the knots are carried on a separate thread, which forms an internal core.

The thread you use for tatting should be smooth, pliable but firm, and tightly twisted, with as little stretch as possible. Cotton thread is an ideal choice.

The shuttle (like a bobbin with pointed ends) conveniently holds your thread—it does not make the stitches. The stitches are formed by the movement of the fingers. The size of the shuttle depends on the size of your thread, not on the size of your project.

The snowflake-like patterns that are typical of tatting are formed by a series of rings and lines. Rings are the most identifiable feature of tatting. They result in the characteristic circular shapes. These patterns were traditionally used to decorate pillows, hankies, and clothing, but we have chosen more decorative projects, such as the flowers and table mat shown here.

Our flowers, made from two different weights of pearl cotton floss, are fanciful adaptations of daisies and roses. You can arrange them for a centerpiece as shown here, or combine them with fresh flowers for a special bridal bouquet, nosegay, and boutonniere.

The square doily consists of 100 of the daisy motifs tatted together.

Complete tatting instructions begin on page 166.

Shuttles are pointed bobbins used to store thread so it can be worked conveniently. To wind the shuttle, pull the end of the thread through the hole in the shuttle post and tie off. Wind the thread counterclockwise around the post. Don't fill the shuttle so full that the thread protrudes beyond the edge of the shuttle.

160

Stitched in a traditional counted-thread technique, these hardanger table accessories found their way to American soil from Norway, where this particular technique evolved. Using even-weave fabric, these designs are embroidered in blocks of satin stitches and then accented with cutwork and delicate needleweaving. The result is a look that is reminiscent of old-fashioned lace.

To add this versatile technique to your needlework repertoire, always embroider the satin stitches before doing any cutwork. Make each satin stitch over four threads of the fabric, and work one more stitch than the number of threads to be cut, so the cut area is sufficiently bound and will not ravel.

Be careful to work the embroidery thread through the spaces between the fabric threads rather than into the threads themselves.

After all the embroidery is finished, use small, sharp scissors to cut away the threads that are bound by the satin-stitched blocks. Don't worry about frayed edges; the fabric will shrink when it is washed and all the rough edges will pull up beneath the blocks of satin stitches.

For how-to instructions and a pattern for the place mat, turn to page 169.

When all of the satin stitching is complete and bound threads have been carefully cut away, work needleweaving around the remaining long threads in the openwork areas. While you weave, add loops and a variety of other decorative lace stitches inside the needle-woven blocks.

Designs from nature adapt beautifully to needlework, and this graceful "mallard in flight" wall hanging is a perfect example. The design is worked in crewel embroidery, a technique that pairs wool yarn and even-weave fabric with the basic embroidery stitches. With wool yarns you can achieve interesting textures and intricate shading for a dramatic effect.

Embroider the design using one, two, or three strands of wool yarn, depending on whether you prefer a "full" look or one that's a little thinner. Accent the design with cotton embroidery floss, if desired.

Simple satin and outline stitches are used to work the 26x26-inch design shown here. (Always mount the fabric in a frame or hoop when working crewel embroidery.) While working your design, refer to these photographs for specific details, such as the direction each stitched area is worked and the placement of the stitches. To work certain areas we used a "close-outline" stitch, which is simply an outline stitch worked in rows that are placed closely together to resemble the satin stitch.

For how-to instructions, turn to page 170.

Frame your finished design according to personal preference. To maximize the texture of your stitches, do not cover the design with glass. (Glass often causes mildew, which eventually discolors and decays the fabric.)

165

DARNING SAMPLER
pages 158-159

Finished size is 18x19 inches.

Materials: 21x22 inches of #28-count even-weave linen; 1 skein each of rose, wine, light blue, navy blue, green, and yellow embroidery floss; embroidery needle and hoop; masking tape.

Instructions: Tape edges of linen to prevent raveling. Separate the 6-ply floss and use 3 strands throughout.

Begin stitching 3¾-inch blocks in running stitches (work floss *over* 3 threads of fabric and *under* 1 thread), starting in the center of the fabric. Using running stitches, work 2 borders for each block; leave 4 threads between each border and between blocks. Stitch 16 blocks (4 across and 4 down), alternating a navy block with a different-colored block. Number blocks from left to right, beginning with the top row.

Following the diagrams (right and opposite), embroider a darning pattern in each block.

Blocks 5 and 15 (not shown) are weaving patterns (with warp and weft threads extending on block 5). Stitch 3 vertical strands of floss next to each other, alternating bands of color as you work. Weave 3 strands of floss over and under vertical strands, also in alternating colored bands to complete the woven block.

Using the photograph as a guide, work a straight-stitch border around alternate darning patterns. Work each straight stitch over 3 horizontal threads; leave 2 vertical threads between each stitch.

Lay a damp cloth over the wrong side of the finished embroidery and press. Frame the sampler, leaving a 1¾-inch border around the design.

TATTED FLOWERS
pages 160-161

General instructions: For tatting, thread and a shuttle are the only materials you need. *Shuttles* are pointed bobbins used to store thread so that it can be worked conveniently. *Thread* used for tatting is traditionally fine white cotton, although any type of thread, string, or yarn may be used.

Block #1   1 Square = 1 Mesh

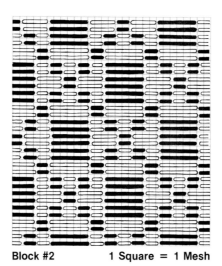

Block #2   1 Square = 1 Mesh

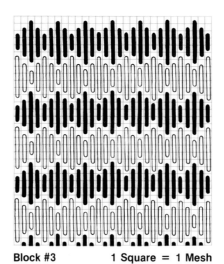

Block #3   1 Square = 1 Mesh

Block #4   1 Square = 1 Mesh

Block #6   1 Square = 1 Mesh

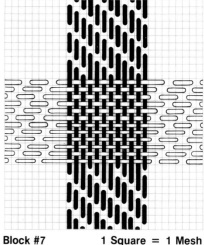

Block #7   1 Square = 1 Mesh

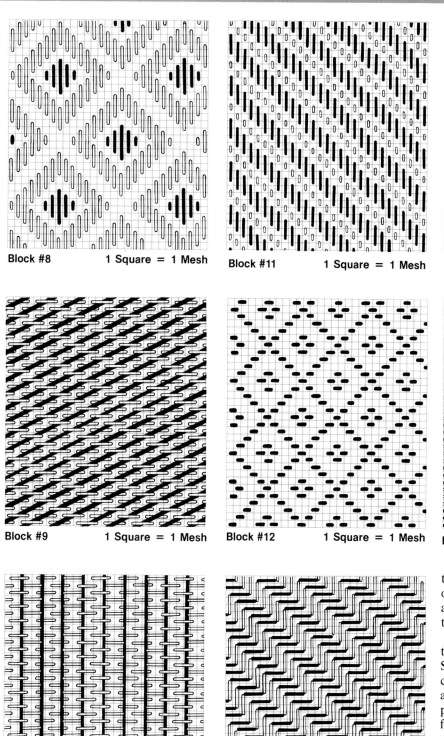

Block #8   1 Square = 1 Mesh

Block #11   1 Square = 1 Mesh

Block #14   1 Square = 1 Mesh

Block #9   1 Square = 1 Mesh

Block #12   1 Square = 1 Mesh

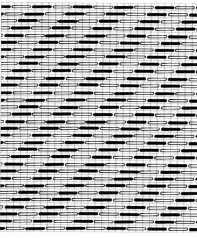

Block #16   1 Square = 1 Mesh

Block #10   1 Square = 1 Mesh

Block #13   1 Square = 1 Mesh

To wind the shuttle, pull end of thread through hole in shuttle post; tie off. Wind the thread counterclockwise around post. Don't fill shuttle so full that thread protrudes beyond the edge.

To position the left hand, grasp end of thread between thumb and forefinger. Spread your other three fingers and encircle them with thread. Bring thread around to form a circle; hold overlapping threads securely with thumb and forefinger. See the top left drawing on page 168.

Bend the little finger to hold the thread against the palm, and bend the middle finger back to catch the loose part of the circle. Adjust the thread so that your fingers don't feel strained. This is called the circle thread.

To position the right hand, unwind shuttle thread so 12 inches of thread
(Continued)

167

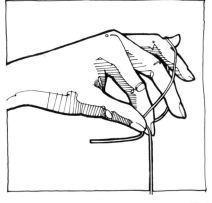 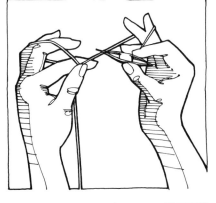 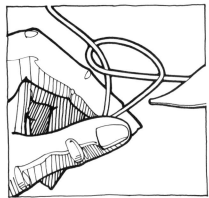

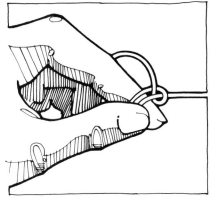 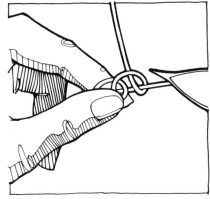 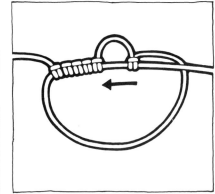

are between the two hands. This is called the shuttle thread. Hold the shuttle so the pointed end faces the left hand and the thread comes off far side of shuttle. Hold flat side of shuttle with thumb and forefinger in a horizontal position, using little finger to hold thread taut and out of the way. See top center drawing.

To begin double stitch, pass shuttle *under* the taut thread of right hand, then *under* the portion of the circle thread between forefinger and middle finger. Bring shuttle up and over this section of circle thread, and down *under* taut shuttle thread. See top right drawing. Let thread around fingers of right hand drop off; pull shuttle to the right until thread between your hands is taut. Keeping the shuttle thread taut and not moving the right hand, slowly *raise* middle, ring, and little fingers of left hand to move this first half of double stitch into place. See drawing 4.

To complete double stitch, pass shuttle over top of, and back under, circle thread. Pull shuttle out to right so it is parallel with the left hand. Keeping your right hand steady, *slowly raise*

middle, ring, and little fingers to pull knot into place. See drawing 5.

These two movements complete a double stitch. If tied correctly, the knot will slide back and forth along the shuttle thread. If the knot does not move, cut it off and begin again.

To make a picot, begin by tying several double stitches in a row. Tie the next double stitch a short distance away from the group of stitches. Slide the last double stitch made along the shuttle thread to form a thread loop. See drawing 6. Size of loop depends upon the amount of thread you leave slack between double stitches.

To close a ring, pull shuttle thread until first stitch touches last. To practice joining rings, make a ring of 3 double stitches, a picot, 3 double stitches, a picot, 3 double stitches, a picot, and 3 double stitches. Close the ring.

To join rings, position first stitch of second ring as close as possible to last stitch of first ring. Tat 3 double stitches of second ring. Insert a crochet hook or pointed end of shuttle through last pi-

cot of previous tatted ring. Pull up a loop of circle thread big enough to pass shuttle through. Pass shuttle all the way through loop to right from back side. Hold shuttle still and slowly raise middle, ring, and little fingers in same manner as for making double stitch.

Tatting abbreviations:

R ....Ring
DS ....Double Stitch
P ....Picot
LP ....Long Picot
SP ....Small Picot
CL ....Close (ring)
* Repeat what follows * as indicated

Tatted Flowers

Materials: (for 10 daisies and 10 roses): Tatting shuttle, 2 balls #5 white pearl cotton (for slightly larger flowers substitute #3 pearl cotton); size 8 or 10 steel crochet hook; 1 ball yellow #5 pearl cotton; lengths of 22-gauge florist's wire for stems; 1 roll green florist's tape; 1 package yellow mum stamen; white glue.

Instructions: *Daisy:* Wind 9 yards of white #5 pearl cotton for 2 flowers, or 5 yards, 9 inches of white #3 pearl cotton for 1 flower.

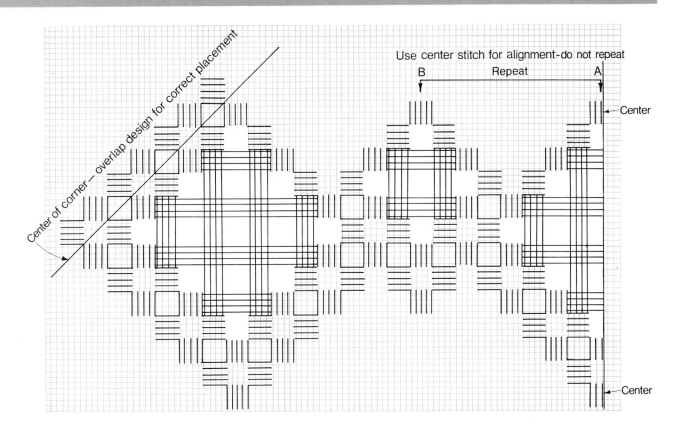

Center of corner — overlap design for correct placement

Use center stitch for alignment—do not repeat

B — Repeat — A

Center

Center

Tat: R of 10 DS, SP, 4 DS, SP, LP, SP, 4 DS, SP, 10 DS, CL R; * R of 10 DS, join to last SP of previous R, 4 DS, SP, LP, SP, 4 DS, SP, 10 DS, CL R. Repeat from * 4 more times. R of 10 DS, join to last SP of previous R, 4 DS, SP, LP, SP, 4 DS, join to first SP of first R, 10 DS, CL R. Cut medallion from shuttle thread. Tie; cut end thread.

Daisy Medallion will have 7 petals that form a cupped shape. For center, wind shuttle with yellow thread. Tat: R of 1 DS, 12 *very long* P, CL R, and cut off. Glue this ring to center of daisy medallion. Poke mum stamen through center hole; glue. Attach flower to florist's wire; wrap with florist's tape.

Rose: Wind 8½ yards of white #5 pearl cotton for 2 roses, or 5 yards of white #3 pearl cotton for 1 rose. Tat: R of 30 DS, CL R. *Do not join rings.* Repeat 4 more times, making each ring as close to previous ring as possible. Then, tat: R of 25 DS, CL R. Repeat 3 more times. R of 7 DS, CL R. Layer rings with 5 large rings on bottom, and successive rings spiraling from base. Glue along bases of rings. Poke wire through center with a tiny portion of wire protruding through flower. Glue;

dry. Wrap wire with florist's tape.

Tatted Doily

Finished size is 18½ x 18½ inches.

Materials: 10 balls white #5 pearl cotton; size 8 or 10 steel crochet hook; 800-1,000 rustproof straight pins; spray starch; sewing needle and white thread.

Instructions: (Note: Doily contains 100 medallions.) Wind shuttle with 9½ yards of thread to make 2 medallions.

Row 1, medallion 1: Tat: R of 10 DS, SP, 4 DS, SP, LP, SP, 4 DS, SP, 10 DS, CL R, * R of 10 DS, join to last SP of previous R, 4 DS, SP, LP, SP, 4 DS, SP, 10 DS, CL R. Repeat from * five times more. (Seven joined rings have been made so far.)

8th R: Tat: R of 10 DS, join to lst SP of previous R, 4 DS, SP, LP, SP, 4 DS, join to first SP of first R, 10 DS, CL R. Cut medallion off; tie.

Row 2, medallion 2: Tat: R of 10 DS, SP, 4 DS, SP, LP, SP, 4 DS, SP, 10 DS, CL R; * R of 10 DS, join to last SP of previous R, 4 DS, SP, LP, SP, 4 DS, SP, 10 DS, CL R. Repeat from * four more times. Tat: R of 10 DS, join to SP of previous R, 4 DS, SP, join in any LP

of *previous medallion,* SP, 4 DS, SP, 10 DS, CL R. R of 10 DS, join to last SP of previous R, 4 DS, SP, join to *next adjacent LP of previous medallion,* SP, 4 DS, join to first SP of first R of second medallion, 10 DS, CL R. Add 8 more medallions to form a strip of ten medallions. *Row 2, medallion 1:* Begin as for first row of medallions; join to first medallion of first row. Continue adding medallions to adjacent medallions.

To finish, whipstitch loose thread ends to back of each medallion.

On blocking surface, pin center 4 medallions flat and square. Continue outward, pinning each ring of each medallion, easing doily to square shape. Pin decorative picots around perimeter. Spray doily with starch until saturated. Blot up excess starch with paper towel. Dry; remove from blocking surface.

HARDANGER PLACE MAT AND NAPKIN
page 163

Materials: 12x17 inches of #22-count white hardanger cloth (for each
(Continued)

mat); 16x16 inches of #22-count white hardanger cloth (for each napkin); white #5 pearl cotton; white #8 pearl cotton; graph paper; tapestry needles.

Instructions: The diagram on page 169 is for a portion of the pattern showing the corner and side. Transfer it to graph paper using a large enough piece so that there are the same number of spaces and lines on the paper as spaces and threads on the mat. In that way, you can see the exact location of each stitch and be sure that stitches are accurately placed.

To complete the pattern, turn the repeat area over so "A" sides match. For the corner, reverse the pattern and match it along the diagonal. Graph the design for the napkin by referring to the photograph.

Before doing cutwork, embroider all satin stitches using #5 pearl cotton. Then, cut only threads that are bound with satin-stitched blocks and indicated on the pattern. Use small, sharp-pointed scissors and cut close to the satin stitching. Cut both ends of block-bound threads and gently lift the cut threads from the fabric with a needle.

Next, thread a smaller needle with #8 pearl cotton and work areas of needleweaving over and under the long threads remaining in the open areas of the design. Begin with the needle at the edge of the open work and in the center of a group of 4 threads. Go over 2 threads on the left, wrapping thread around them, and bring the needle up again in the center. Then go over 2 threads on the right. Continue, pulling threads together tightly as you weave.

If woven threads are distorted at the end of a block, you have woven too many or too few times over the threads. Make necessary adjustments (so woven threads lie flat) and continue. Do not end or start a thread in the middle of a row of weaving.

Plan the needleweaving so that you weave threads that form a square in either a clockwise or counterclockwise direction. Then, when making the tiny loops to join pairs of woven threads (see photograph), work in the opposite direction. Make loops by working the thread through the center of the needle-woven pairs rather than around them.

When the embroidery is finished, turn up a narrow (¼-inch) hem.

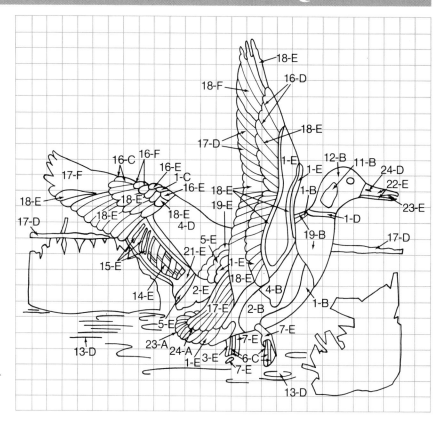

EMBROIDERED MALLARD
pages 164-165

Finished *embroidered* area measures 24½ x23 inches.

Materials: 1 yard fine, even-weave fabric such as linen or cotton blend; 6-strand embroidery floss in gold, gray, and black; embroidery hoop or frame; tissue paper; hot-iron transfer pencil; picture frame; crewel yarn in these amounts and colors:

Yds.	Color	Yds.	Color
29	white	7	dark green
8	ivory	1	dull turquoise
1	peach	1	blue
11	light beige	3	violet
2	dark beige	4	light gray
1	gold	17	dark gray
2	orange	33	blue gray
1	pale olive	8	rust
1	light olive	2	green brown
7	dark olive	4	black
1	light green		

Instructions: Enlarge the pattern (above); transfer to fabric. Place the fabric in a hoop or frame. Embroider the design using 1, 2, or 3 strands of yarn at your discretion. Use all 6 strands of cotton floss.

Color key

1—white		13—dull turquoise	
2—ivory		14—blue	
3—peach		15—violet	
4—light beige		16—light gray	
5—dark beige		17—dark gray	
6—gold		18—blue gray	
7—orange		19—rust	
8—pale olive		20—green brown	
9—light olive		21—black	
10—dark olive		22—gold floss	
11—light green		23—gray floss	
12—dark green		24—black floss	

Stitch Key:

A—outline	D—straight
B—close-outline	E—satin
C—couching	F—split

The close-outline stitch is outline stitch worked in rows placed close together. As you embroider, refer to the photograph for specific details (direction and stitch spacing). The two large areas near the bottom indicate wild grasses. Fill them with split, straight, and couched stitches in colors 8, 9, 10, 12, and 20. When finished, block the needlework; frame it if desired.

PATCHWORK
APPLIQUÉ
RUG MAKING

PATCHWORK

Patchwork can be as complicated as an intricate arrangement of several different shapes or as simple as the fabric checkerboard shown here (opposite). Choosing your basic design is the first step toward making a patchwork project. Select a simple patchwork pattern first (one made up mostly of squares and rectangles), then gradually work up to more difficult designs.

The next step is to select fabrics. Keep in mind washability and durability above all. Also consider color, pattern, and texture so that the overall design will be pleasing.

To begin cutting your pattern pieces, you'll need a cardboard template for each piece. Trace around the templates onto fabric and cut each piece ¼ inch beyond the penciled lines. Cut the pieces individually and sort them according to color and shape.

When "piecing" your patchwork fabrics together, you can use hand or machine sewing. Hold the pattern pieces firmly in place with right sides together. (There is no need to pin or baste short seams. However, long seams should be pinned together so the pieces line up correctly.)

To hand sew the pieces together, use tiny running stitches. To machine sew, use stitches of medium length, stitching along the penciled lines.

Piece one entire block at a time, then press all of the seams to one side (toward the darker patches). Sew the blocks together by forming rows, making sure each block lines up with the one next to it.

1) Preshrink and press all fabrics. (You will need three different fabrics, two solid colors and one print.) Cut cardboard templates and trace them onto fabric, adding ¼-inch seam allowances. Sort the pieces according to color and shape.

2) Stitch the squares together (by hand or machine) into eight rows of eight, alternating colors and using ¼-inch seam allowances. Press all seams open, then pin and stitch the rows together.

3) Stitch four triangles together to make a square; then stitch four squares together to form a row. Repeat this procedure to make a second row.

Cut border strips from print fabric. Stitch all the pieces together by bordering the checkerboard on two sides by fabric strips. Add the two rows along the top and bottom of the gameboard and border the outside edges with fabric strips. Back the design with quilt batting and backing fabric.

4) Baste the three layers together and place the design in a quilting hoop. Quilt the pattern pieces as desired, using threads of matching color. Finish the gameboard by stitching bias strips in place around the outside edges of the design.

APPLIQUÉ

Learning to appliqué is easy if you begin with a simple pattern like this one (opposite). Select a design with straight lines or gradual curves and one with relatively few pattern pieces. If you are appliquéing by hand, choose supple, lightweight or medium-weight fabrics such as cotton, muslin, broadcloth, or sailcloth. (Avoid any fabrics that ravel easily.) It is important that a needle can pass through the fabric easily.

When selecting colors, choose the background fabric first, then develop a color scheme around it.

To begin the project, first trace your pattern onto a large sheet of paper for a master pattern. Make another pattern and cut out each pattern piece. To keep track of the pieces, number or letter the corresponding shapes on the cutting pattern and the master pattern. For each pattern piece, cut a template from cardboard but do not add seam allowances.

Lay out the pattern pieces on your fabric, leaving at least ½ inch between the pieces. Trace around the pieces, using a hard lead pencil. This line represents the fold line (for turning under the seam allowance). Cut the pattern pieces ¼ inch beyond the fold line.

Turn under the seam allowances on all of the pattern pieces and baste. Pin and baste the appliqués to the background fabric and begin appliquéing the pieces in place, using whipstitches, backstitches, or blindstitches.

Remove pins and baste a layer of quilt batting and a layer of backing fabric to your appliquéd piece. Quilt the design as desired, using small running stitches.

Frame your finished appliquéd piece inside a wooden quilting hoop and hang as desired.

1) Cut a cardboard template for each pattern piece and trace the templates onto fabric using a hard lead pencil. Cut the pattern pieces ¼ inch beyond the penciled lines.

2) Turn under the seam allowance and baste it in place. If desired, stay-stitch along the penciled fold line (¼ inch from the raw edges) and clip the seam allowance along curves and corners so turned edges lie flat.

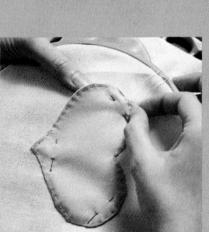

3) Pin the appliqués in place atop the background fabric. The traditional appliqué stitch is the whipstitch: bring the needle up through the appliqué ⅛ to $1/16$ inch from the edge and reinsert it into the background at the edge of the appliqué, making a small diagonal stitch. Bring the needle up again through the background and the appliqué and continue stitching.

You also can use backstitches or blindstitches to securely appliqué pieces in place.

4) Back your appliquéd piece with quilt batting and backing fabric and quilt the design using waxed quilting thread and a size 8 or 9 sharp needle. Take short, even running stitches, making sure each stitch goes through all three layers of fabric. Take two or three running stitches at a time before pulling the thread through the fabric. Stitches should be the same length on both sides of the fabric.

Frame your finished design in a wooden hoop or any frame suited to the design and the fabrics used for your appliqué.

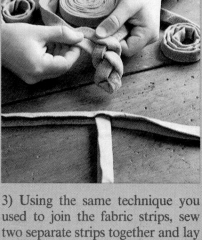

1) To make a braided rug, mark 2½-inch-wide strips of heavy- to medium-weight wool fabrics with tailor's chalk. Cut strips with the grain. Join strips by placing one end perpendicular to and over another and stitching on the bias. Trim seams to ¼ inch; press seams open.

2) Fold in the outside edges of each strip (lengthwise) so they meet in the center. Fold the strip again so the folded edges meet (you will have four thicknesses of fabric). Steam press the strips lightly to "set" the folds. Roll each folded strip into a wheel.

3) Using the same technique you used to join the fabric strips, sew two separate strips together and lay the joined strips flat. Place the end of the third strip on the first two strips between the fold to make a T-formation. As you begin braiding, always keep the open edges of each strip to the left.

To braid, lift the right strand over the center strand and lay it down. Then lift the left strand over the new center strand and lay it down. Next, lift the right strand over the center strand. Continue in this manner, keeping the same tension throughout. (Avoid stretching the braid.) Stitch the new strips to the working strips and continue braiding.

To determine the length of the braided center piece, decide on the width and length of your rug and subtract the width from the length. For example, to make a 3x5-foot finished rug, the center piece would be two feet long.

4) For an oval rug, you must make three "modified square turns" at each end to make your rug lie flat. For a modified square turn, instead of straight braiding, lift the right strand over the center strand, the new right strand over the new center strand again, and the new right over the new center again (three times). Place the center strand under the left strand and fold the right strand up over the center strand. Then fold the center strand down and continue braiding.

5) Lace the braids together using linen thread and a broad lacer (which is a large flat needle with a curved point). Insert the lacing needle into a space on the rug with an upward stroke; then pick up a loop on the braid with a down stroke. This interlocks the braids rather than stitching them side by side. The next up stroke should pick up the adjacent strand of the adjacent braid. Skip one loop at a time on the curves but do not skip loops when lacing on straight lines.

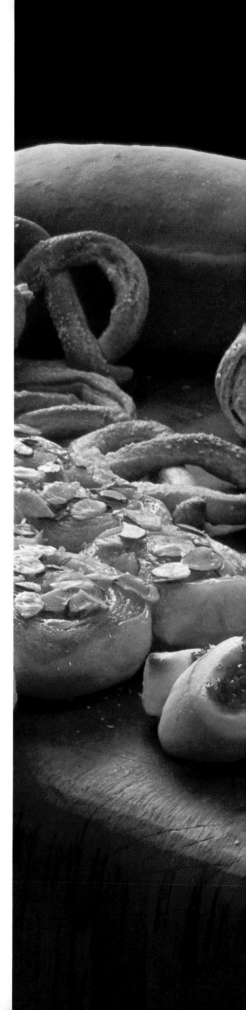

COUNTRY BREAD BAKING

RECIPES WITH DOWN-HOME FLAVOR

Nothing symbolizes country cooking better than home-baked breads right out of the oven, and on the next few pages you'll find recipes for country breads at their best. What's more, you will discover step-by-step hints to help you bake like a pro. Choose from whole grain loaves, light and tasty sweet rolls and coffee cakes, fruit-filled muffins, flaky biscuits, and easy-on-the-cook quick breads. If these breads all sound so tempting that you don't know where to start, look at the options at right. All of these breads (except pretzels) are made from one basic yeast dough. Because each bread requires only half a batch of dough, you can make two kinds at once. Pictured clockwise from back left are Basic Yeast Bread, Cheese-Filled Bread, Coconut-Cherry Coffee Ring, Spicy Butter Knots, Apple-Date Butterhorns, Cranberry Relish Twists, Almond-Lemon Sticky Buns, and Wheat Pretzels. (See index for recipe pages.)

Clockwise from right: Dill-Onion Bread, Sunflower-Apricot Cookies, Molasses-Rye Bread, Whole Wheat Batter Rolls, and Molasses Brown Bread. (See index for recipe page numbers.)

YEAST BREADS

Yeast bread recipes needn't be difficult if you keep a few basic points in mind. Use these handy, step-by-step bread-baking tips to help you with the recipes on pages 182 through 187.

YEAST BREADS

Once you've prepared the dough, turn it out onto a lightly floured surface such as a pastry cloth or counter top. Knead in flour by folding the dough over and pushing down with the heels of your hands (left). Turn the dough a quarter turn and continue kneading until it's smooth and elastic. Shape the dough into a ball and place it in a greased bowl. Turn the ball over to grease the entire surface. Cover the dough and then place it in a warm, draft-free place (an unheated oven is ideal). Position the dough on the upper oven rack and a dish or pan of hot water on the lower rack (center). Keep the oven door closed. Let the dough rise till double. Times suggested in the recipes are guidelines. It is ready to shape when you can lightly press a finger ½ inch into the dough and the indentation remains (right).

To shape the dough into a loaf, roll it on a lightly floured surface into a 12x8- or 12x9-inch rectangle, depending on the size of the loaf pan called for in the recipe. Be sure to roll out from the center of the dough to remove all air bubbles. Roll up the rectangle tightly starting with the narrow edge (left). Then seal the ends of the loaf by pressing down on each end to make a thin strip (center). Fold the strips under the loaf and place the bread in a prepared pan. Cover and let it rise a second time. Bake the bread according to recipe directions. To prevent overbrowning, cover the loaf with foil during the last 20 minutes of baking. To tell whether the bread is done, tap it lightly with your finger (right). You should hear a hollow sound if it is done. Remove the bread from the pans, and cool it on a wire rack.

BASIC YEAST BREAD

*Use this basic dough in the following recipes or make it into three loaves of bread—
See photo, pages 178-179—*

5¾ to 6¼ cups all-purpose flour
2 packages active dry yeast
2 cups milk
⅓ cup sugar
⅓ cup shortening
2 teaspoons salt
2 eggs

In a large mixer bowl combine *2½ cups* of the flour and the yeast. In a saucepan heat together the milk, sugar, shortening, and salt just till warm (115° to 120°), stirring constantly till shortening melts.

Add milk mixture to flour mixture in mixer bowl. Add the eggs. Beat with an electric mixer at low speed for ½ minute, scraping the sides of the bowl constantly. Beat 3 minutes at high speed. Using a spoon, stir in as much of the remaining flour as you can.

Turn out onto a lightly floured surface. Knead in enough remaining flour to make a moderately stiff dough that is smooth and elastic (6 to 8 minutes total). Shape into a ball. Place in lightly greased bowl; turn once to grease surface. Cover; let rise in warm place till double (about 1¼ hours).

Punch dough down; divide in thirds. Cover; let rest 10 minutes. Shape dough into 3 loaves. Place in 3 greased 8x4x2-inch loaf pans. Cover and let rise till nearly double (45 to 60 minutes). Bake in a 375° oven for 35 to 40 minutes or till done, covering with foil the last 15 minutes to prevent overbrowning. Remove from the pans; cool on wire rack. Makes 3 loaves.

COCONUT-CHERRY COFFEE RING

See photo, pages 178-179—

Basic Yeast Bread dough
⅔ cup sugar
½ teaspoon ground cinnamon
¼ cup milk
¼ cup flaked coconut
¼ cup chopped walnuts
¼ cup chopped maraschino
cherries

Prepare a *half recipe* of Basic Yeast Bread dough. Knead dough till smooth and elastic (6 to 8 minutes). Shape into a ball. Place in a greased bowl; turn once to grease surface. Cover. Let rise in warm place till double (about 1¼ hours); punch down. Cover; let rest 10 minutes. Divide dough into 24 pieces; shape into balls.

In a bowl combine sugar and cinnamon. Dip individual dough balls into milk, then into cinnamon-sugar mixture. Place *half* the dough balls in bottom of a greased 10-inch tube pan.

In a bowl combine coconut, walnuts, and the maraschino cherries; sprinkle *two-thirds* of the cherry mixture over balls in pan. Place remaining dough balls over filling. Sprinkle the remaining cherry mixture over all.

Cover and let rise in warm place till nearly double (30 to 40 minutes). Bake in a 375° oven for 30 to 35 minutes or till golden brown. Let cool 15 minutes in pan. Loosen coffee cake and invert onto a wire rack. Turn coffee cake upright to cool. Makes 1 coffee cake.

ALMOND-LEMON STICKY BUNS

See photo, pages 178-179—

Basic Yeast Bread dough
½ cup sugar
⅓ cup dark corn syrup
¼ cup butter
1 teaspoon finely shredded
lemon peel
2 tablespoons lemon juice
¾ cup toasted sliced almonds
2 tablespoons butter, melted
¼ cup sugar
¼ teaspoon ground nutmeg

Prepare a *half recipe* of Basic Yeast Bread dough. Knead dough till smooth and elastic (6 to 8 minutes). Shape into a ball. Place in a greased bowl; turn once. Cover; let rise in warm place till double (about 1¼ hours). Punch down. Cover; let rest 10 minutes.

Meanwhile, in a small saucepan combine the ½ cup sugar, corn syrup, the ¼ cup butter, lemon peel, and lemon juice. Cook and stir just till sugar dissolves and the mixture boils. Pour into the bottom of an ungreased 13x9x2-inch baking pan. Sprinkle toasted almonds atop.

On a lightly floured surface, roll dough into a 16x8-inch rectangle. Brush with the 2 tablespoons of melted butter. Combine the ¼ cup sugar and nutmeg; sprinkle over dough. Beginning with long side, roll up jelly-roll fashion; seal edge. Cut into sixteen 1-inch slices. Place slices, cut side down, in pan. Cover; let rise in warm place till nearly double (30 to 45 minutes).

Bake in a 375° oven for 20 to 25 minutes. Immediately loosen sides and turn out onto wire rack placed atop waxed paper. Makes 16 rolls.

CRANBERRY RELISH TWISTS

See photo, pages 178-179—

Basic Yeast Bread dough
½ **cup cranberry-orange relish**
3 **tablespoons brown sugar**
¾ **teaspoon ground cinnamon**

Prepare a *half recipe* of Basic Yeast Bread dough. Knead dough till smooth and elastic (6 to 8 minutes). Shape into a ball. Place in a greased bowl; turn once to grease surface. Cover. Let rise in a warm place till double (about 1¼ hours); punch dough down.

Cover; let rest 10 minutes. On lightly floured surface roll dough into an 18x12-inch rectangle. In a bowl combine the cranberry-orange relish, brown sugar, and cinnamon. Spread the cranberry mixture over dough rectangle to within ½ inch of the edges.

Starting at long side, fold ⅓ of the dough to the center. Fold opposite side over top, forming three layers. Seal edges with *water*. Cut the dough into eighteen 1-inch-wide strips. Twist each strip twice.

Arrange twists one inch apart in a greased 15x10x1-inch baking pan. Cover; let rise in warm place till nearly double (30 to 45 minutes). Bake in a 375° oven for 22 to 25 minutes or till twists are golden brown. Remove twists from baking pan to wire rack. Cool completely or serve slightly warm. Makes 18.

CHEESE-FILLED BREAD

See photo, pages 178-179—

Basic Yeast Bread dough
½ **cup sliced green onion**
1 **tablespoon butter**
1 **cup shredded Edam cheese**
1 **slightly beaten egg**
¼ **cup snipped parsley**
2 **tablespoons fine dry bread crumbs**
½ **teaspoon dried dillweed**
⅛ **teaspoon salt**
   Few drops bottled hot pepper sauce
   Sesame seed

Prepare a *half recipe* of Basic Yeast Bread dough. Let rise in warm place till double (1¼ hours).

Meanwhile, in a saucepan cook green onion in butter till tender but not brown. Remove from the heat; cool slightly. Stir in cheese, beaten egg, parsley, bread crumbs, dillweed, salt, and pepper sauce.

Punch dough down. Cover; let rest 10 minutes. On lightly floured surface roll dough into 18x12-inch rectangle. Spread cheese mixture over dough. Starting from long side, roll up jelly-roll fashion; seal long edge with *water*.

Grease a 10-inch fluted tube pan; sprinkle bottom and halfway up sides with sesame seed. Place roll, seam side up, in pan; moisten ends with *water;* press together. Cover; let rise in warm place till nearly double (40 to 45 minutes).

Bake in a 375° oven for 40 minutes or till golden, covering with foil after 25 minutes to prevent over-browning. Cool 10 minutes; invert onto wire rack. Serve warm or cool. Makes 1 loaf.

SPICY BUTTER KNOTS

See photo, pages 178-179—

Basic Yeast Bread dough
6 **tablespoons butter *or* margarine, melted**
½ **cup packed brown sugar**
½ **cup finely chopped pecans**
1 **teaspoon pumpkin pie spice**

Prepare a *half recipe* of Basic Yeast Bread dough. Knead dough till smooth and elastic (6 to 8 minutes). Shape into a ball. Place in a greased bowl; turn once to grease the surface. Cover. Let dough rise in warm place till double (about 1¼ hours); punch dough down. Divide dough in half. Cover; let rest 10 minutes.

On a lightly floured surface roll *each* half into an 8x6-inch rectangle. Cut each rectangle into eight 1-inch-wide strips. Tie loosely in knots. Dip knots into melted butter or margarine. Place, 1 inch apart, in 2 greased 9x9x2-inch baking pans or one 15x10x1-inch baking pan.

In a bowl combine brown sugar, pecans, and pumpkin pie spice. Sprinkle the brown sugar mixture over rolls; drizzle any remaining melted butter over tops. Cover; let rise in warm place till nearly double (30 to 40 minutes).

Bake rolls in a 375° oven for 15 to 20 minutes or till golden. Cool completely on wire rack or serve slightly warm. Makes 16 rolls.

APPLE-DATE BUTTERHORNS

See photo, pages 178-179—

**Basic Yeast Bread dough
(see recipe, page 182)**
1½ cups finely chopped
    peeled apple
¾ cup finely snipped
    pitted dates
¼ cup packed brown sugar
2 tablespoons water
½ teaspoon vanilla
    Powdered Sugar Icing

Prepare a *half recipe* of Basic Yeast Bread dough. Knead the dough till smooth and elastic (6 to 8 minutes). Shape into a ball. Place in a greased bowl; turn once to grease surface. Let dough rise in a warm place till double (about 1¼ hours). Punch down; divide in half. Cover; let rest 10 minutes.

In a saucepan combine the apple, dates, brown sugar, and the water. Bring to boiling; reduce heat. Cover and simmer about 10 minutes or till apple is tender. Stir in vanilla; set mixture aside.

On lightly floured surface roll each half of the dough to a 12-inch circle. Spread each with half of the apple-date mixture. Cut each into 12 wedges. Roll wedges up from wide end. Place on a greased baking sheet.

Cover; let rise in a warm place till nearly double (30 to 40 minutes). Bake in a 375° oven for 12 to 14 minutes. Frost rolls with Powdered Sugar Icing. Makes 24 rolls.

Powdered Sugar Icing: In a bowl combine 1 cup *sifted powdered sugar*, ¼ teaspoon *vanilla*, and 4 to 5 teaspoons *milk* to make an icing of spreading consistency.

GRANOLA CASSEROLE BREAD

See photo, pages 16-17—

3 cups all-purpose flour
1 package active dry yeast
1¼ cups water
3 tablespoons light molasses
2 tablespoons butter *or*
    margarine
1 teaspoon salt
1 egg
1½ cups Homemade Granola
    (see recipe, page 314) *or*
    granola
    **Butter *or* margarine, melted
    (optional)**

In a large mixer bowl combine *2 cups* of the flour and the yeast. In a saucepan heat together water, light molasses, the 2 tablespoons butter or margarine, and salt just till warm (115° to 120°), stirring constantly until the butter or margarine almost melts.

Add to flour mixture in mixer bowl. Add egg. Beat ½ minute at low speed with an electric mixer, scraping sides of bowl constantly. Beat 3 minutes at high speed. By hand, stir in remaining flour and granola till dough is well mixed. Place in greased 1½-quart soufflé dish or casserole. Cover loosely.

Let rise in warm place till almost double (about 1 hour). Bake in a 325° oven for 45 minutes, covering with foil the last 25 minutes to prevent overbrowning. Remove from soufflé dish; brush crust with additional melted butter or margarine if desired. Makes 1 loaf.

WHEAT PRETZELS

See photo, pages 178-179—

2¾ to 3¼ cups all-purpose flour
2 packages active dry yeast
1 teaspoon baking powder
2 cups milk
⅓ cup sugar
⅓ cup shortening
2 eggs
3 cups whole wheat flour
1 slightly beaten egg white

In a mixer bowl mix *2½ cups* all-purpose flour, yeast, and baking powder. Heat and stir milk, sugar, shortening, and 2 teaspoons *salt* till warm (115° to 120°). Add to bowl. Add eggs. Beat with electric mixer at low speed for ½ minute, scraping bowl. Beat at high speed for 3 minutes. Stir in whole wheat flour and as much of the remaining all-purpose flour as you can mix in with a spoon. On floured surface knead in enough all-purpose flour to make a moderately stiff dough that is smooth and elastic (6 to 8 minutes). Place in greased bowl. Cover; let rise in warm place till double (1¼ hours).

Punch down. Cover; let rest 10 minutes. On floured surface roll into 15x12-inch rectangle. Cut into 15x½-inch strips; roll each into 20-inch rope. Shape into pretzels. Let rise 30 minutes. In kettle stir 3 tablespoons *salt* into 2 quarts *boiling water*. Add a few pretzels at a time to the water; boil 1 to 2 minutes. Drain on paper toweling; pat dry. Place on greased baking sheet. Mix egg white and 1 tablespoon *water*; brush atop pretzels. Sprinkle with *coarse salt*. Bake in 400° oven about 20 minutes. Cool on wire rack. Makes 24 pretzels.

DILL-ONION BREAD

See photo, page 180—

1 package active dry yeast
½ cup warm water (110° to 115°)
1 beaten egg
½ cup cream-style cottage cheese
⅓ cup finely chopped onion
1 tablespoon butter *or* margarine, melted
2 cups all-purpose flour
½ cup wheat germ
⅓ cup whole bran cereal
1 tablespoon sugar
1 tablespoon dillseed
1 teaspoon salt
¼ teaspoon baking soda

Soften yeast in warm water. In a bowl combine egg, cottage cheese, onion, and butter or margarine; mix well. In another bowl stir together flour, wheat germ, bran cereal, sugar, dillseed, salt, and the baking soda. Add yeast mixture and cottage cheese mixture to the flour mixture, stirring well.

Cover; let rise in warm place till double (1 hour). Stir dough down. On lightly floured surface knead the dough for 1 minute. With greased hands pat into well-greased 9x1½-inch round baking pan. Cover; let rise till nearly double (1 hour).

Gently score top of bread in a diamond pattern. Bake in a 350° oven 40 minutes or till golden. Remove from pan; cool on wire rack. Serve warm. Makes 1.

MOLASSES-RYE BREAD

See photo, page 180—

3 packages active dry yeast
1 cup warm water (110° to 115°)
½ cup dark molasses
½ cup boiling water
2 tablespoons butter *or* margarine
2 tablespoons caraway seed
2 teaspoons salt
½ cup wheat germ
2¾ cups rye flour
2½ to 2¾ cups all-purpose flour

Dissolve yeast in warm water. In a large bowl combine the molasses, the boiling water, butter, caraway, and salt, stirring till butter almost melts. Cool to lukewarm (110° to 115°). Stir the yeast mixture and wheat germ into molasses mixture. Using a spoon, stir in all the rye flour and as much of the all-purpose flour as you can.

Turn out onto lightly floured surface. Knead in enough remaining all-purpose flour to make a moderately stiff dough that is smooth and elastic (6 to 8 minutes). Shape dough into a ball. Place in greased bowl; turn once. Cover; let rise till double (about 1½ hours). Punch dough down. Divide dough in half. Cover; let rest 10 minutes.

Shape the dough into 2 loaves. Place in 2 greased 11x4x3-inch or 9x5x3-inch loaf pans. Cover; let rise till almost double (1 hour). Brush with water. Using a sharp knife, gently score tops of loaves diagonally at 3-inch intervals.

Bake in a 350° oven for 45 minutes. Remove from pans; cool on wire rack. Makes 2 loaves.

WHOLE WHEAT BATTER ROLLS

See photo, page 180—

1 package active dry yeast
1¼ cups warm water (110° to 115°)
2 cups all-purpose flour
1 teaspoon salt
1 teaspoon Italian seasoning
2 tablespoons butter *or* margarine, softened
1 tablespoon honey
1 tablespoon dark molasses
1 cup whole wheat flour
Butter *or* margarine, melted (optional)

In a large mixing bowl dissolve yeast in warm water. Add all-purpose flour, salt, and Italian seasoning. Stir in the 2 tablespoons softened butter or margarine, honey, and molasses; beat well. Add whole wheat flour, mixing well. Cover; let rise 30 minutes.

Punch dough down. Reserve about ½ cup batter. Spoon remaining batter into greased 2½-inch muffin cups, filling ⅔ full. Spoon an additional teaspoon of the reserved batter atop batter in each muffin cup to make a topknot.

Bake in a 375° oven for 10 to 15 minutes or till rolls are golden. Remove from pans. Cool on wire rack. Brush tops of rolls with melted butter or margarine if desired. Makes 16 rolls.

HONEY-RYE BREAD

See photo, page 193—

4 to 4½ cups all-purpose flour
2 packages active dry yeast
2 cups warm water (115°
    to 120°)
¼ cup sugar
¼ cup honey
2 teaspoons salt
2 cups rye meal *or* rye flour
1 beaten egg yolk

In a large mixer bowl combine *3 cups* of the all-purpose flour and the yeast. Combine the warm water, sugar, honey, and salt, stirring till sugar is dissolved. Add to dry ingredients in mixer bowl. Beat with electric mixer at low speed for ½ minute, scraping sides of bowl constantly. Beat 3 minutes at high speed. Using a spoon, stir in rye meal or flour and as much of the remaining all-purpose flour as you can. Turn out onto a lightly floured surface; knead in enough of the remaining all-purpose flour to make a moderately stiff dough that is smooth and elastic (6 to 8 minutes total). Place in greased bowl; turn once. Cover; refrigerate overnight.

Remove dough from refrigerator. Punch dough down; divide into thirds. Shape into loaves and place in 3 greased 7½x3½x2-inch loaf pans. Cover; let rise in warm place till nearly double (about 1¼ hours). Brush tops with a mixture of the egg yolk and 1 tablespoon *water*. Place in a *cold* oven. Turn oven to 300°; bake 15 minutes. Increase oven temperature to 325° and bake 30 minutes more. Remove from pans; cool loaves on wire rack. Makes 3 loaves.

RAISIN-APPLE BREAD

See photo, page 193—

2 packages active dry yeast
½ cup warm water (110° to
    115°)
1 beaten egg
1 cup warm milk (115° to 120°)
¼ cup honey
1½ teaspoons salt
1 cup raisins
1 cup finely chopped, peeled
    tart apple (2 small apples)
1½ cups whole wheat flour
2½ cups all-purpose flour
½ cup cracked wheat flour
1 beaten egg yolk

Soften yeast in the warm water. In bowl combine egg, milk, honey, and salt; add yeast mixture, raisins, and apple. In another bowl combine the whole wheat flour and *1½ cups* of the all-purpose flour; stir in milk mixture and cracked wheat flour. Turn out onto lightly floured surface; knead in the remaining all-purpose flour to make a moderately stiff dough that is smooth and elastic (6 to 8 minutes). Place in a greased bowl; turn once. Cover; let rise in warm place till double (1 hour).

Punch dough down. Divide into thirds. Cover; let rest 10 minutes. Shape into loaves. Place in 3 greased 7½x3½x2-inch loaf pans. Cover; let rise till nearly double (30 to 45 minutes). Beat together the egg yolk and 1 tablespoon *water*. Brush over loaves. Bake in a 375° oven for 30 minutes; cover with foil after 15 minutes to prevent overbrowning. Remove from pans. Cool on rack. Makes 3 loaves.

PUMPKIN BREAD

3¼ to 3½ cups all-purpose flour
2 packages active dry yeast
¼ teaspoon ground ginger
¼ teaspoon ground nutmeg
¼ teaspoon ground cloves
¾ cup milk
¼ cup packed brown sugar
2 tablespoons butter *or*
    margarine
1½ teaspoons salt
½ cup cooked mashed pumpkin
¾ cup raisins

In large mixer bowl stir together *1½ cups* of the flour, the yeast, ginger, nutmeg, and cloves. In a saucepan heat together the milk, brown sugar, butter, and salt just till warm (115° to 120°), stirring constantly till butter almost melts. Add to flour mixture in mixer bowl; add pumpkin. Beat at low speed with electric mixer for ½ minute, scraping sides of bowl constantly. Beat 3 minutes at high speed. Using a spoon, stir in raisins and as much of the remaining flour as you can.

Turn out onto lightly floured surface and knead in enough of the remaining flour to make a moderately stiff dough that is smooth and elastic (6 to 8 minutes). Shape into ball. Place in lightly greased bowl; turn once to grease surface. Cover and let rise in warm place till double (1 hour).

Punch dough down; cover and let rest 10 minutes. Shape into loaf; place in a greased 8x4x2-inch loaf pan. Cover; let rise till nearly double (about 30 minutes). Bake in a 375° oven for 35 to 40 minutes. Remove from pan; cool on rack. Makes 1 loaf.

LUCIA BUNS

2 tablespoons hot water
⅛ teaspoon powdered saffron
3½ to 3¾ cups all-purpose flour
1 package active dry yeast
1 cup milk
½ cup sugar
6 tablespoons butter
1 teaspoon salt
1 egg
½ cup raisins, chopped
¼ cup chopped Brazil nuts

Pour hot water over saffron; let stand. In a large mixer bowl combine *2 cups* of the flour and yeast. In a saucepan heat together the milk, sugar, butter, and salt just till warm (115° to 120°), stirring till butter almost melts. Add to flour mixture along with the egg and saffron mixture. Beat at low speed with electric mixer for ½ minute, scraping sides of bowl constantly. Beat 3 minutes at high speed. Using a spoon, stir in raisins, nuts, and as much of the remaining flour as you can.

Turn onto a floured surface; knead in enough of the remaining flour to make a moderately stiff dough that is smooth and elastic (6 to 8 minutes). Place in a greased bowl; turn once. Cover; let rise till double (1½ to 1¾ hours).

Punch dough down; cover and let rest 10 minutes. Divide dough into 32 pieces. Roll each into a 9-inch rope. On lightly greased baking sheet, form one rope into an S-shape, coiling the ends snail fashion. Repeat with remaining ropes. Cover; let rise till nearly double (30 to 45 minutes). Bake in a 425° oven 8 to 10 minutes. Cool on wire racks. Makes 32.

WHOLE GRAIN MOLASSES BREAD

4¾ to 5 cups all-purpose flour
2 packages active dry yeast
3 cups warm water (115° to 120°)
⅓ cup light molasses
⅓ cup cooking oil
1 tablespoon salt
5 cups whole wheat *or* rye flour
1 beaten egg white
Poppy seed *or* sesame seed

In a large mixer bowl combine *4 cups* of the all-purpose flour and the yeast. Stir together warm water, molasses, oil, and salt; add to flour mixture in bowl. Beat at low speed with electric mixer for ½ minute, scraping sides of bowl constantly. Beat 3 minutes at high speed. Using a spoon, stir in the whole wheat or rye flour and as much of the remaining all-purpose flour as you can.

Turn out onto lightly floured surface; knead in enough of the remaining all-purpose flour to make a moderately stiff dough that is smooth and elastic (6 to 8 minutes). Place in greased bowl; turn once to grease surface. Cover and let rise in warm place till double (50 to 60 minutes).

Punch dough down. Divide into thirds. Cover; let rest 10 minutes. Shape into loaves; place in 3 greased 8x4x2-inch loaf pans or 1½-quart casseroles. Cover; let rise till nearly double (40 to 50 minutes). Brush loaves with egg white; sprinkle with poppy or sesame seed. Bake in a 375° oven for 40 to 45 minutes. Remove from pans; cool on wire racks. Makes 3.

ANADAMA BREAD

4½ to 4¾ cups all-purpose flour
2 packages active dry yeast
2 cups cold water
1 cup cornmeal
½ cup molasses
⅓ cup lard
1 tablespoon salt
2 eggs
2 tablespoons butter *or* margarine, melted

In a large mixer bowl mix *1 cup* of the flour and yeast. In saucepan combine the water and cornmeal. Cook and stir till thickened and bubbly. Remove from heat; stir in molasses, lard, and salt. Cool till just warm (115° to 120°). Add to flour mixture in bowl; add eggs. Beat with electric mixer at low speed for ½ minute, scraping sides of bowl constantly. Beat 3 minutes at high speed. Using a spoon, stir in as much of the remaining flour as you can.

Turn dough out onto a lightly floured surface. Knead in enough of the remaining flour to make a moderately stiff dough that is smooth and elastic (6 to 8 minutes). Place in a greased bowl; turn once to grease surface. Cover and let rise in warm place till double (about 1 hour).

Punch dough down; divide in half. Cover and let rest 10 minutes. Shape into loaves and place in 2 greased 8x4x2-inch loaf pans. Cover; let rise till almost double (about 45 minutes). Brush with butter. Bake in a 375° oven for 40 minutes, covering with foil the last 20 minutes to prevent overbrowning. Remove from pans; cool on wire rack. Makes 2 loaves.

From front left: Pearadise Bread, Spicy Raisin Coffee Cake, Sage-Cornmeal Biscuits, Basic Muffins, Ham 'n' Cheesers, Rye Biscuit Fans, Orange Twists, Banana Muffins, and Pineapple-Bran Bread. (See index for recipe page numbers.)

BREAD BAKING

Whip up loaves of warm fragrant quick breads or batches of delicious muffins or biscuits in minutes with these easy step-by-step hints. See pages 190 through 195 for recipes.

QUICK BREADS OR MUFFINS

Start a quick bread or muffin recipe by greasing and flouring the pan according to recipe directions. Then, in separate bowls combine the liquid and dry ingredients. With a wooden spoon push the dry ingredients against the edge of the bowl to make a well in the center. Add the liquid mixture all at once, pouring into the well (left). Stir the mixture only until it is moistened. Don't try to beat the batter smooth. It should be lumpy (center). Overbeating will give breads a heavy texture with holes or tunnels. Fill the prepared pan only two-thirds full to allow space for rising (right). An easy way to fill muffin pans is to push the batter from the spoon with a rubber spatula. Bake the bread or muffins according to the recipe directions. Don't overbake breads or they will be tough and dry. A crack on the top is typical of many quick breads.

BISCUITS

For biscuits, begin by combining the dry ingredients. Cut the shortening into the flour mixture with a pastry blender till the mixture resembles coarse crumbs (left). For best results, don't blend the fat completely or your biscuits will be mealy. Make a well in the center of the mixture. Add the liquid. Stir quickly till the dough follows the fork around the bowl (center). On a lightly floured surface knead the dough 10 to 12 strokes by curling your fingers over the dough. Pull it toward you, then push it down and away from you with the heel of your hand. Give the dough a quarter turn and repeat (left). On a lightly floured surface, pat the dough to ½-inch thickness. Cut and bake according to recipe directions.

BASIC MUFFINS

Use this basic batter to make several of the recipes on the next few pages—
See photo, page 188—

1 beaten egg
¾ cup milk
⅓ cup cooking oil
1¾ cups all-purpose flour
¼ cup sugar
2½ teaspoons baking powder
¾ teaspoon salt

In a small mixing bowl combine the egg, milk, and cooking oil; set mixture aside.

In a large mixing bowl stir together the flour, sugar, baking powder, and salt. Make a well in the center of dry ingredients. Add egg mixture all at once; stir just till moistened (batter will be lumpy).

Grease muffin cups or line with paper bake cups; fill ⅔ full. Bake in a 400° oven for 20 to 25 minutes or till muffins are golden brown. Remove from the pan; serve warm. Makes 12 muffins.

Self-Rise Muffins: Prepare Basic Muffins as above, *except* use 1¾ cups *self-rising flour* instead of the all-purpose flour and omit the baking powder and salt.

Enriched Muffins: Prepare Basic Muffins as above, *except* stir ⅓ cup *nonfat dry milk powder* into the flour mixture.

Cheese Muffins: Prepare Basic Muffins as above, *except* stir ½ cup shredded *Swiss or Muenster cheese* into the flour mixture.

HAM 'N' CHEESERS

See photo, page 188—

Basic Muffin batter
½ cup shredded American
    cheese (2 ounces)
½ cup finely chopped
    fully cooked ham

Prepare Basic Muffin batter as directed, *except* stir cheese and ham into the liquid ingredients. Proceed as directed in Basic Muffin recipe. Makes 12 muffins.

BANANA MUFFINS

See photo, page 188—

Basic Muffin batter
1 ripe medium banana, mashed
½ cup whole wheat flour
¼ cup wheat germ
¼ teaspoon baking soda
¼ teaspoon ground cinnamon

Prepare Basic Muffin batter as directed, *except* add banana to egg mixture and replace ¾ cup of the all-purpose flour with the whole wheat flour and wheat germ. Stir the baking soda and cinnamon into the flour mixture. Spoon batter into greased 2¾-inch fluted muffin cups. Bake in a 400° oven for 20 to 25 minutes. Makes 12.

HONEY-WHEAT MUFFINS

See photo, page 266—

1 beaten egg
½ cup milk
½ cup honey
¼ cup cooking oil
½ teaspoon finely shredded
    lemon peel
1 cup all-purpose flour
½ cup whole wheat flour
2 teaspoons baking powder
½ teaspoon salt

In a bowl combine the egg, milk, honey, cooking oil, and lemon peel. In another bowl stir together the flours, baking powder, and salt. Add egg mixture to flour mixture all at once. Stir till just moistened (batter will be lumpy). Grease muffin cups or line with paper bake cups; fill ⅔ full. Bake in a 375° oven for about 20 minutes. Makes 10 muffins.

BUTTERMILK BISCUITS

See photo, page 276—

2 tablespoons lard
2 cups self-rising flour
1 cup buttermilk

In a bowl cut lard into flour till mixture resembles coarse crumbs. Make a well in center; add buttermilk all at once. Stir just till dough follows fork around bowl. Form into 15 smooth balls. Place on greased baking sheet. Press to flatten biscuit tops. Bake in a 450° oven 12 to 15 minutes. Makes 15.

BASIC BISCUITS

Use this basic dough to make several of the recipes on the next few pages—

2 cups all-purpose flour
1 tablespoon baking powder
½ teaspoon salt
⅓ cup shortening
¾ cup milk

In a mixing bowl thoroughly stir together the flour, baking powder, and salt. Cut in shortening till mixture resembles coarse crumbs. Make a well in flour mixture; add milk all at once. Stir just till dough clings together.

On a lightly floured surface knead dough gently for 10 to 12 strokes. Pat or roll dough to a ½-inch thickness. Cut with a 2½-inch biscuit cutter, dipping cutter in flour between cuts.

Transfer biscuits to an ungreased baking sheet. Bake in a 450° oven for 10 to 12 minutes or till golden. Serve immediately. Makes 10.

Self-Rising Biscuits: Prepare Basic Biscuits as above, *except* substitute 2 cups *self-rising flour* for the all-purpose flour. Omit the baking powder and salt.

Sour Cream Biscuits: Prepare Basic Biscuits as above, *except* substitute 1 cup dairy *sour cream* for the milk.

Whole Wheat Biscuits: Prepare Basic Biscuits as above, *except* use only *1½ cups* all-purpose flour and add ½ cup *whole wheat flour.*

RYE BISCUIT FANS

See photo, page 188—

Basic Biscuit dough
1 cup rye flour
1 teaspoon finely shredded orange peel
1 tablespoon butter *or* margarine, melted

Prepare Basic Biscuit dough as directed, *except* substitute the rye flour for *1 cup* of the all-purpose flour and stir orange peel into the milk. Roll dough into a 12x9-inch rectangle. Brush with the melted butter. Cut dough in half to make two 9x6-inch rectangles. Cut each rectangle into six 6x1½-inch strips. Make 2 stacks of 6 strips each. Cut each stack into four 1½-inch pieces. Place stacks, cut side down, in greased 2½-inch muffin cups. Bake in a 400° oven for 23 to 25 minutes. Makes 8.

SAGE CORNMEAL BISCUITS

See photo, page 188—

Basic Biscuit dough
½ cup yellow cornmeal
½ to ¾ teaspoon ground sage

Prepare Basic Biscuit dough as directed, *except* substitute the yellow cornmeal for *½ cup* of the all-purpose flour. Stir ground sage into flour mixture. Proceed as directed in Basic Biscuits recipe. Makes 8 biscuits.

ORANGE TWISTS

See photo, page 188—

Basic Biscuit dough
2 tablespoons sugar
½ cup orange marmalade
½ teaspoon rum flavoring
¼ cup flaked coconut

Prepare Basic Biscuit dough as directed, *except* add the sugar to the flour mixture. On floured surface roll dough into a 15x8-inch rectangle. Combine marmalade and rum flavoring; spread over dough. Top with coconut. Fold dough in half lengthwise to make a 15x4-inch rectangle. Cut into fifteen 1-inch strips. Holding strip at both ends, twist in opposite directions twice, forming a spiral. Bake on greased baking sheet in a 450° oven 10 to 12 minutes. Makes 15.

CRANBERRY-NECTAR BREAD

Basic Muffin batter
¼ cup sugar
¾ cup apricot nectar
¾ cup chopped cranberries
½ cup flaked coconut

Prepare Basic Muffin batter as directed, *except* substitute the apricot nectar for the milk and stir the cranberries and coconut into the egg mixture. Add the additional ¼ cup sugar to the flour mixture.

Turn batter into a greased and floured 9x9x2-inch baking pan. Bake in a 350° oven for 30 to 35 minutes. Cool slightly in pan on wire rack. Cut into squares; serve warm. Makes 9 servings.

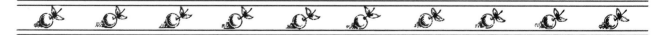

HONEY-ORANGE BREAD

1 cup whole bran cereal
4 teaspoons finely shredded
   orange peel (set aside)
1 cup orange juice
½ cup honey
¼ cup sugar
2 tablespoons shortening
1 egg
2¼ cups all-purpose flour
2½ teaspoons baking powder
½ teaspoon baking soda
½ teaspoon salt

In a bowl combine the whole bran cereal and *half* of the orange juice; let stand several minutes.

In mixing bowl stir together the honey, sugar, and the shortening. Add egg and shredded orange peel; mix well.

In another bowl stir together the flour, baking powder, baking soda, and salt. Add flour mixture and remaining orange juice alternately to honey mixture, beating after each addition. Stir in bran cereal-orange juice mixture. Pour batter into 2 greased 7½x3½x2-inch loaf pans or 1 greased 9x5x3-inch loaf pan.

Bake bread in a 325° oven 45 to 50 minutes for the small pans or 55 to 60 minutes for the large pan. Cool in pans on wire rack. Remove from pans. If desired, wrap bread loaves and let stand 24 hours before slicing. Makes 2 small loaves or 1 large loaf.

HONEY-DATE NUT BREAD

¾ cup boiling water
1 cup pitted whole dates,
   chopped
1 egg
1 cup honey
1 tablespoon butter *or*
   margarine, softened
1 teaspoon vanilla
2 cups all-purpose flour
1 teaspoon baking soda
½ teaspoon salt
1 cup chopped walnuts

In a bowl pour the boiling water over the dates; let stand till cool. *Do not drain.*

In a small mixer bowl beat the egg with an electric mixer at high speed for 2 minutes or till thick and lemon-colored. Beat in the honey, butter or margarine, and vanilla. Stir the undrained dates into the egg mixture.

Stir together the flour, baking soda, and salt. By hand carefully stir flour mixture into egg mixture along with nuts just till combined. Turn the batter into 2 greased 7½x3½x2-inch loaf pans or 1 greased 9x5x3-inch loaf pan.

Bake in a 350° oven about 50 minutes for the small pans or about 65 minutes for the large pan. Cool in pans 10 minutes. Remove bread from pans; cool completely on a wire rack. If desired, wrap bread and let stand for 24 hours before slicing. Makes 2 small loaves or 1 large loaf.

PEARADISE BREAD
See photo, page 188—

1 8½-ounce can pear slices
1 beaten egg
⅓ cup cooking oil
1¾ cups all-purpose flour
¼ cup sugar
2½ teaspoons baking powder
¾ teaspoon salt
½ cup shredded cheddar cheese
   (2 ounces)
½ cup chopped walnuts

Drain pear slices, reserving ½ cup syrup. Chop pears. In a bowl combine chopped pears and reserved syrup with egg and cooking oil.

In a large mixing bowl stir together the flour, sugar, baking powder, and salt. Stir in the cheddar cheese and walnuts. Make a well in the center of the flour mixture. Add the egg mixture all at once. Stir just till the mixture is moistened (batter will be lumpy).

Turn the batter into a greased 8x4x2-inch loaf pan. Bake in a 350° oven for 55 to 60 minutes or till golden. Let cool in pan 10 minutes. Remove from pan; cool on wire rack. Cool thoroughly before slicing. Makes 1 loaf.

Clockwise from back left: Raisin-Apple Bread (see recipe, page 186), Honey-Orange Bread, Honey-Date Nut Bread, and Honey-Rye Bread (see recipe, page 186).

PINEAPPLE-BRAN BREAD

See photo, page 188—

1   8¼-ounce can crushed
        pineappple
     Milk
½   cup whole bran cereal
1   beaten egg
⅓   cup cooking oil
1¾   cups all-purpose flour
½   cup sugar
2½   teaspoons baking powder
¾   teaspoon salt
½   cup chopped pecans

Drain crushed pineapple; reserve ⅓ cup pineapple and 3 tablespoons pineapple syrup. (Save the remaining crushed pineapple for another use.) Add enough milk to reserved syrup to make 1 cup liquid. Pour over bran cereal. Let stand about 15 minutes or till softened.

In a small bowl combine the drained pineapple, the syrup-milk mixture, egg, and cooking oil.

In a large mixing bowl stir together the flour, sugar, baking powder, and salt. Stir in the chopped pecans. Make a well in the center of the flour mixture. Add egg mixture all at once. Stir just till moistened (batter will be lumpy). Turn batter into a greased 8x4x2-inch loaf pan.

Bake in a 350° oven for 50 to 55 minutes. Let cool in pan 10 minutes. Remove from pan; cool on wire rack. Cool thoroughly before slicing. Makes 1 loaf.

SPICY RAISIN COFFEE CAKE

See photo, page 188—

     Boiling water
½   cup raisins
2   cups all-purpose flour
½   cup sugar
1   tablespoon baking powder
½   teaspoon salt
½   teaspoon ground cardamom
⅓   cup shortening
¾   cup milk
2   tablespoons butter *or*
        margarine, softened
¼   cup chopped pecans
¼   cup packed brown sugar
1   teaspoon lemon juice
¼   teaspoon ground cinnamon

Pour boiling water over raisins to cover; let stand 10 minutes. Drain.

In a bowl stir together the flour, sugar, baking powder, salt, and cardamom. Cut in shortening till the mixture resembles coarse crumbs. Make a well in the flour mixture; add milk all at once. Stir just till dough clings together.

On a lightly floured surface knead dough gently for 10 to 12 strokes. Set aside ¼ of the dough. Pat remaining dough in bottom and up sides of a greased 8x1½-inch round baking dish. Spread butter or margarine over dough.

In a bowl toss together the pecans, brown sugar, lemon juice, cinnamon, and drained raisins. Turn into dough-lined pan. On a floured surface, roll the remaining dough to ¼-inch thickness. Cut in ½-inch strips. Arrange in lattice-fashion atop raisin mixture, trimming to fit. Seal edges. Bake in a 375° oven for 25 to 30 minutes or till golden brown. Makes 1 coffee cake.

MOLASSES BROWN BREAD

See photo, page 180—

2¼   cups whole wheat flour
1¾   cups all-purpose flour
2   teaspoons baking soda
1   teaspoon salt
2   beaten eggs
2   cups sour milk* *or*
        buttermilk
½   cup molasses
⅓   cup honey
2   teaspoons finely shredded
        orange *or* lemon peel
1   cup chopped walnuts
¾   cup raisins

In a large mixing bowl stir together the whole wheat flour, the all-purpose flour, baking soda, and salt; set aside.

In another bowl combine eggs, sour milk or buttermilk, molasses, honey, and orange or lemon peel; add to flour mixture, stirring till combined. Stir in walnuts and raisins. Turn batter into 2 greased 8x4x2-inch loaf pans.

Bake in a 350° oven about 55 minutes, covering with foil the last 15 to 20 minutes to prevent over-browning. Remove from pans and cool on wire racks. If desired, wrap and store 24 hours before slicing. Makes 2 loaves.

*For sour milk place 2 tablespoons *lemon juice* or *vinegar* in a large glass measuring cup. Add enough *milk* to make 2 cups liquid. Stir and let stand 5 minutes.

BANANA-NUT LOAF

2 cups all-purpose flour
2 teaspoons baking powder
¾ teaspoon salt
¼ teaspoon baking soda
½ cup shortening
½ cup sugar
2 eggs
1 teaspoon finely shredded
    orange peel
2 ripe medium bananas, cut up
2 tablespoons milk
½ cup chopped pecans *or*
    walnuts

In a mixing bowl thoroughly stir together the flour, baking powder, salt, and baking soda; set aside.

In a small mixer bowl cream the shortening and sugar till mixture is light and fluffy. Add eggs and shredded orange peel; beat well.

In a small bowl mash bananas with fork (mixture should measure about 1 cup); stir in the milk. Add flour mixture and banana mixture alternately to sugar mixture, beating till smooth after each addition. Fold in pecans or walnuts. Pour batter into a greased 9x5x3-inch loaf pan.

Bake in a 350° oven for 45 to 50 minutes or till wooden pick inserted near center comes out clean. Turn out and cool loaf on wire rack. Makes 1 loaf.

CARROT-RAISIN CRUNCH BREAD

2 large carrots, cut into 1-inch
    chunks
1 teaspoon finely shredded
    orange peel
1 teaspoon ground cinnamon
½ teaspoon ground nutmeg
2¼ cups all-purpose flour
2 teaspoons baking powder
½ teaspoon baking soda
½ teaspoon salt
1 cup packed brown sugar
½ cup butter *or* margarine,
    softened
2 eggs
1 teaspoon vanilla
½ cup raisins

In a saucepan cook the carrots in a small amount of boiling water 15 minutes or till tender. Drain, reserving ¼ cup cooking liquid. In blender container or food processor bowl combine the carrots, the reserved liquid, orange peel, cinnamon, and nutmeg. Cover; blend or process till smooth.

In a mixing bowl stir together the flour, baking powder, baking soda, and salt; set aside.

In a large mixer bowl beat together the brown sugar and butter or margarine till light and fluffy. Add eggs and vanilla; beat well. Stir in the carrot mixture. Add the flour mixture to the sugar mixture; mix well. Fold in raisins. Spoon the batter into 2 greased 8x4x2-inch loaf pans.

Bake in a 350° oven for 35 to 40 minutes. Cool in pans 10 minutes. Remove from pans; cool loaves on wire rack. Makes 2 loaves.

PUMPKIN DOT COFFEE CAKE

1 cup sugar
¼ cup butter *or* margarine,
    softened
2 eggs
1 teaspoon vanilla
2 cups all-purpose flour
1 tablespoon baking powder
½ teaspoon salt
1 cup milk
½ cup canned pumpkin
3 tablespoons brown sugar
1 tablespoon butter *or*
    margarine, melted
1 teaspoon ground cinnamon

In a large mixer bowl cream together the sugar and ¼ cup softened butter or margarine. Beat in eggs and vanilla.

In a mixing bowl stir together the flour, baking powder, and salt. Add the flour mixture and milk alternately to creamed mixture. Mix the pumpkin with *¾ cup* of the batter. Spread the remaining batter into a greased 12x7½x2-inch baking dish.

Drop pumpkin mixture over batter by teaspoonfuls. Combine the brown sugar, the 1 tablespoon melted butter or margarine, and cinnamon. Sprinkle over pumpkin mixture.

Bake in a 350° oven for 35 to 40 minutes or till wooden pick inserted just off center comes out clean. Cool slightly in pan on wire rack. Cut coffee cake into squares; serve warm. Makes 1 coffee cake.

COUNTRY WEAR AND WARMERS

Afghans

nterpret the classic granny square in your own special way using a rainbow of colors. This country-style rendition is loaded with vitality, because there are 10 shades of yarn in it in every color combination you can think of. Make handfuls of the bright, easy-to-stitch granny squares, then crochet them together using black borders between each one. Finish the outside edges with bands of color worked in double crochet stitches. To make the super-size afghan shown here (90 granny squares in all), we used a hefty machine-washable acrylic yarn. For a smaller afghan, choose the same colors in a sportweight yarn. A comfortable handmade afghan like this one makes a great decorative accessory for your home. You can display your afghan in any room in your house for a touch of homespun detail. For how-to instructions, see page 202.

Bring a bit of the country indoors with any one of the three springtime-fresh afghan designs shown here. Nothing adds to a favorite room's cozy feeling the way a handcrafted afghan does. To make one of these three, you can choose the technique you prefer, either knitting or crocheting.

The striped patchwork afghan (top right) is made one square at a time using single and double crochet stitches. Alternate the colors and the direction of the stripes when assembling the squares.

Use simple afghan stitches to make the daisy bouquet project (bottom right). Then, embroider the designs in cross-stitches and join the panels.

While cultivating some fresh crocheting ideas, this garden delight afghan (opposite) cropped up, filled with textured stitches and three-dimensional shapes. Even when frost covers your windows, you will be able to glance at this afghan and get a view of sunshine and flowers.

To begin this project, work the background first, then stitch the flowers one at a time and tack them in place along the windowsill and shutters. Cut lengths of lace to adorn the curtains.

For instructions, see page 202.

If you desire, construct a colorful flower basket pillow to match your afghan (opposite), using extra flowers and leaves. Cluster the flowers together on a crocheted background, then arrange some of them inside a "basket" made of single crochet stitches.

Crocheted afghans are just as popular today as they were in the days of homespun yarns and hand-dyed colors. The materials have changed, but the desire for warmth and comfort hasn't. Afghans such as these provide the same warmth and comfort, but they work up faster and easier than their old country counterparts.

The multicolored afghan (below) is worked in a traditional ripple design. The textured ridges are formed by single crocheting into the back loops.

You can quick-stitch great granny squares like these (opposite) into colorful jumbo blocks using six strands of worsted-weight knitting yarn. Work the granny squares in different color combinations, but stitch white centers and black borders throughout.

Instructions begin on page 207.

The finished size of the ripple afghan at right is 46x68 inches. To make your afghan larger or smaller, increase or decrease the total number of rows you crochet, or add fringe along the top and bottom.

GRANNY SQUARE AFGHAN
pages 196-197

The 64x74-inch afghan shown is made of ninety 5x5-inch squares.

Materials: Unger Roly Poly (3½-ounce skeins)—*For squares:* 1 skein each of red, rust, gold, light yellow, medium green, olive green, medium blue, turquoise, lavender; 2 black. *For stripes and border:* 2 skeins each red, rust, gold, medium green, medium blue, lavender; 3 black. Size F aluminum crochet hook, or size to obtain gauge.

Note: For smaller (48x62 inches), lighter weight afghan, use Unger Roly Sport yarn in same colors and amounts. Squares will be about 4x4 inches.

Gauge: 2 rows of 3 dc clusters = 1 inch; (3 dc, ch 1, 3 dc) = 1 inch across work.

Instructions: (*Note:* Each square consists of five rounds worked in different colors and bordered by a sixth round in black. Study the photograph for color combinations. Combine colors freely within the squares group, but reserve yarn for stripes and borders or you may not have enough yarn to complete this part of the afghan.)

Squares: With first color, ch 4, join with sl st to form ring. *Rnd 1:* Ch 3 (counts as first dc), work 2 dc in ring, ch 1, (3 dc, ch 1) in ring 3 times, join with sl st to top of ch-3 (always join end of rnd this way). Fasten off.

Rnd 2: Attach second color in any ch-1 sp, ch 3, 2 dc, ch 1, 3 dc in same sp, (3 dc, ch 1, 3 dc in next ch-1 sp) 3 times, join. Fasten off. *Rnds 3, 4, 5:* Attach next color in any corner sp, ch 3, 2 dc, ch 1, 3 dc in same sp, ch 1, sk 3 dc, 3 dc in next sp. Continue around, making 3 dc, ch 1 in each sp, and making 2 (3 dc) groups in each corner sp. Join with sl st to top of ch-3. Fasten off.

Rnd 6: Attach black in any corner sp, ch 3, 2 dc, ch 1, 3 dc in same sp, ch 1, sk next 3-dc grp, 3 dc in next sp. Continue around, making 3 dc, ch 1 in each sp, and making 2 (3 dc) groups in each corner sp. Join with sl st to top of ch-3. Fasten off.

Assembling the afghan: Make 90 squares. Weave or crochet together 18 squares into a panel 2 squares across and 9 squares down (panel A). Repeat for panel C. These are end panels.

Next, assemble 54 squares to form a piece 6 squares wide and 9 squares long (panel B—the center panel).

Work 1 rnd of black around each rectangular panel: Attach black in any corner sp, ch 3, 2 dc, ch 1, 3 dc in same sp, ch 1. Continue around, making 3 dc, ch 1 in each ch = 1 sp, and making 2 (3 dc) grps in each corner sp. Join with sl st to top of ch-3. Fasten off.

Making stripes and attaching end panels: Stripes—On 9-square side of panel B, attach red in corner sp. *Row 1:* Ch 3, work dc in each st across, end dc in ch-1 sp at other corner. Ch 3, turn. *Row 2:* Still using red, work dc across to last dc. Fasten off. *Row 3:* Attach rust in first dc, ch 3, work dc across row to last dc, ch 3, turn. *Row 4:* Rep Row 2, using rust. For remainder of stripes, rep Rows 3 and 4, changing colors every 2 rows. Work 2 rows each of gold, medium green, blue, lavender. Rep stripe section on opposite 9-square side of panel B. Weave or crochet narrow end panels (A and C) to last rows of lavender stripe on either end.

Border: Attach lavender in any corner sp, ch 3, 2 dc in corner sp. Work dc in each dc of 3-dc grps and in each ch-1 sp (work 2 dc in each row of stripe and work 3 dc in each corner sp to keep work flat). Work around afghan in this manner. Join with sl st to top of ch-3. Work 1 more rnd of lavender, then work 2 rnds each of blue, medium green, gold, rust, red.

Picot edge: Attach black in any corner. Ch 1 and sc around outside edge (counts as Rnd 1). *Rnd 2:* Sl st in first 2 sc, * ch 3, sl st in same st, sl st in next 2 sc. Rep from * around edge. Fasten off.

STRIPED CROCHETED AFGHAN
page 198

Finished size is about 45x67 inches.

Materials: Botany Machine Washable Winsom (2-ounce skeins) or a suitable substitute: 3 each of colors A, B, C, D, E, and F; Size J crochet hook.

Gauge: 10 sts = 3½ inches; 9 rows = 3½ inches.

Instructions: Afghan consists of 54 squares, 9 each in combinations below:

Combination No.	1st Color	2nd Color
1	A	B
2	B	A
3	C	D
4	D	C
5	E	F
6	F	E

When working squares, change yarn color at end of every 2nd row—one stripe—as follows: complete last st by drawing new color through the last 2 loops on hook; break previous color.

Square: Using first color, ch 22 loosely. *Row 1 (right side):* Work 1 dc in 3rd ch from hook, 1 sc in next ch, * 1 dc in next ch, 1 sc in next ch; rep from * 8 times—20 sts. *Row 2:* Ch 1, turn, work 1 dc in first sc, 1 sc in next dc, * 1 dc in next sc, 1 sc in next dc; rep from * 8 times, completing last sc with new color—20 sts. Break off. *Row 3:* Ch 1, turn, work 1 dc in first sc, 1 sc in next dc, * 1 dc in next sc, 1 sc in next dc; rep from * to end. *Row 4:* Rep Row 2.

Rep Rows 3 and 4, alternating first and 2nd colors until 16 rows—eight stripes—are complete, ending with 2nd color; change to first color. Break 2nd color. Work 2 more rows with first color. *Do not break yarn or change color.* Mark right side of last stripe of square. Square should measure 7x7 inches. Continuing with first color, ch 1, turn.

Edging (right side): Work 3 sc in first st for corner, working along upper edge, with care to keep work flat, work 1 sc in each of next 18 sts, 3 sc in last st for corner; work 18 sc evenly spaced along side edge, 3 sc in first st of lower edge for corner, 1 sc in each of next 18 sts, 3 sc in last st for corner, 18 sc evenly spaced along side edge, join with sl st in first sc and fasten off.

Finishing: Block squares to 7½ x 7½ inches; arrange as shown in chart (opposite), alternating vertical and horizontal stripes. Place marked stripe at top for horizontal stripes and at left for vertical stripes. With right sides facing, sew squares tog, st for st, through top loops only.

DAISY BOUQUET AFGHAN
page 198

Finished size is about 50x88 inches including fringe.

Materials: Botany Winsom (2-ounce skeins) or a suitable substitute: 18 color A, and 1 each of colors B, C, and D; Size H afghan hook or size to obtain gauge; Size F aluminum crochet hook.

Gauge: Afghan St: 4 sts = 1 inch; 7 rows = 2 inches.

Instructions: *Center strip, Afghan Stitch*—With A and Size H hook, ch 81 for lower border edge.

Row 1: First half of row—Retaining all loops on hook, draw up a loop in 2nd ch from hook and in each rem ch. There are same number of lps on hook as there were ch sts. *Second half of row:* Yo and draw through one lp, * yo and draw through 2 lps. Rep from * across until 1 lp remains. Remaining lp always counts as first st on the next row.

Row 2: First half of row—Retaining all lps on hook, draw up a lp in 2nd vertical bar (formed by lp of previous row) and in each vertical bar across to last bar, insert hook through last vertical bar and st directly behind it and draw up a lp. *Second half of row:* Yo and draw through 1 lp, * yo and draw through 2 lps. Rep from * across. Rep Row 2 for pat until 48 rows (about 14 inches) have been completed.

Final row: Work a sl st under 2nd and each remaining vertical bar to within 1 bar of end, insert hook under both bars and work a final sl st.

Chain loop inset (wrong side): With F

center panel ↗

← upper and lower borders

right side panel
(reverse for left side)

Color and Stitch Key:
☒ *white cross stitch—color B*
◉ *gold cross stitch—color C*
▣ *green cross stitch—color D*
---- *green outline stitch—color D*
⌇ *white outline stitch—color B*

hook, ch 1, turn, work 1 sc in first sl st, * ch 5, sk next 3 sts, 1 sc in next st; rep from * to end—20 ch lps. *Row 2:* Ch 5, turn, 1 sc in first lp, * ch 5, 1 sc in next lp, rep from * to end, ch 2, 1 dc in sc—19 ch lps with 1 half lp at each end. *Row 3:* Ch 5, turn, 1 sc in first full lp, * ch 5, 1 sc in next lp; rep from * to last lp, ch 5, 1 sc in half lp.

Row 4: Rep Row 2, end 1 dc in first ch of ch 5 lp. Fasten off.

Center afghan stitch panel: Turn, join yarn from right side with H hook, draw up 2 lps in first half lp of ch inset, sk sc, * draw up 4 lps in next ch lp, sk next sc; rep from * to end, draw up 3 lps in last half ch lp—81 lps on hook.

Work off lps as before. Work Afghan Stitch until center panel is 130 rows, *(Continued)* or about 38 inches from beg. Work 1 row sl st. Work inset as before.

Top afghan stitch border: Work as for Center Panel until 48 rows. Work a final row sl st. Mark for top.

Side strips (make 2): With H hook, ch 49 for lower edge. Working as for Center Strip, work 48 rows Afghan St, 4 rows inset, 130 rows Afghan St, 4 rows inset, 48 rows Afghan St.

Using charts on page 203, work cross sts and outline sts on panels. Mark for top.

Note: Strips have more rows and stitches than shown on charts. For center panel, begin on 5th row from top and 41st st in from right edge for center of top flower. For side panels, begin first flower on 12th row from top and 15th st from right edge of right panel. Embroidery for borders begins on 18th row from top edge and 14th st from right edge for first leaf.

Inset and joining between the strips: From right side, working on side edge of left side strip, with F hook and A, beg at lower edge, work 1 sc in end of first row, * ch 5, sk next 3 rows, 1 sc in end of next row *; rep between *'s 10 times, ch 5, 1 sc in end of first inset row, ch 5, 1 sc in end of 2nd row of Afghan St panel, 33 lps on Afghan St panel, 2 lps on inset, 12 lps on Afghan St border—61 lps.

Row 2: Rep Row 2 of ch lp inset. From right side, beg at upper edge of center strip, work 1 row ch lps as for side strip.

Joining row: Ch 2, turn, work 1 sc in first half lp of left side strip, ch 2, 1 sc in first lp of center strip, * ch 2, 1 sc in next lp of left side strip, ch 2, 1 sc in next lp of center strip; rep from * to end, ch 2, 1 sc in last half lp of left side strip. Join center and right side strips in same way.

Loop edging: From right side, join A at upper left corner, work 1 row of ch lps around all 4 sides of afghan.

Fringe: Wind A around a 10-inch cardboard, cut at one end. Fold in half and knot a 6-strand fringe into each loop at upper and lower edges.

WINDOW BOX AFGHAN
page 199

Finished size is 48x58 inches.

Materials: *For afghan:* Unger Roly Poly (3.5-ounce balls): 4 dark blue; 2 light blue; 3 each brick, light yellow, dark yellow; 2 green; 1 each ecru, orange, medium rose, light rose, and purple. *For pillows:* 3 green; 2 brick; scraps of remaining colors from afghan for flowers; aluminum crochet hook size G, or size to obtain gauge; 4 large yarn bobbins; 2¼ yards 2-inch-wide lace.

Gauge: 6 sts = 2 inches; 4 rows = 2 inches.

Instructions: *Afghan—(Note:* To change yarn colors, work last st before changing colors until 2 lps rem on hook. *Always* drop this color to *wrong* side of afghan. Then draw new color through rem 2 lps to complete the st.)

Afghan: With dark blue, ch 149. Break off.

Row 1 (wrong side): With brick, sl st through last ch made, ch 3 to count as first dc and work 36 dc; change to light blue and work 75 dc for flowerpot; attach a second ball of brick and work 37 dc—149 dc; ch 3, turn.

Row 2: Dc in next 7 dc, dc around post *in front of* next 2 dc, dc in next 14 dc, dc around post *in front of* next dc, dc in next 11 dc; change to light blue and work 75 dc for flowerpot; change to brick. Referring to chart (opposite), complete row working a dc around post in front of each square indicated. *Note:* Hereafter work brick-colored dc in each unmarked square; work dc around post from front in each square marked with a black X.

Rows 3-5: Work from chart, changing colors and working dc around post in front of dc as indicated.

Row 6: Work across first 74 sts according to chart; *join pink and (yo, draw up a lp in st) 3 times; yo and draw through all 7 lps*—puff st made. Continue across row according to chart.

Note: Hereafter (for the heart motif) work the pink puff st in each square marked with a small circle; work pink dc in each square marked with a black triangle.

Rows 7-15: Continue working rows according to chart, making puff sts within heart motif and color changes as indicated. Drop pink at end of Row 15.

Rows 16-17: Work in pat as established. *Row 18:* Work in pat as estab-

lished over first 8 sts, drop brick; attach dark blue and dc around post from front over next 30 sts, drop blue; attach ecru and dc around post from front over 73 sts, drop ecru; attach another ball of dark blue and dc around post from front over next 30 sts, drop dark blue; attach brick and complete row. *Note:* Hereafter (for window frame) work ecru dc around post from front in squares marked with black slashes.

Row 19: Work in pat as established over first 8 sts, drop brick; pick up dark blue and dc around post from back over next 30 sts, drop dark blue; pick up ecru and work hdc in front lp over next 73 sts, drop ecru; pick up dark blue and work dc around post from back over next 30 sts, drop dark blue; pick up brick and complete row.

Row 20: Work as for Row 18 until 3 sts of ecru have been worked, drop ecru; attach dark yellow and work (sk hdc, 2 dc in next hdc) 16 times, drop dark yellow; attach a yarn bobbin wound with ecru and work 3 dc around post from front, drop ecru; attach another ball of dark yellow and (sk hdc, 2 dc in next hdc) 16 times, drop dark yellow; attach 2nd yarn bobbin wound with ecru and work 3 dc around post from front, drop ecru; pick up dark blue and complete row as indicated. *Note:* Work areas within window frame (light blue on chart) in dark yellow in st pats as established in Rows 19 and 20.

Row 21: Work in pat as established over first 41 sts (sk dc, 2 dc in next dc) 16 times over the next 32 sts; work 3 sts in ecru as established (sk dc, 2 dc in next dc) 16 times over the next 32 sts; complete row as established.

Rows 22-23: Work in pat established.

Row 24: Work as established over first 8 sts, dc around post from front in next 6 dc, hdc in back lp over next 18 dc, dc around post from front in next 6 dc; work across through 3rd ecru grp of sts; dc around post from front in next 6 dc, hdc in back lp over next 18 dc, dc around post from front in next 6 dc; complete row.

Row 25: Work first 8 sts in pat established, dc around post from back in next 6 dc, hdc in front lp of next 18 hdc, dc around post from back over next 6 dc; complete row, working other dark blue shutter sts similarly.

(Continued)

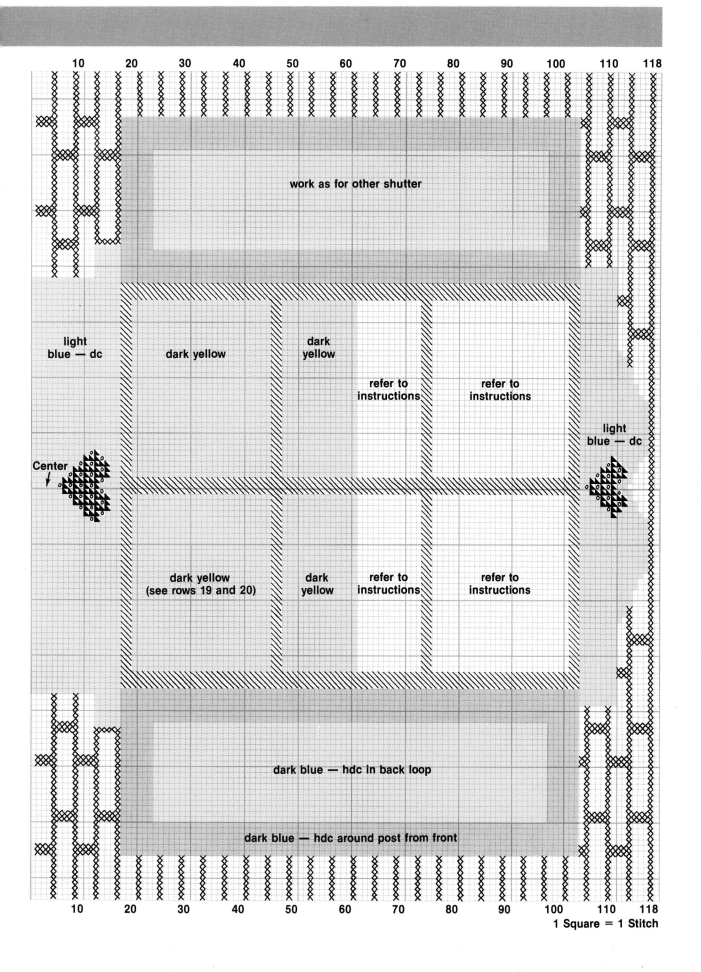

1 Square = 1 Stitch

Rows 26-45: Work in pats as established.

Rows 46-47: Work as established through first 3 ecru sts, do not drop ecru; continue with window frame pat across row to opposite dark blue shutter; complete row.

Rows 48-61: Resume dark yellow window pat.

Now establish curtain panel as follows: *Row 62:* Work across first 41 sts; join light yellow for curtain, dc in next dc, in next st make (*yo, draw up a lp, yo, draw through 2 lps on hook) 4 times; yo, draw through all 5 lps on hook, ch 1*—cluster (cl) made; dc in next dc, drop light yellow; attach dark yellow and work windowpane pat to ecru, drop dark yellow; work ecru in pat over next 3 sts; work dark yellow to 4 sts before end of second "pane"; join another ball of light yellow, sk dc, dc in next dc, cl in next dc, dc in next dc, drop light yellow; complete row. Hereafter, instructions refer to portions of row inside window "frame," the center 67 sts.

Row 63: Cl in dc, sk cl, cl in next dc, pick up dark yellow and work dark yellow as established, ecru as established, and dark yellow as established to within 3 sts of beg of 3rd ecru grp, now pick up light yellow and work cl in dc, sk cl, cl in dc; complete row.

Row 64: Dc in sp before first cl, cl bet next 2 cl, cl in sp following next cl, sk dc, dc in next dc, drop light yellow; pick up dark yellow and work until 13 2-dc grps are completed in 2nd "pane"; pick up light yellow and work dc in next dc, cl in sp bet dc and next cl, cl bet next 2 cl, dc in sp bet cl and dc of "frame"; complete row.

Row 65: Dc in dc, cl in sp bet next 2 cl, cl in sp bet cl and dc, cl in sp bet dc and 2-dc grp, sk dc, dc in next dc, drop light yellow; pick up dark yellow and work across until twelve 2-dc grps have been worked in 2nd "pane," drop dark yellow; pick up light yellow and work dc in next dc, cl in sp bet next 2 dc, cl in sp bet dc and cl, cl in sp bet next 2 cl, dc in dc—3 cl in curtain; complete row.

Row 66: Dc in dc, cl in sp bet dc and next cl (cl in sp bet next 2 cl) twice; cl bet cl and dc, cl bet dc and next 2-dc grp, sk dc, dc in next dc; work as established across panes—eleven 2-dc grps; pick up light yellow and work dc in

next dc, cl bet dc grp and dc, cl bet dc and cl (cl bet next 2 cl) twice; cl bet cl and dc, dc in dc—5 cl in curtain; complete row.

Row 67: Dc in dc (cl in sp bet next 2 cl) 4 times; cl bet cl and dc, cl bet dc and 2-dc grp, sk dc, dc in next dc, work in pat across panes—ten 2-dc grps; pick up light yellow and work dc in dc, cl bet 2-dc grp and dc, cl bet dc and cl (cl bet next 2 cl) 4 times; dc in dc—6 cl in curtains; complete row.

Row 68: Dc in dc, cl in sp bet dc and cl (cl in sp bet next 2 cl) 5 times; cl bet cl and dc, sk dc, dc in next dc; work in pat across panes—nine 2-dc grps; pick up light yellow and work dc in dc, cl bet dc and cl (cl bet next 2 cl) 5 times; cl in sp bet cl and dc, dc in dc—7 cl in curtain; complete row.

Refer to chart (below) for center 67 sts for curtain line. Maintain the correct numbers of 2-dc grps and cl in each row. Work rem 41 sts in pat as established.

Row	No. of 2-dc grps	No. of cl
69-70	9	7
71-73	8	8
74-75	Rep Rows 46, 47 for frame	
76-79	6	9
80-83	5	10
84-87	4	11
88-91	3	12
92-95	2	13
96-99	1	14
100-101	0	15

Rows 102-103: Rep Rows 46 and 47 for top of window frame.

Row 104: Drop ecru and dark blue; work according to chart.

Rows 105-117: Work according to chart; add pink heart as indicated. *Row 118:* With brick, dc across. Fasten off.

Border: With right side facing, attach dark blue in any corner, ch 3, work 2 more dc in corner and dc evenly spaced around afghan, working 3 dc in each corner; sl st to top of ch-3. *Next rnd:* Sc around ch-3 in rnd below, ch 2, dc around post from the front of each dc around, working 2nd dc in corner 3-dc grps as follows: dc in top of st, dc around post, dc in top of st once more. When rnd is completed, join to top of ch-2. Edge of work will roll to front.

Note: Follow directions below for flowers; sew in place after completion.

Pats below are for several of the flowers shown on left and right shutter and window box. Alter the pats slightly as desired.

Flower no. 1 (make 5): Ch 5, sl st to form ring. *Rnd 1:* (Ch 4, dc in ring, ch 4, sc in ring) 5 times; join with sl st to first ch of ch-4 at beg of rnd. Break off. When flower is secured to afghan, embroider a French knot in center.

Flower no. 2 (make 5): With light yellow, beg as for flower no. 1. *Rnd 1:* Ch 3, work 14 dc in ring; join with sl st to top of ch-3. Break off. *Rnd 2:* Attach new color in any dc, ch 4, in same st work hdc and trc; in each dc around work trc, hdc, trc; join with sl st to top of ch-4. Break off.

Flower no. 3 (make 17): Beg as for flower no. 1. *Rnd 1:* Ch 3, 4 dc in ring, *drop hook from work, insert hook in top of ch-3 at beg of rnd, draw dropped lp through, ch 1 tightly*—popcorn (pc) made; ch 1, (5 dc in ring, drop hook from work and insert hook in first dc of the 5-dc grp just made and draw dropped lp through; ch 1 tightly, ch 1) 4 times; join with sl st to top of pc.

Window box flowers: Flower no. 4 (make 3): With light yellow, beg as for flower no. 1. *Rnd 1:* Work same as Rnd 1 of flower no. 2. *Rnd 2:* Join petal color in back lp of any dc, ch 4 in same lp and work hdc, trc; in back lps around, work trc, hdc, trc; join with sl st to top of ch-4 at beg of rnd; ch 3. *Rnd 3:* Now working in front lps of same dc, in each lp work hdc, trc, and hdc; join with a sl st to first hdc. Break off.

Flower no. 5 (make 2): With light yellow, beg as for flower no. 1. *Rnd 1:* (Ch 1, sc in ring, ch 3) 5 times; join last ch-3 to first sc—5 ch-3 lps. *Rnd 2:* Sl st into ch-3 lp (ch 5, trc in same lp, ch 5, sc in same lp, sc in next ch-3 lp) 5 times, ending with join the ch-5 to sl st at beg of rnd. Break off. *Rnd 3:* Attach a 3rd color in any sc (ch 7, sc in first sc bet *next* 2 petals) 5 times; ending with join ch-7 to first sc. *Rnd 4:* Ch 1, sc in ch-7 lp; in each ch-7 lp around work sc, 2 hdc, 2 dc, trc, ch 1, trc, 2 dc, 2 hdc, sc; join with sl st. Break off.

Flower no. 6: This tulip is worked in 2 sizes; changes for larger size follow in parentheses. Make 2 large and 1 small tulip.

For flower sides (make 2), ch 16 (19). *Row 1:* Sc in 2nd ch from hook and in next 2 (3) ch, hdc in next 3 (3) ch, dc in next 2 (2) ch, trc in next 3 (5) ch, dc in next ch (2 ch), hdc in next 2 (1) ch, sc in last ch; ch 1, turn. *Row 2:* Sc in first 2 (3) sts, hdc in next 1 (2) sts, 2 dc in each of next 2 (3) sts, 2 hdc in next 1 (1) st, hdc in next 0 (1) st, sc in next 4 (4) sts, sl st in next 5 (5) sts. Break off.

For flower center (make 1): Ch 5. *Row 1:* In 5th ch from hook *work 2 dc, ch 2, 2 dc*—shell made; ch 3, turn. *Row 2:* Work shell in ch-2 sp of shell, dc in ch-2 sp bet shell and turning ch; ch 3, turn. *Rows 3-4:* Rep Row 2. For larger flower only, rep Row 2 once more. *Row 5:* Dc in sp bet dc and shell; in ch-2 sp of shell work 2 dc, ch 3, 2 dc; 2 dc in sp bet shell and turning ch; ch 3, turn. *Row 6:* Dc in next dc, ch 2, in ch-3 sp of next shell work 2 dc, ch 3, 2 dc; ch 2, sk 2 dc, dc in next dc and in top of turning ch; ch 1, turn. *Row 7:* Sc in 2 dc, 2 dc in next ch-2 sp, sc in 2 dc, 5 sc in ch-3 sp, sc in 2 dc, 2 sc in next ch-2 sp, sc in 2 dc. Break off.

Tulip leaves: Make 2 leaves per flower. Instructions are for shorter leaves; changes for longer leaves follow in parentheses.

Ch 40 (50), sc in 2nd ch from hook and next 4 (6) ch, hdc in next 5 (6) ch, dc in next 5 (6) ch, trc in next 6 (8) ch, dc in next 6 (6) ch, hdc in next 6 (6) ch, sc in next 6 (10) ch; do not turn, continue down other side of ch row; 2 (2) sc in same ch, sc in next 5 (6) ch, hdc in next 6 (8) ch, dc in next 6 (6) ch, trc in next 4 (6) ch, dc in next 5 (8) ch, hdc in next 6 (7) ch, sc in next 6 (6) ch, sl st in last st and first sc on other side of work. Break off.

Single leaf: Leaf is made in 2 sizes. Instructions are for small leaf; changes for larger leaf follow in parentheses. Leave a 6-inch tail at beg and end of each leaf to tack to afghan.

Ch 9 (12), sc in 2nd ch from hook, hdc in next 2 (3) ch, dc in next 2 (4) ch, 2 trc in next ch, 2 dc in next ch, 2 hdc and sc in next ch; do not turn, continue work along other side of ch, 2 dc in next ch, 2 trc in next ch, dc in next 2 (3) ch, hdc in next 2 (4) ch, sc in next ch, sl st in last ch and first sc on other side of work. Break off.

Stems: Leaves on vine of left shutter were made separately and attached to 2 stems. For longer stem, ch about 160. For shorter stem, ch about 40. To as-

semble stems on left shutter, position flowers on shutter; wind stems up the stem. Stitch stem to shutter. Tack flowers in place.

Stem on right shutter includes all leaves and stem.

For first side of leaf ch 9, * sc in 2nd ch from hook, hdc in next ch, dc in next 2 ch, 2 trc in next ch, dc in next ch, hdc in next ch, sc in sl st in next ch, ch 19. Rep from * until 22 leaves are completed for 1 stem. Make another stem with 8 leaves.

Complete other side of each leaf by joining yarn in ch where sc and sl st were made and work along other side as follows: Sc in next ch, dc in next 2 ch, 2 trc in next ch, 2 dc in next ch, hdc in next ch, sc in next ch, sl st in sc on opposite side of leaf. Break off.

Arrange flowers for right shutter in pleasing position; wind stem and tack in place at leaf tips only.

Stems for window box are various lengths of ch. Arrange flowers, adding tulips and long leaves.

Make smaller leaves as for left shutter and tack all flowers and leaves. Cut lace to fit along curved edge of curtain; fold edges under and sew in place.

RIPPLE AFGHAN
page 200

Finished size is 46x68 inches.

Materials: Unger Roly Poly (3.5-ounce balls): 8 balls natural, 1 ball each of blue, pink, green, gold, maroon; size G aluminum crochet hook, or size to obtain gauge given below.

Gauge: 9 sc = 2 inches.

Instructions: With natural, ch 311. *Pat row:* Sc in 2nd st from hook and in next 10 sts, * 3 sc in next st, sc in each of next 12 sts, sk 2 sts, sc in each of next 11 sts. Rep from * across, ending with 3 sc in next st, sc in next 10 sts, sk 1 st, sc in front of last st; ch 1, turn.

Working in back lp only, work 9 more pat rows with natural. Then work stripe pat as follows: 3 rows blue, 2 rows natural, 3 rows pink, 2 rows natural, 3 rows green, 2 rows natural, 3 rows gold, 2 rows natural, 3 rows maroon, 10 rows natural. The last 33 rows form pat rep. Rep pat rep 5 times more;

then work 10 rows more of pat row in natural. Fasten off. To block, dampen afghan and pin out to measurements. Let dry away from heat and light.

GREAT SCOT GRANNY AFGHAN
pages 200-201

Finished size is 50x64 inches.

Materials: Lion Brand Sayelle 4-ply knitting worsted (4-ounce skeins): 3 skeins white, 12 skeins black, 6 skeins *each* green, blue, and red; size S plastic crochet hook, or size to obtain gauge.

Gauge: One 5-rnd square measures 14 inches.

Instructions: *Note on afghan construction:* This afghan is worked using 6 strands of yarn at once. (To prevent tangling, place ball in jar.)

If you intend to duplicate the design shown using 3 colors plus black and white, there is a total of six color combinations when alternating colors for the squares. You will need to make 2 of each of the 6 combinations to most efficiently use the amounts of yarn specified above.

The following color references for the 6 squares are to be used for Rnds 2, 3, and 4 of each square (Rnd 1 is worked with white; Rnd 5 is worked with black.) Refer to these square numbers during assembly *(see below)*.

Square no. 1: Green, blue, red
Square no. 2: Green, red, blue
Square no. 3: Red, blue, green
Square no. 4: Red, green, blue
Square no. 5: Blue, red, green
Square no. 6: Blue, green, red

Granny square: Refer to instructions for Granny Square Afghan, page 202, and work a square containing 5 rnds.

Assembly: Arrange 12 squares according to photo, in four horizontal rows of three squares. To join, hold two adjacent squares right sides tog, and crochet tog, making one sc in each sp and dc across; fasten off. Repeat until all 12 squares have been joined.

Border: Attach black in any ch-3 corner sp. Work sc around, making 3 sc in each corner so that work lies flat, and working sc in each dc and in each adjacent corner sp around. Rep with one rnd blue, one rnd red, ending one rnd green. Tie in yarn ends.

207

COUNTRY WEAR AND WARMERS

Family Sweaters

Before brisk autumn winds begin to blow, gather up your knitting needles and yarn and make these fall family sweaters. Country-style dressing is never out of fashion, and you can wear these sweaters wherever you go, in town or country. The sweaters shown here are quick-knit versions of traditional Fair Isle patterns. Fair Isle knitting is a combination of horizontal stripes and multicolored patterns that originated in Spain and traveled to Fair Isle on the Spanish Armada. Pattern motifs may be worked later in duplicate stitches or knitted in as a sweater is made. (Our directions are for knitted-in patterns.) When worked in easy-care yarns and versatile colors, these sweaters are right for almost any occasion. With casual daytime clothes they're great for a beach side outing, and with evening clothes they're right for dressy occasions. For how-to instructions, see page 214.

Sweaters like these are naturals for a fall family outing. Besides being easy to knit in simple knit and purl stitches, they pick up the rugged, earthy colors of this beautiful Virginia countryside. Features such as dropped shoulders and boat necks make them especially stylish and easy to make. You'll find the classic styling makes these sweaters a permanent addition to your family's fall wardrobe.

When you select yarns, choose something that is practical, such as the half wool, half acrylic yarn shown here. The wool and acrylic blend makes these sweaters warm and easy to care for. If you choose a different yarn, remember that colors, textures, and yardage requirements may vary. Check your gauge to make sure it matches the one given in the instructions, which begin on page 217.

Finishing and assembling these handmade sweaters is easy if you follow proper blocking instructions. Pin each piece to measurement to a padded surface, cover with a damp cloth, and let dry. Do not press. Then weave the seams together.

hat better reminder of our knitting heritage than the classic crew-neck sweater, a remarkably versatile exercise in design and technique that has been interpreted countless ways through the years. Even if your knitting repertoire consists of just two basic stitches, you can still make these comfortable outdoor sweaters. The knit-purl patterning is easy, even for beginning knitters.

To work these patterns, use two strands of yarn on size 15 knitting needles. You'll love the variegated pattern you get when you mix a solid color with a tweed. Notice the garter stitching along the neck, the cuffs, and the bottom edge of each sweater, which adds to the interesting texture.

Complete your sweater sets with coordinated caps sized for both kids and adults. Simply work several inches of ribbing along the bottom edges, then change to a straight stockinette stitch.

For instructions, see page 218.

Use two strands of yarn throughout when working these sweaters, one in a solid color and one in a tweed. This will result in a pleasing pattern. It also gives your sweaters extra body and weight for outdoor activities.

212

213

WOMAN'S PATTERNED PULLOVER
page 208

Instructions are for size Small (6-8); changes for Medium (10-12) and Large (14-16) are in parentheses.

Materials: Bucilla Softex Spectrum Shades (3-ounce balls) or a suitable substitute: Color A (medium blue)—2 (2, 3), Color B (light brown)—1 (2, 2), Color C (light blue)—2 (2, 3); Bucilla Softex (4-ounce balls) or a suitable substitute: 1 each Colors D (winter white), E (rose), and F (navy); sizes 4 and 6 knitting needles or sizes needed to obtain gauge below.

Gauge: St st using size 6 needles, 5 sts = 1 inch; 7 rows = 1 inch.

Knitting abbreviations: See the stitch glossary, page 371.

Finished measurements: Bust—33 (36½, 39½) inches. Width of back or front at underarm—16½ (18¼, 19¾) inches. Width of sleeves at underarm—11½ (12½, 13½) inches.

Instructions: (*Note:* Pattern motifs may be worked later in duplicate st or knitted in as given in directions. When knitting in, use a separate 2-yard strand of each color for each motif.)

Always bring color to be used from under color last used to prevent a hole. Carry yarn not in use loosely across wrong side, twisting with working yarn every 3 sts.

Back: With size 4 needles and A, cast on 83 (91, 99) sts. *Ribbing—Row 1* (wrong side): P 1, * k 1, p 1; rep from * across. *Row 2:* K 1, * p 1, k 1; rep from * across. Rep Rows 1 and 2 until 2 inches from beg, end with Row 1. Break A, join B.

Change to size 6 needles. Work in st st (k 1 row, p 1 row), working stripe pat of 4 rows each of B, C, A. Break A, join color C.

Heart band: Work 2 rows even. *Row 3:* K 1 (5, 9) C, * k 1 E, k 9 C; rep from * 8 times more, end last rep k 1 (5, 9) C.

Beg with chart Row 4 and working thru Row 12, follow chart from left to right for p rows and right to left for k rows.

Work stripe pat of 4 rows each of A, C, and B. Break B, join D.

Flower band: Work 3 rows even. *Row 4:* P 1 (5, 9) D, * p 1 F, p 9 D; rep

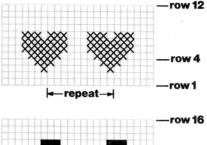
1 Square = 1 Stitch
WOMAN'S PATTERNED PULLOVER

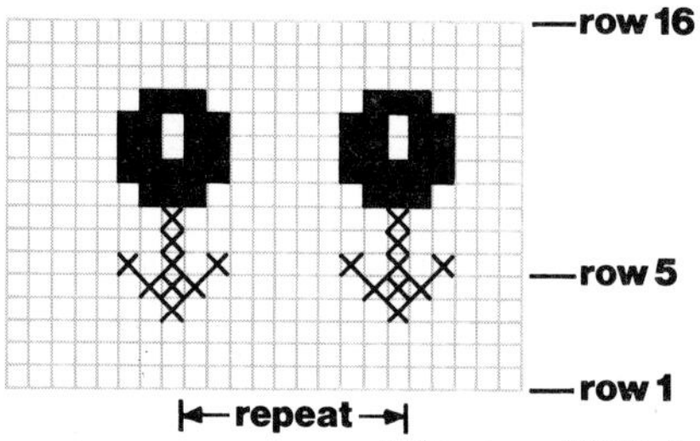

from * 8 times more, end last rep p 1 (5, 9) D.

Beg with chart Row 5, follow chart thru Row 16.

Work stripe pat of 4 rows each B, C, and A. Rep heart band once. Work 4 rows each of A and C. Mark last row. Break C, join B.

Shape armholes: Bind off 5 (6, 6) sts at beg of next 2 rows. *Next row—Dec row:* K 1, sl 1, k 1, psso, k to within last 3 sts, k 2 tog, k 1. Working in stripe pat of 4 rows each of D, B, C and A, rep Dec row every k row 2 (3, 4) times more; 67 (71, 77) sts. Break A, join D.

Flower band: Work 3 rows even. *Row 4:* P 3 (5, 8) D, * p 1 F, p 9 D. Rep from * 6 times more, end last rep p 3 (5, 8) D. Follow chart Rows 5 thru 16.

Work in stripe pat of 4 rows of A, C, and B until 6¾ (7¼, 7¾) inches above underarm marker, end with p row.

Shape shoulders: Bind off 11 (11, 12) sts at beg of next 2 rows, then 10 (11, 12) sts at beg of next 2 rows; 25 (27, 29) sts. Sl sts to holder for neck.

Front: Work same as back to beg of 2nd flower band: 67 (71, 77) sts. Work 3 rows even with D. *Row 4:* P 3 (5, 8) D, * p 1 F, p 9 D, p 1 F, p 39 D, p 1 F, p 9 D, p 1 F, p 3 (5, 8) D. Work 4 motifs as established, following chart, until 4¼ (4½, 4¾) inches above underarm marker, end with p row.

Shape neck: Next row: K in pat across first 26 (27, 29) sts, join 2nd ball of D, k next 15 (17, 19) sts and sl to

holder for neck, k in pat to end. Working each side separately in pat as for back, at each neck edge dec 1 st every row twice, then every other row 3 times; 21 (22, 24) sts. Work even until same length as back to beg of shoulder.

Shape shoulders: At each armhole edge bind off 11 (11, 12) sts once, then 10 (11, 12) sts once.

Sleeves: With size 4 needles and A, cast on 41 (47, 51) sts. Work ribbing same as back until 2 inches from beg, end with Row 1. Break A, join C. Change to size 6 needles.

(*Note:* Sleeve is planned for 17 inches in length to underarm; to adjust length, add or delete a stripe.) Working in st st, work 4 rows each of C and B. Break B, join D.

Flower band: Inc 1 st each side edge in first row of D and rep inc every 12th row 7 times more, work a total of 3 rows D. *Row 4:* P 1 (4, 6) D, * p 1 F, p 9 D; rep from * 4 times more, end last rep p 1 (4, 6) D.

Follow chart Rows 5 thru 16. Work 4 rows each of B, C, and A.

Heart band: Work 2 rows C; 47 (53, 57) sts. *Row 3:* K 3 (6, 8) C, * k 1 E, k 9 C; rep * 4 times more, end last rep k 3 (6, 8) C. Follow chart Rows 4 thru 12. Work 4 rows each A, C, and B.

Flower band: Work 3 rows D. *Row 4:* P 5 (8, 10) D, * p 1 F, p 9 D; rep from * 4 times more, end last rep p 5 (8, 10) D. Follow chart as before. Work 4 rows each of B, C, and A.

Heart band: Work 2 rows C; 55 (61, 65) sts. *Row 3:* K 7 (10, 2) C, * k 1 E, k 9 C; rep from * 4 (4, 5) times more, end last rep k 7 (10, 2) C. Follow chart as before. Work 4 rows each A and C; 57 (63, 67) sts. Break C, join B.

Shape cap: Bind off 5 (6, 6) sts at beg of next 2 rows. Dec 1 st each side edge every k row 16 (17, 18) times, working pat as follows: 2 rows more of B, 4 rows each of D, B, C, and A.

Flower band: Work 3 rows D; 25 (29, 33) sts. *Row 4:* P 12 (14, 16) D, p 1 F, p 12 (14, 16) D.

Continuing to dec every k row, follow chart for 1 motif, then work with D only until all dec are completed; 15 (17, 19) sts. Bind off.

Finishing: Sew left shoulder seam.

Neckband: Right side facing, with size 4 needles and A, k 25 (27, 29) sts from back holder, pick up 20 (22, 24) sts along left side edge, k 15 (17, 19) sts from front holder, pick up 21 (23, 25) sts along right side edge; 81 (89, 97) sts. Work ribbing as for back for 1 inch. Using size 6 needles, bind off loosely in ribbing.

Sew right shoulder and neckband seam. Matching stripes, sew side and sleeve seams, sew in sleeves.

CHILD'S STRIPED PULLOVER
page 208

Instructions are for size Small (4-6); changes for Medium (8-10) and Large (12-14) are in parentheses.

Materials: Bucilla Softex Spectrum Shades (3-ounce balls) or a suitable substitute: Color A (light blue)—1 (2, 2), Color B (medium blue)—1 (1, 2), Color E (light brown)—1 (1, 2); Bucilla Softex (4-ounce balls) or a suitable substitute: Color C (off-white)—1 (1, 1), Color D (navy)—1 (1, 1); sizes 4 and 6 knitting needles or sizes needed to obtain gauge below.

Gauge: St st using size 6 needles, 5 sts = 1 inch; 7 rows = 1 inch.

Knitting abbreviations: See the stitch glossary, page 371.

Finished measurements: Chest—25 (28, 33) inches. Width of front at underarm—12½ (14, 15½) inches. Width of sleeve at underarm—10 (11, 11½) inches.

Instructions: *Stripe pattern:* Work in st st (k 1 row, p 1 row) in the following color sequence: * 4 rows of B, 4 rows of C, 4 rows of D, 4 rows of E, 4 rows of A. Rep from *.

Back: With size 4 needles and A, cast on 63 (69, 77) sts. *Ribbing—Row 1* (wrong side): P 1, * k 1, p 1; rep from * across. *Row 2:* K 1, * p 1, k 1; rep from * across. Rep Rows 1 and 2 until 2½ inches from beg, end with Row 1. Break A, join B.

Change to size 6 needles. Work in stripe pat until the 3rd (4th, 4th) A (B, D) stripe is completed—approximately 11 (12, 13) inches from beg—or until desired length to underarm; end with a p row. Mark last row.

Shape armholes: Keeping pat, bind off 3 (4, 4) sts at beg of next 2 rows. *Dec row:* K 1, skp, k to within last 3 sts, k 2 tog, k 1. Rep dec row every k row 1 (1,

2) times more; 53 (57, 63) sts. Work until 5¼ (6, 6½) inches above underarm marker, end with p row.

Shape shoulder: Bind off 8 (9, 10) sts at beg of next 4 rows; 21 (21, 23) sts. Sl sts to holder for neck.

Front: Work same as back until 3 (3½, 3¾) inches above the underarm marker, end with p row.

Shape neck: Next row: K 20 (22, 24) sts, join 2nd ball of yarn, k next 13 (13, 15) sts and sl to holder for front neck, k 20 (22, 24) sts.

Working each side separately, at each neck edge dec 1 st every row twice, then every other row twice; 16 (18, 20) sts. Work even until same length as back to beg of shoulder.

Shape shoulders: At each armhole edge bind off 8 (9, 10) sts twice.

Sleeves—Note: Sleeves are planned so the striping matches body striping at the underarm. Sleeve length to underarm is about 10½ (11½, 14½) inches. To adjust length, beg stripe sequence with color before or after the color specified.

With size 4 needles and A, cast on 35 (37, 39) sts. Work ribbing same as back until 2½ inches from beg, end with Row 1. Break A, join D (B, E). Change to size 6 needles.

Work stripe pat beg with 4 rows D (B, E), and inc 1 st each side in 4th row, then every 6th row 7 (8, 9) times more; 51 (55, 59) sts. Work even until 3rd (4th, 4th) A (B, D) stripe is completed.

Shape cap: Keeping pat, bind off 3 (4, 4) sts at beg of next 2 rows. Dec 1 st each side edge every k row 9 (9, 10) times, then every row 7 (8, 8) times; 13 (13, 15) sts. Bind off.

Finishing: Sew left shoulder seam.

Neckband: Right side facing, with size 4 needles and A, k across 21 (21, 23) sts from back holder, pick up 19 (21, 21) sts along left side edge, k 13 (13, 15) sts from front holder, pick up 20 (22, 22) sts along right side edge; 73 (77, 81) sts.

Work ribbing the same as for the back for 1 inch. Using size 6 needles, bind off loosely in ribbing.

Sew right shoulder and neckband seam. Matching stripes, sew side and sleeve seams, sew in sleeves, easing in fullness at top.

MAN'S STRIPED V-NECK VEST
page 208

Instructions are for size Small (36-38); changes for Medium (40-42) and Large (44-46) are in parentheses.

Materials: Bucilla Softex Spectrum Shades (3-ounce balls) or a suitable substitute: Color A (medium brown) —2 (2, 3), Color B (beige)—2 (2, 2), Color C (rust)—2 (2, 3); Bucilla Softex (4-ounce balls) or a suitable substitute: Color D (dark brown)—1 (1, 2); sizes 4 and 6 knitting needles or sizes needed to obtain gauge below.

Gauge: St st using size 6 needles, 5 sts = 1 inch; 7 rows = 1 inch.

Knitting abbreviations: See the stitch glossary, page 371.

Finished measurements: Chest—38 (42, 46) inches. Width of back or front at underarm—19 (21, 23) inches.

Instructions: *Stripe pattern:* Work in st st (k 1 row, p 1 row) in the following color sequence: * 4 rows D, 4 rows A, 4 rows B, 4 rows C, 4 rows B, 4 rows A, 4 rows D, 10 rows C, 4 rows D, 4 rows A, 4 rows B, 4 rows A, 4 rows D, 10 rows A; rep from * for pat.

Back: With size 4 needles and A, cast on 95 (105, 115) sts. *Ribbing—Row 1* (wrong side): P 1, * k 1, p 1; rep from * across. *Row 2:* K 1, * p 1, k 1; rep from * across. Rep Rows 1 and 2 until 3 inches from beg, end with Row 1.

Change to size 6 needles. Work in st st and stripe pat, beg with 3 rows A, until 17 inches from beg or desired length, end with p row. Mark last row.

Shape armholes: Keeping pat, bind off 8 sts at beg of next 2 rows. *Dec row:* K 1, sl 1, k 1, psso, k to within last 3 sts, k 2 tog, k 1. Rep dec row every k row 5 times more; 67 (77, 87) sts. Work even until 10 (11, 12) inches above underarm marker, end with p row.

Shape shoulders: Bind off 9 (11, 13) sts at beg of next 4 rows; 31 (33, 35) sts. Sl sts to holder for back neck.

Front: Work same as back until 1 inch less than back to underarm, end with p row; 95 (105, 115) sts.

Divide V neck and shape armholes: K 47 (52, 57) sts, join 2nd ball of yarn, k 1 st and sl to pin for center front, k 47 (52, 57).

(Continued)

Working each side separately, at each neck edge dec 1 st every k row 7 (8, 9) times, then every other k row 8 times; at same time when same length as back to underarm, at each side edge bind off 8 sts once, then dec 1 st every k row 6 times; 18 (22, 26) sts each side. Work even until same length as back to beg of shoulder.

Shape shoulders: At each armhole edge, bind off 9 (11, 13) sts twice.

Finishing: Sew left shoulder seam.

Neckband: Right side facing, with size 4 needles and A, k 31 (33, 35) sts from back holder, pick up 63 (68, 73) sts along left side edge, place a marker on needle, k st from pin, pick 64 (69, 74) sts along right side edge; 159 (171, 183) sts. *Ribbing—Row 1:* Work same as back, p center st. *Row 2:* Work in k 1, p 1 ribbing to within 2 sts of marker, dec 1 st, k center st, dec 1 st, rib to end. Rep last 2 rows twice. Bind off loosely in ribbing.

Sew the right shoulder and neckband seam.

Armhole bands: Right side facing, with size 4 needles and A, pick up 135 (141, 147) sts evenly spaced along armhole edge. Work ribbing same as back for 7 rows. Bind off loosely in ribbing. Sew side seams, matching stripes.

CHILD'S PATTERNED PULLOVER
page 209

Instructions are for size Small (4-6); changes for Medium (8-10) and Large (12-14) are in parentheses.

Materials: Bucilla Softex Spectrum Shades (3-ounce balls) or a suitable substitute: Color A (medium red)—2 (2, 3), Color B (light blue)—1 (1, 2), Color C (light red)—1 (1, 2); Bucilla Softex (4-ounce balls) or a suitable substitute: Color D (winter white)—1 (1, 2); ½ ounce each colors E (rose) and F (navy) for pattern; sizes 4 and 6 knitting needles or sizes to obtain gauge below.

Gauge: St st using size 6 needles, 5 sts = 1 inch; 7 rows = 1 inch.

Knitting abbreviations: See the stitch glossary, page 371.

Finished measurements: Chest—25 (28, 33) inches. Width of front or back at underarm—12½ (14, 15½) inches.

Width of sleeves at underarm—10 (11, 12) inches. Length from lower edge to underarm—10¼ (11, 11) inches.

Instructions: *Stripe pattern:* Work in st st (k 1 row, p 1 row), working 4 rows of each color in the following sequence, except as noted for pat bands: C, B, A, C, A, B, C, *14 rows* D, C, A, B, D, B, A, C, *14 rows* D, C, A, B, C, A, C.

Note: Pattern motifs may be worked later in duplicate stitch, or knitted in as given in the directions. When knitting pattern in, use a separate 2-yard strand of each color for each motif.

To prevent a hole, always bring color to be used from under color last used. Carry yarn not in use loosely across wrong side, twisting every 3 sts with working yarn.

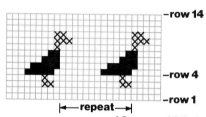

1 Square = 1 Stitch
CHILD'S PATTERNED PULLOVER

Back: With size 4 needles and A, cast on 63 (71, 77) sts. *Ribbing—Row 1* (wrong side): P 1, * k 1, p 1; rep from * across. *Row 2:* K 1, * p 1, k 1; rep from * across. Rep Rows 1 and 2 until 2½ inches from beg, end with Row 1. Change to size 6 needles.

Beg with 4 rows of B (C, C) at the start of the stripe sequence, work in stripe pat until the 2nd row of the first band of D is completed.

Pattern—Row 3: K 4 (8, 15) D, * k 2 F, k 11 D; rep from * 4 times more, end last rep k 5 (9, 16) D. Beg with chart Row 4, follow chart for pat, from left to right for p rows and right to left for k rows, thru Row 14. Continue in stripe pat until 2nd row of 4th A stripe is completed. Mark last row.

Shape armholes: Keeping pat, bind off 4 (5, 5) sts at beg of next 2 rows. *Dec row:* K 1, sl 1, k 1, psso, k to within last 3 sts, k 2 tog, k 1. Rep dec row every k row 2 (2, 3) times more; 49 (55, 59) sts. When 2 rows of next D band are completed, work pat as follows: *Row 3:* K 10 (13, 15) D, * k 2 F, k 11 D; rep from

* twice more, end k 11 (14, 15) D. Follow chart for pat as before.

Continue stripe pat until 5½ (6, 6½) inches above underarm marker, end with p row.

Shape shoulders: Keeping pat, bind off 5 (6, 6) sts at beg of next 4 rows, then 5 (5, 6) sts at beg of next 2 rows; 19 (21, 23) sts. Sl sts to holder for neck.

Front: Work same as back until 3 (3½, 3¾) inches above the underarm marker, end with p row; 49 (55, 59) sts.

Shape neck: Next row: K 19 (21, 22) sts, join 2nd ball of yarn, k next 11 (13, 15) sts and sl to holder for neck, k 19 (21, 22) sts.

Working each side separately in pat as for back, at each neck edge dec 1 st every row twice; every other row twice; 15 (17, 18) sts each side. Work even until same length as back to beg of shoulder, end with same row of stripe.

Shape shoulders: At each armhole edge, bind off 5 (6, 6) sts twice, then 5 (5, 6) sts once.

Sleeves: With size 4 needles and A, cast on 49 (53, 57) sts. Work ribbing same as back until 1 inch from beg, end with Row 1. Change to size 6 needles.

Beg with A (C, C) work stripe sequence that follows first pat band until 2nd row of 2nd A stripe is completed.

Shape cap: Continuing stripe pat, bind off 4 (5, 5) sts at beg of next 2 rows. Dec 1 st each side edge every k row 9 (10, 11) times, then every row 4 times, at same time, when 2 rows of D band are completed, work pat as follows: *Row 3:* K 1, sl 1, k 1, psso, k 13 (14, 16) D, k 2 F, with D k to within last 3 sts, k 2 tog, k 1. Work 1 pat, following chart.

When D band is completed, work stripe sequence same as body until dec is completed. Bind off 2 sts at beg of next 2 rows. Bind off rem 9 (9, 11) sts.

Finishing: Sew left shoulder seam.

Neckband: Right side facing, with size 4 needle and A, k 19 (21, 23) sts from back holder, pick up 20 (23, 26) sts along side neck edge, k 11 (13, 15) sts from front holder, pick up 21 (24, 27) sts along side edge; 71 (81, 91) sts. Work ribbing same as back for 1 inch. Using size 6 needle, bind off loosely in ribbing.

Sew the right shoulder and neckband seam. Matching stripes, sew side and sleeve seams; sew in sleeves.

WOMAN'S BOATNECK PULLOVER
page 210

Instructions are for size Small; the changes for size Medium are in parentheses. (See the note below on *finished measurements.*)

Materials: Bernat Icespun (2-ounce skeins) or a suitable substitute: 6 (7) skeins (Natural) Main Color (MC), 3 (4) skeins (Chestnut) First Contrasting Color (A), 2 (2) skeins (Copper) Second Contrasting Color (B), 1 (1) skein (Barley Mist) Third Contrasting Color (C). Knitting needles—Bernat-Aero, 1 pair each No. 8 and No. 10 or sizes needed to obtain gauge below.

Gauge: On larger needles—7 sts = 2 inches; 5 rows = 1 inch.

Knitting abbreviations: See the stitch glossary, page 371.

Finished measurements: Bust = 36 inches (40 inches); width across back or front at underarms = 18 inches (20 inches); width across sleeve at upper arm = 13½ inches (14½ inches).

Instructions: *Back:* With the smaller needles and A, cast on 64 (72) sts.

Ribbing—Row 1: K 1, * p 2, k 2; rep from * across, ending with p 2, k 1. *Row 2:* P 1, * k 2, p 2; rep from * across, ending with k 2, p 1. Rep these 2 rows until ribbing measures 2 inches, ending with Row 2.

Change to larger needles and MC and work in body pat as follows: *Row 1 (right side):* K across. *Row 2:* K 2, * p 4, k 4; rep from * across, ending p 4, k 2. Rep last 2 rows for body pat until total length (including ribbing) is 15 (15½) inches, ending with Row 2.

Change to B. Working in garter st (k each row), work stripe pat as follows, cutting and attaching colors as needed: K 2 rows B, 6 rows A, 2 rows B, 6 rows C, 2 rows B, 6 rows MC, 2 rows B, 6 rows A, 2 rows B, 6 rows MC, 2 rows B, 6 rows C, 2 rows B, 4 (10) rows A.

To shape shoulders: Continuing in garter st with A, bind off 5 (6) sts at beg of each of next 6 rows. Bind off rem 34 (36) sts for neck.

Mark each end of first row of second B stripe for beg of armholes.

Front: Work same as for back.

Sleeves: With smaller needles and A, cast on 28 (32) sts. Work in ribbing same as for back for 2½ inches, ending with Row 2 of ribbing.

Change to larger needles and B; working in garter st (k each row), work stripe pat as follows.

Increasing one st at each end of next row, then every 8th row 5 more times, k 2 rows B, 6 rows MC, 2 rows B, 6 rows C, 2 rows B, 6 rows A, 2 rows B, 6 rows MC, 2 rows B, 6 rows A, 2 rows B—40 (44) sts.

Change to MC and work in pat as follows: *Row 1:* K across.

Row 2: K 2 (4), * p 4, k 4; rep from * across, ending with p 4, k 2 (4).

Keeping continuity of body pat as established and working increased sts in pat, inc one st at each end of every 6th row 3 times; work even in pat over 46 (50) sts until the total length (including ribbing) is 13½ (14) inches, ending with a wrong-side row.

Work top portion of stripe pat in garter st as follows: K 2 rows B, 6 rows A, 2 rows B, 6 rows MC, 2 rows B, 6 rows C, 2 rows B. With B, bind off loosely.

Finishing: Pin each section to measurements on a padded surface, cover with a damp cloth, and allow to dry; do not press.

Weave shoulder seams. Weave top edges of sleeves to armhole sections, between markers, adjusting to fit. Weave side and sleeve seams.

CHILD'S BOATNECK PULLOVER
page 210

Instructions are for size Small. The changes for size Medium are given in parentheses. (See note below for *finished measurements.*)

Materials: Bernat Icespun (2-ounce skeins) or a suitable substitute—5 (6) skeins (Barley) Main Color (MC), 2 (3) skeins of (Chestnut) First Contrasting Color (A), 1 skein each of (Copper) Second Contrasting Color (B) and (Natural) Third Contrasting Color (C). Knitting needles—Bernat-Aero, 1 pair each No. 8 and No. 10 or any size needles to obtain gauge below.

Gauge: On larger needles—7 sts = 2 inches; 5 rows = 1 inch.

Knitting abbreviations: See the stitch glossary, page 371.

Finished measurements: Chest = 30 inches (34 inches); width across back or front at underarms = 15 inches (17 inches); width across sleeve at upper arm = 11 inches (12½ inches).

Instructions: *Back:* With the smaller needles and A, cast on 52 (60) sts. Work in ribbing as for Woman's Boatneck Pullover (above) until ribbing measures 1¾ (2) inches, ending with Row 2; inc one st at each end of last row—54 (62) sts.

Change to larger needles and MC and work in body pat as follows.

Row 1 (right side): K across. *Row 2:* K 1, * p 4, k 4; rep from * across, ending with p 4, k 1. Rep last 2 rows for body pat until length is 8 (9) inches above ribbing, ending with Row 2.

Working in garter st, work stripe pat as follows, cutting and attaching colors as needed.

Knit 2 rows B, * 6 rows A, 2 rows B, 6 rows C, 2 rows B, 6 rows MC, 2 rows B; rep from * once more. Change to A and k 2 (8) rows.

To shape shoulders: Continuing in garter st with A, bind off 5 (6) sts at beg of each of next 4 rows. Bind off rem 34 (38) sts for neck. Mark each end of first row of 3rd B stripe for beg of armholes.

Front: Work same as back.

Sleeves: With smaller needles and A, cast on 24 (28) sts. Work in ribbing as for back for 2 (2½) inches, ending with Row 2.

Change to larger needles and MC and work in body pat as follows.

Row 1 (right side): K across, inc one st at each end—26 (30) sts on needle.

Row 2: K 3 (1), * p 4, k 4; rep from * across, ending with p 4, k 3 (1).

Row 3: K across.

Rows 4, 5, 6: Rep Rows 2, 3, and 2.

Keeping continuity of pat as established and working increased sts in pat, inc one st at each end of 7th row, then every 6th row until total length (including ribbing) is 8 (9) inches, ending with a wrong-side row.

Change to B.

Continuing to inc one st at each end every 6th row until there are 38 (44) sts on needle (then work even to end), work stripe pat as follows: K 2 rows B, 6 rows A, 2 rows B, 6 rows MC, 2 rows

(Continued)

B, 6 rows C, 2 rows B. With B, bind off loosely.

Finishing: Follow the directions included in the how-to for the Woman's Boatneck Pullover (page 217).

MAN'S BOATNECK PULLOVER
page 211

Instructions are for size Medium. The changes for size Large are given in parentheses. (See note below for *finished measurements.*)

Materials: Bernat Icespun (2-ounce skeins) or a suitable substitute: 8 (10) skeins (Chestnut) Main Color (MC), 4 (5) skeins (Barley Mist) First Contrasting Color (A), 2 (3) skeins each of (Copper) Second Contrasting Color (B) and (Natural) Third Contrasting Color (C). Knitting needles—Bernat-Aero, 1 pair each No. 8 and No. 10 or any size needles to obtain gauge below.

Gauge: On larger needles—7 sts = 2 inches; 5 rows = 1 inch.

Knitting abbreviations: See the stitch glossary, page 371.

Finished measurements: Chest = 46 inches (50 inches); width across back or front at underarms = 23 inches (25 inches); width across sleeve at upper arm = 16½ inches (17½ inches).

Instructions: *Back:* With the smaller needles and A, cast on 80 (88) sts. *Ribbing*—*Row 1:* K 1, * p 2, k 2; rep from * across, ending with p 2, k 1. *Row 2:* P 1, * k 2, p 2; rep from * across, ending with k 2, p 1. Rep these 2 rows until ribbing measures 2½ (3) inches, ending with Row 2.

Change to larger needles and MC and work in body pat same as for Woman's Boatneck Pullover (see page 217) until the total length (including ribbing) is 16 (17) inches, ending with a wrong-side row.

Change to B. Working in garter st, work stripe pat as follows, cutting and attaching colors as needed: K 2 rows B, * 6 rows A, 2 rows B, 6 rows C, 2 rows B, 6 rows MC, 2 rows B; rep from * once more. Change to A and k 14 (20) rows A.

To shape shoulders: Continuing in garter st with A, bind off 7 (8) sts at beg of each of next 6 rows. Bind off rem 38 (40) sts for neck.

Mark each end of first row of second B stripe for beg of armholes.

Front: Work same as for back.

Sleeves: With smaller needles and A, cast on 40 (44) sts. Work in ribbing same as for back for 3 inches, ending with Row 2 of ribbing.

Change to larger needles and B; working in garter st, work stripe pat as follows: Increasing one st at each end of next row, then every 8th row 5 more times, k 2 rows B, 6 rows MC, 2 rows B, 6 rows C, 2 rows B, 6 rows A, 2 rows B, 6 rows C, 2 rows B, 6 rows A, 2 rows B—52 (56) sts.

Change to MC and work in body pat as follows: *Row 1:* K across. *Row 2:* K 4 (2), * p 4, k 4; rep from * across, ending with p 4, k 4 (2). Keeping continuity of body pat as established, working increased sts in pat, continue to inc one st at each end every 8th row (from last inc) 3 more times; then work even in body pat over 58 (62) sts until total length (including ribbing) is 15½ (16) inches, ending with a wrong-side row.

Work top portion of stripe pat as follows: K 2 rows B, 6 rows A, 2 rows B, 6 rows MC, 2 rows B, 6 rows C, 2 rows B. With B, bind off loosely.

Finishing: Same as for Woman's Boatneck Pullover.

WOMAN'S OR MAN'S CREWNECK PULLOVER
pages 212-213

Instructions are for size 36; changes for sizes 38, 42, and 44 are given in parentheses.

Materials: Bucilla Machine Washable Frisky (2-ounce skeins) or a suitable substitute: 6 (7, 7, 8) skeins of color No. 3, "Salt 'n' Pepper"; Bear Brand, Fleisher's, or Botany Machine Washable Winsom (2-ounce skein) or a suitable substitute: 4 (4, 5, 5) skeins of gray for woman's sweater, same amount of black for man's sweater; Size 15 knitting needles, or size needed to obtain gauge below.

Note: Use two strands of yarn throughout, one of tweed and one of solid color.

Gauge: 5 sts = 2 inches; 7 rows = 2 inches.

Knitting abbreviations: See the stitch glossary, page 371.

Blocking measurements: Chest = 35½ (38½, 42, 44½) inches; back at underarm = 17¾ (19¼, 20¾, 22¼) inches; sleeves at underarm = 16 (16, 18, 19) inches.

Instructions: *Back:* Cast on 44 (48, 52, 56) sts. K 6 rows for the garter st border.

Work st st (p 1 row, k 1 row) until 17 (17, 19, 19) inches from beg. End on wrong side. Mark for underarm. Continue to work st st until 8 (8, 9, 9½) inches above underarm marker.

Shoulders: Bind off 6 (6, 7, 7) sts at beg of next 2 rows, 6 (7, 7, 8) sts at beg of next 2 rows. Bind off rem 20 (22, 24, 26) sts.

Front: Work same as back until 4½ (4½, 5, 5) inches above underarm marker. End on wrong side.

Divide for right front: K 16 (18, 19, 21) sts and place on holder for left front. Bind off 12 (12, 14, 14) sts for front neck, k rem 16 (18, 19, 21) sts for right front. P 1 row.

Next row (dec row): K 1, s 1, k 1, psso, k to end; 15 (17, 18, 20) sts. Rep dec row every second row 3 (4, 4, 5) times more; 12 (13, 14, 15) sts. Work even until same length as back above underam marker. End on right side.

Shoulder: Bind off 6 (6, 7, 7) sts at beg of next row. K 1 row. Bind off rem 6 (7, 7, 8) sts.

Left front: From wrong side, sl sts from holder to needle, join yarn at neck edge, p to end.

Next row (dec row): K to within 3 sts of end, k 2 tog, k 1. Complete to correspond with right front, reversing the shaping.

Sleeves: Cast on 28 (28, 33, 35) sts. K 6 rows for garter st border. Work st st for 5 rows. End on wrong side.

Next row (inc row): K 1, inc 1 st in next st, k to within 2 sts of end, inc 1 st in next st, k 1. Rep inc row every 8th (8th, 10th, 10th) row 5 times more; 40 (40, 45, 47) sts.

Work even until 19 (19, 21, 21) inches, or desired length from beg. End on wrong side. Bind off. Sew left shoulder seam.

Neck edging: From right side, pick up and k 20 (20, 22, 24) sts of back neck, pick up and k 11 (11, 13, 15) sts on left front neck, 12 (12, 14, 14) sts of neck, 11 (11, 13, 15) sts on right front neck; 54 (54, 62, 68) sts. K 6 rows for garter st edging. Bind off loosely.

Finishing: Sew right shoulder seam. Sew sleeve and side seams. Sew in the sleeves, matching the underarms.

To block: Steam the sweater lightly, but do not press.

CHILD'S CREWNECK PULLOVER
page 213

Instructions are for sizes 6-8 (small); changes for sizes 10-12 (medium) are in parentheses.

Materials: Bucilla Machine Washable Frisky (2-ounce skein) or a suitable substitute: 4 (5) skeins of color No. 3, "Salt 'n' Pepper"; Bear Brand, Fleisher's, or Botany Machine Washable Winsom (2 ounce skeins) or a suitable substitute: 2 (3) skeins of white; Size 15 knitting needles or size needed to obtain gauge below.

Gauge: 5 sts = 2 inches; 7 rows = 2 inches.

Knitting abbreviations: See the stitch glossary, page 371.

Blocking measurements: Chest = 27 (31) inches; back at underarm = 13½ (15½) inches; sleeves at underarm = 13½ (14½) inches.

Instructions: *Back:* Cast on 34 (40) sts. Work as for back of woman's and man's pullover (above) until 12 inches from beg. End on wrong side.

Mark for underarms. Work even until 7 (7½) inches above underarm marker. End on wrong side.

Shoulders: Bind off 4 (5) sts at beg of next 2 rows, 5 (6) sts at beg of next 2 rows. Bind off rem 16 (18) sts.

Front: Cast on 34 (40) sts. Work as for back until 4 (4½) inches above underarm marker. End on wrong side.

Divide for right front: K 12 (15) sts and place on holder for left front. Bind off 10 sts for front neck, k rem 12 (15) sts for right front. P 1 row. Dec 1 st at neck edge on next row, then every second row 2 (3) times more: 9 (11) sts. Work even until the same length as the back above the underarm marker. End on right side.

Shoulder: Bind off 4 (5) sts at beg of next row. K 1 row, bind off 5 (6) sts at beg of next row.

Left front: From wrong side, sl sts from holder to needle, join yarn at neck edge and complete to correspond with right front, reversing shaping.

Sleeves: Cast on 24 (26) sts. K 6 rows for garter st cuff. Work st st for 3 rows. Inc 1 st each side of next row, then every 8th row 4 times more; 34 (36) sts. Work even until 13½ (14½) inches from beg. End on wrong side. Bind off. Sew left shoulder seam.

Neck edging: From right side, pick up and k 16 (18) sts of back neck, pick up and k 8 sts along left front neck, 10 sts on front neck; 8 sts along right front neck; 42 (44) sts. K 6 rows for garter st edging. Bind off loosely.

Finishing: Sew right shoulder seam. Sew sleeve and side seams. Sew in the sleeves, matching the underarms.

To block: Steam lightly, but do not press.

KNITTED CAPS
pages 212-213

Instructions are given for child's version; changes for women's and men's caps are in parentheses.

Materials: Bucilla Machine Washable Frisky (2-ounce skein) or a suitable substitute: 1 skein (1, 1) of color No. 3, "Salt 'n' Pepper"; Bear Brand, Fleisher's, or Botany Machine Washable Winsom (2-ounce skein) or a suitable substitute: 1 skein white, gray, *or* black (all sizes); Size 12 knitting needles; large-eyed crewel embroidery needle; 3 rings for markers.

Note: Throughout this project use two strands of yarn, one of tweed and one of solid color.

Instructions: Cast on 48 (56, 60) sts. Work k 1, p 1 ribbing for 5 (7½, 6) inches. Work even in st st 12 (10, 16) rows.

Dec rows: * Sl 1, k 1, psso, k 8 (10,11), k 2 tog, slide on marker, rep from * twice, k to within last 2 sts, k 2 tog (8 sts decreased). P 1 row.

Continue working in st st and dec in this manner—1 st at each end of row and 1 st before and after each marker on each k row until 16 (24, 28) sts rem.

P 1 row. K 2 tog across k row; 8 (12, 14) sts rem on needle. Set aside.

Cut yarn 30 inches long and thread it into a crewel needle. Run yarn through 8 (12,14) rem sts on the needle and pull up tightly; fasten and, with the right sides together, weave sts tog from top to bottom of cap. Fasten off and weave in yarn ends.

TIPS FOR BLOCKING AND ASSEMBLING KNITS

Fine finishing of your knitted sweaters can make the difference between garments that look handcrafted and those that simply look homemade. So take the time to carefully block and assemble any sweater that you make.

Blocking is shaping your knitted piece to fit body measurements. Unless pattern instructions indicate otherwise, block each sweater piece individually to smooth out wrinkles and to simplify sewing the pieces together. Occasionally, a pattern will call for another blocking after the sweater is assembled.

Since different yarns react differently to blocking procedures, yarn labels usually carry blocking instructions. If the label does not give blocking directions, dampen the sweater pieces with cool water and lay them on a folded sheet or towel. Gently shape them to the dimensions given in the pattern. Cover the pieces with a damp towel and allow them to dry.

Assemble your garment by weaving, overcasting, backstitching, or crocheting the seams. Use the method that is best suited to the yarn and the pattern.

To weave seams together, hold the wrong sides adjacent; draw matching stitches together with yarn and needle. To overcast seams, hold right sides together; sew with whipstitches. Reserve this method for sewing ribbed cuffs or attaching collars.

Backstitching works best for curved seams and tapered shoulder seams. Hold right sides together and make running stitches with a backstitch. If the yarn is nubby or tweedy, any of these methods may result in bumpy seams. If so, hold right sides together and slip-stitch crochet the seams.

Always use matching yarn for assembling. If the yarn is even-textured, and too thick for sewing seams, split it and use half the plies.

219

COUNTRY WEAR AND WARMERS

Folkwear and Aprons

Hale and hardy ethnic fashions like these are never out of style because they celebrate the magnificent treasury of our folk art heritage. The warmers shown here evoke the memory of another era, and the care, skill, and quality invested in these projects give them a timeless charm. Inspired by Swedish heirlooms, these crocheted and embroidered warmers are a rich source of design motifs. Although they're made with today's yarns, they still retain old country character. To make the adult-size warmer, use a No. 1 steel crochet hook and choose acrylic yarns in rich, robust colors. The child's warmer is stitched from brown wool fabric and then embroidered, using Persian wool yarn and a variety of different stitches. Complete instructions begin on page 224.

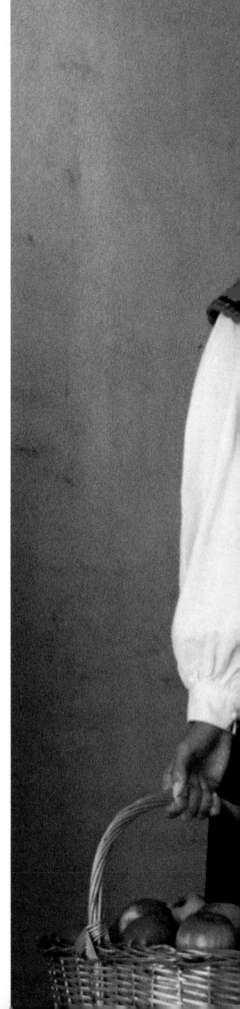

S traight from the prairie come these three apron designs, reflecting a sense of history and a pride in the past.

To wear these designs today is to remember a simpler time in America's past. Whether you choose the striped tabard knitted with stockinette and garter stitches (below), the antique-looking apron embroidered with satin and outline stitches (right), or our lacy, crocheted apron (opposite), you'll be perfectly suited for any casual occasion. These three country styles blend old-fashioned charm with up-to-date fashion.

See page 226 for instructions.

The embroidered apron above is actually an old-timer that you can easily reproduce. Modern-day thread and material, and basic embroidery techniques of satin and outline stitching will produce the same good country looks.

SWEDISH WARMER
page 221

Materials: Coats & Clark Red Heart 3-ply Sock and Sweater yarn (2-ounce skeins) or a suitable substitute: 3 skeins main color (MC), 1 skein each of A, B, C, and D; size 1 steel crochet hook, or size to obtain gauge given below.

Gauge: 8 dc = 1 inch; 7 rows = 2 inches.

For crochet abbreviations and stitch diagrams, see pages 371 and 373.

Instructions: *Foundation:* At long edge, with MC, ch 674 to measure 86 inches (mark every 50th ch with a small safety pin for easier counting). Dc in 4th ch from hook, dc in each ch across—672 dc, counting beg ch-3 as 1 dc. Fasten off. (*Note:* All rows are worked on right side of previous row. Every dc is worked in back lp of each st. Fasten off at end of every row.)

Row 1: Sk first 332 dc, attach MC to *back* lp of next dc, ch 1, sc in same st where yarn was attached, dc in 2 dc, 2 dc in next dc, ch 1 for center st, 2 dc in next dc, dc in 2 dc, sc in next dc.

Row 2: Attach MC to *back* lp of 3rd ch (on foundation) before beg of last row; ch 1, sc in same dc, dc in 2 dc on foundation, dc in 5 sts of last row, 3 dc, in ch-1 sp, dc in 5 sts of last row, dc in 2 dc on foundation, sc in next dc—19 sts.

Row 3: Attach MC as for Row 2; ch 1, sc in same dc, dc in 2 dc on foundation, dc in each st to within center dc of 3-dc grp, 2 dc in center st; *ch 4, sc in 2nd ch from hook, sc in 2 ch, sc in top of last dc made*—arm made; dc in same place as last 2 dc to complete a center 3-dc grp, dc in each rem st of last row, dc in 2 dc on foundation, sc in next st.

Row 4: Work as for last row to within center dc of 3-dc grp, dc in center dc; working along opposite side of ch of arm, make dc in 2 ch, 2 dc in end sc, ch 4 and complete an arm, make dc in 2 ch, 2 dc in end sc, ch 4 and complete an arm, dc in same place as last 2 dc to complete a center 3-dc grp, dc in next 3 sc; complete as for last row. *Row 5:* Work same as for Row 4. *Rows 6-9:* Attach MC to 12th dc before beg of last row, ch 1, sc in same dc, dc in 11 dc, work as for 4th row ending with dc in 11 dc of foundation, sc in next dc.

Row 10: Attach MC to 67th dc be-

fore beg of last row, ch 1, sc in same dc, * holding A along top of last row and working over it in order to conceal it, with MC make dc in 11 dc, *yo, draw up a lp in next st, yo, and draw through 2 lps on hook, drop MC, pick up A, draw through rem 2 lps on hook*—color changed in last st of grp; with A, *yo, draw up a lp in next st, yo, draw through 2 lps, drop A, pick up MC, draw through rem 2 lps on hook*—color changed again. Rep from * 11 times more; drop A to back of work, mark with safety pin the dc directly opposite last A dc made; with MC, dc in each st to center dc of 3-dc grp, dc in center dc, dc in 2 ch, 2 dc in end sc, ch 8, sc in 2nd ch from hook, sc in 6 ch, sc in top of last dc made, dc in same place as last 2 dc, dc in each st to within 1 st of pin-marked st, change color in next st, make an A dc in pin-marked st, change to MC. Work rem of row to correspond with beg of row.

Row 11: Attach MC to 12th dc before beg of last row, ch 1, sc in same dc; carrying A as before, dc in each st to within next A dc, changing to A in last st, * changing color as before, make 2 A dc, 2 MC dc, 1 A dc, 8 MC dc. Rep from * 10 times more, ending with 2 A, 2 MC, 1 A; drop A to back, with MC dc in each st to end sc of arm, 2 dc in end sc, ch 8, complete arm same as for last row, dc in each st to within 4 sts of next A dc changing color in last dc; then reversing pat, ** work 1 A, 2 MC, 2 A, 8 MC. Rep from **, ending same as for beg.

Row 12: Work same as for 11th row to within first A dc, * 3 A, 1 MC, 2 A, 2 MC, 1 A, 4 MC. Rep from * 10 times more, ending with 3 A, 1 MC, 2 A; work MC dc in each st to end sc of arm, 2 dc in end sc, ch 4, complete arm, dc in each st to 1 st before next A dc; then reversing pat, ** work 2 A, 1 MC, 3 A, 4 MC, 1 A, 2 MC. Rep from **, ending same as for beg.

Row 13: Work same as for 11th row to within first A dc, * 6 A, 1 MC, 3 A, 3 MC. Rep from * 11 times more, ending with MC dc in each st to end sc of arm; work same as for last row to 4 sts before next A dc, ** 3 A, 1 MC, 6 A, 3 MC. Rep from ** ending same as for beg.

Row 14: Work same as for 11th row

to first A dc, * 3 A, 2 MC, 4 A, 4 MC. Rep from * 11 times; working over B and A, with MC make 4 dc changing directly to B in last dc, 1 B, mark the dc directly opposite the B dc; working over both colors with MC, work as for last row to and across arm to marked st; with B dc in marked st, with MC, dc in each st, dc in first A dc. Break off B, ** 4 A, 2 MC, 3 A, 4 MC. Rep from **, ending same as for beg.

Row 15: Omitting A, work as for 11th row to first B dc, 2 B, 1 MC, 1 B, work as before to and across arm to 3 sts before next B dc; 1 B, 1 MC, 2 B. Break off B after 6th dc; complete row, ending same as for beg.

Row 16: Work same as for last row to first B dc; 3 B, 1 MC, 2 B; work same as for last row, reversing B pat on other side of point. Fasten off B.

Row 17: Work same as for last row until there are 11 dc, working over C dc in 5 sts changing to C, * 1 C, 12 MC. Rep from * 17 times. Fasten off C; with MC working over B, dc to first B dc; 6 B, 1 MC, 3 B, 1 MC, 1 B; work around point as for last row; complete row, reversing B pat on the other side of the point. Fasten off B; mark the st opposite last C dc, with MC dc to marked st, ** C dc in next st, 12 MC. Rep from ** ending same as for beg.

Row 18: Carrying C work same as for 11th row to first C dc, * 2 C, 2 MC, 1 C, 8 MC. Rep from *17 times. Fasten off C; carrying B and D, with MC make dc to first B dc; 8 B, 2 D, 4 B, 1 MC, 1 B; work around point as for last row reversing pats on other side and ending same as for beg. *Row 19:* Work same as for last row to first C dc, * 3 C, 1 MC, 2 C, 2 MC, 1 C, 4 MC. Rep from * 17 times. Fasten off C. Carrying B and D dc to 2nd B dc; 5 B, 2 D, 2 MC, 2 D, 6 B, 1 MC, 1 B; make point as before and complete row reversing pats and ending same as for beg.

Row 20: Work same as for last row to first C dc, *6 C, 1 MC, 3 C, 3 MC. Rep from * 17 times. Fasten off C; carrying B and D, dc to 2nd B dc; 4 B, 2 D, 2 MC, 2 D, 8 B, 1 MC, 1 B; make point, complete row reversing pats and ending same as for beg.

Row 21: Work same as for last row to first C dc; * 3 C, 2 MC, 4 C, 4 MC. Rep from * 17 times. Fasten off C; carrying B and D, dc to 2nd B dc; 5 B, 2

D, 4 B, 2 MC, 7 B, 1 MC, 1 B; make point, complete same as for last row.

Row 22: Work same as for last row to first B dc; 9 B, 2 MC, 7 B, 2 MC, 5 B, 1 MC, 1 B; make point and finish same as for last row.

Row 23: With MC, work same as for last row to end sc of arm at point; 2 dc in end sc, ch 11, sc in 2nd ch from hook, sc in 9 ch, sc in top of last dc made, complete row same as for other side.

Row 24: Attach C to top of ch-3 at beg of foundation, ch 3, working over D make 3 C, * 3 D, 4 C. Rep from * to end sc at point; keeping to pat make 5 dc in end sc, continue in pat along other side and in rem sts of foundation ending with 4 C. (*Note:* Inc or dec as necessary to retain pat.) Fasten off.

Row 25: Attach MC in top of ch-3 of last row, ch 3, working over B make 5 MC, * 1 B, 1 MC, 3 B, 1 MC, 1 B, 12 MC. Rep from * to last st before 5-dc grp at point in any stitch of rep; with MC dc in 2 dc, 2 dc in center dc, ch 4, complete arm, dc in center dc, dc in 2 dc; complete row reversing pat.

Row 26: Sk first pat B, attach MC to 6th dc before next B dc; working over B, with MC sc in same place, dc to 1 st before next B dc; * 4 B, 1 MC, 4 B, 10 MC. Rep from * to end sc of arm at point; with B, 2 dc in end sc, ch 4, complete arm, dc in same end sc; complete row reversing pat and ending same as for beg.

Row 27: Attach MC, work same as for last row to 1 st before first B dc on 2nd pat, * 4 B, 1 MC, 1 B, 1 MC, 4 B, 8 MC. Rep from * to end sc of arm; with MC, 2 dc in end sc, ch 4, complete arm, dc in same end sc; complete row, reversing pat and ending same as for beg.

Row 28: Work same as for Row 26 to end sc of arm, 3 MC dc in end sc; complete row reversing pat and ending same as for beg.

Row 29: Attach MC, work same as for last row to 2nd B dc on next pat. Rep from * on Row 25 to 1 st before 3-dc grp at point; with B, dc in next dc, 2 dc in next dc; with MC, 3 dc in center dc; with B, 2 dc in next dc, dc in next dc; complete row as before.

Row 30: Attach D to end of beg ch where foundation was made, ch 3, work over C make 3 D over end st of foundation, 4 C over end st of next row,

3 D over end st of next row; * working in sts of previous row, make 4 C, 3 D. Rep from * to st before the 9-dc point; keeping in pat (dc in next dc, 2 dc in next dc) 4 times; dc in next dc. Continue pat across ending same as for beg.

Row 31: Attach MC to top of ch-3 at beg of last row, (2 dc in next dc, dc in next dc) 3 times; dc in each st inc 5 sts across point, ending same as for beg.
Edging: Row 1: Attach C same as for last row, ch 3, working over B and D dc where yarn was attached, (1 D in next st, 2 C in next st, 1 B in next st, 2 C in next st) twice; * dc in each st in following order: 1 D, 2 C, 1 B, 2 C. Rep from * making 3 dc in center st of point and ending same as for beg; then work in pat along opposite side to beg ch of foundation; join with sl st to top of beg ch-3.

Rnd 2: Attach B to top of first C dc on last rnd, ch 3, dc in next dc, sc in next 2 dc, * inc as necessary at both ends and point, dc in 4 dc, sc in 2 dc. Rep from * around, ending with dc in last 2 dc. Fasten off.

Tie (make 2): Cut two 45-inch-long strands of each color. Twist all the strands together tightly in one direction; fold them in half and twist them in the opposite direction. Tie an overhand knot about 1½ inches from the free ends. Trim the strands to form a tassel. Sew a tie to the center of each end of the warmer.

To block, lay warmer out flat. Cover with a wet towel and allow to dry.

CHILD'S WARMER
page 221

Fits girls sizes 5-10.

Materials: ⅔ yard of brown wool fabric; ⅔ yard lining fabric; 3-ply Persian wool (8.8-yard skeins) or a suitable substitute in the following amounts and colors: 2 skeins each of red, purple, and gold, and 1 skein of aqua; 3⅔ yards of red ½-inch-wide purchased trim; crewel needle; tailor's chalk or dressmaker's carbon paper.

For abbreviations, see page 371.

Instructions: Enlarge the diagram (right) and make a pattern on brown

wrapping paper. Fold the fabric in half lengthwise; the fold should be along the true grain of the fabric. Place the pattern on the fold of the fabric; pin. Cut out the V-shaped body of the scarf, adding ½ inch all around edges (except at fold) for the seam allowance. Cut a piece of lining fabric to match.

Using tailor's chalk or dressmaker's carbon, lightly sketch each line of embroidery on the right side of the fabric. You need not sketch each stitch, just mark the lines each series of stitches will follow. Sketch circles approximately 1¼ inches in diameter, spaced about 1¼ inches apart, as general stitching guides for red flowers.

Work the design in the stitches indicated on the pattern. Use two strands of yarn for all embroidery.

Work flowers in red (freehand clusters composed of eight detached chain stitches each). Work checkered chain-stitched borders in gold and purple. Work the single line of chain stitches in aqua. Work the line of spaced buttonhole stitches in purple.

When the embroidery is complete, steam press the entire scarf.

(Continued)

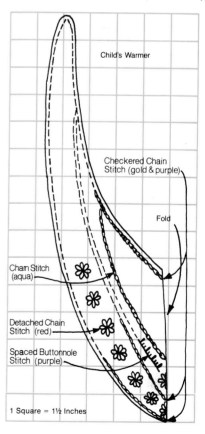

Child's Warmer

Checkered Chain Stitch (gold & purple)

Fold

Chain Stitch (aqua)

Detached Chain Stitch (red)

Spaced Buttonhole Stitch (purple)

1 Square = 1½ Inches

Baste the crocheted edging in place ½ inch from the edge of the scarf, with the edging facing the body of the scarf. With right sides together, pin the backing to the embroidered piece. Machine-stitch ½ inch from the edge, leaving 6 inches open at the point of the scarf for turning. Turn the scarf right side out, steam press again, and slip-stitch the opening closed.

Yarn ties (make two): For each string, cut 2 strands of each color 45 inches long. Twist all strands together tightly in one direction. Fold the twisted strand in half and twist in the opposite direction. Tie an overhand knot at the loose ends about ½ inch from the end. Trim yarn ends evenly to form a tassel.

Tack one tie to the center of each end of the scarf.

KNITTED APRON
page 222

One size fits all.

Materials: Tahki Creole Cotton 100-percent cotton yarn (100-gram skeins) or a suitable substitute in the following colors and amounts: 4 skeins light blue (A), 1 skein lavender (B), 1 skein purple (C); Size 9 knitting needles, or size to obtain gauge given below; Size J aluminum crochet hook; stitch holder; ¾-inch-wide ribbon: 2 yards for waist ties and 3 yards for bodice trim and neck ties.

Gauge: 4 sts = 1 inch, 5 rows = 1 inch.

For knitting abbreviations, see page 371.

Instructions: *Pocket*—With A, cast on 18 sts. Work even in st st (k one row, p one row) for 15 rows. Break off and sl sts onto a holder.

Apron: Beg at hem and with A, cast on 70 sts. Work even in st st for 6 rows. Change to B, and work 3 rows in st st. Change to A, and work 6 rows in st st. Change to C, and work 3 rows in st st. These 18 rows constitute stripe pat. Rep pat for about 23½ inches, ending with any right side (knit) row in the 6-row band of color A.

Pocket insert: P first 9 sts, cast off next 18 sts, p to end. *Next row:* K 43, sl pocket lining from the holder to the right-hand needle, k 9—70 sts. Work

even until total length measures about 28 inches, or length desired to waist, ending with the fifth row of a 6-row band of color A.

Waistband dec row: * Work 2 sts tog. Rep from * across—35 sts. Work 10 rows even in color A. For the next narrow stripe, rep the color of the last one made before waistband, and then continue in stripe pat as established until total length from dec row measures 10¾ inches. Cast off.

Crochet border: With A and one strand of yarn, sc 2 rnds along outer edge, making 3 sc in each corner so that work lies flat. Finish off, and run in all yarn ends.

To block the apron, dampen it thoroughly and pin it out to shape on a padded surface. Allow to dry.

Finishing: Stitch a piece of ribbon along the top of the apron bodice. Cut the remaining ribbon trim for the bodice and neckline in half and stitch one piece to each side of the bodice, leaving the long ends for neck ties. Be sure to cover raw edges of ribbon trim along the top of the apron bodice. Fold under and stitch the ends of the neck ties.

Center the ribbon trim on the waistline, leaving the same amount of excess ribbon at each side. Stitch it in place. Fold under and stitch ends of waist ties.

EMBROIDERED APRON
page 222

Materials: 1½ yards of 36-inch-wide natural-colored linen; yellow, gold, and pink pearl cotton thread; embroidery needle; ½-inch-diameter button.

Instructions: Cut a 19x54-inch piece of linen for the apron and two 4x33-inch pieces of linen for the sash (see patterns, above). Cut a pocket from the remaining fabric. Turn under the raw edges and stitch 1-inch hems along the two long edges of the apron.

With right sides facing, stitch the two sash pieces together, using a 1-inch seam and leaving a 6-inch opening in the center of one long edge. Trim the seams and clip the corners and carefully turn the sash right side out.

Gather and pleat one of the apron's 17-inch edges until it measures 6 inches

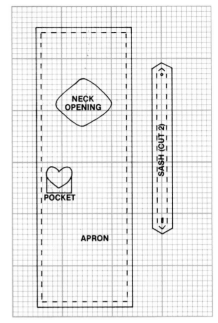

1 SQUARE = 1 INCH

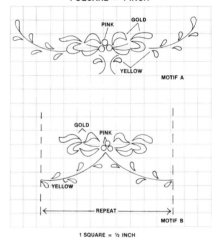

1 SQUARE = ½ INCH

wide. Tuck 1 inch of this gathered edge inside the 6-inch opening in the sash; pin and stitch.

Turn up a 1-inch hem in the bottom edge of the apron and embroider a row of gold feather stitches 1 inch above the bottom, securing the hem.

Center motif B 1 inch above the featherstitching and embroider the design, using outline and satin stitches. Repeat the motif two more times to finish the row.

Using gold pearl cotton thread, embroider a row of buttonhole stitches around the neck opening, making a scalloped edge. Cut away the fabric inside the stitching to make the neck opening (see the photograph). Embroider motif A on the front of the apron below the scalloped edge.

Embroider a heart on the pocket, making gold buttonhole stitches across the top and featherstitches along the two sides. Turn up ½-inch hems along three sides of the pocket and stitch them in place.

Embroider the sash with an outline of gold featherstitches. Sew a button in place at one end of the sash and hand- or machine-stitch a buttonhole at the other end.

CROCHETED APRON
page 223

Finished length measures 18 inches.

Materials: J. & P. Coats Knit-Cro-Sheen (400-yard balls) or a suitable substitute: 2 balls of white, 1 ball of blue; Size 8 steel crochet hook, or size to obtain gauge given below.

Gauge: Width of Pattern 1 = 3 inches; 7 rows of Pattern 1 = 2 inches.

For crochet abbreviations and diagrams, see pages 371 and 373.

Instructions: *Apron waistband and ties:* With white, ch 22. *Row 1:* Dc in 4th ch from hook, dc in next ch, (ch 2, sk 2 ch, dc in next dc) 5 times; dc in last 2 ch; ch 3, turn.

Row 2: Sk first dc, dc in next 2 dc, (ch 2, dc in next dc) twice; 2 dc in ch-2 sp, dc in next dc, (ch 2, dc in next dc) twice; dc in next dc and top of turning ch; ch 3, turn.

Row 3: Sk first dc, dc in next 2 dc, ch 2, dc in next dc, 2 dc in ch-2 sp, dc in next dc, ch 2, sk 2 dc, dc in next dc, 2 dc in ch-2 sp, dc in next dc, ch 2, dc in each of next 2 dc and top of turning ch; ch 3, turn.

Row 4: Sk first dc, dc in next 2 dc, ch 2, dc in next dc, ch 2, sk 2 dc, dc in next dc, 2 dc in ch-2 sp, dc in next dc, ch 2, sk 2 dc, dc in next dc, ch 2, dc in next 2 dc and top of turning ch; ch 3, turn.

Row 5: Sk first dc, dc in next 2 dc, (ch 2, dc in next dc) twice; ch 2, sk 2 dc, dc in next dc, (ch 2, dc in next dc) twice; dc in next dc and top of turning ch; ch 3, turn.

Rep Rows 2-5 72 times, or for desired length. Fasten off.

Apron skirt: (*Note:* Apron skirt is made of 9 sections combined to make 1 row across. The instructions [*below*] refer to the sections as *Patterns,* and although they may be repeated across a row, they are referred to as patterns for clarity.)

Row 1, Pattern 1: Join white thread in the 108th row of the waistband section around the turning ch-3 bar. Ch 3 (to count as first dc), in same sp work *2 dc, ch 2, 3 dc*—shell made; (sk next row of tie, in next turning ch-3 sp work *dc, ch 3, dc*—V-st made; sk row, work shell of 3 dc, ch 2, 3 dc in next row) twice; sk next row; V-st in next row. *Pattern 2:* Ch 3, sk next row, sc in next row, ch 3. *Pattern 3:* Rep bet ( )'s of Pat 1 twice. *Pattern 4:* Sk next row, in next row work 2 dc, ch 2, 2 dc, place marker in ch-2 sp and carry from row to row. (*Note:* It is in this pattern, *increasing shell,* that the work increases—rem of pats are worked even.) *Pattern 5:* Rep bet ( )'s of Pat 1 three times. *Pattern 6:* Rep Pat 4. *Pattern 7:* (Sk next row, shell in next row, sk row, V-st in next row) twice. *Pattern 8:* Rep Pat 2. *Pattern 9:* Rep bet ( )'s of Pat 7 three times; ch 3, turn.

Row 2, Pattern 1: In ch-3 sp of V-st work 3 dc, ch 2, 3 dc—shell over V-st made; *work V-st in ch-2 sp of shell*—V-st over shell made; (shell over V-st, V-st over shell) twice. *Pattern 2:* Ch 5 (for Row 1 of lacet st), sk next 2 ch-3 lps. *Pattern 3:* (Shell over V-st, V-st over shell) twice. *Pattern 4:* Sk the first dc of the *next* shell grp, dc in next dc; in ch-2 sp work 2 dc, ch 2, 2 dc, dc in next dc, carry marker (see instructions for *increasing shell,* Rows 4-53). *Pattern 5:* (V-st over shell, shell over V-st) 3 times. *Pattern 6:* Rep Pat 4. *Pattern 7:* (V-st over shell, shell over V-st) 2 times. *Pattern 8:* Ch 5, sk next 2 ch-3 lps. *Pattern 9:* (Shell over V-st, V-st over shell) 3 times; ch 3, turn.

Row 3, Pattern 1: (Shell over V-st, V-st over shell) 3 times. *Pattern 2:* Ch 3, sc in 3rd ch of ch-5 lp, ch 3 (for Row 2 of lacet st). *Pattern 3:* (V-st over shell, shell over V-st) twice. *Pattern 4:* Sk first dc of next shell, dc in each of next 2 dc; in ch-2 sp of shell work dc, ch 2, dc; dc in each of next 2 dc (see instructions for *increasing shell,* Rows 4-53). *Pattern 5:* (V-st over shell, shell over V-st) 3 times. *Pattern 6:* Rep Pat 4. *Pattern 7:* (Shell over V-st, V-st over shell) twice. *Pattern 8:* Rep Pat 2. *Pattern 9:* (Shell over V-st, V-st over shell) 3 times; ch 3, turn.

Rep Rows 2 and 3 for apron skirt for all pats except 4 and 6. The following instructions apply for Patterns 4 and 6: *Increasing Shell Pattern (*Rows 4-53): *Row 4:* Sk the first dc of the increasing shell grp, dc in each of next 2 dc; in ch-2 sp work dc, ch 2, dc; dc in each of next 2 dc. *Row 5:* Sk first dc of the increasing shell grp, dc in each dc to the ch-2 sp; in ch-2 sp work 2 ch, ch 2, 2 dc; dc in each dc except the last dc of the grp. (*Note:* Inc row has just been completed.) *Row 6:* Sk first dc of the increasing shell grp, dc in each dc to the ch-2 sp; in ch-2 sp work dc, ch 2, dc; dc in each dc of the shell grp except the last one. *Rows 7-8:* Rep Row 6.

Rep Rows 5-8 for this pat throughout the apron skirt. There will be 32 dc in each shell grp when apron skirt is completed.

Work: 19 rows in white,
2 rows in blue,
8 rows in white,
3 rows in blue,
8 rows in white,
4 rows in blue,
9 rows in white. Fasten off.

Waistband edgings: (*Note:* This edging is worked across top of waistband only, not ties.) Attach thread in top edge of waistband, opposite row apron skirt began, * ch 3, sl st in 3rd ch from hook—picot made; ch 1, sc in next row. Rep from * until edging across waistband is completed. Fasten off.

Apron skirt: Attach thread in same sp where V-st is made on first row of apron skirt, *ch 3, sc around turning ch of next shell, ch 3, sc in same sp. Rep from * along side of apron to bottom edge, then work similarly, except working sc in each ch-2 sp of shell and in each ch-3 sp of V-sts. Work other side as established.

Care of hand-crocheted items: Fine crocheted and knitted pieces should be hand washed in lukewarm water and a mild detergent. Rinse them thoroughly in cold water.

To block, lay out work on a flat surface that is large enough to accommodate the piece. Pad the surface with bath towels. Using rustproof pins, gently pull and stretch piece to shape, pinning in place as you go. Let dry away from heat and light. If you desire, add starch or other stiffening as you rinse the article.

227

CHILDREN'S CORNER
Toys and Dolls

ou won't find a happier home than this one, filled with doll-size country crafts and collectibles. Handmade Early American-style furniture fills this playroom. The reproduction pieces include a settle, hutch, dry sink, and cradle. Craft each of the furnishings from pine, using a jigsaw to cut and shape the wood. For a dark, rich wood tone, use brown stain and then varnish. The country-clad dolls are crafted from a variety of different materials, including fabric, yarn, papier-mâché, and acrylic paints. Our pioneer ancestors knew the virtue of saving every scrap of fabric and the joy of crafting the fabric into small quilts for their children's dolls. This mini-postage-stamp quilt, made of one-inch squares, is just the right size to nestle inside the cradle. See page 236 for complete instructions.

From such humble beginnings as burlap and buckskin, you can create these beguiling country-lass dolls. Everything you use to make these dolls, including calico fabric, felt, straw bonnets, and rope, will add to their charm.

Begin with wire supports fashioned from coat hangers, then add the one-piece skirts, blouses, cloaks, and shawls. Individualize each doll with your own touches, such as the tiny wooden bucket for the milkmaid, the box of wares for the peddler, the crook for the shepherdess, and the straw flowers for the flower girl. Remember to use miniature laces and trims and small print fabrics to keep everything in scale.

Fashion farm animals from leftover pieces of leather and rope.

Complete how-to instructions begin on page 238.

To make the doll hair, cut 20-inch lengths of rope and unravel the strands. Machine-stitch a "part" down the center of the strands and glue a wig in place to the top of each doll's head. Shape and style the strands into braids, pigtails, or twists.

231

Growing up country usually meant lots of plain and simple childhood toys, mostly crafted by hand from the simplest materials around. Fabric and yarn dolls like those shown here have always been favorites, from the mountains of Kentucky to the plains of Kansas.

You'll be enchanted by the 10 heritage dolls shown at right. Each is a distinctive personality from the pioneer era.

Fashioned from plain muslin fabric, the dolls appeal to kids and adults alike. Your children will enjoy decorating these delightful characters with crayons. Or, use a brush and different colors of fabric paint for one-of-a-kind touches.

When painting fabric, leave a sliver of space between each color to prevent paints from "bleeding." Also, let each painted area dry thoroughly before painting an adjacent area a different color.

By using crayons or paints on the dolls, you'll create a soft background for the finishing touch: delicate embroidery that highlights the design details. When decoratively stitched, then sewn together and stuffed, the dolls are transformed into choice collectibles to be used in a variety of ways.

Bestow them as gifts or hang them on a country-style Christmas tree. Or, use the dolls as package trims, sachets, or special residents of your child's dollhouse.

The fetching knitted doll (opposite), complete with her own wardrobe, is a knitting challenge you'll enjoy. Knit the doll on size 3 needles using sportweight yarn, then work the bonnet, pinafore, and pantaloons separately. The doll is worked in sections: first the body and head, then the arms and legs. Each knitted piece is stuffed firmly with polyester fiberfill. The facial features are embroidered with leftover knitting yarn.

Because most of the doll's clothes are detachable, you can choose the number of pieces of clothing you want to make. (Only the shawl is tacked in place to the doll's body.)

Instructions begin on page 238.

To make a set of pioneer dolls like the ones above, trace the designs onto fabric using a tracing wheel and light-colored dressmaker's carbon paper. Go over the lines with a permanent fine-tip brown marking pen.

232

W hat youngster wouldn't be delighted with these lovable pets? They're crafted by hand from fabric, yarn, and other sewing basket remnants.

The needlepoint bears (above) are worked in just one basic stitch. Make a front and back side for each bear, then stitch the two sides together along the outside edges. Add a touch of stuffing for shape and dimension.

To stitch the bears in different sizes, simply change the size of the needlepoint canvas and vary the number of plies you use with each strand of yarn.

Create a fabric menagerie like the one shown at right using country quilts that are too old and tired to save. Cut out simple animal shapes,

making the best use of color and pattern. (Keep your patterns simple to enhance the primitive, rustic charm of these animals.) Avoid using torn spots or fabric that is badly worn or faded.

See page 242 for instructions.

Other possible quilt animals are rabbits, roosters, sheep, goats, and pigs. Use your imagination for a few special touches such as the cow's braided tail or the horse's mane made of yarn loops. If you desire, embroider a few facial features.

234

DOLL FURNITURE
pages 228-229

Finished sizes are as follows: the settle is 16x17 inches; the hutch is 24x12x6 inches; the cradle is 9½x8x12 inches; the dry sink is 12½x18x17 inches.

Materials: ½-inch C-select pine; 2-inch-wide lattice (for settle and dry sink); ¾-inch-wide screen molding (for cradle); 5 shutter knobs; jigsaw; nails; glue; sandpaper; stain; varnish.

General instructions: Enlarge diagrams (below). Cut out pieces; assemble using butt joints, nails, and glue.

After assembling, sand the edges to make them safe for children. Countersink nails; fill holes. Stain and varnish.

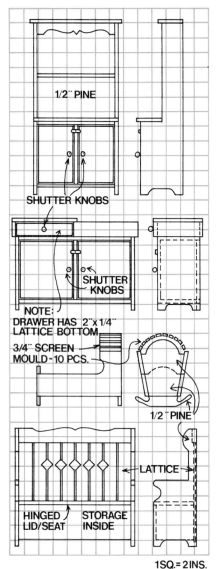

1 SQ. = 2 INS.

Settle: Assemble from pine except cut the back from strips of lattice. Make V cuts in lattice as shown; assemble with the cutouts in a diamond pattern. The back is dadoed into the bench top and sides.

After assembling back and sides, attach the front of seat and bottom. Seat is 6 inches above the floor and is mounted with pivoting nail hinges to make a lid for the storage box inside.

Hutch: Assemble entirely using ½-inch pine, adding a 2½-inch-deep shelf to the top as shown. Mount doors on pivoting nail hinges and attach a small wood dog between doors to keep them closed. For handles, use shutter knobs.

Cradle: Assemble from pine except for top, which is cut from ¾-inch screen molding. Cut rockers from a separate piece, with grain running horizontally, to prevent breaking.

Dry sink: Assemble from pine except for bottom of drawer, which is made of lattice. Build the two-door chest first; mount tray-and-drawer piece on top. Mount doors on pivoting nail hinges; add a wood dog between them to hold doors closed. Add shutter knobs to doors and drawer for handles.

PARLOR DOLLS
pages 228-229

Materials for each head: 5-inch egg-shaped plastic foam head; other foam scraps; brown grocery bag; wallpaper paste; glue; lightweight cardboard; acrylic paints; air-drying clay or papier-mâché powder to form nose; water-base varnish; 6 yards jute or yarn; ¼x12-inch dowel for each head; miscellaneous items (wig and jewelry).

Instructions: Carve a thumb-size hole in the narrow end of the foam egg slightly behind the point for a chin, using scissor points or a kitchen knife. Model the nose from plastic foam scraps, air-drying clay, or papier-mâché powder. Attach it with straight pins. Cut ears about 1 inch long from cardboard; insert them in place.

Soak 3x5-inch pieces of grocery bag in warm water. Meanwhile, mix a small amount of wallpaper paste (1 part white glue to 8 parts water). Remove

paper from water, crumple; return to water. Rub the paste mixture into the hole in the egg. Wring out the brown paper, tear it into small pieces, and dip it into the paste mixture. Cover the entire head with paper pieces, overlapping the edges ¼ inch. Smooth the edges with your fingers.

Cover the dowel using paper pieces. Allow the covering on the dowel to dry and insert the dowel into the neck. Stand the dowel in a weighted tumbler. When the dowel is thoroughly dry, sand any rough spots. Repeat this procedure twice.

Coat with water-base varnish to seal; sand lightly before applying base coat of white water-base enamel. Paint head flesh color; rub red into cheeks for a rosy blush. Paint eyes and brows with brush or markers.

Hair for doll with purple blouse: Cut 6 yards of jute into 9-inch lengths. Set 1 piece aside; stitch other fiber on wig base strips (see sketch below).

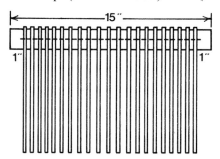

Trim the base strip ¼ inch on each side. Bead glue along the stitch line (hair side up); set aside for a few minutes. When the glue is tacky, pin the center of the wig to the head, hair side down, with long ends hanging over the center of the forehead.

Continue around the head at the hairline, behind the ears, and to the nape of the neck, overlapping ends slightly. Allow hair to dry completely before removing pins. Smooth hair using a wide-tooth comb and comb it into a loose ponytail. Wind the ponytail into a circle, gluing and wrapping as you go. Glue topknot to back of the head above the nape of the neck.

Braided hairstyle: Cut 6 yards of fiber into 36-inch lengths. Make 1 braid of 3 lengths; make 2 smaller braids of the remaining 3 lengths that you divide in two. Apply glue to the back of the large braid; when tacky, press the center of the braid to the center of the forehead; pin into place. Continue, positioning the braid around the hairline, behind the ears, and to the nape of the neck. Turn braids upward along the back center part, continue to the top of the head, then follow around, filling in previous oval to end of braid on both sides. Wind the braids around the doll's head, pinning and gluing as you go. Let glue dry before removing pins.

Jewelry: Pierce earlobes using large needle. Cut ¼ inch off regular ear wires; rebend to hook. Hang small bead on wire, insert in ear, and close.

Earring studs: Make indentation in earlobe using sharp object. Drop in a spot of glue; apply small rhinestone.

Materials for each body: ¼ yard of unbleached muslin; ⅛ yard of striped cotton for stocking legs; small bag of polyester fiberfill; acrylic paint—both flesh and red; 2 chenille stems.

Instructions: Enlarge the body pattern (below). Cut arms and neck from muslin. With right sides facing stitch as indicated, clip curves and turn.

Using fiberfill, stuff each arm to the elbow. Insert a chenille stem into the arm with half on either side of the elbow, then stitch across the elbow so that the arm seam runs through the middle of the flattened area. Stuff the upper arm firmly to within 1 inch of the top.

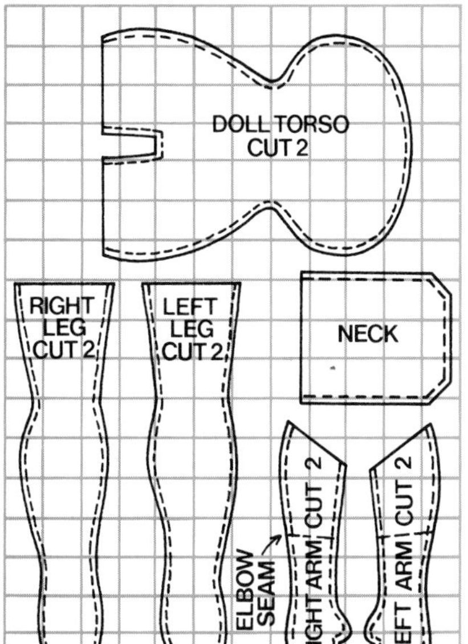

Cut out and stitch stocking legs to torso (cut from muslin) at thigh, right sides together. Stuff legs firmly and torso lightly.

Stitch the arms into the shoulders, leaving an opening at the neck. Insert glue-coated neck into head; dry. Insert dowel; stuff neck, leaving rod in center. Work dowel into torso. Dowel rod should come to within ¼ inch of the bottom of the torso. Cut to length. Pin neck inside shoulders. Add more stuffing if needed; stitch. Paint arms from elbow to fingertip in flesh tone. Rub a little red into backs of hands for blush; paint neck to match the head.

Materials for wardrobe: ⅜ yard of blouse fabric; ⅛ yard for ruffled apron; ¼ yard for plain apron; ⅜ yard each for skirt and petticoat; 1 yard lace for petticoat; ¼ yard lace for hankie; ¼ yard of ¼-inch-wide elastic; 1 kid glove from thrift shop for shoes; small beads for necklace; 3 blouse buttons.

Instructions: *For doll with braided hair:* Cut out the skirt (10¼ x 36 inches), petticoat (10½ x 33 inches), apron sash (2 x 30 inches), bow tie (3 x 25 inches), apron ruffle (1½ x 32 inches), and tied cuffs (2¾ x 4 inches).

Enlarge the clothing patterns (below), then cut blouse, apron, and handkerchief. Sew ¼-inch hem on skirt. Sew the lace trim onto the petticoat.

Run a gathering thread along the top of the skirt, petticoat, and apron. Gath-

er the petticoat and skirt to 12 inches. Anchor the ¼-inch-wide elastic, then stretch it and sew it along the gathering thread. Stitch right sides of skirt and petticoat together at ends.

Press under ¼ inch around pocket; sew to apron. Gather ruffle to fit edge of apron (first turn up a ¼-inch hem; press and stitch). Stitch apron to ruffle.

Stitch sash to apron, right sides facing, matching center fronts. With right sides facing, stitch sash; leave piece already sewn to apron free. Turn sash through free piece; press. Turn under raw edge of waistband front; sew.

Insert hankie into pocket. Stitch the blouse. Gather wrists 1 inch above the edge of the fabric; put the blouse on the doll. Next, pull gathering threads tight and knot firmly; trim ends. Sew, clip, turn, and press the cuffs. Wrap cuffs around wrists, tucking in raw edges; stitch them closed. Add buttons.

Tuck in raw edges around neck. Overlap blouse front; fold under one edge, tack at neck. Sew buttons to front, tacking blouse closed. Sew neck bow tie, leaving an opening; turn. Tie bow around neck. Put skirt on doll, then petticoat.

For doll with purple blouse: Follow directions for above doll to make the skirt, petticoat, and basic blouse. When attaching bow tie, simply loop it 4 times, tacking instead of tying a bow. Cuffs are wrapped around wrist, then knotted instead of buttoned. Make an apron from a scrap of print. Hem, stitch, and gather to 5 inches. Attach waistband as for doll above.

Shoes: Using an old kid glove, cut 2 of larger fingertips off at 2¼ inches; slit down front 1½ inches. From the glove, cut 4 strips ⅛ to ¼ inch wide and as long as you can cut them. Stuff tips of shoes with cotton. Put shoes on feet, tacking corners at top of slit. Tack long strips at back of slit. Tack long strips at back of ankle. Bring strips forward; lace up leg. Tack to leg at bow.

POSTAGE STAMP QUILT
page 229

Materials: Fabric scraps in assorted colors and prints; complementary fabric for backing; quilt batting.

(Continued)

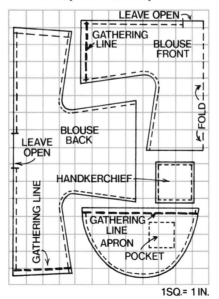

DOLL TORSO CUT 2

RIGHT LEG CUT 2

LEFT LEG CUT 2

NECK

ELBOW SEAM

RIGHT ARM CUT 2

LEFT ARM CUT 2

1 SQ.= 1 IN.

LEAVE OPEN

GATHERING LINE

BLOUSE FRONT

FOLD

BLOUSE BACK

LEAVE OPEN

HANDKERCHIEF

GATHERING LINE

GATHERING LINE

APRON

POCKET

1 SQ.= 1 IN.

Instructions: Make a 10-inch-square mini-quilt by cutting and joining 1½-inch fabric squares. Use ¼-inch seams.

The quilt shown has a red center block surrounded by a 5-inch square of blocks in assorted prints. Prints are bordered by green, pink, red, purple, blue, and black squares.

Stitch blocks into diagonal rows. Join rows, then trim outer edges so they are straight. Cut backing fabric to size. Assemble layers into a quilt.

BUCKSKIN AND BURLAP DOLLS
pages 230-231

Materials: 1 yard of good quality burlap; buckskin remnants (available from leather supply outlets); wire coat hangers or aluminum welding rods (which are easier to bend; available where welding supplies are sold); polyester fiberfill; ¼ yard of calico; 1 yard of manilla rope; white glue; masking tape; pliers; wire cutters; small metal file; buttonhole or carpet thread.

Instructions: For doll bodies, cut armature pieces from hangers: one 10-inch piece for the arms, one 9-inch piece for the body, and two 6-inch pieces for leg supports. Round all sharp edges with a file, and wrap the ends of the arm and leg pieces with tape to contour hands and feet.

Cut 1-inch-wide strips of burlap to cover the wires, making the strips ½ inch longer than the wires. Fold the edges inward, tuck wire into the fold, and sew fabric tightly around wires.

Stitch the two 6-inch burlap-covered wires tightly to the body wire; keep ends flush at the bottom. Separate the wires to form a tripod. The protruding end of the body wire will be used for attaching the head.

Enlarge the head pattern (above right) and transfer it to a sheet of paper. This is your master pattern.

Cut two pieces of buckskin or burlap that are slightly larger than the pattern pieces (placing the pattern along the length of the buckskin grain). Trace the pattern onto the wrong side of the buckskin. Place the right sides together and double-stitch around the lines. Leave the seam open from point A to B to allow for stuffing. Trim the seams to

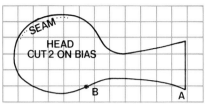

1 Square = ½ Inch

¼ inch, then turn right side out and stuff the head.

Position the head atop the body wire. Stitch the stuffing opening closed, and sew the neck to the body. (For buckskin head, use white glue to close the seam, and glue the head to the body.) Stitch arms 1 inch below neck.

For the blouse, cut a 10x4-inch piece of calico. Fold in half lengthwise, right sides together, and fold again from top to bottom. Clip a small piece from the folded corner for the neck opening. While still folded, cut along the short edge (through one thickness) from the neck to the open side to make the blouse back opening.

With right sides together, sew sleeve seam 1½ inches from folded edge. Sew to within 1 inch of the back opening. Turn blouse at a right angle and sew to the open edge. This forms sleeves and blouse shape. Clip seams to ¼ inch. Bend the doll's arms to the front of the body. With the blouse on the doll, sew the back seam closed and turn the remaining raw edges under.

For the skirt, cut a 9x13-inch piece of burlap. Sew the short sides together, stitching twice. Fold under the top edge ¼ inch and gather it to the body of the doll. Tack the skirt to the waist.

Gather the bottom of the skirt. Fold the skirt up around the tripod until it is even with the feet and the doll stands balanced. (Foot can be revealed by cutting a small hole at the hemline.)

For the hair, cut a 20-inch length of rope and unravel it. Separate the rope into individual strands, lay them out side by side, then carefully machine-stitch through the strands along the center. Glue the wig to the doll's head and style the rope hair into braids, pigtails, or twists.

For the shepherdess, cut a vest from a buckskin scrap. Punch six holes (three on each side) for lacing. Glue one

shoulder seam; place vest around doll, then glue the other shoulder seam. Cut a thin strip of buckskin for lacing; lace it through the holes. For a staff, attach a long twig to the hand, or use a wire with a crook in one end covered with buckskin, burlap, or thread.

For the shepherdess' cloak, cut a 12x4-inch rectangle from burlap or calico. Fold in half lengthwise (to measure 6 inches) and seam one side. Fold the open edge back and under 1 inch; press. Place it on the doll's head and mark where the neck of the doll falls on the cloak. Gather for 2 inches at center back to form a hood shape. Fray or hem the bottom edge.

For flower girl, dress with vest as for shepherdess and add a calico scarf.

For peddler lady, cut a 10-inch-diameter burlap circle for a cape. Fold over one edge of the circle to form a 7-inch-long straight side, making the neck and collar opening. Press.

Gather across the opening (½ inch from the fold) to form a ruffled collar, and turn under a ¼ inch hem around the remaining edge of the circle. Drape the cape around the doll's head, and tack it into place. Fashion a small box filled with beads, dried flowers, and lace for wares; suspend box around doll's neck with a length of buckskin.

PIONEER DOLLS
page 232

Materials: White or off-white fabric; dressmaker's carbon paper; permanent brown fine-tip marking pen; embroidery floss in a variety of colors; metallic threads; acrylic or fabric paints; paint brushes; crayons or fabric crayons; colored pencils; embroidery hoop; embroidery needle; fiberfill; ribbons.

Instructions: Enlarge the drawings of the dolls (pages 240-241) on brown paper, adding ½ inch for seams. Transfer the patterns onto fabric using dressmaker's carbon. Or tape patterns to a window, tape fabric atop patterns, and transfer design lines with a hard lead pencil. Then trace outlines with brown marking pen to define the designs. (*Note:* Test the pen on a scrap of fabric first to make sure it does not bleed.) Before cutting the dolls apart, decorate them as follows:

To embellish dolls: Choose fine-tip markers or acrylic paints that do not bleed and that will not cause the brown outlines to bleed. If you use paints, thin colors with water to the consistency of light cream, then paint them onto the fabric using a relatively dry brush. Paint up to but not over the brown outlines. For best results, leave a sliver of unpainted fabric between colors. Allow one area of color to dry thoroughly before painting adjacent areas.

Work all embroidery on the faces with a single strand of floss; for the costumes use 2 strands of floss. Use simple stitches to outline and highlight design details.

To assemble dolls: Cut out fronts and backs of each doll. With right sides facing, pin, baste, and sew fronts to backs, placing the stitching line approximately ⅛ inch beyond the outlines of the dolls. Leave an opening for turning at the base of each doll. Trim seams, clip curves, and turn dolls right side out. Stuff carefully and slip-stitch the opening closed.

Or, leave the entire bottom edge open and cut a fabric oval for the base of each doll. Stuff the doll, then sew the oval in place, inserting cardboard ovals for extra firmness if desired. Slip-stitch the opening closed.

KNITTED DOLL
page 233

Finished size is 18 inches tall.

Materials: Coats & Clark Red Heart Sport Yarn, 2 ounces of cranberry and 1 ounce each of eggshell, camel, black, gray, and blue; Size 3 knitting needles, or size to obtain gauge below; polyester fiberfill.

Gauge: 13 sts = 2 inches; 9 rows = 1 inch.

Instructions: *Body and head:* Beg at lower edge with eggshell, cast on 54 sts. Work even in st st until total length measures 4½ inches; drop eggshell and attach cranberry. Work even in cranberry until total length measures 9 inches; drop cranberry and attach eggshell. Work even until total length measures 12 inches. Cast off. Fold work in half lengthwise and sew back seam; sew lower edge. Stuff firmly, leaving top open. Draw a strand of eggshell yarn

through sts of first row of eggshell; pull slightly to form neck and secure.

Hair section: Beg at back of neck and with black, cast on 8 sts. *Row 1* (wrong side): K in front and back of first st, k to last st, k in front and back of last st—2 incs made. *Row 2:* P in front and back of first st, p to last st, p in front and back of last st. Rpt Rows 1 and 2 alternately until there are 68 sts on the needle. Work even in st st for 1 inch more. Break off yarn, leaving a 20-inch tail. Thread this end into a needle and draw through sts on needle. With another strand of black, sew edges of last 1 inch tog. With the seam at center front and cast-on sts ½ inch above neck, pin hair section in place as shown in the photograph and sew. Add more fiberfill as necessary to fill in hair section. Draw sts on yarn tightly tog and secure. Wind a 1-inch-diameter black ball for bun; tack in place.

Embroider eyes with black; embroider mouth and cheeks with cranberry.

Leg (make 2): Beg at upper edge with black, cast on 26 sts. Work in st st for 5 inches, ending with a p row. Now work in pat as follows: *Rows 1 and 2:* P across. *Row 3:* K across. *Rows 4-8:* P each row. *Row 9:* * P 2 tog. Rpt from * across. Break off, leaving a 20-inch tail. Thread this end into a needle and draw through rem sts. Draw tog tightly and secure; then sew seam, leaving top open. Stuff firmly. Sew top seam tog and sew to body.

Arm (make 2): Beg at top edge with cranberry, cast on 4 sts. Work in st st, cast on 3 sts at end of next 6 rows—22 sts. Work even until total length measures 5 inches. Fasten off cranberry, attach eggshell and continue in st st for 1¼ inches more. Break off, leaving a 20-inch tail. Thread this end into a needle and draw through sts on needle. Draw tog tightly and secure; then sew seam, leaving top open. Stuff firmly. With cast-on sts on top, sew arm opening to body 1 inch below neck.

Bloomers: Front—first leg section: Beg at lower edge with camel, cast on 16 sts. *Row 1:* K across. *Row 2:* P across. *Rows 3-4:* Rpt rows 1 and 2. *Row 5* (first eyelet row): K 1, * k 2 tog, yo. Rpt from * across, ending k 1. *Row 6:* P across. *Rows 7-10:* Rpt rows 1 and

2 alternately. *Row 11* (second eyelet row): K 2 (k 2 tog, yo, k 3) twice; k 2 tog, yo, k 2. *Row 12:* P across. Work even in st st until total length measures 3½ inches, ending with a p row. Break off, sl sts onto a holder to be used later. Make another leg section in the same way; do not break off.

Joining row: K across sts on needle, cast on 4 sts, then k across sts on holder—36 sts. Work even in st st for 3 inches; cast off.

Back: Work same as for Front. Sew side seams and crotch seam. Fold first 4 rows to wrong side on first eyelet row and sew in place. Pull on bloomers; add more fiberfill to round out body. Sew top edge to body. Thread needle with a 15-inch double strand of eggshell yarn. Draw through sts of each leg section ¼ inch above second eyelet row and tie at the side.

Petticoat: Beg at lower edge with camel, cast on 116 sts. *Rows 1-10:* Work as for Rows 1-10 of Leg Section of Bloomers. *Row 11:* K 2, * k 2 tog, yo, k 3. Rpt from * to last 4 sts; k 2 tog, yo, k 2. Beg with a p row, work in st st until total length measures 5½ inches. Fasten off yarn end, leaving a 20-inch tail. Thread this end into a needle and draw through sts on needle. Fold first 4 rows to wrong side on first eyelet row and sew in place. Pull on petticoat, draw sts on yarn end tog to fit around body and sew in place ½ inch above bloomers.

Skirt: Beg at lower edge with cranberry, cast on 124 sts. *Rows 1-4:* Rpt Rows 1-4 of Leg Section of Bloomers. *Next row:* P across for turning ridge. Beg with a p row, work even in st st until the total length measures 6 inches. Break off, leaving a 20-inch tail. Draw yarn end through sts on needle. Turn first 4 rows to wrong side on turning ridge and sew in place. Draw sts on yarn end tog to fit waistline and sew in place.

Apron: Lower part: Beg at lower edge with gray, cast on 46 sts. K 6 rows, then work in pat as follows: *Row 1* (right side): K 4, p to last 4 sts, k 4. *Row 2:* K across. Rpt Rows 1 and 2 alternately until total length measures 5 inches. Break off, leaving a 20-inch tail; draw ends through sts on needle. *Upper part:* Beg at lower edge with gray, cast on 20 sts. K 4 rows, then work in pat as

(Continued on page 242)

These patterns can be enlarged on grids, or you can scale them up to the desired size using an opaque projector or a photoduplication service.

Opaque projectors are often available in public libraries or school media centers. To use one, slide the scaled-down pattern into the projector and it will transfer the image to a wall. Tape paper onto the wall and transfer the pattern outlines onto the paper with a pencil.

A photo engraving shop can enlarge the patterns photostatically. This is a quick process (often while you wait), but it can be expensive, so it is a good idea to ask for a cost estimate first.

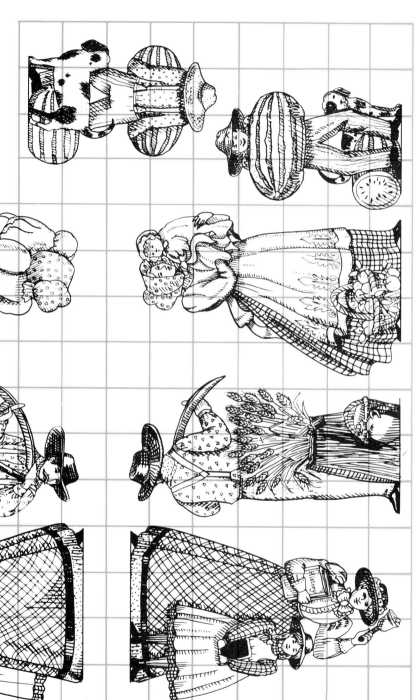

1 Square = 1 Inch

240

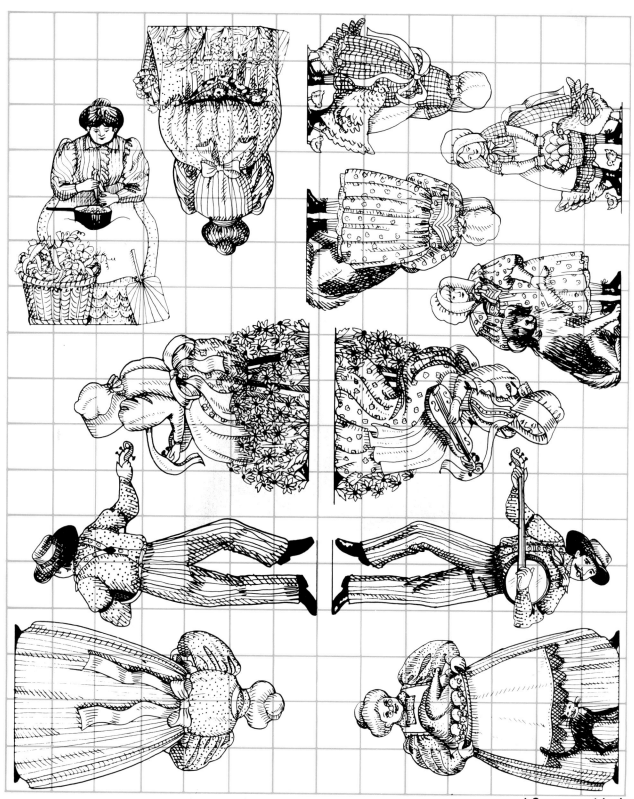

1 Square = 1 Inch

241

follows: *Row 1* (right side): K 3, p to last 3 sts, k 3. *Row 2:* K across. Rpt rows 1 and 2 alternately until length is 2 inches. *Next 4 rows:* K across. Cast off. Draw sts on yarn end of lower part to width of upper part; secure and sew tog. For tie, cast on 90 sts; k 6 rows and cast off. Place center of tie at center of apron on seam; tack in place.

Shawl: With blue, cast on 3 sts. *Row 1:* K 2; with yarn in front of needle, sl 1 as to p. Always sl last st in this way. *Row 2:* K 1; k in front and back of next st—inc made; sl 1. *Row 3:* K 3, sl 1. *Row 4:* K 2, inc in next st, sl 1. *Row 5:* K 4, sl 1. *Row 6:* K 3, inc in next st, sl 1. *Row 7:* K 5, sl 1. *Row 8:* K to last 2 sts, inc in next st, sl 1. *Row 9:* K to last st, sl 1. Rpt Rows 8 and 9 alternately until there are 40 sts on the needle, ending with Row 8. Work 3 rows even. *Next row:* K to last 3 sts, k 2 tog, sl 1. *Following row:* K to last st, sl 1. Rpt last 2 rows until 3 sts rem. Cast off. Drape shawl over shoulders, crossing points at front. Tack each point to waist at side. Tie apron at back. Tack each corner of upper apron part to shawl.

Bonnet: Beg at center back with eggshell, cast on 18 sts. *Row 1:* K across. *Row 2:* P across. *Row 3:* Inc one st in each st across—36 sts. *Row 4:* P across. *Rows 5-6:* Rpt Rows 1 and 2. *Row 7:* * K 1, inc one st in next st. Rpt from * across—54 sts. *Row 8:* P across. *Rows 9-12:* Rpt Row 1 and 2 alternately. With a different color yarn, mark each end of last row. *Rows 13-18:* Work as for Rows 7-12—81 sts. *Row 19:* Inc one st in first st, * k 1, inc one st in next st. Rpt from * across—122 sts. Beg with a p row, work even in st st until length is 3½ inches. Break off, leaving 20-inch tail. Draw yarn through sts on needle.

Brim: With eggshell, cast on 66 sts. Work even in st st for 1¼ inches, ending with a p row. *Next row:* P across for turning ridge. Beg with a p row, continue in st st for 1¼ inches; cast off. Draw cast-on sts at center back tightly tog and secure. Sew seam to marker. Draw sts on yarn end to length of brim and secure. Fold brim on turning ridge. Place gathered end of bonnet bet the two layers of brim and sew in place.

Cord: Cut two 72-inch strands of yarn. Twist these strands tightly in one direction, then fold twisted strands in half and twist in opposite direction. Cut

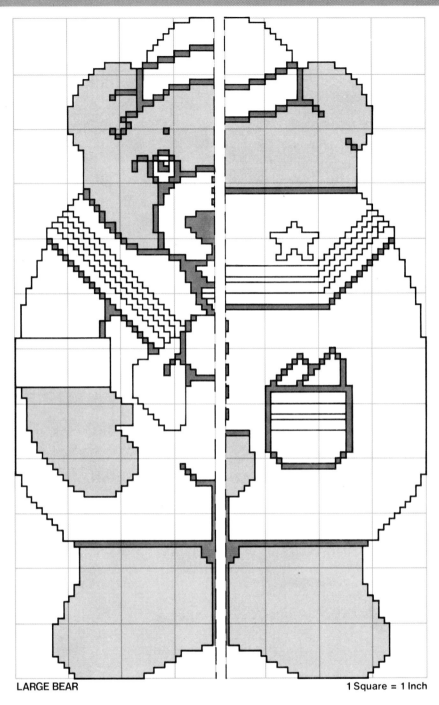

LARGE BEAR　　　　1 Square = 1 Inch

in half and knot at each end. Tack one cord to each side of bonnet; tie.

NEEDLEPOINT BEARS
page 234

Materials: *For large bears* (about 8x11 inches): ½ yard of #10-count in-

terlock needlepoint canvas for one complete bear; 3-ply Persian wool yarn (or a suitable substitute) in the colors and amounts listed below; #18 tapestry needle.

For medium bears (about 6x8½ inches): ¼ yard of #14-count interlock needlepoint canvas for a complete bear; 3-ply Persian wool yarn (or a suitable substitute) in colors and amounts listed below; #20 tapestry needle.

For small bears (about 4x5½ inches): ¼ yard of #22-count needlepoint canvas for two complete bears; 3-ply Persian wool yarn (or a suitable substitute) in colors and amounts listed below; #22 tapestry needle.

Additional supplies: Masking tape; needlepoint frame; polyester fiberfill; 10-squares-per-inch graph paper; colored pencils.

Sailor Bear (in yards)

	Large	Medium	Small
Brown	44½	35½	9
Light brown	2½	2	1
Black	18	13½	5½
White	13½	9	5½
Navy blue	62	49	12½
Red	2½	2	1
Rust	1	1	1

Lady Bear (in yards)

	Large	Medium	Small
Brown	35½	22	7
Light brown	2½	2	1
Black	18	9	2½
White	31	22	7
Yellow	13½	4½	2
Blue-green	133	67	12½
Dark green	9	7	3½
Pink	18	6	2
Dark pink	1	1	1
Rust	1	1	1

Instructions: All of the bears are stitched from the same patterns. To change the size of the bears, simply change the size of the needlepoint canvas—from #10-count to #14-count to #22-count canvas. Work the bears in basket-weave stitches to minimize distortion.

Enlarge patterns (right and opposite) onto 10-squares-per-inch graph paper so 1 square = 1 stitch. To complete patterns, finish drawing second half of each bear so patterns are symmetrical. The bears on your graph paper are equal to the size of the large bears.

Bind canvas edges with masking tape and mount canvas in a needlepoint frame to minimize distortion. Begin working bears using 3-ply strands on #10-count canvas, 2-ply strands on #14-count canvas, and 1-ply on #22-count canvas. Work one area of color at a time, referring to the graphed patterns and carefully counting the number of stitches in each section.

The shaded areas on the patterns represent colors brown and black; refer to the photograph for other colors.

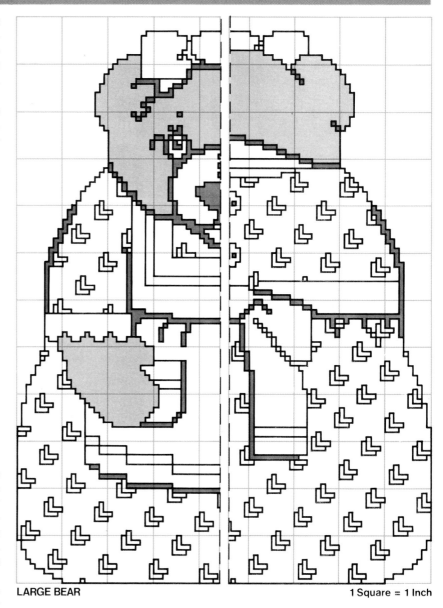

LARGE BEAR   1 Square = 1 Inch

When bears are completely stitched, remove the canvas from the frame and block it if necessary.

Trim the canvas edges to ½ inch beyond the needlepoint and fold the edges to the back, leaving one row of unworked canvas all the way around. Carefully clip into the margin of the canvas if necessary (not including row of unworked canvas) so it lies flat.

To hold the edges in place, steam press the back side of the canvas using a damp cloth.

With wrong sides facing, match the front and back sides of each bear. Join the two pieces, placing small safety pins every 1 to 2 inches. (As you pin, be sure the two sides are aligned.)

Begin stitching the two sides together using a binding stitch and single strands of leftover yarn. Work the binding stitch through the row of unworked canvas.

After you have stitched halfway around the bears, begin stuffing them with fiberfill. Tear stuffing into small pieces before inserting it so bears will not be lumpy. Stuff the bears lightly so they do not pucker when finished. Fill small, rounded areas such as ears and feet with small pieces of stuffing.

Finish stitching bears together, adding small pieces of stuffing as you go. Remove safety pins and clip yarn ends.

243

CHILDREN'S CORNER

Country Crafts Kids Can Make

ost children love the idea of craft projects they can make themselves, so here and on the next two pages are some easy country-like crafts for them to choose from. These delightful leaf projects are naturals for kids because most children love to search out special fall leaves to save. Whether you choose to frame your leaves, make leaf collection books, or assemble a colorful catchall, here are a few tips you should remember for gathering and pressing. Gather leaves singly or in small sprays and slip each leaf or spray between folds of newspaper. When you get home, sandwich the leaves between several sheets of clean, dry newspaper. Weight your stack of pressed leaves with magazines or books. Leaves usually take one to two weeks to dry. When leaves are dry, store them between single sheets of newspaper until you are ready to start a project. Instructions for leaf projects begin on page 248.

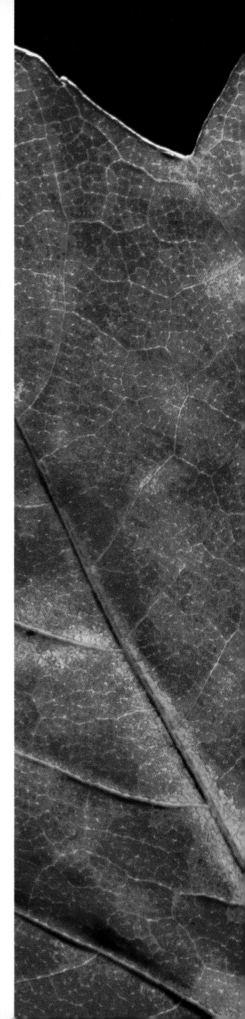

W hen setting out to make something from wood, whether it be a log cabin built entirely by hand or a simple toy carved or whittled from pine, our pioneer ancestors had to make good on the old adage "waste not, want not." For little more than a song, woodsmiths made beautiful like-new crafts from materials that were too good to throw away.

Here are two examples of how you can make something special from nothing, just as our country predecessors used to do. With a little adult supervision, your child can help make these projects, too.

You'll find everything you need in your basement toolbox to make the rustic wooden mosaic (right). All it takes are a few scraps of lumber, a hammer, some nails, and a dab of white glue.

After you've cut the pieces and arranged them in a picturesque, pastoral setting like the one shown here, secure the pieces to a hardboard backing cut to size.

Then, add color to each piece of wood by applying watercolor paints or highly diluted liquid fabric dyes. Frame the mosaic with pine strips, mitering the corners.

The Noah's ark and paired-off animals (opposite) are a child's delight. They're easy to make and provide hours of playtime fun when finished. The simple wooden shapes make this a good beginner's project.

Cut the animals from ¾-inch pine and sand the edges lightly. If

you desire, drill a hole in the top of each wooden shape so you can hang them as Christmas ornaments.

Build the ark from pieces of pine, curving the bottom edges of the sides so the ark rocks back and forth. Top the deck with a shelter, with simple doorways cut into the sides. Then, add a pitched roof made of small cedar shakes.

Although the ark and animals pictured here are shown without a finish, you may wish to paint yours or finish them with stain and varnish. Be sure to select non-toxic materials if you have toddlers at home.

For complete instructions and patterns for the wooden mosaic and animals, see page 249.

When teaching your child how to work with wood, emphasize tool maintenance and safety. Using a tool that has been properly stored and maintained will improve your chances of getting professional-looking results.

246

LEAF COLLECTOR'S BOOK
page 245

To make your leaf-hunting more enjoyable, we have included drawings (right) and some information to help you identify the leaves you collect for your scrapbook.

Horse chestnut: A horse-chestnut leaf is divided into five or seven smaller leaflets arranged in a circle around the leaf stem. Mature leaves may measure 8 to 10 inches in diameter.

Locust: These leaves are made up of many pairs of small leaflets. In fact, there are so many small leaflets that each leaf resembles a large fern frond.

Maple: There are five major kinds of maples: silver, sugar, Norway, black, and red. All produce star-shaped leaves that are easy to identify.

Oak: Oak trees produce bright green lobed leaves. Some species of oak native to the southern United States have unlobed leaves.

Sassafras: The low-growing, aromatic, shrublike sassafras tree produces a leaf that resembles the foot of a goose. This tree is most commonly seen in wooded regions of the South.

Ash: Each ash leaf is composed of smaller leaflets arranged in pairs along the leaf's stem. One slightly larger leaflet always grows at the tip.

Basswood: Basswood trees (also known as linden trees) have large, almost round leaves with a point on one end. The leaves have rough edges and may be 4 or 5 inches in diameter.

Birch: Birch trees produce leaves that look much like elm leaves. But birch leaves are even at the base, and elm leaves are uneven.

Elm: Elm trees produce oval leaves that are pointed on one end. They are uneven at the base and have ragged edges.

Gingko: Because gingkos are not native to this country, they are most commonly found planted along city streets and in parks. The leaves are fan-shaped and are about 3 inches wide.

Poplar: The poplar family includes poplars, cottonwoods, and aspens. All have triangular leaves, and leaf size may differ from species to species. Several species produce leaves with silver or gray undersides.

Horse chestnut   Locust   Maple   Oak

Sassafras   Ash   Basswood   Birch

Elm   Gingko   Poplar   Sweetgum

Sycamore   Tulip   Walnut   Willow

Sweetgum: The star-shaped leaf of the sweetgum is easy to recognize. The sweetgum tree is found mainly in the southern parts of the United States.

Sycamore: The sycamore produces leaves that look like large maple leaves. Mature leaves may measure 12 inches in diameter.

Tulip tree: The tulip tree or yellow poplar produces a bright green, blunt, maple-like leaf. This tree is found mainly in the southern United States.

Walnut: Walnut leaves have long stems with pairs of small leaflets along each side. Unlike ash leaves, walnut leaves do not have a leaflet on the tip of the stem.

Willow: Willow trees have long slender leaves that are easy to recognize. Mature leaves may be 4 inches long.

Materials: Dried leaves (see leaf collecting guide above); construction paper; scrapbook; clear adhesive-backed vinyl; white glue or rubber cement.

Instructions: Cut construction paper the same size or slightly smaller than the front of the scrapbook or notebook you want to cover. Lightly glue dried leaves onto the paper. (It's a good idea to arrange all the leaves before you start to glue.)

When leaves are in place, glue construction paper to the scrapbook. If you wish, use a second piece of construction paper slightly larger than the first to frame the leaf arrangement.

Next, cut a piece of vinyl large enough to wrap all the way around the notebook. Gently press the vinyl into place, removing all the air bubbles as you work.

SCRAP WOOD MOSAIC
page 246

Materials: Pieces of leftover pine lumber; ¼-inch hardboard; glue; acrylic paints, watercolors, or fabric dyes.

Instructions: Cut a 12x16-inch piece of ¼-inch hardboard for the backing. Rip scrap pieces of 2x4-inch pine and ¾-inch pine into ⅛-inch-thick strips.

Place pine strips on hardboard to make a design similar to the one in the photograph. Use a coping saw or jigsaw to cut the pieces to fit. Secure each piece to hardboard with white glue and weight the mosaic until the glue dries. Paint the wood pieces as desired.

To make a frame, rip scrap pine into ¾x1¼-inch pieces and nail the pieces in place, mitering the corners.

NOAH'S ARK
page 247

Materials: Scraps of ¾-inch-thick pine; sandpaper.

Instructions: Enlarge the patterns at right and cut 2 animals each from scrap lumber. Sand the edges lightly.

To make the ark, cut two side pieces from pine, curving the bottom edges and leaving the top edges flat (see photograph). Join the two side pieces with a pine strip deck. Build a small shelter atop the deck, cutting portholes or doors. Add a pitched roof made of small cedar shakes if you wish.

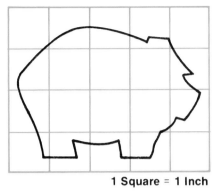

1 Square = 1 Inch

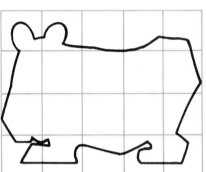

1 Square = 1 Inch

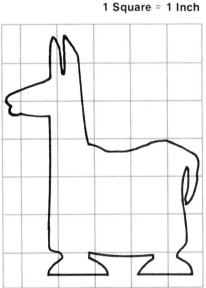

1 Square = 1 Inch

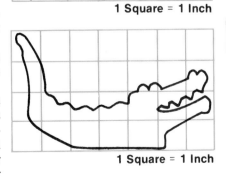

1 Square = 1 Inch

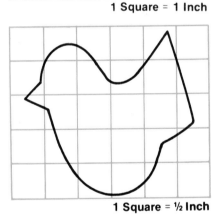

1 Square = 1 Inch

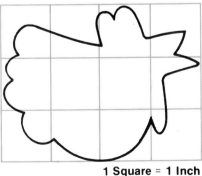

1 Square = 1 Inch

249

CHILDREN'S CORNER

Crafts to Decorate a Child's Room

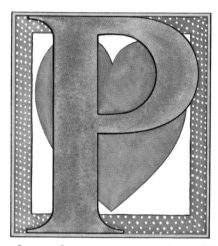

ure and simple designs like these were inspired by our country heritage. By combining good design, beautiful materials, and careful craftsmanship, you can achieve attractive, cheerful results that will appeal to the young at heart of any age. The small-scale furniture and the stitchery ideas shown here are examples of lovingly handcrafted items you can make for your child. The in-between bed and matching rocker are toddler size. The bed measures 20 inches high and sits 11 inches from the floor (length and width depend on the size of your mattress). The rocker is about 27x36 inches. For more country accents, stitch a quilt, pillows, or rug in updated country-style designs. Scatter stylized versions of two basic country motifs, the heart and the tulip, on the stitchery projects. The quilt and pillows are painted, then quilted and stitched. The throw rug is worked in needlepoint on jumbo canvas. For complete instructions, see page 254.

Country Crafts to Decorate a Child's Room

This roomful of imaginative, decorative furniture was inspired by designs from our country past. Each piece, including two chairs, rocking horse, and trunk, is embellished with a fanciful array of woodburning patterns and painted in sprightly colors.

To achieve interesting shapes like the ones shown here, gather a selection of hardware and tools such as nails, hinges, springs, and pipes. Heat each item, then "brand" the shape of the tool onto the wooden furniture to make an imprint.

Protect each piece with a coat of varnish. Sand, then trim the furniture with painted details inspired by your own creativity. When adding touches of color, follow the excellent guidelines the branded designs provide. Then simply fill in the woodburned shapes and add rows of dots or outlines as desired. Finish with two more coats of varnish.

For instructions, see page 254.

Practice this woodburning technique on scrap lumber before you begin the actual projects. To heat the hardware and tools you need for your designs, arrange them around a gas burner set at medium-high. Handle the heated items with a pair of tongs.

IN-BETWEEN BED
page 251

Bed size depends on size of mattress.

Instructions: Add 3 inches to both the length and width of the mattress. Cut a piece of ¾-inch plywood to these dimensions.

Join lengths of 1-inch-thick pine lumber (by splining) to create the headboard, footboard, and sides. The headboard measures 20 inches high. The footboard is 13 inches high. The sides are 11 inches high. (Add 1½ inches to the length to allow for mitered joints.)

Contour the footboard as shown in the photograph; shape the headboard similarly.

Cut a heart-shaped motif in the top center of each. Cut an area in each side piece to allow for easy access. Miter ends; glue and nail together.

Glue and nail plywood bottom inside the frame so that the top of the plywood is recessed 7¾ inches from the top of the sides. Glue and screw 2x2-inch legs to inside corners so that tops of sides are 18½ inches from the floor. Sand; finish as desired.

CHILD-SIZE ROCKER
page 250

Instructions: Enlarge the rocker side pattern (below) and transfer it to pieces of 1-inch-thick pine lumber that have been splined together.

Cut out two shapes for the sides. Cut out a 13x14-inch pine seat and a 13x15-inch pine back. Cut heart-shaped motif from back and contour edges as shown in the photograph.

Glue and nail the seat and back to the sides. Sand and finish as desired.

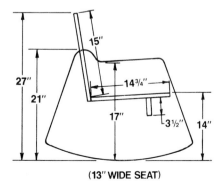

(13" WIDE SEAT)

BLOCK PRINT QUILT
page 251

Finished size is 27½x54½ inches.

Instructions: Enlarge the tulip pattern (below) and cut heart pattern from 4x4 inches of paper; transfer them to linoleum blocks. Cut away nonprinting areas according to manufacturer's directions; prepare ink for printing.

Cut twenty 6¼x6¼-inch pieces of white fabric. Cut two 13½x20-inch pieces of white fabric. Print squares with red heart design; print rectangles with tulip design.

Join 2 tulip-printed panels as shown in the photograph. Cut two 2½x53-inch and two 2½x14-inch red polka dot strips for inside borders. Stitch to tulip panel using ½ inch seams.

For each side heart panel, join 8 heart-printed squares alternately with 7 2½x6¼-inch red dotted strips, with a heart square on each end. For each end panel, sew a 3½x6¼-inch red dotted strip between 2 heart squares. Sew end and side panels to tulip panel.

Cut a 32x58½-inch red polka dot backing and a 27½x54½-inch piece of

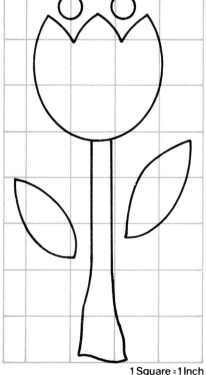

1 Square = 1 Inch

polyester quilt batting. Center top, batting, and backing; baste together. Quilt along seams. Fold excess backing to the right side. Miter corners, fold raw edges under ½ inch; sew to top of quilt.

QUICKPOINT RUG
page 251

Finished size is 28½x37½ inches.

Instructions: Using linoleum blocks from quilt, print motifs on 7-mesh-per-inch rug canvas. Allow ink to dry thoroughly. Work design with rug yarn in continental or basket-weave stitches. Bind edges with rug tape. Add a coating of liquid latex to the back of the rug to prevent skidding.

WOODBURNED FURNITURE AND HORSE
pages 252-253

Materials: Acrylic paints; metal tools for woodburning patterns such as hinges, nails, large springs, heavy pipe ends, wrenches, chrome sleeves for plumbing pipes, base of a cleat; aluminum foil; tongs; heat-proof pad; gas flame; unfinished furniture or rocking horse; scrap wood; stain and varnish; sponges; sandpaper; tack rag.

Instructions: Gather tools. Each tool must have a projection to grasp when in use. Wrap that area with crushed foil; use tongs to handle when hot.

Place heat-proof pad beside the gas burner; arrange tools in circle around gas jet so ends touch blue flame. Turn burner to medium high. Using tongs, lift tool and brand its imprint into scrap wood. This serves as a sampler and teaches you the heating times required.

To prepare wood for burning: Apply thinned acrylics to unfinished surface using a wet sponge. Wipe off excess; dry, sand, and wipe with tack rag.

Plan the design using the shapes on your sampler board. On scrap paper trace shape of area to be burned, then add shapes of tools in a pleasing arrangement. Transfer design to wood. Heat tools; woodburn the pieces. Apply one coat of varnish; sand when dry.

With thinned acrylics, paint furniture with decorative shapes; dry, then finish with 2 coats of varnish.

CORN HUSKS
POTPOURRI
NATURAL DYES

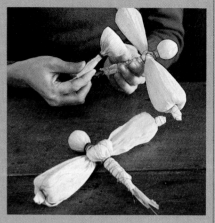

1) To make a corn husk doll like these (opposite), soak corn husks in warm water and work with the husks while they're still damp. For the doll's head, place a small foam ball in the center of a corn husk and cover the ball completely. Wrap the corn husk with thread around the bottom of the ball to form a neck. Insert a six-inch wire into the bottom of the foam ball.

2) For arms, cut an 11-inch wire; bend ends into small loops. Wrap husks around loops, continuing to middle of wire; secure with thread. For sleeves, gather husks around wrists, extending husks over hands; wrap with thread and pull back over arms. Wrap husks with thread near center of wire (shoulders). Push head wire through center of arms; wrap with thread.

3) For bust and waist, place two cotton balls side by side in the center of a corn husk and fold the long sides toward the center; then fold the husk in half across the width. Wrap thread around the bottom of the husk to form the waist. Place this piece on the head wire ½ inch below the neck. Wrap thread over the shoulders and around the waist to join the pieces.

Center a three-inch-wide corn husk on each shoulder for the dress bodice. Cross husks over the bust in front and back, gathering at the waist. Secure with thread and repeat with two more husks, pleating them across the shoulders.

4) For the doll's skirt, cut a 15-inch-diameter half-circle from cardboard. Wrap the cardboard into a cone, leaving a five-inch opening in the bottom of the cone and a one-inch opening in the top.

Wrap half of the cone with husks, overlapping pieces slightly and pinning them at the bottom. Repeat for the rest of the skirt, wrapping with thread until dry.

5) Insert bodice through top of skirt and glue in place. Remove pins and thread and position doll as desired before husks dry.

For apron, cut curved edge along top of husk; gather straight edge to waistline. For shawl, drape a husk over doll's shoulders and tie ends. To make a bonnet, place folded edge of a corn husk next to doll's face, lay husk across the head, and secure with pins.

POTPOURRI

To make a potpourri, you'll need to gather a variety of garden-fresh flowers. Pick the flowers at midday during the summer months, when the dew has dried and flowers are at full bloom. The flowers must then be dried, using one of the four methods listed here.

Air drying: Gather flowers in small bunches and hang the bunches upside down in a dark, well-ventilated room for two to three weeks. Or, dry flowers and petals on a rack made of wire screen for one week; then dry them for four hours in a 100-degree oven.

Silica gel: Pour one to two inches of silica gel (available at craft and hobby shops) into a container and place whole flowers face up in the granules. Sprinkle the flowers with more silica gel until they are completely covered. Cover the container tightly and leave it in a dark, dry place for two to six days (petals should feel brittle and paper-like).

Borax: Using ordinary household borax, follow the drying instructions for silica gel except place the flowers face down and do not cover the container while flowers are drying. Drying time is four to 12 days.

Pressing: Spread facial tissue on the pages of a telephone book at one-inch intervals. Place flattened flowers on the tissue until the book is filled. Place weight on the book and store it in a dry, dark place for three to four weeks.

Flowers that are well-suited for potpourris include roses, marigolds, calendulas, clematis, bachelor buttons, pansies, apple blossoms, delphiniums, nasturtiums, alyssum, azaleas, forsythia, peonies, and camelias.

1) Once you've gathered your fresh flowers, dry them according to one of the four techniques explained at left. Here we used a drying rack made of wire screen. Store the flowers in airtight containers, stirring them every few days until you are ready to make your potpourri.

2) Stir together a mixture of lavender, tonka bean, sandalwood, lemon verbena, frankincense, myrrh, cloves, and cinnamon until you get a pleasing scent combination. (Experiment with one teaspoon of each herb or spice until you achieve a fragrance you like.)

3) Add the herbs and spices to the flower mixture, stirring carefully. (Choose a dry day for mixing the potpourris.) Sprinkle orris root, a scent preservative available at most pharmacies, on the potpourri.

4) Add several drops of essential oil to the potpourri and stir well. Carefully pour the mixture into an airtight container and cure it for three to four weeks, stirring often. After curing, use the potpourri mix in sachets, in jars (opened occasionally to add fragrance to a room), or in open bowls for constant fragrance.

NATURAL DYES

1) Dyeing with natural materials is another step in the art of creating a one-of-a-kind craft project entirely by hand. By dyeing your own wool flannel or wool yarn, you can work the "Naphtali" (leaping hart) wall hanging (opposite) in the tapestry hooking technique shown here or in crewel embroidery.

All of the colors for this project were achieved by using onionskins (yellow, red, and mixed) and four different mordants—alum, chrome, copper, and tin. (A mordant is a chemical fixative agent that fixes the final color so it does not fade or bleed. Mordants may be purchased in small quantities from pharmacies or craft shops.) The final yarn color will vary according to the mordant you use so you can achieve different yarn colors from the same dyebath.

Measure the mordant according to the amount of yarn you plan to dye. Our yarn was mordanted in one pound lots. We treated each lot with one of the mordants, then divided the yarn into ¼-pound skeins for dyeing.

Dissolve the mordant in a pot of warm water and add the yarn. Let the yarn steep for one hour.

2) While the yarn is soaking in the mordant, prepare an onionskin dyebath. (For four ounces of wool, use two quarts of onionskins.) Simmer the onionskins for one hour in a pot of water on your kitchen stove.

If you're interested in experimenting with other natural dyes, gather a selection of plant materials from your backyard (such as flowers, leaves, berries, barks, roots, hulls, pods, grasses, weeds, stems, twigs, and vines). To preserve colors, store your plant materials in paper bags and freeze the bags until you are ready to use them.

The most common colors in natural dyes are browns, yellows, greens, oranges, and violets. Be sure to keep a record of the plants you experiment with and the colors you get so you can repeat the successful recipes.

After dyeing flannel or yarn in a variety of colors (see step 3, above right), you can make the wall hanging (opposite). Enlarge the pattern at right onto high-quality and tightly woven burlap and work the design in tapestry hooking (using wool flannel strips) or in crewel embroidery (using wool yarn).

3) When the dyebath is ready, remove plant material, straining if necessary to remove small particles. Remove the wool from the mordant and squeeze gently to remove excess water. Place wool directly in the dyebath; simmer for one hour, stirring occasionally (do not boil).

Rinse the wool in water the same temperature as the dyebath, then wash the wool in lukewarm water with liquid dishwashing detergent. Rinse the wool thoroughly and hang it in a shady place to dry.

All natural fibers can be dyed with natural dyes, including wool, silk, cotton, jute, and linen.

COUNTRY FOODS

FROM SOUPS TO DESSERTS

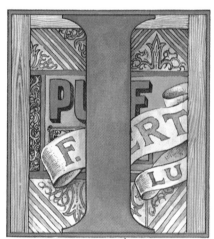

In years past, mealtime in many country homes called for loading the table with a variety of delicious foods. Often the recipes used were favorite family dishes handed down for generations, and each was prepared and brought to the table with loving care. In this chapter you'll find a sampling of those old-fashioned favorites. The list includes hearty main dishes, steaming soups and stews, refreshing salads, versatile vegetable dishes, crisp pickles and relishes, tempting homemade jellies and jams, and mouth-watering desserts of all types. Five country favorites are pictured at right. Clockwise from front left are: Popover Pizza, Beerwurst Soup, Chorizo-Stuffed Eggplant, Italian Sausage Kabobs, and Kielbasa Pasta Salad. (See index for recipe pages.)

MAIN DISHES

LAYERED HAMBURGER BAKE

4 ounces medium noodles
1 pound ground beef
1 15-ounce can tomato sauce
1 teaspoon sugar
½ teaspoon salt
¼ teaspoon garlic salt
⅛ teaspoon pepper
1 8-ounce package cream cheese, softened
½ cup dairy sour cream
3 tablespoons milk
2 tablespoons finely chopped onion
1 10-ounce package frozen chopped spinach, cooked and drained
½ cup shredded cheddar cheese (2 ounces)

Cook noodles in large amount of boiling salted water about 10 minutes or till tender; drain.

Meanwhile, brown ground beef in a skillet; drain off fat. Add tomato sauce, sugar, salt, garlic salt, pepper, and the cooked noodles. Set aside. Combine cream cheese, sour cream, milk, and onion.

In 2-quart casserole layer *half* of the ground beef-noodle mixture, *half* of the cream cheese mixture, all of the spinach, and the remaining ground beef and noodle mixture. Cover and bake in a 350° oven about 40 minutes or till bubbly. Uncover and spread remaining cream cheese mixture atop; sprinkle with the cheddar cheese. Bake about 10 minutes more or till cheese melts. Makes 6 servings.

COLOSSAL CORNBURGER

1 slightly beaten egg
1 cup fresh corn cut from cob
½ cup coarsely crushed cheese crackers
¼ cup sliced green onion
¼ cup snipped parsley
1 teaspoon Worcestershire sauce
½ teaspoon salt
½ teaspoon dried sage, crushed
2 pounds ground beef
Catsup, warmed (optional)

In a medium bowl combine the beaten egg, fresh corn, the crushed cheese crackers, sliced green onion, snipped parsley, the Worcestershire sauce, salt, and sage.

Divide beef in half. On separate sheets of waxed paper, pat each half into a 9-inch circle. Spoon corn mixture over one circle of meat to within 1 inch of edge. Invert the second circle of meat atop corn mixture; peel off waxed paper and seal edges well.

Invert meat patty onto a well-greased grill basket; peel off remaining waxed paper. Sprinkle with salt and pepper.

Grill over *medium* coals 12 to 15 minutes on each side or till done. Cut into wedges. Serve with some warmed catsup if desired. Makes 6 servings.

STUFFED CABBAGE ROLLS

See photo, pages 18-19—

12 large cabbage leaves
1 beaten egg
½ cup water
1 cup Homemade Granola (see recipe, page 314)
¼ cup chopped onion
1 teaspoon salt
¼ teaspoon pepper
¼ teaspoon dried thyme, crushed
1 pound ground beef
1 15-ounce can tomato sauce
2 tablespoons brown sugar
2 tablespoons lemon juice

Remove 2 inches of heavy center vein from the bottom of each cabbage leaf. Immerse cabbage leaves in boiling water for 3 minutes or just till limp; drain.

In a bowl combine the egg and water. Add Homemade Granola, onion, salt, pepper, and thyme. Add ground beef; mix thoroughly.

Place about ¼ cup of the meat mixture in the center of each leaf; fold in sides and roll ends over meat. Fasten with wooden picks. Place in a 10-inch skillet.

In a bowl combine the tomato sauce, brown sugar, and the lemon juice. Pour over cabbage rolls. Simmer, covered, for 55 minutes, basting occasionally. Remove cover; cook about 5 minutes more or till sauce reaches desired consistency. Makes 6 servings.

CORN MOUSSAKA

1 17-ounce can whole kernel
   corn, drained
1½ pounds ground beef
1 tablespoon all-purpose flour
1 8-ounce can tomato sauce
½ teaspoon garlic salt
¼ teaspoon ground cinnamon
2 slightly beaten eggs
1½ cups cream-style cottage
   cheese with chives,
   drained
¼ cup grated Parmesan cheese
   (1 ounce)
1 4-ounce package (1 cup)
   shredded mozzarella
   cheese
   Slivered almonds (optional)

Spread drained corn in an un-greased shallow 1½-quart casserole or a 10x6x2-inch baking dish.

In a medium skillet brown the ground beef; drain off fat. Add flour; cook and stir for 1 minute. Stir in tomato sauce, garlic salt, and cinnamon; pour over corn in dish. Bake in a 350° oven for 15 minutes.

Meanwhile, combine eggs and cottage cheese with chives; spread over meat mixture. Top with Parmesan cheese and the mozzarella cheese; sprinkle slivered almonds atop if desired. Bake 10 to 15 minutes more or till mozzarella is just melted. Makes 6 servings.

RED FLANNEL HASH

⅓ cup finely chopped onion
¼ cup shortening
3 cups finely chopped cooked
   potatoes
1 16-ounce can diced beets,
   drained and finely
   chopped
1½ cups finely chopped cooked
   corned beef
⅓ cup milk
1 to 2 drops bottled hot pepper
   sauce

Cook onion in hot shortening till tender. Lightly mix onion, remaining ingredients, and ½ teaspoon *salt*. Spread in skillet. Cook over medium heat till brown. Serves 4.

PEACH-GLAZED CORNED BEEF

1 3-pound corned beef brisket
2 medium acorn squash,
   quartered and seeded
4 small apples, cored and
   quartered
½ cup peach preserves
½ teaspoon ground ginger

Rinse meat in cold water. Place meat, fat side up, on rack in shallow roasting pan. Add 2 cups *water*; cover. Bake in a 350° oven for 2 to 2¼ hours. Drain. Add squash and apples, skin side down, to pan. Sprinkle the squash with salt. Add ½ cup hot *water*. Cover; bake 45 minutes. Mix the preserves and ginger; spoon over the meat, apples, and squash. Bake, uncovered, 10 minutes more. Serves 6 to 8.

BAKED CORNED BEEF BURGERS

1 slightly beaten egg
1½ cups soft bread crumbs
   (2 slices bread)
½ cup finely chopped onion
¼ cup mayonnaise *or* salad
   dressing
   Dash pepper
1 12-ounce can corned beef,
   flaked
⅓ cup fine dry bread crumbs
2 tablespoons cooking oil
   Celery Sauce
3 slices sharp American
   cheese, halved diagonally
3 English muffins, halved and
   toasted

In a bowl combine egg, soft bread crumbs, onion, mayonnaise or salad dressing, and pepper. Stir in corned beef; mix well. Shape mixture into 6 patties.

Coat the patties with dry bread crumbs. In a skillet brown patties in hot cooking oil about 2 minutes per side. Spoon *half* of the Celery Sauce into a 12x7½x2-inch baking dish. Add patties. Spoon remaining sauce atop.

Bake, uncovered, in a 400° oven for 15 to 20 minutes. Top each patty with a halved cheese slice. Bake 2 to 3 minutes more. Serve patties atop the English muffin halves. Makes 6 servings.

Celery Sauce: In a bowl combine one 10¾-ounce can of condensed *cream of celery soup;* one 8½-ounce can *mixed vegetables,* drained; and 1 teaspoon of *prepared horseradish mustard.* Stir in ⅓ cup *milk* till sauce is smooth.

EASY OVEN-BAKED SWISS STEAK

1½ pounds beef round steak, cut
  ¾ inch thick
¼ cup all-purpose flour
1 teaspoon salt
2 tablespoons shortening *or*
  cooking oil
1 16-ounce can tomatoes,
  cut up
½ cup finely chopped celery
½ cup finely chopped carrots
½ teaspoon Worcestershire
  sauce

Cut round steak into 6 serving-size portions. In a bowl combine flour and salt. With meat mallet, pound *1 tablespoon* of the flour mixture into meat on each side.

In a skillet brown meat on both sides in the hot shortening or cooking oil. Transfer meat pieces to a 12x7½x2-inch baking dish. Blend the remaining 2 tablespoons flour mixture into the pan drippings in a skillet. Stir in the *undrained* tomatoes, chopped celery, chopped carrots, and the Worcestershire sauce. Cook and stir till mixture is thickened and bubbly; pour over meat in baking dish.

Bake steak, covered, in a 350° oven about 1 hour and 20 minutes or till meat is tender. Serves 6.

From back to front: Pheasant with Wild Rice (see recipe, page 268), Honey-Wheat Muffins (see recipe, page 190), and Easy Oven-Baked Swiss Steak.

CHICKEN-FRIED STEAK

See photo, page 270—

1½ pounds beef top round steak
1 beaten egg
1 tablespoon milk
1 cup finely crushed saltine
  crackers (28 crackers)
¼ cup cooking oil

Pound beef to a ¼-inch thickness; cut into serving-size pieces. In a bowl mix egg and milk. Dip meat pieces in egg mixture, then in the crushed crackers. In a skillet brown meat in hot oil; turn once. Cover; cook over low heat 45 to 60 minutes. Makes 6 servings.

BARBECUED SHORT RIBS

4 pounds beef short ribs
⅔ cup catsup
¼ cup light molasses
¼ cup lemon juice
1 tablespoon dry mustard
½ teaspoon chili powder
  Dash garlic powder

Trim fat from ribs. Season with salt and pepper. Place ribs in large kettle and add enough water to cover ribs. Cover kettle; simmer about 2 hours or till tender. Drain; place ribs on rack of unheated broiler pan. In a bowl mix the catsup, molasses, lemon juice, mustard, chili powder, and garlic powder; brush over ribs. Broil 4 to 5 inches from heat for 10 to 15 minutes. Turn often; baste with the catsup mixture. Makes 4 servings.

CORNISH BEEF PASTIES

2 cups all-purpose flour
1 teaspoon salt
⅔ cup shortening
5 to 6 tablespoons cold water
1 medium potato, peeled
1 pound beef round steak, cut
  into ¼-inch cubes
⅔ cup peeled turnip, carrot, *or*
  rutabaga cut into ¼-inch
  cubes
½ cup finely chopped onion
1 teaspoon salt
¼ teaspoon pepper
  Milk
1 tablespoon sesame seed

In a large mixing bowl stir together the flour and 1 teaspoon salt. With a pastry blender, cut in the shortening till the mixture resembles coarse crumbs. Add cold water, 1 tablespoon at a time, tossing with a fork to moisten. Form pastry into a ball. Cover; chill 1 hour.

Meanwhile, coarsely chop potato. Combine with beef; turnip, carrot, or rutabaga; onion; 1 teaspoon salt; and pepper. Set aside.

Divide dough into 5 portions. On a lightly floured surface roll each portion into a 7-inch circle. Place about ⅔ cup filling in the center of each circle; bring sides of pastry over filling. Pinch edges to seal. Cut slits in the pastry to allow steam to escape.

Place on ungreased baking sheet; brush lightly with milk and sprinkle with sesame seed. Bake in a 375° oven for 35 to 40 minutes or till golden. Makes 5.

PHEASANTS WITH WILD RICE

See photo, page 266—

- 1 cup chopped onion
- 1 cup chopped carrot
- 1 cup chopped celery
- ⅓ cup butter *or* margarine
- 1½ cups wild rice, rinsed
- 3 cups sliced fresh mushrooms
- ¾ teaspoon dried sage, crushed
- ¾ teaspoon dried thyme, crushed
- ¾ teaspoon dried savory, crushed
- 2 2- to 3-pound domestic pheasants
- 6 slices bacon

Cook onion, carrot, and celery in butter. Stir in rice, 5¼ cups *water,* and 1 tablespoon *salt.* Cover; cook 35 to 40 minutes or till rice is nearly tender. Stir in the mushrooms, sage, thyme, and savory. Cover and cook 10 minutes. Rinse birds and pat dry with paper toweling. Sprinkle with salt. Spoon rice mixture loosely into the neck cavities. Pull the neck skins to the back; fasten with skewers. Lightly spoon more rice mixture into body cavities. Tie legs to tail. Twist wing tips under back. Place, breast side up, on rack in shallow roasting pan. Lay bacon over birds. Insert meat thermometer in center of inside thigh muscle, not touching bone. Place remaining stuffing in a 1-quart casserole. Cover. Roast birds, uncovered, in a 350° oven for 1½ to 2 hours or till meat thermometer registers 185°. During last 30 minutes, cut string between legs and bake stuffing in casserole. Serves 6.

CORNISH HENS WITH GRANOLA-RICE STUFFING

See photo, pages 18-19—

- 1 small orange
- 1½ cups cooked rice
- 1 cup Homemade Granola (see recipe, page 314)
- 1 small apple, peeled, cored, and chopped (⅔ cup)
- ½ teaspoon salt
- ¼ teaspoon ground cinnamon
- ¼ cup chopped celery
- ¼ cup chopped onion
- 2 tablespoons butter *or* margarine
- 6 1-pound Cornish game hens Cooking oil

Peel and section orange over a bowl to catch juice; set juice aside. Chop orange sections. In a large bowl combine orange sections, cooked rice, Homemade Granola, apple, salt, and cinnamon. Set aside.

In a saucepan cook celery and onion in butter or margarine till tender but not brown. Add to rice mixture, tossing lightly till well mixed. (Add reserved orange juice to moisten if desired.)

Season cavities of hens with salt. Lightly stuff hens with rice mixture. Pull neck skin, if present, to back. Twist wing tips under back, holding skin in place. Tie legs to tail. Place, breast side up, on a rack in a shallow roasting pan. Brush with cooking oil. Roast Cornish hens, loosely covered with foil, in a 375° oven for 30 minutes; uncover and roast hens about 1 hour more. Serves 12.

FRIED QUAIL WITH SAWMILL GRAVY

See photo, page 276—

- ⅔ cup all-purpose flour
- 1½ teaspoons salt
- 8 4- to 6-ounce quail *or* one 2½- to 3- pound broiler-fryer chicken, cut up
- Shortening
- ¾ teaspoon salt
- ¾ cup milk
- Hot cooked rice

In a bag mix *half* of the flour, the 1½ teaspoons salt, and ⅛ teaspoon *pepper.* Add the quail or chicken pieces two at a time; shake well to coat. In a deep 12-inch skillet heat ½ inch shortening to 375°. Add quail or chicken pieces. Fry, uncovered, on one side about 4 minutes for quail or 5 minutes for chicken. Turn pieces. Cover skillet; cook till second side is brown. Allow 3 to 4 minutes for quail and 4 to 5 minutes for chicken. Uncover; turn once more. Cook 2 to 3 minutes more for quail and 5 minutes more for chicken or till crisp. Remove to platter; keep warm.

Drain fat, reserving ¼ cup. Return reserved fat to skillet; stir in remaining flour, the ¾ teaspoon salt, and ¼ teaspoon *pepper.* Cook and stir over medium heat about 8 minutes or till mixture has a dark brown color. Mix milk and ¾ cup *water*; add to flour mixture. Cook and stir till mixture is thickened and bubbly. Cook and stir 1 minute more. Season to taste. Arrange the birds atop rice and garnish with snipped parsley if desired. Serve with gravy. Makes 4 servings.

SIX-WAY CHICKEN BASE

2 2½- to 3-pound broiler-
   fryer chickens, cut up, *or*
   one 6-pound stewing hen,
   cut up
1¼ pounds chicken wings *or*
   backs (about 6)
4 stalks celery with leaves
1 carrot, quartered
1 small onion, cut up
2 sprigs parsley
2 teaspoons salt
¼ teaspoon pepper
2½ quarts water

Place chicken pieces, celery, carrot, onion, and parsley in a large Dutch oven or kettle. Sprinkle with the salt and pepper. Add the 2½ quarts water. (Add more water to cover chicken if necessary.) Bring to boiling. Reduce heat; cover and cook over low heat for about 1 hour (1½ to 2 hours for stewing hen) or till chicken is tender. Transfer meat to shallow baking pan to cool; refrigerate broth or chill in pan of ice water.

When chicken is cool enough to handle, remove meat from bones; discard skin and bones. Cube the meat. Cover meat and refrigerate. When broth is chilled, skim fat from broth. Strain broth.

In each of three 1-quart freezer containers, pack *2 cups* of the cubed chicken and *2 cups* of the chilled broth. Pour the remaining broth into two 1-pint containers. Seal, label, and freeze. Makes 3 quarts of cubed chicken with broth and 2 pints of broth.

BRUNSWICK STEW

1 quart frozen Six-Way
   Chicken Base
1 pint frozen Six-Way
   Chicken Base broth
1 10-ounce package frozen cut
   okra
1 10-ounce package frozen
   baby lima beans
1 16-ounce can tomatoes,
   cut up
2 cups diced peeled potatoes
½ cup chopped onion
1½ teaspoons salt
½ teaspoon dried marjoram,
   crushed
½ teaspoon dried rosemary,
   crushed
1 bay leaf
¼ teaspoon pepper

Place the frozen Chicken Base, the frozen Chicken Base broth, the cut okra, and the baby lima beans in a large kettle or a Dutch oven.

Drain tomato juice into pan. Cover and cook over medium heat for 15 to 20 minutes or till chicken mixture is thawed.

Add tomatoes, diced potatoes, the chopped onion, salt, marjoram, rosemary, bay leaf, and pepper to chicken mixture. Bring to boiling. Cover and simmer for 15 to 20 minutes or till potatoes are tender. Remove bay leaf. Serve in soup bowls. Makes 8 servings.

SAUCY CHICKEN PIE

1 quart frozen Six-Way
   Chicken Base
½ cup milk
½ cup chopped onion
6 tablespoons butter *or*
   margarine
6 tablespoons all-purpose flour
1 teaspoon salt
1 cup dairy sour cream
1 10-ounce package frozen
   peas and carrots, cooked
   and drained
¼ cup chopped pimiento
   Packaged instant mashed
   potatoes (enough for
   4 servings)
1 cup milk
1 beaten egg
1 cup herb-seasoned stuffing
   mix

In a saucepan mix frozen Chicken Base and the ½ cup milk. Cover; cook over medium heat about 20 minutes or till chicken is thawed.

In another saucepan cook onion in butter or margarine till tender. Stir in flour and salt. Add chicken mixture. Cook and stir till mixture thickens and bubbles. Remove mixture from heat; stir in sour cream. Stir in peas and carrots and pimiento. Turn into a 12x7½x2-inch baking dish. Bake in a 425° oven about 15 minutes or till mixture is bubbly.

Prepare mashed potatoes according to package directions, *except* use the 1 cup milk. Beat in egg. Fold in stuffing mix. (Potato mixture will be very wet.) Drop potato mixture by spoonfuls onto the bubbling chicken mixture. Sprinkle with paprika if desired. Bake 5 to 8 minutes more. Makes 6 servings.

CLUB CHICKEN

1 quart frozen Six-Way
   Chicken Base (see recipe,
   page 269)
⅔ cup long-grain rice
3 tablespoons butter
3 tablespoons all-purpose flour
1½ teaspoons salt
1 13-ounce can (1⅔ cups)
   evaporated milk
1 10-ounce package frozen
   chopped broccoli, cooked
   and drained
1 3-ounce can sliced
   mushrooms, drained
¼ cup toasted slivered almonds

In saucepan combine frozen Six-Way Chicken Base and ½ cup *water*. Cover; cook over medium heat about 20 minutes or till thawed. Remove chicken. Cook rice in the chicken broth according to package directions.

In a saucepan melt butter. Stir in the flour and salt. Add evaporated milk; cook and stir till mixture thickens. Stir in the cooked rice, cooked chicken, broccoli, and the mushrooms. Turn into a 10x6x2-inch baking dish. Bake in a 350° oven for 30 to 35 minutes or till hot. Top with nuts. Serves 6.

Clockwise from the top: Raspberry-Cherry Pie (see recipe, page 318), Fig-Apple Pie (see recipe, page 319), boiled potatoes, Nutmeg Squash (see recipe, page 291), sliced cucumbers and onions, Chicken and Homemade Noodles, Cabbage Slaw (see recipe, page 297), sliced tomatoes, Chicken-Fried Steak (see recipe, page 267), and bacon-topped cooked green beans.

CHICKEN AND HOMEMADE NOODLES

2 beaten eggs
¼ cup milk
¾ teaspoon salt
2 cups all-purpose flour
1 5- to 6-pound stewing
   chicken, cut up, *or two*
   2½- to 3-pound broiler-
   fryer chickens, cut up
1 medium onion, chopped
4 teaspoons salt
¼ teaspoon pepper
3 carrots, thinly sliced
¼ cup cold water
2 tablespoons all-purpose flour

To prepare noodles, combine eggs, milk, and the ¾ teaspoon salt. Add as much of the 2 cups flour as you can mix in with a spoon to make a stiff dough. Divide dough in half. Roll very thinly on floured surface; let stand 20 minutes. Roll up loosely; slice ¼ inch wide. Unroll; cut into desired lengths. Let dry 2 hours.

Place the chicken in kettle with enough water to cover (about 8 cups). Add onion, the 4 teaspoons salt, and pepper. Cover; bring to boiling. Reduce heat; simmer 2 to 2½ hours for stewing chicken or 1 hour for broiler-fryers. Remove the chicken; cool. Remove meat from bones; discard skin and bones. Cut meat into bite-size pieces.

Bring broth to boiling; add noodles and carrots. Cover and simmer 10 minutes. Add chicken. Combine ¼ cup cold water and the 2 tablespoons flour; add to the chicken and noodle mixture. Cook, stirring constantly, till slightly thickened and bubbly. Makes 6 to 8 servings.

BEAN CASSOULET

1 pound dry navy beans
   (2 cups)
1 cup chopped celery
1 cup diced carrot
2 teaspoons instant beef
   bouillon granules
1 2½- to 3-pound broiler-
   fryer chicken, cut up
½ pound bulk pork sausage
1 cup chopped onion
1½ cups tomato juice
1 tablespoon Worcestershire
   sauce

In a 6-quart Dutch oven combine beans and 8 cups *water*. Bring to boiling; boil 2 minutes. Remove from heat. Cover; let stand 1 hour. (*Or*, let beans and water stand overnight.) Drain beans. Combine the beans, celery, carrot, bouillon granules, neck and giblets from chicken, 8 cups *water*, and 1 teaspoon *salt*. Bring to boiling; reduce heat. Cover; simmer 1 hour.

Meanwhile, shape sausage into small balls; brown in a skillet. Remove sausage; set aside. Reserve drippings in skillet. Sprinkle chicken pieces with salt and pepper. Brown chicken in the drippings and set aside.

In the same skillet cook onion in drippings till tender. Stir in the tomato juice and the Worcestershire sauce. Drain bean mixture, reserving liquid. Combine bean mixture, sausage, and tomato mixture. Turn into Dutch oven. Top with chicken pieces; pour *1½ cups* of the reserved liquid over all. Sprinkle with paprika if desired. Cover; bake in a 325° oven for 1 hour, adding more bean liquid if necessary. Makes 8 servings.

CHORIZO-STUFFED EGGPLANT

See photo, pages 262-263—

    3 medium eggplants (1 pound
        each)
 1¼ pounds bulk chorizo *or*
        Italian sausage, crumbled
    1 small onion, thinly sliced
    1 green pepper, cut into strips
    1 tablespoon snipped chives
   ¾ teaspoon dried oregano,
        crushed
   ¼ teaspoon pepper
   ⅓ cup grated Parmesan cheese
    2 medium tomatoes, sliced and
        halved
        Cooking oil

Halve eggplants lengthwise. Carefully scoop out pulp, leaving a ½-inch-thick shell; reserve pulp.

In a large saucepan cook eggplant shells, uncovered, in a large pan of boiling water for 2 minutes or till tender. Drain; sprinkle with salt. Set aside.

In a large skillet cook sausage, uncovered, on low heat for 5 minutes; drain off fat. Stir onion, green pepper, chives, oregano, and pepper into skillet; cook till vegetables are tender but not brown. Chop reserved eggplant pulp; add to sausage mixture. Cook, covered, for 5 minutes more. Spoon mixture into the eggplant shells. Sprinkle Parmesan cheese atop.

Place the stuffed eggplant shells in an ungreased 15x10x1-inch baking pan; cover lightly with foil. Bake in a 350° oven for 20 minutes; remove foil. Place two tomato slice halves atop each shell; brush tomatoes lightly with cooking oil. Bake, uncovered, for 5 to 10 minutes longer. Makes 6 servings.

POPOVER PIZZA

See photo, pages 262-263—

   12 ounces mortadella, cubed
   ½ cup chopped onion
    1 tablespoon butter *or*
        margarine
    1 15½-ounce jar spaghetti
        sauce
   ½ teaspoon fennel seed
    1 6-ounce package sliced
        mozzarella cheese
    2 eggs
    1 cup milk
    1 tablespoon cooking oil
    1 cup all-purpose flour
   ½ teaspoon salt
   ½ cup grated Parmesan cheese

In a skillet cook the mortadella and chopped onion in the butter or margarine till onion is tender but not brown; drain. Stir in the spaghetti sauce and fennel seed. Pour mixture into an ungreased 13x9x2-inch baking pan. Arrange sliced mozzarella cheese atop.

In a mixing bowl combine the eggs, milk, and cooking oil; add the flour and salt. Beat with a rotary beater till mixture is smooth. Pour egg mixture evenly over cheese in pan. Sprinkle the grated Parmesan cheese over all.

Bake in a 400° oven about 30 minutes or till the crust is golden brown. Cut the pizza into squares. Serve at once. Makes 6 servings.

ITALIAN SAUSAGE KABOBS

See photo, pages 262-263—

   ¼ cup finely chopped onion
    2 tablespoons butter *or*
        margarine
   ½ cup apple cider *or* juice
   ¼ cup red wine vinegar
    2 tablespoons honey
    1 tablespoon bottled steak
        sauce
    1 teaspoon salt
   ⅛ teaspoon pepper
    2 pounds mild Italian sausage
        links
    8 small white onions (1 pound)
    8 medium to large mushroom
        caps
    8 cherry tomatoes

To prepare sauce, in a small saucepan cook chopped onion in butter or margarine till tender but not brown. Stir in apple cider or juice, the red wine vinegar, honey, steak sauce, salt, and pepper. Bring to boiling; simmer, uncovered, for 20 minutes, stirring occasionally.

Meanwhile, in large saucepan add sausage to large amount of boiling water. Reduce heat; simmer, covered, for 10 minutes. Drain. Cut crosswise into 2-inch pieces. Cook onions, uncovered, in boiling water for 3 to 5 minutes or till nearly tender; drain.

On eight 10-inch skewers alternately thread sausage pieces, onions, and mushrooms. Grill over *hot* coals for 10 to 12 minutes, turning and brushing often with sauce. Garnish ends of skewers with cherry tomatoes. Heat and pass remaining sauce. Makes 8 servings.

KIELBASA-PASTA SALAD

See photo, pages 262-263—

12 ounces kielbasa *or* Polish
    sausage links
½ cup water
1½ cups small-shell macaroni
6 slices bacon
1 cup sliced fresh mushrooms
3 tablespoons sugar
2 tablespoons all-purpose flour
½ teaspoon salt
⅛ teaspoon pepper
¾ cup water
¼ cup tarragon vinegar
2 tablespoons snipped parsley
    Snipped parsley (optional)

In a skillet simmer sausage, covered, in the ½ cup water for 20 minutes. Meanwhile, cook macaroni according to package directions; drain. Drain and slice the sausage; set aside.

In a large skillet cook bacon till crisp; drain, reserving 3 tablespoons drippings in skillet. Crumble bacon; set aside.

Cook the mushrooms in reserved drippings for 2 minutes. Stir in sugar, flour, salt, and pepper; add the ¾ cup water and the vinegar. Cook and stir till thickened and bubbly. Add the cooked sausage, cooked shell macaroni, crumbled bacon, and the 2 tablespoons of snipped parsley. Toss together lightly. Garnish with additional snipped parsley if desired. Serve at once. Makes 4 to 6 servings.

SALAMI BAGELWICHES

4 bagels, split and toasted
2 tablespoons butter
2 hard-cooked eggs, chopped
2 tablespoons mayonnaise
1 tablespoon chopped onion
2 teaspoons toasted sesame
    seed
4 ounces sliced Genoa salami
4 slices Swiss cheese
½ medium cucumber, sliced

Spread bagels with the butter. Mix eggs, mayonnaise, onion, and sesame seed. Spread the cut side of *each* bagel bottom with *2 teaspoons* of egg mixture; place a *fourth* of the salami, cheese, and cucumber atop *each*. Spread cut side of *each* bagel top with *2 teaspoons* of egg mixture; place atop sandwich. Makes 4.

METTWURST PÂTÉ

8 ounces cooked mettwurst *or*
    teawurst
½ cup cream-style cottage
    cheese
⅓ cup chopped walnuts
2 tablespoons crumbled blue
    cheese (½ ounce)
    Assorted crackers

Place mettwurst or teawurst, cottage cheese, walnuts, and the blue cheese in blender container. Cover and blend till smooth, stopping to scrape down sides as necessary. Turn into oiled 2-cup bowl or mold; cover and chill for several hours. Unmold. Serve with assorted crackers. Makes 1½ cups.

SWISS-BRATWURST MELT

2 tablespoons butter *or*
    margarine
4 teaspoons all-purpose flour
¼ teaspoon salt
¼ teaspoon dry mustard
¾ cup milk
¾ cup shredded process Swiss
    cheese (3 ounces)
1 8-ounce can sauerkraut
4 cooked bratwurst links
    (about 1 pound)
4 large slices pumpernickel
    bread, toasted
4 slices tomato
4 green pepper rings
    Ground nutmeg (optional)

Melt butter or margarine in a small saucepan. Stir in flour, salt, and dry mustard; add milk all at once. Cook and stir till mixture is thickened and bubbly. Stir in Swiss cheese till melted; cover and keep warm. Heat sauerkraut in a small saucepan.

Meanwhile, halve the bratwurst links lengthwise; place, cut side down, on unheated broiler pan or baking sheet. Broil 3 to 5 inches from heat for 3 minutes. Drain the sauerkraut.

To make each sandwich, place 2 bratwurst halves on a bread slice. Top with a *fourth* of the hot sauerkraut and a tomato slice; spoon a *fourth* of the cheese sauce over. Garnish with a green pepper ring and a dash of ground nutmeg if desired. Makes 4 servings.

CHILI-PORK BAKE

1 pound ground pork
¼ cup chopped onion
1 16-ounce can stewed
  tomatoes
4 ounces medium noodles,
  cooked and drained
1 12-ounce can whole kernel
  corn, drained
1 16-ounce can tomato paste
1 teaspoon chili powder
¼ teaspoon garlic powder
1 cup shredded cheddar cheese

Cook meat and onion till meat is browned; drain. Stir in tomatoes, noodles, corn, tomato paste, chili powder, garlic powder, 1 teaspoon *salt*, and dash *pepper*. Turn into 1½-quart casserole; cover. Bake in a 350° oven for 40 minutes. Top with cheese. Bake, uncovered, 5 minutes. Serves 6.

PORK SKILLET

4 pork shoulder chops, cut
  ½ inch thick (2 pounds)
1 16-ounce can (2 cups)
  sauerkraut, snipped
1 8-ounce can applesauce
¼ cup finely chopped onion
2 tablespoons brown sugar
¾ teaspoon caraway seed

Trim fat from chops. In skillet cook fat till 1 tablespoon drippings accumulates. Discard the trimmings. Brown chops in skillet. Drain; remove chops. Mix kraut, applesauce, onion, brown sugar, and caraway seed. Add to skillet. Add chops. Cover; simmer for 35 to 45 minutes. Serves 4.

UPSIDE-DOWN POLENTA CASSEROLE

1 pound bulk pork sausage
1 cup chopped onion
1 16-ounce can tomatoes,
  cut up
1 8-ounce can tomato sauce
1 4-ounce can sliced
  mushrooms, drained
1 teaspoon salt
¼ teaspoon dried oregano,
  crushed
⅛ teaspoon garlic powder
¾ cup all-purpose flour
¾ cup cornmeal
¾ cup grated Parmesan cheese
1 tablespoon sugar
1 tablespoon baking powder
¾ teaspoon salt
¾ cup milk
1 well-beaten egg
3 tablespoons cooking oil
1 cup shredded cheddar cheese
2 tablespoons snipped parsley

In a saucepan cook sausage and onion till meat is brown and onion is tender; drain off fat. Stir in *undrained* tomatoes, tomato sauce, mushrooms, the 1 teaspoon salt, the oregano, garlic powder, and a dash *pepper*. Bring to boiling. Simmer, covered, for 5 minutes.

In a bowl mix flour, cornmeal, the Parmesan cheese, sugar, baking powder, and the ¾ teaspoon salt; make a well in center of dry ingredients. Add milk, egg, and oil, stirring till combined. Spread in an ungreased 13x9x2-inch baking dish. Spoon tomato mixture atop. Bake in a 400° oven for 20 minutes. Sprinkle with the cheddar cheese and parsley. Bake about 5 minutes more. Makes 8 servings.

LIMA BEANS AND PORK SAUSAGE

1 pound dry lima beans
  (2½ cups)
12 cups water
½ teaspooon salt
1 pound bulk pork sausage
2½ cups tomato juice
1 teaspoon dried basil, crushed
¼ teaspoon chili powder
⅛ teaspoon pepper

Rinse beans. In a Dutch oven or kettle combine beans with *half* of the water. Bring to boiling and simmer 2 minutes; remove from heat. Cover; let stand 1 hour. (*Or*, let beans and *half* the water soak overnight.) Drain beans.

In a kettle combine beans, remaining water, and salt. Bring to boiling. Cover; simmer 45 to 60 minutes or till beans are tender. Drain and set aside.

In the same pan cook sausage till brown; drain. Stir in tomato juice, basil, chili powder, pepper, and drained beans. Simmer, uncovered, about 10 minutes or till hot, stirring often. Serve in soup bowls. Makes 8 servings.

From front to back: Upside-Down Polenta Casserole, Calico Bean Bake (see recipe, page 278), and Anything-Goes Quiche (see recipe, page 277).

PORK CHOP ROYALE

6 pork chops, cut 1 inch thick
   (2 pounds)
   Garlic salt
3 cups cooked brown rice
½ cup coarsely chopped
   cashews
½ cup chopped celery
¼ cup finely chopped onion
3 tablespoons soy sauce
¼ teaspoon ground ginger
1 10¾-ounce can condensed
   cream of mushroom soup
½ cup dairy sour cream
¼ cup milk

Trim fat from chops. Place fat in skillet; cook till about 2 tablespoons of drippings accumulate. Remove trimmings and discard. Brown the meat on both sides in hot fat. Season with a little salt, pepper, and garlic salt.

In a bowl combine the cooked brown rice, cashews, celery, onion, soy sauce, and ginger. Spread in a 12x7½x2-inch baking dish; arrange chops atop. Cover and bake in a 350° oven for about 1 hour or till meat is tender.

Meanwhile, in a saucepan combine the cream of mushroom soup, the sour cream, and milk. Heat through but *do not boil.* Serve over chops and rice. Makes 6 servings.

From front to back: Garden Salad (see recipe, page 297), Country Ham with Red-Eye Gravy, Fried Quail with Sawmill Gravy (see recipe, page 268), Buttermilk Biscuits (see recipe, page 190), and mixed fresh fruit.

COUNTRY HAM

1 12- to 14-pound bone-in
   country ham

Throughly scrub and rinse ham. In a large bowl or kettle cover ham with water. Place ham in the refrigerator to soak overnight. Drain ham. Place ham in a large kettle; add water to cover. Bring to boiling. Reduce heat and simmer 20 minutes per pound (4 to 4½ hours). Transfer ham from water to platter and thinly slice. Cover and chill any remaining ham to serve with Red-Eye Gravy.

HAM WITH RED-EYE GRAVY

3 slices country ham, cut
   ⅛ to ¼ inch thick
½ cup water *or* coffee
   Biscuits, grits, *or* rice

In a large heavy skillet (preferably cast iron) cook ham 4 to 5 minutes per side. Transfer ham to warm platter; keep warm.

Quickly add water or coffee to hot skillet, being careful to avoid splattering. Cook, scraping pan to remove crusty bits, till mixture boils vigorously. Continue cooking about 3 minutes more or till mixture is reduced by half. Serve gravy with ham over biscuits, grits, or rice. Makes 3 servings.

ANYTHING-GOES QUICHE

See photo, page 274—

1 9-inch unbaked pastry shell
8 slices bacon, diced, *or* ½
   cup diced fully cooked
   ham *or* cooked shrimp
3 beaten eggs
1½ cups milk
1 tablespoon all-purpose flour
¼ teaspoon salt
   Dash ground nutmeg
1½ cups shredded Swiss cheese
   (6 ounces)
½ cup shredded Monterey
   Jack, mozzarella,
   cheddar, *or* brick cheese
   (2 ounces)

Bake unpricked pastry shell in a 450° oven for 10 to 12 minutes or till pastry is nearly done. Remove from oven; reduce oven temperature to 325°. (Pastry shell should be hot when filling is added; do not partially bake ahead of time.)

Meanwhile, if using the bacon, cook the pieces in skillet till crisp; drain. In bowl thoroughly stir together the eggs, milk, flour, salt, and nutmeg. Stir in the cooked bacon pieces, ham, or shrimp, Swiss cheese, and choice of remaining cheeses; mix well.

Pour into the *warm* pastry shell. Cover edge of crust with foil to prevent overbrowning. Bake in a 325° oven for 35 to 40 minutes. Remove foil; bake 10 to 15 minutes more or till knife inserted just off-center comes out clean. Let stand 5 to 10 minutes before serving. Trim with parsley and cherry tomatoes if desired. Makes 6 servings.

CALICO BEAN BAKE

See photo, page 274—

- ½ cup chopped onion
- 1 tablespoon butter
- 1 16-ounce can red kidney beans
- 1 16-ounce can lima beans
- 1 16-ounce can pork and beans in tomato sauce
- ½ cup bottled barbecue sauce
- ⅛ teaspoon garlic powder
- 5 slices fully cooked ham, cut ¼ inch thick

Cook onion in butter till tender. Drain kidney and lima beans. Combine all ingredients *except* ham. Turn into a 1½-quart casserole. Top with ham. Cover; bake in a 350° oven for 25 minutes. Uncover; bake 25 minutes. Serves 6.

ORANGE-GLAZED CANADIAN BACON

- 8 slices Canadian-style bacon, cut ½ inch thick
- 1 tablespoon butter
- ¼ cup pineapple preserves
- 3 tablespoons frozen orange juice concentrate, thawed
- 2 teaspoons lemon juice
- 1 teaspoon prepared mustard
- ⅛ teaspoon ground cloves

In a skillet brown bacon, half at a time, in butter. Return all to skillet. In a bowl mix preserves, orange juice concentrate, lemon juice, mustard, and cloves. Pour over bacon. Bring to boiling; reduce heat. Cook about 5 minutes. Serves 4.

ROAST LAMB WITH PLUM SAUCE

- 1 4- to 5-pound leg of lamb
- 1 clove garlic, halved
- 1 tablespoon snipped parsley
- 1 teaspoon salt
- 1 teaspoon celery salt
- ½ teaspoon pepper
- ¼ teaspoon paprika
- ¼ cup butter *or* margarine, softened
- 2 tablespoons all-purpose flour
- ¼ cup finely chopped carrot
- 1 tablespoon finely chopped onion
- ¼ bay leaf, crumbled
  Plum Sauce

Rub leg of lamb all over with cut side of garlic. In a bowl combine parsley, salt, celery salt, pepper, and paprika; rub into lamb. Place lamb, fat side up, on rack in a shallow roasting pan. Insert a meat thermometer so it does not touch bone. Roast in a 325° oven for 2 hours.

In a bowl combine butter or margarine and flour. Stir in carrot, onion, and bay leaf; spread over lamb. Continue roasting the lamb about 1 hour more or till meat thermometer registers 175° to 180°. Serve with warm Plum Sauce. Makes 8 to 10 servings.

Plum Sauce: In a saucepan combine ¾ cup *plum jelly*, ¼ cup *unsweetened pineapple juice*, 1 tablespoon *orange juice*, 1 teaspoon all-purpose *flour*, ¼ teaspoon *dry mustard*, and dash *ground mace*. Cook and stir till mixture is thickened and bubbly. Simmer 2 to 3 minutes more; stir occasionally.

NUTTY TUNA-NOODLE BAKE

- 3 cups medium noodles
- 2 tablespoons butter *or* margarine
- 2 tablespoons all-purpose flour
- 1⅓ cups milk
- 1 10¾-ounce can condensed cream of mushroom soup
- ¾ cup shredded American cheese (3 ounces)
- 1 12½-ounce can tuna, drained and flaked
- 1 8-ounce can peas and carrots, drained
- 2 tablespoons chopped pimiento
- ½ cup chopped peanuts

Cook noodles according to package directions; drain well. Meanwhile, in a saucepan melt the butter or margarine; stir in the flour. Add the milk and cream of mushroom soup all at once. Cook and stir till mixture is thickened and bubbly. Remove the soup mixture from heat; stir in the American cheese till melted. Stir tuna, peas and carrots, and pimiento into soup mixture. Fold in noodles.

Turn the soup-tuna mixture into a 2-quart casserole. Sprinkle the chopped peanuts atop. Bake, uncovered, in a 350° oven for 30 to 35 minutes or till mixture is heated through. Makes 6 servings.

CAPE COD DINNER

1½ pounds salt cod
4 ounces salt pork, diced
4 medium beets, peeled and sliced
4 medium potatoes, peeled and quartered
2 large carrots, cut into chunks
8 small whole onions
  Cream Sauce

In a bowl soak salt cod in enough water to cover for about 12 hours, changing water once. In a saucepan cook the salt pork till crisp. Drain; set the salt pork aside. Discard drippings. Drain salt cod well. In the same saucepan cover cod with fresh cold water. Bring to boiling; reduce heat and simmer about 20 minutes or till the fish is tender. Drain.

Meanwhile, in a second saucepan cook beets, covered, in a small amount of boiling salted water for about 20 minutes or till tender. In a third saucepan cook potatoes, carrots, and onions, covered, in boiling salted water for about 20 minutes or till tender. Drain all vegetables. Arrange fish and vegetables on a warm platter. Stir salt pork into Cream Sauce. Spoon some of the sauce over fish. Top with hard-cooked egg slices if desired. Pass any remaining sauce. Makes 4 servings.

Cream Sauce: In small saucepan melt 2 tablespoons of *butter or margarine*. Stir in 2 tablespoons all-purpose *flour*, ¼ teaspoon *salt*, ⅛ teaspoon *white pepper*, and ⅛ teaspoon ground *nutmeg*. Add 1 cup *milk* all at once. Cook and stir till bubbly. Makes 1½ cups.

HADDOCK PROVENÇALE

6 fresh *or* frozen haddock fillets (1½ pounds)
  Paprika
¼ cup chopped onion
1 clove garlic, minced
1 tablespoon butter *or* margarine
½ cup dry white wine
2 tomatoes, peeled, seeded, and coarsely chopped, *or* one 16-ounce can tomatoes, drained and cut up
1 3-ounce can chopped mushrooms, drained
2 tablespoons snipped parsley
1 vegetable bouillon cube
1 teaspoon sugar
¼ cup cold water
2 teaspoons cornstarch

Thaw fish fillets, if frozen. Sprinkle each fillet with salt and paprika. Roll up fillets and secure them with wooden picks.

In a medium skillet cook onion and garlic in butter or margarine till onion is tender but not brown. Add wine. Stir in tomatoes, mushrooms, parsley, vegetable bouillon cube, and sugar; bring to boiling. Add fish; reduce heat. Cover and simmer 15 to 20 minutes or till fish flakes easily.

Transfer cooked fish to platter; keep warm. Combine cold water and cornstarch. Add to liquid in skillet. Cook and stir till mixture thickens and bubbles. Spoon sauce over fish. Makes 6 servings.

CASHEW-TOFU STIR-FRY

See photo, page 280—

2 tree ears* *or* one 4-ounce can sliced mushrooms, drained
1 vegetable bouillon cube
2 tablespoons soy sauce
2 teaspoons cornstarch
¼ cup cooking oil
2 medium carrots, thinly bias-sliced
1 head Chinese cabbage, cut into 1-inch slices
8 ounces tofu (bean curd), cubed
1 8-ounce can bamboo shoots, drained
¾ cup cashews
1 5-ounce can chow mein noodles

If using tree ears, cover with *hot* water; let stand 30 minutes. Rinse under running water; squeeze to drain. Cut into thin strips.

Combine vegetable bouillon cube and ½ cup *boiling water*; stir to dissolve bouillon cube. Stir together soy sauce and cornstarch. Stir into bouillon mixture.

In large skillet or wok heat *half* of the oil. Stir-fry carrots for 3 minutes. Add cabbage and stir-fry 2 minutes more. Add more oil if necessary. Add the tofu, the bamboo shoots, cashews, and the tree ears or the mushrooms. Stir-fry 1 minute more. Stir bouillon mixture; add to skillet or wok. Cook and stir till mixture is thickened and bubbly. Cover and cook 2 minutes more. Serve with chow mein noodles. Makes 4 servings.

*Note: Tree ears are Oriental mushrooms that are available at most Oriental food shops.

FETA-KALE PIE

2 10-ounce packages frozen
    chopped kale, thawed
3 cups sliced fresh mushrooms
1 cup chopped onion
2 tablespoons cooking oil
6 beaten eggs
2 cups feta cheese, crumbled
2 tablespoons grated
    Parmesan cheese
¼ cup snipped parsley
½ teaspoon dried oregano,
    crushed
½ teaspoon dried basil, crushed
    Pastry

Squeeze moisture from kale; finely chop. Cook mushrooms and onion in oil till tender. Mix eggs and cheeses. Stir in kale, mushroom mixture, parsley, oregano, and basil. On floured surface, roll *half* of the Pastry into a 14x10-inch rectangle. Fit into a 10x6x2-inch baking dish. Trim edges to ½ inch beyond edge of dish. Spoon the kale mixture into crust. Roll the remaining Pastry into an 11x7-inch rectangle. Cut into four 11x1½-inch strips. Space evenly atop filling; trim the edges. Crimp edges. (If desired, use a small leaf-shaped cutter to cut leaves from the remaining pastry. Moisten edge of pie with water; overlap leaves around edge, pressing firmly. Use any remaining pastry to decorate center strips.) Bake in a 375° oven about 50 minutes. Serves 6.

Pastry: Mix 2 cups all-purpose *flour* and 1 teaspoon *salt.* Cut in ⅔ cup *shortening* till the size of small peas. Sprinkle 6 to 7 tablespoons *cold water,* one at a time, over mixture; gently toss with a fork. Form dough into 2 balls.

FETTUCINI WITH MUSHROOM-WINE SAUCE

10 ounces fettucini *or* other
    pasta
1 cup sliced fresh mushrooms
½ cup chopped onion
2 tablespoons butter *or*
    margarine
1 cup dry white wine
2 vegetable bouillon cubes
½ teaspoon dried thyme,
    crushed
⅛ teaspoon pepper
1 15½-ounce can red kidney
    beans, drained
1 cup fresh pea pods *or* one
    6-ounce package frozen
    pea pods, thawed
3 tablespoons butter *or*
    margarine
½ cup grated Parmesan cheese
½ cup snipped parsley
    Grated Parmesan cheese

Cook pasta in a large amount of boiling salted water for 9 to 12 minutes or till tender. Drain.

Meanwhile, in a saucepan cook the mushrooms and onion in the 2 tablespoons of butter or margarine till tender. Stir in wine, vegetable bouillon cubes, thyme, and pepper. Simmer, covered, about 10 minutes. Stir in the drained kidney beans. Simmer, uncovered, for 5 to 10 minutes more.

If using fresh pea pods, cook the pods in boiling water for 1 minute; drain. To serve, toss pasta with the 3 tablespoons butter or margarine. Then toss with the ½ cup Parmesan cheese, parsley, wine mixture, and pea pods. Sprinkle pasta with additional Parmesan cheese. Makes 5 servings.

VEGETARIAN BEAN PITAS

¼ cup chopped onion
1 clove garlic, minced
1 tablespoon cooking oil
1 15-ounce can pinto beans,
    drained and mashed
1 3-ounce package cream
    cheese, softened
½ teaspoon salt
¼ teaspoon pepper
1 cup shredded zucchini
1 tablespoon oil and vinegar
    salad dressing with
    seasonings
5 pita bread rounds
½ cup pumpkin seeds, toasted
1 medium tomato, chopped
½ cup shredded brick cheese
    (2 ounces)

In a saucepan cook onion and garlic in hot cooking oil till onion is tender but not brown. Stir in the mashed beans, cream cheese, salt, and pepper. Heat through.

In a bowl combine zucchini and salad dressing. For each sandwich cut off a small portion of each pita round. Spread inside of the pita rounds with bean mixture; sprinkle with pumpkin seeds. Top with zucchini mixture, chopped tomato, and shredded cheese. Makes 5 servings.

From back to front: Feta-Kale Pie, Vegetarian Bean Pitas, Cashew-Tofu Stir-Fry (see recipe, page 279), and Fettuccini with Mushroom-Wine Sauce.

SOUPS AND STEWS

EASY VEGETABLE-BEEF SOUP

5 cups water
1½ pounds beef shank crosscuts
1 16-ounce can tomatoes, cut up
1 10-ounce package frozen mixed vegetables
1 cup frozen loose-pack hash brown potatoes
½ envelope (¼ cup) *regular* onion soup mix
¼ cup sliced celery
1 teaspoon sugar
1 teaspoon seasoned salt
½ teaspoon Worcestershire sauce
⅛ teaspoon pepper
Dash bottled hot pepper sauce

In a 3-quart saucepan combine the water and the beef shanks. Bring to boiling. Reduce heat; simmer, covered, for 1½ to 2 hours or till meat is tender. Chill beef and broth till a layer of fat forms; remove and discard fat. Cut meat from shanks into bite-size pieces. Set broth aside.

In a large saucepan combine the meat, *3 cups* of the broth (save remaining broth for another use), the *undrained* tomatoes, the mixed vegetables, hash brown potatoes, dry onion soup mix, sliced celery, sugar, the seasoned salt, Worcestershire sauce, pepper, and bottled hot pepper sauce. Bring to boiling. Reduce heat; cover and simmer for 15 to 20 minutes or till vegetables are tender. Makes 6 servings.

PEPPERONI-BULGUR SOUP

10 cups water
2⅓ cups dry lentils (1 pound)
8 ounces pepperoni, thinly sliced and halved
1 large onion, chopped (1 cup)
1 6-ounce can tomato paste
2½ teaspoons salt
½ teaspoon dried oregano, crushed
¼ teaspoon ground sage
¼ teaspoon ground red pepper
4 tomatoes, cut up
2 medium carrots, sliced
2 stalks celery, sliced
Cooked Bulgur Wheat

In a large Dutch oven combine water, lentils, pepperoni, chopped onion, tomato paste, salt, oregano, sage, and the ground red pepper. Bring to boiling. Reduce heat; cover and simmer for 30 minutes, stirring occasionally.

Stir in tomatoes, sliced carrot, and sliced celery; cover and simmer for 40 minutes more. Ladle lentil mixture into serving bowls. Mound some of the Cooked Bulgur Wheat in the center of each serving. Makes 10 to 12 servings.

Cooked Bulgur Wheat: In a 3-quart saucepan combine 3 cups hot *water* and 1½ teaspoons *salt*. Bring to boiling; stir in 1½ cups *bulgur wheat*. Reduce heat; cover and simmer for 25 minutes.

OXTAIL-VEGETABLE SOUP

2 pounds oxtails, cut into 1½-inch pieces
3 tablespoons all-purpose flour
2 tablespoons cooking oil
1 16-ounce can tomatoes
1 10½-ounce can condensed beef broth
1 medium onion, chopped
½ cup water
½ cup dry red wine
1 teaspoon sugar
½ teaspoon salt
½ teaspoon dried thyme, crushed
1 bay leaf
4 medium carrots, cut into julienne strips
4 medium parsnips, peeled and cut into julienne strips
½ cup frozen peas

Trim fat from oxtails. Coat oxtails with flour. In a Dutch oven brown meat in hot cooking oil. Add the *undrained* tomatoes, the beef broth, chopped onion, water, wine, sugar, salt, thyme, bay leaf, and ¼ teaspoon *pepper*. Bring to boiling. Reduce heat; cover and simmer about 2 hours or till meat is just tender. Skim off fat. Add carrots and parsnips; cover and simmer for 25 minutes. Add peas; cook for 5 minutes more. Makes 4 servings.

Hot and Hearty Ham Soup (see recipe, page 285), Easy Vegetable-Beef Soup, and Pork and Cabbage Soup (see recipe, page 285).

MORMON SPLIT PEA SOUP

1 pound dry green split peas
    (2¼ cups)
8 cups cold water
1 large onion, chopped
    (1 cup)
½ cup chopped celery
2 teaspoons salt
½ teaspoon dried marjoram,
    crushed
¼ teaspoon pepper
1 pound ground pork
¾ teaspoon salt
¾ teaspoon ground sage
⅛ teaspoon pepper
3 medium potatoes, peeled and
    diced (1 pound)

Rinse split peas. In a large kettle or Dutch oven combine the split peas, the cold water, the chopped onion, chopped celery, the 2 teaspoons salt, marjoram, and the ¼ teaspoon pepper. Bring to boiling. Reduce heat; cover and simmer about 1 hour or till the peas are tender. *Do not drain.*

Meanwhile, in a bowl combine the ground pork, the ¾ teaspoon salt, sage, and the ⅛ teaspoon pepper. Mix thoroughly. Shape pork-sage mixture into l-inch meatballs. Gently drop meatballs and diced potatoes into soup mixture; return soup to boiling. Reduce heat; cover and simmer 20 minutes longer or until meatballs and potatoes are done. Season to taste with salt and pepper. Makes 10 to 12 servings.

BEERWURST SOUP

See photo, pages 262-263—

1 cup chopped celery
½ cup chopped onion
2 tablespoons butter *or*
    margarine
1 tablespoon cornstarch
½ teaspoon dry mustard
¼ teaspoon garlic powder
¼ teaspoon dried oregano,
    crushed
¼ teaspoon dried basil, crushed
¼ teaspoon dried thyme,
    crushed
1 12-ounce can (1½ cups)
    beer
1 10¼-ounce can (1¼ cups)
    condensed beef broth
4 slices French bread
1 cup shredded mozzarella
    cheese (4 ounces)
12 ounces beerwurst (beer
    salami), thinly sliced and
    quartered

In a large skillet cook celery and onion in butter or margarine till vegetables are tender.

Stir in the cornstarch, dry mustard, garlic powder, oregano, basil, and thyme; add beer and beef broth. Cook and stir till thickened and bubbly. Cook and stir 2 minutes more. Reduce heat; cover and simmer the soup for 30 minutes, stirring occasionally.

Meanwhile, arrange the French bread slices on a baking sheet; sprinkle mozzarella cheese atop. Broil 3 inches from heat for 3 minutes or till cheese is melted and lightly browned.

Add thinly sliced beerwurst to soup; simmer 2 to 3 minutes to heat through. Top soup with hot bread slices. Makes 4 servings.

BOUILLABAISSE GUMBO

2½ cups water
1 16-ounce can stewed
    tomatoes
1 10¾-ounce can condensed
    tomato soup
1 10¾-ounce can condensed
    chicken gumbo soup
1 medium sweet potato, peeled
    and chopped (1 cup)
½ cup chopped celery
⅓ cup sliced green onion
1 tablespoon snipped parsley
1 tablespoon Worcestershire
    sauce
1 clove garlic, minced
2 dashes bottled hot pepper
    sauce
1 bay leaf
1 7½-ounce can minced clams
1 4½-ounce can shrimp,
    drained

In large saucepan combine water, *undrained* tomatoes, tomato soup, chicken gumbo soup, sweet potato, the celery, green onion, parsley, Worcestershire sauce, garlic, hot pepper sauce, and bay leaf. Bring to boiling; reduce heat. Cover and simmer about 30 minutes or till the vegetables are tender.

Add *undrained* minced clams and shrimp; simmer about 10 minutes or till the mixture is heated through. Season to taste with salt and pepper. Remove bay leaf. Ladle into bowls. Serves 6 to 8.

PORK AND CABBAGE SOUP

See photo, page 283—

1 pound boneless pork, cut into ½-inch cubes
1 tablespoon cooking oil
1 small head cabbage, shredded (4 cups)
2 soup cans (2½ cups) water
1 10¾-ounce can condensed tomato soup
1 10½-ounce can condensed beef broth
½ cup chopped onion
¼ cup dry sherry
1 teaspoon salt
½ teaspoon paprika
1 bay leaf
  Dash pepper
  Dairy sour cream
  Snipped parsley (optional)

In a 4½-quart Dutch oven cook pork cubes in hot oil till browned. Drain off fat. Add the shredded cabbage, the water, the condensed tomato soup, condensed beef broth, chopped onion, dry sherry, the 1 teaspoon salt, paprika, bay leaf, and the dash pepper. Bring to boiling. Reduce heat; cover and simmer about 40 minutes or till meat is tender.

Season the soup to taste with salt and pepper. Ladle into soup bowls. Dollop each serving with dairy sour cream. Garnish with parsley if desired. Makes 5 or 6 servings.

HOT AND HEARTY HAM SOUP

See photo, page 283—

8 cups water
1 1½- to 1¾-pound meaty ham bone *or* 1½ pounds smoked ham hocks
8 whole black peppercorns
5 whole cloves
1 teaspoon salt
1 clove garlic, halved
½ head cabbage, coarsely chopped
2 large potatoes, peeled and thinly sliced
3 large carrots, peeled and thinly sliced
1 medium onion, chopped
6 to 8 thick slices rye bread
¼ cup grated Parmesan cheese
  Swiss cheese, cut into strips

In a 4½-quart Dutch oven combine water, ham bone or hocks, whole peppercorns, cloves, the 1 teaspoon salt, and garlic; bring to boiling. Reduce heat; cover and simmer for 2½ hours. Remove ham bone or hocks; when cool enough to handle, cut meat off bones. Strain broth.

Return broth and meat to the Dutch oven. Add chopped cabbage, sliced potatoes, sliced carrots, and chopped onion. Cover and simmer about 40 minutes or till vegetables are tender. Season to taste with salt and pepper.

Meanwhile, toast rye bread. Ladle soup into heat-proof bowls. Top each serving with a slice of toast; sprinkle with the Parmesan cheese and top with strips of Swiss cheese. Place under broiler about 2 minutes or till Swiss cheese melts. Makes 6 to 8 servings.

NEW ENGLAND CLAM CHOWDER

See photo, pages 18-19—

1 pint shucked clams *or* two 7½-ounce cans minced clams
4 ounces salt pork, finely chopped
4 cups diced potatoes
1½ cups water
½ cup chopped onion
1¾ cups milk
1 cup light cream
¼ cup milk
3 tablespoons all-purpose flour
1½ teaspoons salt
  Dash pepper

Drain clams, reserving ½ cup liquid. Strain clam liquid. If using shucked clams, finely chop and set aside. In a large saucepan fry salt pork till crisp. Remove bits of salt pork; set aside. To drippings in pan add the reserved clam liquid, diced potatoes, water, and the chopped onion. Cook, covered, for 15 to 20 minutes or till potatoes are tender.

Stir in clams, the 1¾ cups milk, and the light cream. Stir together the ¼ cup milk and flour; stir into clam mixture. Cook and stir till chowder is slightly thickened and bubbly. Cook and stir 1 minute more. Stir in salt and pepper. Sprinkle the reserved salt pork bits atop. Serve clam chowder in soup bowls. Makes 6 servings.

RIO GRANDE STEW

2 pounds beef stew meat, cut
    into 1½-inch cubes
2 tablespoons cooking oil
1 10½-ounce can condensed
    beef broth
½ cup chopped celery
½ cup chopped onion
2 cloves garlic, minced
1 tablespoon dried oregano,
    crushed
1 tablespoon ground coriander
2 teaspoons ground cumin
2 bay leaves
3 medium carrots, cut into
    chunks
2 ears fresh corn, cut into
    1-inch pieces
1 15-ounce can garbanzo beans
1 small head cabbage, cut
    into 8 wedges
    Salsa

In a large Dutch oven brown beef, half at a time, in hot oil; return all meat to pan. Stir in the next 8 ingredients, 3 cups *water*, and 1½ teaspoons *salt*. Bring to boiling; reduce heat. Cover; simmer about 2 hours or till meat is almost tender. Skim off fat. Stir in carrots, corn, and *undrained* garbanzo beans; arrange cabbage atop. Simmer, covered, 20 to 30 minutes. Discard bay leaves. Season to taste. Serve with Salsa. Serves 8.

Salsa: Stir together one 16-ounce can *tomatoes,* cut up; ½ cup finely chopped *onion;* one 4-ounce can green *chili peppers,* rinsed, seeded, and finely chopped; ¼ cup snipped *parsley;* 1 clove *garlic,* minced; and ½ teaspoon *salt.*

Beef-Wine Stew

BEEF-WINE STEW

2 cups dry red wine
1 medium onion, chopped
2 cloves garlic, minced
1 tablespoon vinegar
1 teaspoon salt
½ teaspoon dried rosemary,
    crushed
½ teaspoon dried thyme,
    crushed
½ teaspoon finely shredded
    orange peel
¼ teaspoon pepper
2 to 2½ pounds beef stew
    meat, cut into 1-inch cubes
2 ounces salt pork
½ cup water
½ teaspoon instant beef
    bouillon granules
6 carrots, bias-sliced
    into 1-inch pieces
3 onions, quartered
1 cup pitted ripe olives
2 tablespoons cornstarch

In a bowl combine first 9 ingredients. Add beef cubes; stir to coat. Cover and marinate at room temperature for 2 hours.

Drain meat, reserving the marinade; pat meat dry with paper toweling. In a 4-quart Dutch oven cook salt pork till 2 to 3 tablespoons of fat accumulate; discard the pork. Brown beef in the hot fat. Add marinade, the ½ cup water, and beef bouillon granules; bring to boiling. Reduce heat; cover and simmer 1 hour. Add carrots, quartered onions, and olives. Simmer, covered, 30 to 40 minutes. Blend cornstarch and 2 tablespoons cold *water;* add to Dutch oven. Cook, stirring constantly, till thickened and bubbly. Garnish with snipped parsley if desired. Serves 8 to 10.

TURKEY FRAME SOUP

1 meaty turkey frame
1 medium onion, quartered
3 medium tomatoes, quartered
1 teaspoon dried thyme,
    crushed
½ teaspoon dried oregano,
    crushed
8 cups chopped fresh
    vegetables*
    Egg Noodles

Place turkey frame in large Dutch oven with onion, 5 quarts *water,* and 4 teaspoons *salt.* Bring to boiling. Reduce heat; simmer, covered, 1½ hours. Remove frame from the broth; cool till easy to handle. Remove meat from bones; discard bones. Strain broth. Return meat to broth with the tomatoes, thyme, and oregano. Stir in vegetables. Bring to boiling; cover and simmer 45 minutes. Add the Egg Noodles. Cook 15 minutes more. Makes 12 servings.

Egg Noodles: In mixing bowl combine 1 beaten *egg,* 2 tablespoons *milk,* and ½ teaspoon *salt.* Using 1 to 1¼ cups all-purpose *flour,* add enough flour to make a stiff dough. Roll dough thinly on floured surface. Let stand 20 minutes. Roll up loosely. Slice ¼ inch wide. Unroll cut noodles; spread out. Let dry 2 hours.

*Vegetables can be any combination of carrot, rutabaga, broccoli, celery, cabbage, or cauliflower.

CORN-ZUCCHINI BAKE

3 to 4 medium zucchini
¼ cup chopped onion
1 tablespoon butter *or* margarine
2 beaten eggs
1 10-ounce package frozen whole kernel corn, cooked and drained
1 cup shredded process Swiss cheese (4 ounces)
¼ teaspoon salt
¼ cup fine dry bread crumbs
2 tablespoons grated Parmesan cheese
1 tablespoon butter *or* margarine
Cherry tomatoes, halved
Parsley sprigs

Slice unpeeled zucchini about 1 inch thick. In a covered saucepan cook the sliced zucchini in a small amount of boiling salted water 15 to 20 minutes or till tender. Drain and mash with fork.

In the same saucepan cook the onion in 1 tablespoon of butter till tender. Add the mashed zucchini, eggs, corn, Swiss cheese, and salt. Turn into 1-quart casserole. Combine crumbs, Parmesan cheese, and 1 tablespoon melted butter; sprinkle atop corn mixture.

Place on baking sheet; bake in a 350° oven about 40 minutes or till knife inserted off-center comes out clean. Let stand 5 to 10 minutes before serving. Garnish with the tomatoes and parsley. Serves 6.

SUNSHINE CARROTS

See photo, page 290—

7 *or* 8 medium carrots, bias-sliced ½ inch thick
1 tablespoon brown sugar
1 teaspoon cornstarch
¼ teaspoon ground ginger
¼ teaspoon salt
¼ cup orange juice
2 tablespoons butter

In a saucepan cook carrots in boiling salted water 10 to 15 minutes; drain. In saucepan mix brown sugar, cornstarch, ginger, and salt. Stir in orange juice; cook and stir till mixture is thickened. Boil 1 minute; remove from heat. Stir in butter. Toss with hot carrots. Top with parsley and an orange slice if desired. Makes 6 servings.

LEMON MUSHROOMS

1 pound fresh mushrooms
½ cup olive *or* salad oil
3 tablespoons lemon juice
1 tablespoon Dijon-style mustard

Cut the mushrooms into ⅛-inch slices. In a screw-top jar combine olive or salad oil, lemon juice, mustard, ½ teaspoon *salt*, and ¼ teaspoon *pepper*. Cover and shake well. In a bowl toss mixture with the mushrooms. Let stand at room temperature for 1 hour; stir occasionally. Serves 3 or 4.

ARTICHOKES PARMESAN

6 medium artichokes
1 tablespoon sliced green onion
1 clove garlic, minced
¼ cup butter *or* margarine
3 cups soft whole wheat bread crumbs
2 medium tomatoes, peeled, seeded, and chopped
½ cup grated Parmesan *or* Romano cheese (2 ounces)
¼ cup snipped parsley

Remove stems and outer leaves from artichokes. Cut off 1 inch from tops; snip off sharp leaf tips. In large covered kettle cook artichokes in boiling salted water for 20 to 30 minutes or till a leaf pulls out easily. Drain the artichokes upside down on paper toweling. Remove center leaves and choke. Sprinkle insides with salt.

Meanwhile, in a saucepan cook onion and garlic in butter till onion is tender but not brown. In a bowl combine bread crumbs, tomatoes, cheese, and parsley. Add onion mixture; mix lightly. Spoon into the artichokes.

Arrange in 13x9x2-inch baking pan so artichokes won't tip over. Cover; bake in a 375° oven for 15 minutes. Uncover; bake about 10 minutes more. Makes 6 servings.

Back: Corn-Zucchini Bake.
Front: Corn Relish Molds (see recipe, page 295).

CORN 'N' SQUASH PUDDING

1 12-ounce package frozen mashed cooked winter squash
1 10-ounce package frozen whole kernel corn
½ cup chopped onion
5 tablespoons butter *or* margarine
2 slightly beaten eggs
¼ cup evaporated milk *or* milk
1 tablespoon sugar
¼ teaspoon salt
⅛ teaspoon pepper
1 cup herb-seasoned stuffing mix

In separate pans cook squash and corn according to package directions. Drain corn; set vegetables aside. In a small skillet cook onion in butter or margarine till tender but not brown. Set aside.

In a bowl combine eggs, evaporated milk or milk, sugar, salt, and pepper; stir in onion mixture. Add stuffing mix, cooked squash, and drained corn; mix well.

Turn mixture into a 10x6x2-inch baking dish. Bake, uncovered, in a 350° oven for 30 minutes or till knife inserted just off-center comes out clean. Let stand 5 minutes before serving. Serves 6.

From front to back: Cheese-Sauced Cauliflower, Sunshine Carrots (see recipe, page 288), and Italian Cauliflower.

CHEESE-SAUCED CAULIFLOWER

1 head cauliflower
1½ cups sliced fresh mushrooms (4 ounces) *or* one 4-ounce can sliced mushrooms, drained
2 tablespoons butter *or* margarine
2 tablespoons all-purpose flour
¼ teaspoon salt
Dash white pepper
1 cup milk
1 cup shredded sharp American cheese (4 ounces)
1 teaspoon prepared mustard
1 tablespoon snipped parsley

In a saucepan cook the whole cauliflower, covered, in a small amount of boiling salted water about 20 minutes or just till cauliflower is tender. Drain thoroughly; keep the cauliflower warm.

Meanwhile, in a saucepan cook the fresh mushrooms in butter or margarine about 4 minutes or till tender. (*Or*, if using canned mushrooms, just melt the butter or margarine.) Blend the flour, salt, and white pepper into butter-mushroom mixture (or into melted butter or margarine). Add milk all at once. Cook and stir till mixture is thickened and bubbly. Stir in the American cheese and mustard. If you are using canned mushrooms, stir them into sauce. Heat till cheese melts.

Place the cooked head of cauliflower on a platter; spoon some of the sauce over it. Sprinkle with snipped parsley. Pass the remaining sauce. Makes 6 servings.

ITALIAN CAULIFLOWER

1 tablespoon chopped onion
1 small clove garlic, minced
2 tablespoons Italian salad dressing
3 cups small cauliflower flowerets
½ teaspoon salt
2 tablespoons chopped green pepper
⅛ teaspoon dried basil, crushed
1 cup cherry tomatoes, halved

In saucepan cook onion and garlic in salad dressing about 2 minutes or till tender. Add cauliflower, salt, and ¼ cup *water*. Cook, covered, over low heat for 10 minutes. Add green pepper; cook about 5 minutes more or till vegetables are tender. Stir in basil. Add tomatoes; heat through. Serves 6.

NUTMEG SQUASH

3 pounds Hubbard squash, cut into chunks
2 tablespoons butter *or* margarine
2 tablespoons brown sugar
½ teaspoon salt
½ teaspoon ground nutmeg

In a large saucepan cook squash, covered, in boiling salted water about 25 minutes or till tender. Drain. Scoop pulp from rind; discard rind. Mash pulp. If squash seems too thin, return to saucepan; cook, uncovered, to desired consistency. Stir in butter or margarine, the brown sugar, salt, and nutmeg. Makes 6 servings.

ZUCCHINI MEXICALI

1 pound zucchini, thinly sliced
    (4 cups)
1 large carrot, shredded
1 large onion, chopped (1 cup)
¾ cup chopped celery
½ medium green pepper, cut
    into thin strips
½ teaspoon garlic salt
¼ teaspoon dried basil, crushed
¼ cup cooking oil
⅓ cup taco sauce
2 teaspoons prepared mustard
2 medium tomatoes

In a 10-inch skillet cook and stir the
zucchini, the carrot, onion, celery,
green pepper, garlic salt, basil, and
dash *pepper* in hot oil, covered, over
medium-high heat for 4 minutes.
Mix taco sauce and mustard; stir
into vegetables. Cut tomatoes into
wedges. Add to skillet. Cook, uncovered, for 3 to 5 minutes more.
Makes 4 to 6 servings.

SAUCY BAKED BEANS

3 16-ounce cans pork and
    beans in tomato sauce
½ cup chopped onion
1 medium green pepper,
    chopped
¼ cup packed brown sugar
¼ cup catsup
2 tablepoons Worcestershire
    sauce
3 slices bacon

In a 2-quart casserole mix beans,
onion, pepper, brown sugar, catsup,
and Worcestershire. Top with bacon. Bake in a 325° oven for 1½
hours. Serves 10.

CARAWAY BEANS

2 9-ounce packages frozen cut
    green beans
½ cup dairy sour cream
1 tablespoon all-purpose flour
¼ cup milk
2 tablespoons chopped onion
½ teaspoon sugar
4 ounces caraway cheddar
    cheese, crumbled

In saucepan cook beans according
to package directions; drain. In
saucepan mix sour cream and flour.
Stir in milk, onion, sugar, ½ teaspoon *salt*, and das*h pepper*. Cook
and stir over low heat till bubbly.
Stir in cheese till melted. Toss with
beans. Serves 6.

GREEN BEANS PIQUANT

2 9-ounce packages frozen cut
    green beans
1 medium onion, thinly sliced
4 slices bacon
3 tablespoons red wine vinegar
2 teaspoons sugar
1 teaspoon Worcestershire
    sauce

In a saucepan cook beans, onion,
and ½ teaspoon *salt* according to
directions on the bean package.
Drain. In skillet cook bacon till
crisp; drain, reserving 3 tablespoons
drippings. Crumble the bacon; set
aside. Return drippings to skillet;
stir in vinegar, sugar, Worcestershire sauce, and ¼ teaspoon *salt*.
Bring to boiling. Add beans to vinegar mixture; toss. Cover; heat for 2
to 3 minutes. Serves 6.

TURNIP-BACON PUFF

1 pound turnips, peeled and
    shredded (3 cups)
4 egg yolks
¼ cup milk
¼ cup mayonnaise *or* salad
    dressing
1 teaspoon lemon juice
2 tablespoons all-purpose flour
½ teaspoon salt
    Dash pepper
4 slices bacon, crisp-cooked,
    drained, and crumbled
2 tablespoons snipped parsley
4 egg whites

In a saucepan cook shredded turnips, covered, in a small amount of
boiling salted water about 15 minutes or till tender. Drain.

In a small mixer bowl beat egg
yolks, milk, mayonnaise or salad
dressing, and lemon juice at high
speed with electric mixer about 5
minutes or till mixture is thick and
lemon-colored. Beat in flour, salt,
and pepper. Stir in turnips, bacon,
and snipped parsley.

Thoroughly wash beaters. In a
large mixer bowl beat egg whites till
stiff peaks form (the tips stand
straight). Fold egg yolk mixture
into egg whites.

Turn the turnip-bacon mixture
into an 8x1½-inch round baking
dish. Bake in a 350° oven for 30 to
35 minutes or until a knife inserted
just off-center comes out clean.
Makes 6 to 8 servings.

NAPA-STYLE MARINATED VEGETABLES

1½ cups dry white wine
⅔ cup cooking oil
½ cup lemon juice
¼ cup sugar
2 teaspoons salt
1 teaspoon mustard seed
2 cloves garlic, minced
½ teaspoon whole peppercorns
1½ cups halved brussels sprouts
1½ cups cauliflower flowerets *or*
     broccoli cuts
1½ cups carrot sticks
1½ cups sliced cucumber
1½ cups cherry tomatoes
1 small onion, thinly sliced and
     separated into rings

In a screw-top jar combine the white wine, the cooking oil, lemon juice, sugar, salt, mustard seed, garlic, and peppercorns; cover and shake well.

In separate saucepans cook the brussels sprouts, the cauliflower or broccoli, and the carrots in small amounts of lightly salted boiling water till crisp-tender; drain.

In a deep bowl layer brussels sprouts, the cauliflower or broccoli, carrot, sliced cucumber, and cherry tomatoes, pouring some of the wine mixture over each layer. Pour any leftover wine mixture over top layer. Place onion slices atop. Cover; chill several hours or overnight. Serve with a slotted spoon. Makes 12 servings.

BRUSSELS SPROUTS AU GRATIN

1 pound fresh brussels sprouts
     or two 10-ounce packages
     frozen brussels sprouts
⅓ cup finely chopped onion
3 tablespoons butter *or*
     margarine
2 tablespoons all-purpose flour
½ cup finely shredded sharp
     cheddar cheese (2 ounces)
¼ cup grated Parmesan cheese
     (1 ounce)
   Paprika

Cut large fresh brussels sprouts in half. In a saucepan cook sprouts, covered, in a small amount of lightly salted boiling water about 5 minutes or till crisp-tender. (Or, cook frozen brussels sprouts according to package directions.) Drain, reserving the cooking liquid; add enough water to reserved liquid to make 1 cup. Keep the vegetables warm.

In a small saucepan cook the onion in the butter or margarine till tender but not brown. Stir in flour; add reserved cooking liquid all at once. Cook, stirring constantly, till mixture is thickened and bubbly. Stir in the finely shredded cheddar cheese; cook and stir 1 to 2 minutes more or till cheese melts. Season with salt and pepper.

Pour some of the cheese sauce into a greased 10x6x2-inch baking dish. Add cooked brussels sprouts; pour remaining sauce atop. Sprinkle with the Parmesan cheese and paprika. Broil 4 inches from heat about 5 minutes or till top is lightly brown. Serve at once. Serves 6.

GARDEN STUFFED PEPPERS

4 large green peppers
3 or 4 fresh ears of corn *or*
     one 10-ounce package
     frozen whole kernel corn
¼ cup chopped onion
2 tablespoons butter *or*
     margarine
1 8½-ounce can lima beans,
     drained
1 large tomato, chopped
½ teaspoon dried rosemary,
     crushed

Remove tops from green peppers; discard. Cut the peppers in half lengthwise and remove seeds. In a saucepan cook pepper halves in boiling salted water for 3 to 5 minutes; invert pepper halves on paper toweling to drain.

Cut off tips of fresh ears of corn. Carefully scrape cobs with dull edge of knife; measure 1½ cups corn. In saucepan cook fresh corn, covered, in a small amount of boiling salted water 12 to 15 minutes or till done. (Or, cook frozen whole kernel corn according to package directions. Drain.)

In a saucepan cook onion in butter or margarine till tender. Stir in cooked corn, lima beans, tomato, and rosemary.

Season green peppers with salt and pepper. Fill peppers with vegetable mixture. Place stuffed peppers in a 13x9x2-inch baking dish. Bake in a 350° oven for 30 minutes. Makes 8 servings.

CORN RELISH MOLDS

See photo, page 288—

1¾ cups water
1 7-ounce can whole kernel corn, drained
1 3-ounce package lemon-flavored gelatin
2 tablespoons white tarragon vinegar
1 tablespoon sugar
¼ teaspoon celery salt
½ cup chopped tomato
¼ cup chopped green pepper
   Bibb lettuce
   Mayonnaise *or* salad dressing (optional)

In a medium saucepan combine water, drained whole kernel corn, lemon-flavored gelatin, white tarragon vinegar, sugar, and celery salt; bring to boiling. Reduce the heat and simmer, uncovered, for 3 minutes.

Chill gelatin mixture till the consistency of unbeaten egg white (partially set). Fold in the chopped tomato and chopped green pepper.

Turn gelatin mixture into six ½-cup molds. Chill molds at least 6 hours or till firm. Unmold onto lettuce-lined plates. Pass mayonnaise or salad dressing if desired. Makes 6 servings.

Back: Fresh Herb Dressing and Chive Mayonnaise. Front: Sprouting Mini Garden.

CHIVE MAYONNAISE

1 cup mayonnaise *or* salad dressing
¼ cup snipped chives
1 tablespoon lemon juice
2 teaspoons tarragon vinegar
   Dash salt

In a bowl stir together the mayonnaise or salad dressing, chives, lemon juice, tarragon vinegar, and salt. Store covered in the refrigerator. Use for lettuce salads, with fish, or with cold meat or poultry. Makes 1¼ cups.

FRESH HERB DRESSING

¼ cup salad oil
3 tablespoons dry white wine
2 tablespoons lemon juice
1 tablespoon sugar
1 tablespoon snipped fresh basil *or* 1 teaspoon dried basil, crushed
1 teaspoon salt
   Several dashes bottled hot pepper sauce
¼ teaspoon pepper

In a screw-top jar combine salad oil, the white wine, lemon juice, sugar, fresh or dried basil, salt, bottled hot pepper sauce, and pepper. Cover and shake to mix well. Chill thoroughly. Shake again before serving. Use as dressing for tossed salads. Makes ½ cup.

SPROUTING MINI-GARDEN

Lentils, alfalfa seed, curly cress seed, radish seed, mustard seed, mung beans, garbanzos, dried peas, lima beans, *or* pinto beans*

Wash desired seeds thoroughly. In separate small bowls soak seeds in lukewarm water (use four times as much water as seeds) overnight or till seeds swell to double in size. Drain; rinse seeds thoroughly.

Wash three 1-quart jars; place about ¼ cup soaked beans in each jar. Cover tops of the jars with two layers of cheesecloth or nylon netting; fasten each with two rubber bands or a screw-type canning lid band.

Place jars with seeds on their sides in a warm, dark place (68° to 75°). Once a day rinse the sprouts by pouring lukewarm water into the jars, swirling to moisten all the sprouts, then pouring off the water. (Curly cress will develop a gelatinous coating; don't remove it.)

In 3 or 4 days, the sprouts should be 1½ to 2½ inches long and ready to use. Snip off tops and add to main dishes and salads.

Note: Do not buy seeds that have been chemically treated for farming. Some treated seeds can be poisonous.

GARDEN SALAD

See photo, page 276—

3 cups torn mustard *or* turnip
   greens
2 cups torn kale
½ cup sliced radishes
¼ cup sliced green onion
2 hard-cooked eggs, chopped
3 small slices cooked
   country ham cut
   $\frac{1}{16}$ inch thick
½ cup water *or* coffee

In a serving bowl combine torn mustard or turnip greens, the kale, sliced radishes, sliced green onion, and chopped eggs.

In a large heavy skillet (preferably cast iron) cook country ham slices 4 to 5 minutes per side or till ham is crisp enough to crumble. With fingers protected with paper toweling, crumble ham. Set aside.

To make dressing, quickly add water or coffee to hot skillet, being careful to avoid splattering. Cook, scraping pan to remove crusty bits, till mixture boils vigorously. Continue cooking, uncovered, about 3 minutes more or till mixture is reduced by half. Pour hot dressing over the greens in bowl, tossing till greens are well-coated. Sprinkle the greens with the crumbled ham. Makes 4 or 5 servings.

24-Hour Salad.

24-HOUR SALAD

1 head lettuce, torn
   Sugar
6 hard-cooked eggs, sliced
1 10-ounce package frozen
   peas, thawed
1 pound bacon, crisp-cooked,
   drained, and crumbled
2 cups shredded Swiss cheese
1 cup mayonnaise

In a large bowl place *3 cups* of the lettuce; sprinkle with sugar, salt, and pepper. Layer eggs atop lettuce; stand some slices on edge if desired. Sprinkle with salt. Next, layer the peas, the remaining lettuce, *three-fourths* of the bacon, and Swiss cheese. Spread mayonnaise atop, sealing to edge of bowl. Cover; refrigerate 24 hours or overnight. Top with remaining bacon and sliced green onion if desired. Toss to serve. Serves 12 to 15.

CABBAGE SLAW

See photo, page 270—

6 cups shredded cabbage
1 cup shredded carrot
¼ cup chopped green pepper
1 cup mayonnaise *or* salad
   dressing
2 tablespoons sugar
2 tablespoons vinegar
1 teaspoon prepared mustard
1 teaspoon celery seed
½ teaspoon salt

In a bowl combine cabbage, carrot, and green pepper; chill. Mix mayonnaise, sugar, vinegar, mustard, celery seed, and salt. Toss with vegetables. Serves 12.

ASPARAGUS-SPAGHETTI TOSS

6 ounces spaghetti
1 pound fresh asparagus, cut
   into 1-inch pieces *or* two
   8-ounce packages frozen
   cut asparagus
½ teaspoon dried basil, crushed
½ teaspoon dried thyme,
   crushed
½ teaspoon dried rosemary,
   crushed
½ teaspoon onion powder
½ teaspoon garlic powder
2 medium tomatoes, seeded
   and chopped
¾ cup Italian salad dressing
2 tablespoons lemon juice
   Leaf lettuce

Cook spaghetti according to package directions; drain.

Meanwhile, in a saucepan cook fresh asparagus pieces in a small amount of boiling salted water, covered, 8 to 10 minutes or till crisp-tender. (*Or*, prepare the frozen cut asparagus according to package directions.) Drain.

In a bowl toss spaghetti with basil, thyme, rosemary, onion powder, and garlic powder. Add chopped tomatoes, the Italian salad dressing, lemon juice, and cooked asparagus. Toss. Season with salt and pepper. Cover; chill well.

To serve, place the pasta mixture on individual lettuce-lined plates. Makes 6 servings.

SPANISH BULGUR SALAD

¾ cup dry yellow split peas
1 clove garlic, minced
1 teaspoon salt
⅛ teaspoon pepper
¾ cup bulgur wheat
4 ounces cheddar cheese, cut into ½-inch cubes
1 cup alfalfa sprouts
½ cup chopped green pepper
¼ cup olive *or* cooking oil
¼ cup lemon juice
1 teaspoon dried basil, crushed
Leaf lettuce
3 medium avocados, seeded and peeled
3 medium tomatoes, cut into thick slices and halved
Lemon wedges (optional)

Rinse peas. In a saucepan combine peas, garlic, salt, pepper, and 4 cups *water*. Bring to boiling; cover and simmer 25 to 30 minutes or till peas are tender. Drain peas. In bowl soak bulgur in 2 cups *water* about 30 minutes. Drain, squeezing out excess water.

In a mixing bowl combine the drained peas, the drained bulgur, cheese cubes, alfalfa sprouts, and green pepper. Combine olive or cooking oil, lemon juice, and basil. Add *half* to pea-bulgur mixture; toss. Cover and chill.

To serve, line individual serving plates with lettuce leaves. Slice avocados. Alternate slices of avocado with half-slices of tomato on each plate. Drizzle remaining oil-lemon juice mixture over tomato and avocado. Top each serving with some of the bulgur mixture. Garnish with lemon wedges if desired. Makes 6 servings.

HARVEST FRUIT MOLD

1 11-ounce package mixed dried fruit
¼ cup sugar
1 6-ounce package orange-flavored gelatin
2 cups boiling water
½ cup dry sherry
Leaf lettuce
Frosted Grapes
Candied kumquats, halved lengthwise

In a saucepan combine dried fruit and enough water to cover the fruit. Cover and simmer gently for 25 minutes. Add sugar; simmer 5 to 10 minutes more. Drain fruit, reserving syrup. Add water to syrup to make 1½ cups liquid. Dissolve gelatin in boiling water. Stir in reserved syrup mixture and sherry. Chill till consistency of unbeaten egg whites (partially set).

Pit prunes; cut up all fruit. Fold into gelatin mixture. Pour into 6-cup ring mold. Chill till firm. Unmold on lettuce-lined platter. Fill center of the mold with Frosted Grapes. Trim with kumquat halves. Makes 8 to 10 servings.

Frosted Grapes: Dip 1½ pounds *green grapes* into 2 slightly beaten *egg whites*. Drain. Dip grapes in ½ cup *sugar*. Place grapes on rack to dry for 2 hours.

CUCUMBER RING SUPREME

1½ teaspoons (½ envelope) unflavored gelatin
1 tablespoon sugar
2 tablespoons lemon juice
½ medium cucumber, sliced
1 envelope unflavored gelatin
2 tablespoons sugar
2 tablespoons lemon juice
1 8-ounce package cream cheese, softened
6 medium cucumbers, peeled
1 cup mayonnaise
3 tablespoons chopped onion
¼ cup snipped parsley

In a saucepan mix the 1½ teaspoons gelatin, the 1 tablespoon sugar, and ½ teaspoon *salt*. Add ¾ cup *water*; heat and stir till gelatin dissolves. Stir in 2 tablespoons lemon juice. Pour into a 6½-cup ring mold. Chill till consistency of unbeaten egg whites (partially set). Overlap the cucumber slices in the mold. Chill till *almost* firm.

Meanwhile, mix the 1 envelope gelatin, the 2 tablespoons sugar, and ¾ teaspoon *salt* in a saucepan. Add ⅔ cup *water*; heat and stir till dissolved. Stir in 2 tablespoons lemon juice. Gradually beat hot gelatin mixture into cream cheese with rotary beater till smooth. Halve the 6 cucumbers; scrape out seeds. Shred cucumbers. Measure 2 cups of the drained cucumber and add with mayonnaise, onion, and parsley to cream cheese mixture. Pour over gelatin in mold. Chill till firm. Unmold onto a watercress-lined plate and garnish with cherry tomatoes if desired. Serves 8.

Cucumber Ring Supreme.

CHERRY-CIDER SALAD

2 cups apple cider *or* apple
  juice
1 6-ounce package
  cherry-flavored gelatin
1 16-ounce can pitted dark
  sweet cherries
½ cup thinly sliced celery
½ cup chopped walnuts
1 3-ounce package cream
  cheese, softened
1 8½-ounce can (1 cup)
  applesauce
Leaf lettuce
Mayonnaise *or* salad
  dressing

In a saucepan bring apple cider or juice to boiling. Dissolve gelatin in boiling cider. Drain cherries, reserving syrup. Halve cherries and set aside. Add enough water to reserved syrup to measure 1½ cups liquid; stir into gelatin. Set aside *2 cups* of the gelatin mixture; keep at room temperature.

Chill remaining gelatin till partially set. Fold cherries, celery, and walnuts into partially set gelatin. Pour into 6½-cup ring mold. Chill till *almost* firm.

In a bowl gradually add reserved gelatin to softened cream cheese, beating till smooth. Stir in applesauce. Spoon cream cheese mixture over cherry layer in mold. Chill till firm. Unmold on lettuce-lined platter. Serve with mayonnaise or salad dressing. Makes 10 to 12 servings.

FIVE-FRUIT SALAD WITH PEANUT BUTTER DRESSING

1 6-ounce can frozen pineapple
  juice concentrate, thawed
¼ cup creamy peanut butter
¾ cup salad oil
4 cups torn lettuce
1 cup fresh pineapple chunks
  or one 8-ounce can
  pineapple chunks, drained
  (juice pack)
1 cup fresh sliced peaches,
  1 cup frozen loose-pack
  sliced peaches, thawed* *or*
  one 8-ounce can sliced
  peaches, drained
  (juice pack)
¼ medium cantaloupe, peeled
  and cut into wedges
½ cup seedless green grapes,
  halved
½ cup fresh strawberries,
  halved

For dressing, in blender container or food processor bowl place pineapple juice concentrate and peanut butter. Cover and blend till smooth. Keeping blender running at high speed, gradually add the salad oil through hole in lid or with lid ajar till mixture is well blended. Turn into storage container; cover. Store dressing in refrigerator till serving time.

Line a large platter with torn lettuce; arrange the pineapple chunks, peach slices, cantaloupe wedges, grapes, and strawberries atop. Stir dressing; pass with salad. Makes 8 servings.

*Note: If desired, coat fresh or frozen peaches with lemon juice to prevent darkening.

STRAWBERRY SOUFFLÉ SALADS

1 10-ounce package frozen
  sliced strawberries,
  thawed
1 3-ounce package
  strawberry-flavored
  gelatin
¼ teaspoon salt
1 cup boiling water
2 tablespoons lemon juice
¼ cup mayonnaise *or* salad
  dressing
¼ cup chopped walnuts
  Romaine
  Canned pineapple slices
  Mayonnaise *or* salad
  dressing
  Chopped walnuts (optional)

Drain strawberries, reserving syrup. Add enough water to syrup to make ¾ cup liquid. Dissolve gelatin and salt in boiling water. Stir in reserved syrup and lemon juice. Beat in the ¼ cup mayonnaise or salad dressing. Chill till the consistency of unbeaten egg whites (partially set).

In mixer bowl whip gelatin mixture with electric mixer till fluffy. Fold in strawberries and the ¼ cup walnuts. Pour into 4 to 6 individual molds. Chill till firm. Unmold onto a lettuce-lined platter, setting each salad atop a pineapple slice. Serve with additional mayonnaise or salad dressing. Sprinkle salads with additional chopped walnuts if desired. Makes 4 to 6 servings.

Five-Fruit Salad with Peanut Butter Dressing.

PROSCIUTTO MELON SALAD

8 ounces thinly sliced
    prosciutto, ham, *or*
    salami
½ medium honeydew melon
½ medium cantaloupe
    Lettuce leaves
1 large peach, peeled, pitted,
    and sliced

1 cup fresh strawberries,
    halved
¼ cup whipping cream
½ cup mayonnaise *or* salad
    dressing
¼ cup crumbled blue cheese
    (1 ounce)
1 tablespoon milk
    Pistachio nuts

Roll up prosciutto, ham, or salami slices. Secure with wooden picks if desired. Scoop out the honeydew and the cantaloupe with a melon-ball cutter.

On 4 individual lettuce-lined salad plates, arrange the honeydew and cantaloupe balls, the peach slices, strawberries, and rolled prosciutto, ham, or salami slices.

For salad dressing, in a small mixer bowl whip cream with electric mixer to soft peaks; fold in the mayonnaise or salad dressing, the crumbled blue cheese, and milk. Spoon over fruit mixture. Sprinkle pistachio nuts over salads. Makes 4 servings.

JAMS, JELLIES, PICKLES, & RELISHES

DILL CUCUMBER STICKS

See photo, page 307—

2½ pounds 4-inch-long
    cucumbers
  8 cups water
  ¼ cup salt
  4 hot red *or* green chili peppers
  1 large clove garlic, quartered
  4 small heads fresh dill *or* 2
    teaspoons dried dillweed
  3 cups water
1¼ cups white vinegar

Wash cucumbers; cut lengthwise into eighths. Place in a large bowl. Combine the 8 cups water and the salt. Pour over the cucumbers. Let stand for 24 hours.

Drain well; pat dry with paper toweling. Pack cucumber sticks in clean pint jars. Add *1* pepper, *¼* garlic clove, and *1* head dill or *½ teaspoon* dillweed to *each* jar.

In a large saucepan combine the 3 cups water and vinegar. Bring to boiling. Reduce heat; cover and simmer for 5 minutes.

Pour the hot mixture over the cucumbers, leaving ½-inch headspace. Prepare the lids according to the manufacturer's directions and wipe the jar rims. Adjust lids. Process in boiling water bath for 10 minutes. (Start timing when water returns to boiling.) Makes 4 pints.

CINNAMON PICKLE SLICES

4 to 5 pounds cucumbers,
    3 to 4 inches long
  ½ cup pickling salt
  6 cups sugar
  4 cups vinegar
  ½ cup prepared horseradish
  8 inches stick cinnamon
  ¾ teaspoon celery seed

Wash cucumbers. Stir the pickling salt into 4 cups *boiling water*; pour over cucumbers in a large bowl. Cool. Cover with a weighted plate or lid to keep cucumbers in brine. Let stand 7 days.

Drain cucumbers. Cover with hot water; let stand for 24 hours. Drain. Cover again with hot water; let stand 24 hours. Drain; slice cucumbers. In a saucepan mix sugar, the vinegar, horseradish, cinnamon, and celery seed; bring to boiling. Slowly pour over the cucumbers. Cool; cover. Let stand overnight.

Each day for 4 days, drain syrup from cucumbers. Reheat; pour over cucumbers. Cool; cover. On fifth day, remove cinnamon. Place cucumbers and sugar mixture in a saucepan; bring to boiling. Pack into hot pint jars, leaving ½-inch headspace. Prepare lids according to manufacturer's directions. Wipe jar rims. Adjust lids. Process in a boiling water bath 5 minutes. (Start timing when water returns to boiling.) Makes 5 or 6 pints.

GARLIC-OKRA PICKLES

3 pounds fresh whole okra
    pods, 3 to 4 inches
    long
3 cups water
1 cup white vinegar
¼ cup pickling salt
2 cloves garlic, minced

Thoroughly wash the fresh okra; drain well. Pack the okra pods into hot clean pint jars, leaving ½-inch headspace.

In a saucepan combine the water, white vinegar, pickling salt, and minced garlic. Bring the mixture to boiling. Pour the hot liquid over the okra pods in the jars, leaving ½-inch headspace.

Prepare jar lids according to the manufacturer's directions. Wipe jar rims. Adjust lids. Process in a boiling water bath for 5 minutes. (Start timing when the water returns to boiling.) Makes 4 pints.

From left to right: Pepper Relish (see recipe, page 305), basil Herb Jelly (see recipe, page 308), Cinnamon Pickle Slices, Garlic-Okra Pickles, Brandied Peaches (see recipe, page 306), rosemary Herb Jelly (see recipe, page 308), Hot Pickled Peppers (see recipe, page 304), and red Pepper Relish (see recipe, page 305).

HOT PICKLED PEPPERS

See photo, page 303—

  8 cups red, green, *or* yellow
      chili peppers (1 pound)
  4 heads fresh dill *or* 2
      tablespoons dillseed
  3 cups water
  1 cup white vinegar
  2 tablespoons pickling salt
  1 tablespoon sugar
  2 cloves garlic, minced
 ¼ teaspoon crushed red
      pepper

Wash the peppers; drain. Make 2 small slits in each pepper. (Wear rubber gloves to avoid burning your hands.) Pack the chili peppers into hot pint jars, leaving ½-inch headspace. Place *1 head* fresh dill or *1½ teaspoons* dillseed in *each* jar.

In a saucepan combine remaining ingredients. Bring to boiling; pour over peppers, leaving ½-inch headspace. Prepare lids according to manufacturer's directions. Wipe rims. Adjust lids. Process in a boiling water bath 10 minutes. (Start timing when water returns to boiling.) Makes 4 pints.

APPLE-STICK RELISH

  2 tart apples, cored
 ¼ cup chopped onion
 ¼ cup chopped dill pickle
 ¼ cup sugar
  2 tablespoons vinegar

Chop apples. In bowl mix apples, onion, and pickle. Combine sugar and vinegar. Toss with apple mixture; cover. Chill. Makes 3 cups.

LIME CUCUMBER PICKLES

See photo, page 307—

  2 pounds whole small
      cucumbers
  8 cups water
 ¾ cup pickling lime
  2 teaspoons mixed pickling
      spices
2¾ cups sugar
  3 cups vinegar

Thoroughly wash cucumbers and cut into slices. (You should have about 8 cups.) In a large bowl throughly mix water and pickling lime. Add cucumber slices. Let stand for 24 hours, stirring occasionally. Drain slices; cover with fresh cold water. Replace water after 4 hours. Repeat 3 or 4 times more. Drain.

Tie pickling spices in a cheese-cloth bag. In a large saucepan combine sugar and spice bag. Stir in vinegar. Bring to boiling. Reduce heat; cover and simmer for 5 minutes. Pour hot mixture over cucumbers. Let stand overnight. Drain, reserving vinegar mixture.

In a large saucepan bring vinegar mixture to boiling. Pack the cucumber slices in hot clean half-pint jars, leaving ½-inch headspace. Pour boiling mixture over slices, leaving ½-inch headspace. Prepare lids according to manufacturer's directions. Wipe the jar rims. Adjust lids. Process in boiling water bath for 10 minutes. (Start timing when water returns to boiling.) Makes 7 half-pints.

PICKLED BEETS

See photo, page 307—

Wash 2 pounds whole medium *beets*; leave on root and 1 inch of tops. Place in kettle; cover with boiling water. Simmer, covered, for 25 minutes. Drain. Slip off skins; trim. Cut into quarters. In kettle mix 2 cups *sugar*, 2 cups *vinegar*, and 2 cups *water*. Tie 2 tablespoons *mixed pickling spices* in a cheese-cloth bag. Add to kettle. Bring to boiling; add beets. Simmer 10 minutes. Pack beets into clean hot pint jars; leave ½-inch headspace. Cover with sugar mixture; leave ½-inch headspace. Prepare lids according to manufacturer's directions. Wipe rims. Adjust lids. Process in boiling water bath 30 minutes. (Start timing when water returns to boiling.) Makes 3 pints.

BEAN RELISH

  1 16-ounce can whole green
      beans
 ⅓ cup vinegar
  2 tablespoons sugar
  1 teaspoon dillseed
  1 teaspoon mixed pickling
      spices
  1 medium onion, sliced
  1 tablespoon cooking oil

Drain beans; reserve liquid. Mix reserved liquid with vinegar, sugar, dillseed, pickling spices, and 1 teaspoon *salt*; bring to boiling. Reduce heat; cover. Simmer 5 minutes. Add beans; heat through. Cool; drain. Toss with onion and oil. Cover; chill. Makes 2 cups.

304

PEPPER RELISH

See photo, page 303—

12 sweet green *or* red peppers, ground
6 medium onions, ground
1 cup sugar
1 cup vinegar
1½ teaspoons dillseed

Cover vegetables with boiling water. Let stand 5 minutes; drain. Add remaining ingredients, ½ cup *water*, and 1½ teaspoons *salt*. Boil gently 5 minutes. Pack into hot clean half-pint jars; leave ½-inch headspace. Prepare lids according to manufacturer's directions. Adjust lids. Process jars in boiling water bath 10 minutes. (Start timing when the water returns to boiling.) Makes 10 half-pints.

PICKLED CABBAGE

16 cups chopped cabbage
2 cups chopped onion
½ cup pickling salt
4 cups sugar
3 cups vinegar
1 tablespoon mixed pickling spices

Mix first 3 ingredients; let stand overnight. Rinse; drain. In kettle combine vegetables, remaining ingredients, and 1½ cups *water*. Boil gently 5 minutes. Remove spices. Pack into hot clean pint jars; leave ½-inch headspace. Prepare the lids according to the manufacturer's directions. Adjust lids. Process in a boiling water bath for 10 minutes. (Start timing when water returns to boil.) Makes 6 pints.

DILL GREEN PEPPERS

See photo, page 307—

12 medium green peppers
5 tiny hot green chili peppers, about 1 inch long
5 cloves garlic
5 small heads fresh dill *or* 1¼ teaspoons dried dillweed
Alum
5 cups water
3 cups vinegar
¼ cup salt

Thoroughly wash green peppers. Remove the tops and seeds from green peppers; cut into 1½-inch squares. Arrange in 5 hot clean wide-mouth pint jars, leaving 1-inch headspace.

Place *one* chili pepper, *one* clove garlic, *one small head* dill or ¼ *teaspoon* dried dillweed, and ⅛ *teaspoon* alum in *each* jar.

In a saucepan bring water, vinegar, and salt to boiling. Reduce heat; simmer about 5 minutes. Cover the pepper mixture in the jars with boiling vinegar mixture, leaving ½-inch headspace.

Prepare the jar lids according to manufacturer's directions. Wipe jar rims. Adjust lids. Process in boiling water bath for 10 minutes. (Start timing when the water returns to boiling.) Makes 5 pints.

CARROT-CELERY RELISH

4 medium carrots, cut into 3-inch pieces
1½ cups bias-sliced celery
1 medium onion, chopped (½ cup)
½ cup chopped green pepper
½ cup white tarragon vinegar
¼ cup dry white wine
2 tablespoons sugar
2 tablespoons cooking oil
1 clove garlic, minced
1 teaspoon mustard seed
1 teaspoon whole coriander, crushed
¼ teaspoon salt
Dash pepper

In a medium covered saucepan cook carrots and celery in a small amount of boiling water for 5 minutes or till crisp-tender; drain. Cut carrots into thin sticks. Place carrots and celery in a bowl.

In saucepan combine chopped onion, chopped green pepper, tarragon vinegar, white wine, sugar, cooking oil, garlic, mustard seed, coriander, salt, and pepper. Bring to boiling.

Pour the hot vinegar mixture over carrots and celery in bowl, tossing to coat evenly. Cool. Cover and refrigerate at least 4 hours or for as long as 2 weeks. Stir the vegetable mixture occasionally to distribute the marinade. Drain the vegetable mixture before serving. Makes about 3 cups.

PICKLED BANANA PEPPERS

2 pounds banana peppers
4 cups water
⅓ cup salt
3 cups water
1½ cups vinegar
4 teaspoons dried basil, crushed
1 tablespoon dried oregano, crushed
5 or 6 cloves garlic

Slice the banana peppers in half lengthwise. Rinse and discard the seeds as well as any interior pulp. Combine the 4 cups water and the salt. In a large bowl cover peppers with the salt solution. Let stand overnight. Drain; rinse well.

In a large saucepan combine the 3 cups water, the vinegar, basil, and oregano. Bring to boiling. Reduce heat; simmer, uncovered, about 10 minutes.

Meanwhile pack banana peppers in hot clean half-pint jars, leaving ½-inch headspace. Add *one* clove of garlic to *each* jar.

Pour the hot vinegar mixture over peppers, stirring the mixture to keep the herbs evenly distributed. Leave ½-inch headspace in each jar. Prepare the lids according to manufacturer's directions. Wipe jar rims. Adjust lids; process in boiling water bath for 10 minutes. (Start timing when water returns to boiling.) Makes 5 or 6 pints.

SHERRIED APPLE BUTTER

4 pounds tart cooking apples, cored and quartered (16 medium)
4 cups apple cider or apple juice
1 cup cider vinegar
5 cups sugar
1 cup sweet sherry
1 lemon, seeded and finely ground (⅓ cup)
1½ teaspoons ground cinnamon
½ teaspoon ground cloves
½ teaspoon ground allspice

In a 6-quart Dutch oven combine the quartered apples, apple cider or juice, and vinegar. Bring the mixture to boiling. Reduce heat and simmer, covered, for 1 hour or till apples are very tender. Puree apple mixture through food mill into a large bowl. (There should be about 10 cups of puree.)

Return apple puree to Dutch oven. Stir in sugar, sherry, ground lemon, cinnamon, cloves, and allspice. Bring mixture to boiling. Reduce heat and boil gently for 1½ hours or till the mixture is very thick. Stir mixture frequently to prevent scorching.

Ladle the hot apple butter into hot clean pint jars, leaving ½-inch headspace. Prepare lids according to manufacturer's directions. Wipe jar rims. Adjust lids. Process in boiling water bath for 10 minutes. (Start counting time when water returns to boiling.) Makes 4 pints.

BRANDIED PEACHES

See photo, page 303—

2 cups sugar
2 cups water
2 inches stick cinnamon
6 to 8 small peaches, peeled (2 pounds)
Brandy

In medium saucepan combine the sugar, water, and stick cinnamon; bring the mixture to boiling. Boil hard, uncovered, for 5 minutes. Add a few whole peaches at a time to boiling syrup and cook 5 to 10 minutes or till peaches can be easily pierced with a fork. Remove fruit from syrup; pack cooked peaches in hot clean jars. Repeat till all peaches have been cooked.

Boil remaining syrup, uncovered, till thickened or until syrup registers 222° on candy thermometer. Remove from heat and cool to room temperature; discard the stick cinnamon. Measure syrup; add ⅓ *cup brandy* for *each 1 cup* of the syrup. Stir well. Fill jars with brandy-syrup mixture; seal. Store peaches in the refrigerator. Makes 2 quarts or 4 pints.

In dishes from back to front: Dill Cucumber Sticks (see recipe, page 302), Lime Cucumber Pickles (see recipe, page 304), Pickled Beets (see recipe, page 304), Pickled Banana Peppers, and Dill Green Peppers (see recipe, page 305).

HERB JELLY

See photo, page 303—

6½ cups sugar
2 cups water
1 cup white vinegar
6 drops green *or* yellow food
   coloring
1 cup fresh basil *or* rosemary
   leaves
1 6-ounce package
   liquid fruit pectin

In saucepan mix sugar, water, vinegar, and food coloring. Tie basil or rosemary in cheesecloth bag; crush with rolling pin. Add to pan; bring to boiling. Stir in pectin; return to full rolling boil. Boil hard 1 minute; stir constantly. Remove from heat; discard herb bag. Quickly skim off foam. Pour into hot, sterilized jars; seal with metal lids or paraffin. Makes 7 half-pints.

FRUIT JUICE JELLY

4 cups unsweetened apple,
   grape, *or* orange juice
1 1¾-ounce package
   powdered fruit pectin
¼ cup lemon juice
4½ cups sugar

In 8- to 10-quart kettle combine your choice of fruit juice, pectin, and lemon juice. Bring to full rolling boil. Stir in sugar. Return to full rolling boil. Boil hard, uncovered, for 1 minute; stir constantly. Remove from heat; quickly skim off foam. Ladle fruit syrup into hot, sterilized jars, leaving ¼-inch headspace. Seal with metal lids or paraffin. Makes 6 half-pints.

PEACH JAM

2½ to 3 pounds peaches (10 to
   12 medium)
1 1¾-ounce package
   powdered fruit pectin
2 tablespoons lemon juice
5½ cups sugar

Peel, pit, and coarsely grind the peaches (mixture should measure 4 cups). In an 8- to 10-quart kettle or Dutch oven combine the 4 cups ground peaches, pectin, and lemon juice. Bring to full rolling boil (a boil that cannot be stirred down); stir constantly. Stir in sugar. Return to full rolling boil. Boil hard, uncovered, for 1 minute, stirring constantly.

Remove from heat and quickly skim off foam with metal spoon. Ladle at once into hot clean half-pint jars, leaving ¼-inch headspace. Prepare lids according to manufacturer's directions. Wipe jar rims; adjust lids. Process jam in boiling water bath for 15 minutes. (Start timing when water returns to boiling.) Makes 6 to 7 half-pints.

Peach-Banana Jam: Prepare the Peach Jam as above, *except* chop 1 slightly green medium *banana* and add to kettle or Dutch oven with ground peaches, pectin, and lemon juice.

Peach-Plum Jam: Prepare Peach Jam as above, *except* coarsely grind only *1¼ pounds* peaches (5 to 6 medium); measure *2 cups* of ground peaches. Pit and finely chop ¾ pound fully ripe *purple plums* (about 12 medium); measure 2 cups. Add the plums to kettle or Dutch oven with peaches, pectin, and lemon juice.

FREEZER JAM

4 cups raspberries *or*
   strawberries
4 cups sugar
¼ teaspoon ground nutmeg
½ of a 6-ounce package
   (1 foil pouch) liquid fruit
   pectin
2 tablespoons lemon juice

Remove caps from berries; crush berries. Measure 2 cups. In bowl mix berries, sugar, and nutmeg. Let stand 10 minutes. Mix pectin and lemon juice. Add to bowl; stir for 3 minutes. Ladle into clean half-pint freezer containers, leaving ½-inch headspace. Seal; label. Let stand at room temperature till jam is set. Store up to 1 year in freezer. Makes 5 half-pints.

ALMOND-APRICOT JAM

2 pounds ripe apricots
3 cups sugar
⅓ cup lemon juice
½ cup sliced almonds
½ teaspoon almond extract

Pit and chop apricots; measure 4 cups. In saucepan mix apricots, sugar, and lemon juice. Bring to rolling boil. Boil hard, stirring for 5 minutes. Remove from heat. Stir in almonds and almond extract. Stir for 5 minutes, skimming the foam. Pour into hot clean half-pint jars, leaving ¼-inch headspace. Wipe jar rims; adjust lids. Process in boiling water bath for 15 minutes (start timing when water boils). Makes 3 half-pints.

Apple Marmalade

GOLDEN LEMON MARMALADE

1 pound carrots
2 medium lemons, quartered
  and seeded
3¾ cups sugar
½ cup water
½ teaspoon salt
⅓ cup sliced maraschino
  cherries

Put carrots and lemon through fine blade of food grinder or chop very finely. (You should have about 3 cups chopped carrot and ¾ cup chopped lemon.)

In a large kettle or Dutch oven combine the chopped carrot, the chopped lemon, sugar, water, and salt. Bring the mixture to full rolling boil (a boil that cannot be stirred down). Cook over medium-high heat for 10 minutes.

Add the sliced cherries; cook an additional 3 to 5 minutes or till mixture is thickened and sheets from a metal spoon. Pour into hot clean half-pint jars, leaving ¼-inch headspace. Wipe jar rims; adjust lids. Process in boiling water bath for 15 minutes (start timing when water boils). Makes about 4 half-pints.

APPLE MARMALADE

1 medium orange, quartered
6 medium apples, peeled,
  cored, and chopped
3 tablespoons lemon juice
5 cups sugar

Seed and thinly slice orange. In kettle mix orange, apples, lemon juice, and 2 cups *water*. Boil gently 10 minutes. Add sugar; cook and stir till mixture comes to rolling boil. Cook and stir till candy thermometer registers 220°. Ladle into hot, clean half-pint jars, leaving ¼-inch headspace. Wipe jar rims; adjust lids. Process in boiling water bath for 15 minutes. Makes 6.

DESSERTS

MOCHA STEAMED PUDDING

- 3 slices white bread, torn
- ¾ cup milk
- 2 eggs
- ¾ cup sugar
- 1 teaspoon instant coffee granules
- ¼ cup cooking oil
- 1 cup all-purpose flour
- ¼ cup unsweetened cocoa powder
- 2 teaspoons baking powder
- ¼ teaspoon salt
- 1 cup raisins, chopped
- ½ cup chopped walnuts
  Coffee-Butter Sauce

In a small mixer bowl combine bread and milk; let stand for 5 to 10 minutes. Beat smooth with electric mixer. Beat in eggs and sugar. Dissolve coffee granules in ¼ cup *hot water*; stir into bread along with oil. Stir together flour, the cocoa powder, baking powder, and salt. Stir into bread mixture; fold in raisins and nuts.

Pour into a well-greased 1½-quart mold. Cover with foil; tie with string. Place on wire rack in deep kettle; add *boiling water* to kettle to a depth of 1 inch. Cover; steam 2 hours, adding more water if needed. Cool 10 minutes; unmold. Serve warm with Coffee-Butter Sauce. Makes 6 servings.

Coffee-Butter Sauce: In a bowl cream 2 cups sifted *powdered sugar* and ½ cup *butter or margarine*. Beat in 3 tablespoons *coffee liqueur* and 1 teaspoon *vanilla*.

DATE-NUT CAKE ROLL

- 1 cup pitted whole dates, snipped
- ¼ cup sugar
- 3 eggs
- ½ cup sugar
- 1 cup all-purpose flour
- 1 teaspoon baking powder
- ½ teaspoon ground allspice
- ¾ cup chopped walnuts
  Sifted powdered sugar
  Cream Cheese Filling

In a small saucepan combine the dates, the ¼ cup sugar, 1 cup *water*, and ⅛ teaspoon *salt*. Bring to boiling. Cook and stir over low heat about 4 minutes or till thickened. Remove from heat; cool to room temperature. Beat the eggs at high speed of electric mixer for 5 minutes. Gradually beat in the ½ cup sugar. Stir together flour, baking powder, allspice, and ½ teaspoon *salt*. Fold into egg mixture. Spread batter in a greased and floured 15x10x1-inch jelly-roll pan. Top with nuts. Bake in a 375° oven for 12 to 15 minutes. Turn out onto a towel sprinkled with powdered sugar. Starting at the narrow end, roll up cake and towel together; cool. Unroll cake and spread with Cream Cheese Filling. Reroll and chill. Serves 10.

Cream Cheese Filling: With an electric mixer beat together two 3-ounce packages of *cream cheese*, softened; ¼ cup *butter or margarine*; and ½ teaspoon *vanilla*. Beat in 1 cup sifted *powdered sugar*.

PERSIMMON PUDDING

See photo, page 317—

- 1 cup sugar
- 1 cup all-purpose flour
- 1 teaspoon baking soda
- 1 cup mashed persimmons (about 5 persimmons)
- ½ cup milk
- 1 tablespoon shortening, melted
- 1½ cups sifted powdered sugar
- ½ cup butter, softened
- 2 teaspooons vanilla

In a bowl mix sugar, flour, baking soda, and ¼ teaspoon *salt*. Combine persimmons, milk, and shortening. Stir into dry ingredients. Pour batter into a greased 9-inch quiche dish or pie plate. Place dish in a large shallow pan. Set pan on oven rack. Pour *boiling water* into pan to a depth of ½ inch. Bake in a 350° oven for 1 to 1¼ hours, adding more water if needed. Cool on wire rack. Serve pudding warm or cool completely and refrigerate to serve cold.

Meanwhile, in small mixer bowl cream the powdered sugar and butter together till fluffy. Beat in vanilla. Serve with pudding. Sprinkle each serving with ground nutmeg if desired. Makes 6 to 8 servings.

Clockwise from back left: Alaskan Trifle (see recipe, page 313), Mocha Steamed Pudding, Cherry-Mincemeat Pie (see recipe, page 318), and Date-Nut Cake Roll.

APPLE JONATHAN

8 to 10 tart cooking apples, peeled, cored, and thinly sliced (6 cups)
½ cup maple *or* maple-flavored syrup
½ cup sugar
¼ cup butter *or* margarine
1 egg
1 cup all-purpose flour
2 teaspoons baking powder
1 teaspoon finely shredded orange peel
½ teaspoon salt
½ cup orange juice

In a mixing bowl toss apples with syrup till well coated. Spread evenly in a 10x6x2-inch baking dish or 1½-quart oval au gratin dish. Cover; bake in a 350° oven 25 minutes.

Meanwhile, in small mixer bowl beat together sugar and butter or margarine till light. Beat in egg. Stir together flour, baking powder, orange peel, and salt; add to creamed mixture alternately with the orange juice, beating the mixture well after each addition.

Uncover baking dish. Spread batter over hot apples. Return to oven; bake 25 to 30 minutes more or till cake tests done. Serve warm or cool. Top with the unsweetened whipped cream and halved orange slices if desired. Serves 6 to 8.

Back to front: Black Walnut Cake (see recipe, page 314), Apple Jonathan, and Raspberry-Cherry Pie (see recipe, page 318).

ALASKAN TRIFLE

See photo, page 311—

1⅓ cups all-purpose flour
1 cup sugar
3 tablespoons unsweetened cocoa powder
½ teaspoon baking soda
1 egg
⅓ cup cooking oil
1 teaspoon vanilla
¾ cup apricot preserves
Sherry Filling
1 cup whipping cream
1 tablespoon sugar

In a mixer bowl mix flour, the 1 cup sugar, cocoa powder, soda, and ½ teaspoon *salt*. Add the egg, oil, *half* of the vanilla, and ¾ cup *water*. Beat with electric mixer till combined. Beat 2 minutes more. Turn into greased and floured 8x8x2-inch baking pan. Bake in a 350° oven about 35 minutes. Cool 10 minutes; remove from pan. Cool. Cut cake in half horizontally; spread the bottom half with preserves. Replace top half. Cut cake into 1-inch cubes. Line a 2½-quart bowl with clear plastic wrap. Spread *½ cup* Sherry Filling in bowl. Add *one-third* of the cake cubes; spoon in another *½ cup* filling. Repeat layers twice more. Cover; chill. Invert onto plate; remove wrap. Whip together cream, the 1 tablespoon sugar, and the remaining vanilla till soft peaks form; frost the cake. Trim with toasted sliced almonds if desired. Serves 10.

Sherry Filling: Prepare one 4-serving-size package *regular vanilla pudding mix* according to package directions, *except* use 1¾ cups milk. Stir in ¼ cup *sherry*. Cover with plastic wrap; cool 1 hour.

SALZBERGER NOCKERL

See photo, pages 22-23—

6 egg whites
½ teaspoon finely shredded lemon peel
1 tablespoon lemon juice
½ teaspoon vanilla
¼ cup sugar
4 egg yolks
1 tablespoon all-purpose flour
5 tablespoons butter *or* margarine
Powdered sugar

In a large mixer bowl combine egg whites, lemon peel, lemon juice, and vanilla; beat at medium speed of electric mixer till soft peaks form (tips curl over). Gradually add sugar, beating at high speed till stiff peaks form (tips stand straight).

In a small mixer bowl beat egg yolks at high speed with electric mixer about 5 minutes or till thick and lemon-colored; fold in flour. Gently fold egg yolk mixture into stiff-beaten egg whites.

In a 350° oven melt butter or margarine in a 12x7½x2-inch baking dish or shallow oval baking dish. Remove from oven.

Spoon egg mixture into baking dish, forming 5 or 6 even mounds. Bake in 350° oven for 20 to 22 minutes or till outside is a light golden brown. Sift powdered sugar lightly over top. Serve immediately. Drizzle some of the melted butter in bottom of dish over each serving. Makes 5 or 6 servings.

313

BLACK WALNUT CAKE

See photo, page 312—

3 cups sifted powdered sugar
1 cup butter *or* margarine
1 teaspoon vanilla
4 egg yolks
2¾ cups all-purpose flour
1 tablespoon baking powder
½ teaspoon ground cinnamon
¼ teaspoon salt
1⅓ cups milk
1 cup chopped black walnuts
4 egg whites
Sifted powdered sugar

In a large mixer bowl cream the 3 cups powdered sugar, butter or margarine, and the vanilla till light and fluffy.

Add egg yolks, one at a time, beating well after each. Stir together the flour, baking powder, cinnamon, and salt. Add flour mixture and milk alternately to creamed mixture, beating well after each addition. Stir in black walnuts.

Wash beaters thoroughly. In a small mixer bowl beat egg whites till stiff peaks form (tips stand straight). Fold beaten egg whites into creamed mixture.

Pour into a greased and floured 10-inch fluted tube pan. Bake in a 350° oven for 50 to 55 minutes or till cake tests done. Cool in pan 10 minutes. Invert onto wire rack; remove pan. Cool completely. Dust the cake with additional powdered sugar. Makes 12 to 14 servings.

GRANOLA RIPPLE CAKE

See photo, pages 18-19—

1 package 2-layer-size white cake mix
1 4-serving-size package *instant* butterscotch pudding mix
½ cup cooking oil
4 eggs
2 cups Homemade Granola

In a mixer bowl combine cake mix, pudding mix, oil, and 1 cup *water.* Beat at medium speed with electric mixer for 2 minutes. Add eggs, one at a time, beating well after each. Pour *three-fourths* of the batter into a well-greased and floured 10-inch fluted tube pan. Top with Homemade Granola. Spoon remaining batter over the granola. Bake in a 350° oven for 50 to 55 minutes. Cool 10 minutes. Invert cake onto wire rack; remove the pan. Cool. Sprinkle with sifted powdered sugar if desired. Makes 12 to 14 servings.

Homemade Granola: In a large mixing bowl combine 2½ cups *rolled oats,* 1 cup *shredded coconut,* ½ cup coarsely chopped *almonds,* ½ cup *sesame seeds,* ½ cup *sunflower nuts,* and ½ cup *toasted wheat germ.* Combine ½ cup *honey* and ¼ cup *cooking oil.* Stir into oat mixture. Spread in a 13x9x2-inch baking pan. Bake in a 300° oven 45 to 50 minutes or till light brown, stirring every 15 minutes. Transfer to another pan; stir in ½ cup *dried apricots,* snipped, and ½ cup *raisins.* Cool completely, stirring occasionally to prevent lumps. Store in tightly covered container. Makes 6½ cups.

BLACKBERRY-BUTTERMILK CAKE

See photo, page 317—

2 cups sugar
1 cup butter *or* margarine
4 eggs
4¾ cups all-purpose flour
1 teaspoon baking powder
1 teaspoon baking soda
½ teaspoon salt
1 cup buttermilk
1 teaspoon vanilla
2 cups fresh *or* frozen unsweetened blackberries
1½ cups sifted powdered sugar
1 tablespoon milk

In a mixer bowl cream together sugar and butter or margarine. Add eggs, one at a time, beating well after each.

Stir together flour, baking powder, baking soda, and salt. Combine buttermilk and vanilla. Add the dry ingredients and the buttermilk mixture alternately to the creamed mixture, beating after each addition. Fold in fresh or frozen blackberries.

Spread batter into a greased and floured 10-inch fluted tube pan. Bake in a 350° oven for 1¼ hours. Cool 10 minutes in pan. Invert on wire rack; remove pan. Cool completely. Combine powdered sugar and enough of the milk to make of drizzling consistency. Drizzle the powdered sugar mixture over the cake. Makes 12 to 14 servings.

CHRISTMAS CAKE

See photo, page 317—

 1 cup butter or margarine,
    softened
 1 cup packed brown sugar
 9 eggs
2¼ cups all-purpose flour
 1 teaspoon ground cinnamon
 ⅓ cup orange juice, brandy,
    or rum
 2 cups currants
 2 cups raisins
 4 ounces whole blanched
    almonds
 ⅔ cup chopped candied citron
 ⅔ cup chopped candied orange
    peel
 ⅓ cup red candied cherries,
    halved
    Orange juice, brandy,
    or rum

In a large mixer bowl beat together butter or margarine and brown sugar till fluffy. Add eggs, one at a time, beating well after each. Stir together flour and cinnamon. Add dry ingredients and the ⅓ cup orange juice, brandy, or rum alternately to creamed mixture, beating well after each addition.

In a large bowl stir together currants, raisins, almonds, citron, orange peel, and cherries; fold into batter. Turn into two greased and floured 8x4x2-inch loaf pans. Bake in a 300° oven for 1¼ to 1½ hours or till done. Cool 10 minutes before removing from pans. Cool completely on wire rack.

Wrap in orange juice- or liquor-soaked cheesecloth. Then wrap in foil. Chill; store at least 2 days before slicing. Makes 2 loaves.

CASSATA

See photo, pages 22-23—

 1 cup sugar
 1 cup butter *or* margarine,
    softened
 6 egg yolks
 2 cups sifted cake flour
 ½ teaspoon baking powder
 ½ teaspoon salt
 ½ cup milk
 6 egg whites
 ¾ cup sugar
    Orange-Ricotta Filling
    Vanilla Frosting
 ¼ cup coarsely chopped
    pistachio nuts

In a large mixer bowl beat together the 1 cup sugar and butter or margarine about 7 minutes or till very light and fluffy. Add egg yolks, one at a time, beating well after each. Beat about 5 minutes more or till very fluffy.

Sift together the cake flour, the baking powder, and salt. Add dry ingredients and milk alternately to creamed mixture, beating well after each addition.

Wash beaters thoroughly. Beat egg whites with electric mixer till soft peaks form (tips curl over); gradually add the ¾ cup sugar, beating till stiff peaks form (tips stand straight). Fold into creamed mixture. Pour batter into an ungreased 10-inch tube pan. Bake in a 350° oven for 50 to 55 minutes or till cake tests done. Invert; cool in pan. Remove from pan.

Cut cake horizontally into 3 layers. Spread the Orange-Ricotta Filling between cake layers. Frost top and sides of cake with the Vanilla Frosting, sprinkling nuts around edge of top. Chill. Serves 16.

ORANGE-RICOTTA FILLING

 ¾ cup sugar
 3 tablespoons cornstarch
 ¾ cup milk
 1 pound ricotta cheese
 2 tablespoons orange liqueur
1½ teaspoons vanilla
 3 ounces semisweet chocolate,
    chopped (½ cup)
 ¼ cup finely chopped candied
    citron

In a saucepan combine the sugar and cornstarch. Stir in the milk all at once. Cook and stir till mixture is thickened and bubbly. Cook and stir 2 minutes more. Remove from heat. Cover surface with clear plastic wrap. Cool *without stirring*. In mixer bowl beat ricotta cheese with electric mixer till creamy. Blend in the cooled cornstarch mixture, the orange liqueur, and vanilla. Stir in the chocolate and citron. Makes about 3 cups.

VANILLA FROSTING

 ¾ cup shortening
 1 teaspoon vanilla
 3 cups sifted powdered sugar
 5 tablespoons milk

In small mixer bowl cream together shortening and vanilla thoroughly with electric mixer. Beat in powdered sugar just till mixed. Beat in as much milk as necessary to make a frosting of spreading consistency. Quickly frost the top and sides of one 10-inch cake.

DOUBLE CHOCOLATE CRUMBLE BARS

¾ cup sugar
½ cup butter *or* margarine, softened
2 eggs
1 teaspoon vanilla
¾ cup all-purpose flour
½ cup chopped pecans *or* walnuts
2 tablespoons unsweetened cocoa powder
¼ teaspoon baking powder
¼ teaspoon salt
2 cups tiny marshmallows
1 6-ounce package (1 cup) semisweet chocolate pieces
1 cup peanut butter
1½ cups crisp rice cereal

In a large mixer bowl cream sugar and butter or margarine together thoroughly with electric mixer; beat in eggs and vanilla. Stir together flour, chopped nuts, cocoa, baking powder, and the salt; stir into egg mixture.

Spread in bottom of a greased 13x9x2-inch baking pan. Bake in 350° oven for 15 to 20 minutes or till cookies test done. Sprinkle the marshmallows evenly atop; bake 3 minutes more. Cool.

In small saucepan combine the chocolate pieces and peanut butter; cook and stir over low heat till chocolate is melted. Stir in cereal. Spread mixture atop cooled bars. Chill; cut into bars. Refrigerate. Makes 3 to 4 dozen.

MAID OF HONOR CUPCAKES

1 8-ounce can crushed pineapple
1 cup all-purpose flour
1 teaspoon sugar
½ teaspoon salt
⅓ cup shortening
¼ cup sugar
2 tablespoons shortening
1 egg
⅔ cup all-purpose flour
1 teaspoon baking powder
Dash salt

Drain pineapple, reserving syrup. Set fruit aside. For pastry, in a bowl stir together the 1 cup flour, 1 teaspoon sugar, and ½ teaspoon salt. Cut in the ⅓ cup shortening till mixture is the size of small peas. Stir in ¼ *cup* of the pineapple syrup till mixture forms a ball.

Add water to remaining syrup to make ¼ cup liquid; set aside. Set aside *one-fourth* of the pastry. Press remaining pastry on bottom and halfway up sides of twelve 2½-inch muffin cups.

In a mixer bowl cream together the ¼ cup sugar and 2 tablespoons shortening. Beat in egg. Stir together the ⅔ cup flour, the baking powder, and dash salt. Stir the dry ingredients and pineapple syrup-water mixture alternately into the creamed mixture.

Place *2 teaspoons* of the drained pineapple in each muffin cup. Fill each with a *rounded tablespoon* of batter. Roll reserved pastry into a 6x4-inch rectangle. Cut into twenty-four 2x½-inch strips. Crisscross *two* strips atop each muffin. Bake in a 350° oven for 20 minutes. Serve warm. Makes 12.

WALNUT-CHERRY SNACKS

½ cup butter *or* margarine, softened
½ cup sugar
2 egg yolks
1 teaspoon vanilla
1½ cups all-purpose flour
1 cup packed brown sugar
½ cup flaked coconut
2 egg whites
½ cup chopped walnuts
¼ cup maraschino cherries, drained and cut up

In a large mixer bowl thoroughly cream together the softened butter or margarine and sugar with an electric mixer. Beat in the egg yolks and vanilla. Stir in the flour.

Pat the flour mixture into an ungreased 9x9x2-inch baking pan. In a bowl combine the brown sugar, flaked coconut, and egg whites. Stir in chopped walnuts and cut-up maraschino cherries. Spread over flour mixture in pan.

Bake in a 350° oven for 30 to 35 minutes. Cool cookies in pan on wire rack. Cut into diamonds or squares when cool. Makes 24.

Clockwise from top left: Persimmon Pudding (see recipe, page 310), Blackberry-Buttermilk Cake (see recipe, page 314), Walnut-Cherry Snacks and Maid of Honor Cupcakes, a wedge of Persimmon Pudding, and Christmas Cake (see recipe, page 315).

CHERRY-MINCEMEAT PIES

See photo, page 311—

Double-Crust Pastry (double recipe)
2 cups prepared mincemeat
1 21-ounce can cherry pie filling
½ cup orange marmalade
1 tablespoon all-purpose flour
¼ cup chopped walnuts

Prepare Double-Crust Pastry. On a lightly floured surface roll *1 ball* of dough into a 12-inch circle. Repeat with a second ball of dough. Line a 9-inch pie plate with each pastry circle. Trim to ½ inch beyond edge.

In a bowl mix mincemeat, pie filling, marmalade, flour, and walnuts. Divide mixture between the two pastry shells. Roll each of the 2 remaining balls of dough into a 12-inch circle. Cut into ½-inch-wide strips. Weave the strips atop pies to make lattice tops; flute edges. Bake in a 400° oven for 35 to 40 minutes. Makes 2 pies.

DOUBLE-CRUST PASTRY

Combine 2 cups all-purpose *flour* and 1 teaspoon *salt*. Cut in ⅔ cup *shortening* till pieces are the size of small peas. Sprinkle *1 tablespoon water* over part of mixture; gently toss with a fork. Repeat with 5 to 6 tablespoons more *water* till all is moistened. Form into 2 balls. Use to prepare double-crust or lattice-topped pie. Makes pastry for one 9-inch pie.

RASPBERRY-CHERRY PIE

See photos, pages 270 and 312—

1 10-ounce package frozen red raspberries, thawed
¾ cup sugar
3 tablespoons cornstarch
¼ teaspoon salt
2 cups fresh *or* frozen pitted tart red cherries
Double-Crust Pastry

Drain raspberries, reserving syrup. Add enough water to syrup to measure 1 cup liquid. In a medium saucepan mix together sugar, cornstarch, and salt. Stir in reserved raspberry liquid. Stir fresh or frozen cherries into mixture in saucepan. Cook, stirring constantly, over medium-high heat till thickened and bubbly. Cook and stir 1 minute more. Remove from heat; stir in drained raspberries. Cool 15 to 20 minutes.

Meanwhile, prepare the Double-Crust Pastry. On floured surface roll out *half* of the pastry into a 12-inch circle. Line a 9-inch pie plate with pastry; trim ½ inch beyond edge of pie plate. Fill with partially cooled fruit mixture. On floured surface roll out remaining pastry into a 12-inch circle. Cut into ½-inch-wide strips with a knife or pastry wheel. Weave the strips atop filling to make a lattice top. Trim. Seal and flute edges high. Cover edges of pie with foil to prevent overbrowning. Bake in a 375° oven for 20 minutes. Remove foil; bake 15 to 20 minutes more. Cool on wire rack.

RUM-WALNUT PUMPKIN PIE

Pastry Shell
1½ cups canned pumpkin
¾ cup packed brown sugar
1 teaspoon ground cinnamon
½ teaspoon ground ginger
½ teaspoon ground nutmeg
3 eggs
1 cup evaporated milk
3 tablespoons dark rum
¾ cup chopped walnuts

Prepare Pastry Shell, fluting edge high. Do not prick. In bowl combine the pumpkin, brown sugar, spices, and ½ teaspoon *salt*. Lightly beat eggs into mixture. Stir in evaporated milk and rum; mix well. Stir in nuts. Place *unbaked* shell on oven rack; pour pumpkin mixture into shell. To prevent overbrowning, cover edge of pie with foil. Bake in a 375° oven for 25 minutes. Remove foil; bake 20 to 25 minutes more or till a knife inserted just off-center comes out clean. Cool on wire rack.

Pastry Shell: In a bowl combine 1¼ cups all-purpose *flour* and ½ teaspoon *salt*. Cut in ⅓ cup *shortening or lard* till pieces are the size of small peas. Sprinkle 1 tablespoon *water* over part of the mixture; gently toss with fork. Repeat with 2 to 3 tablespoons more *water* till all is moistened. Form the dough into a ball. On a lightly floured surface, roll dough into a 12-inch circle. Ease into a 9-inch pie plate. Trim to ½ inch beyond edge; flute edges.

For a baked pie shell, prick bottom and sides with tines of fork. Bake in a 450° oven for 10 to 12 minutes. Makes one 9-inch shell.

BLUEBERRY CREAM CHEESE PIE

1 8-ounce package cream
   cheese, softened
¼ cup sugar
¼ cup dairy sour cream
½ teaspoon vanilla
1 *baked* 9-inch Pastry Shell,
   cooled
2 to 3 cups fresh blueberries
½ cup water
½ cup sugar
2 tablespoons cornstarch
1 tablespoon lemon juice
3 tablespoons powdered sugar
   Dash ground cinnamon
   Dash ground nutmeg

In a small bowl stir together the cream cheese, the ¼ cup sugar, sour cream, and the vanilla till smooth. Spread evenly in cooled Pastry Shell; chill till firm.

For glaze, in a small saucepan mash *1 cup* of the blueberries. Add the water and bring to boiling. Strain; add additional water to the blueberry juice to make 1 cup. In the same saucepan combine the ½ cup sugar and the cornstarch; stir in the blueberry liquid. Cook, stirring constantly, till the mixture thickens and bubbles. Cook and stir 1 minute more. Remove from heat; stir in lemon juice. Cool.

Place the remaining blueberries over cream cheese layer. Spoon glaze evenly over all. Chill at least 3 hours. To serve, combine powdered sugar, cinnamon, and nutmeg. Sift over pie.

FIG-APPLE PIE

See photo, page 270—

1 cup sugar
½ teaspoon salt
½ teaspoon ground cinnamon
¼ teaspoon ground cloves
¼ teaspoon ground nutmeg
4 medium apples, cored,
   peeled, and thinly sliced
   (4 cups)
1 cup snipped dried figs
½ cup jellied cranberry sauce
½ teaspoon finely shredded
   lemon peel
¼ cup lemon juice
   Double-Crust Pastry
1 tablespoon butter *or*
   margarine
1 teaspoon sugar
¼ teaspoon ground cinnamon

In a mixing bowl combine the 1 cup sugar, the salt, the ½ teaspoon cinnamon, the cloves, and nutmeg. Add apples, figs, cranberry sauce, lemon peel, and the lemon juice; mix well.

On floured surface roll *half* of the Double-Crust Pastry into a 12-inch circle. Line a 9-inch pie plate. Trim ½ inch beyond edge of plate. Fill with apple mixture; dot with the butter or margarine. On floured surface roll out remaining pastry into a 12-inch circle. Cut slits in top crust for escape of steam. Place top crust over apple mixture. Seal and flute edge.

Sprinkle with mixture of 1 teaspoon sugar and ¼ teaspoon of cinnamon. To prevent overbrowning, cover edge with foil. Bake in 375° oven for 25 minutes. Remove foil; bake for 20 to 25 minutes more or till crust is golden. Cool on rack.

PEAR-CRANBERRY PIE

   Double-Crust Pastry
½ cup sugar
3 tablespoons all-purpose flour
⅛ teaspoon ground cloves
   Dash salt
1 16-ounce can whole
   cranberry sauce
1 tablespoon lemon juice
3 cups sliced, peeled fresh
   pears *or* one 29-ounce can
   pear halves, drained and
   sliced
1 tablespoon butter *or*
   margarine
   Sugar (optional)

Prepare Double-Crust Pastry; roll out *half* the pastry. Line a 9-inch pie plate. Trim pastry to ½ inch beyond edge of pie plate.

In a mixing bowl combine the ½ cup sugar, flour, cloves, and salt. Stir in cranberry sauce and lemon juice; mix well. Gently stir in sliced pears. Turn into pastry-lined pie plate. Dot with butter or margarine. Roll out the remaining pastry; cut into ½-inch-wide strips. Weave the strips atop filling to make a lattice top; flute edges.

Sprinkle top lightly with additional sugar if desired. To prevent overbrowning, cover edge of pastry with foil. Bake in a 375° oven for 30 minutes. Remove foil; bake 25 to 30 minutes more or till crust is golden. Cool on wire rack.

STRAWBERRY ICE CREAM PIE

1 quart vanilla ice cream
1 *baked* 9-inch Pastry Shell
   (see recipe, page 318)
4 cups fresh strawberries
⅓ cup sugar
1 tablespoon cornstarch
½ cup water

Stir ice cream till slightly softened; spread in bottom of pastry shell. Freeze firm. Mash and sieve *1 cup* of the strawberries; set remaining strawberries aside.

In saucepan combine sugar and cornstarch; stir in water. Stir in sieved berries. Cook, stirring constantly, till thickened and bubbly. Cool to room temperature.

About 20 minutes before serving, arrange remaining whole berries, stem end down, atop ice cream. Spoon thickened mixture over berries. Store in freezer till serving time (avoid longer freezing or strawberries will harden).

SUNDAE SPECIAL

In *each* of 4 banana split dishes place 2 scoops *vanilla ice cream* and 1 scoop *chocolate ice cream*. For each dish spoon *chocolate-flavored ice cream topping* over the vanilla ice cream and *marshmallow ice cream topping* over the chocolate ice cream. Top each with *whipped cream*, *chopped pecans*, and *maraschino cherries*. Makes 4 servings.

CARAMEL CRUNCH SUNDAE

1 cup butter *or* margarine,
   softened
1 cup packed brown sugar
1 beaten egg yolk
1 teaspoon vanilla
2 cups all-purpose flour
8 ounces caramels (24)
⅓ cup milk
   Vanilla *or* butter brickle ice
   cream

In a mixer bowl cream the butter or margarine and brown sugar till fluffy. Beat in egg yolk and vanilla. Stir in flour. Spread in an ungreased 15x10x1-inch baking pan. Bake in a 350° oven for 18 to 20 minutes. Cool. Cut into twelve pieces.

In a small saucepan combine caramels and milk; stir till melted and smooth. For each serving, place a baked square on a dessert plate. Top with a scoop of ice cream. Spoon the warm caramel sauce atop. Trim with pecan halves if desired. Serves 12.

PEPPERMINT DREAMBOAT

Place 3 scoops of *peppermint ice cream* in a dessert dish. Drizzle with *marshmallow ice cream topping*, then drizzle with heated *fudge ice cream topping*. Garnish with *whipped cream*, *chopped pecans*, and *maraschino cherries*. Serves 1.

CHOCOLATE MALTS

1 pint vanilla ice cream
¾ cup cold milk
¼ cup malted milk powder
3 tablespoons chilled
   chocolate-flavored syrup
   Chocolate ice cream
   (optional)

In a blender container combine vanilla ice cream, milk, malted milk powder, and chocolate syrup. Cover and blend about 1 minute. Pour into 2 tall glasses. Top each with a small scoop of chocolate ice cream if desired. Makes 2.

RAINBOW SHERBET PARFAIT

Orange sherbet
Lime sherbet
Pineapple ice cream topping
4 strawberry halves
   (optional)

In four parfait glasses alternate layers of orange sherbet, lime sherbet, and pineapple topping. Freeze. To serve, garnish with the strawberry halves if desired. Makes 4 servings.

Clockwise from bottom left: Sundae Special, Strawberry Ice Cream Pie, Rainbow Sherbet Parfait, Chocolate Malts, assorted ice creams, Caramel Crunch Sundae, and Peppermint Dreamboat.

COUNTRY FESTIVITIES
A Homespun Christmas

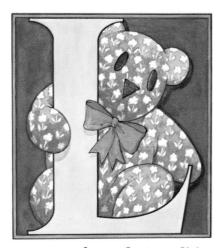

iving in the country taught our pioneer ancestors the worth and beauty of hand-made things. At Christmas-time especially, they took pleasure in creating gifts and trims for the holiday season. Nowadays we take pride in the heritage that has taught us to appreciate American handmades and we pass along that tradition by presenting "a homespun Christmas," six pages filled with projects to make and share with family and friends. The projects, made from the simple materials of home and farm, include wool patch stockings, a homespun prairie doll, wooden barnyard animal puzzles, and spatter-painted gift wrap. On the tree you will find soft sculpture candles, miniature spoon doll ornaments, cross-stitched greetings-of-the-season, and macramé snowflakes. Instructions for these projects begin on page 328.

Christmas treasures abound on these two pages. They're all projects you can give with pride to anyone on your Christmas list, or display in your home as wondrous decorations.

To make the countrified pincushion dolls (right), assemble the bodies from pieces you cut from pine, then carefully whittle the facial features. Dress them in calico fabrics and stuff the full skirts tightly with fiberfill to form the handy cushion for your pins.

The "Little Women" dolls (right) are fashioned from porcelain rather than wood. Buy porcelain doll kits at craft or hobby shops and follow the manufacturer's instructions for dressing the dolls. Or, design your own versions of the ruffled skirts and lace-trimmed blouses.

Use your leftover scraps of fabric by making an assortment of patchwork greeting cards (right). The traditional quilt patterns shown here have been favorites since pioneer days.

On the beautifully carved bedside table (opposite) are some traditional patterns you can work into tablecloths, runners, hand towels, and any manner of linens. The popular pine tree design on the tablecloth is worked in cross-stitches all along the outer edges of the fabrics. The woven towels are embellished with traditional mountain motifs that you can work in simplified darning stitches.

For instructions, see page 330.

For another look at the spatter-painted wrapping paper shown above, see pages 322-323. This is a delightful family-style project for one and all, whether you are a novice at crafts or highly skilled. All it takes is paint and a paintbrush, plus sheets of newspaper to catch the splatters as you sprinkle the paint on the wrapping paper in random designs.

W inter is the time to stay at home and make all kinds of things for Christmas. The assortment of gifts and trims shown here is made entirely from corn husks. To make these projects you can dry corn husks from your garden or use store-bought husks. Use natural-colored husks for the nativity (above) and angel (right) or dye the husks soft prairie colors using liquid fabric dyes, as was done for the tree trimming dolls (opposite).

Complete how-to instructions begin on page 333.

If your cornhusks are especially brittle or thick, add a few drops of glycerin to warm water and soak the husks for several minutes. Always work the cornhusks when they are still damp so they will be pliable enough to bend and shape.

WOOLEN PATCHWORK STOCKING
page 322

Materials *(for each stocking):* Wool fabric scraps; quilt batting; 1¼ yards cable cord; muslin for lining; 12x18 inches wool plaid (backing); 27 inches of 1½-inch-wide grosgrain ribbon.

Instructions: Cut out and piece 2-inch squares of wool fabric, using ¼-inch seams, until you have a piece of patchwork large enough to cut pattern. Cut batting and lining to match pieced "fabric." Sandwich the lining, batting, and front fabric; baste. Tie layers together in corners of squares.

Enlarge pattern (below). Cut stocking front and cuff from pieced fabric. Cut the back from plaid, the cuff lining from muslin.

Cover cable cord with wool; baste to stocking front. Sew front to back, leaving top open. Clip curves; turn.

Stitch short ends of cuff together (side seams). Repeat for cuff lining.

For cuff trim, cut white fabric into eight or nine 4½-inch squares. Fold squares in half diagonally, then in half again to form triangular petals. Pin petals along cuff's lower seam line, raw edges even, with folded edge of each petal tucked slightly inside open edge of adjoining petal; baste.

Stitch cuff to cuff lining along lower edge. Press; turn; baste raw edge of cuff and lining to stocking top. Stitch; cover raw edge with 2-inch-wide bias tape.

Sew on eight inches of ribbon for hanging loop. Tie remaining ribbon into a bow; tack to stocking front.

RUSTIC DOLL
page 322

Materials: ¼ yard natural-colored linen (for body); ¼ yard calico (dress); 1 skein sport-weight yarn or linen thread (hair); red, black felt-tipped pens; fiberfill; red embroidery floss.

Instructions: Enlarge the patterns (below). Cut the pieces, adding ¼-inch seam allowances.

Sew body pieces together, leaving armholes and bottom of body open; turn. Stitch, stuff arms; insert into body; stitch. Stuff body firmly. Stitch, stuff legs. Insert tops of legs into body (toes should point straight up); stitch across. Add facial features with pens.

Cut out dress, adding ½-inch seam allowances. Hem skirt, sleeves, neckline. Buttonhole-stitch around neckline; thread floss through loops; tie.

For hair, spread ½ skein of yarn into 3x12-inch piece. Stitch "part" down center. Stitch hair to head along part. Braid pigtails; tie ends with floss.

WOODEN ANIMAL PUZZLES
page 323

Materials: 2-inch-thick pine lumber; jigsaw; sandpaper; fabric dyes (optional); carbon paper.

Instructions: Enlarge patterns (below and opposite); trace them onto lumber using carbon paper. Cut out shapes with a jigsaw; sand the edges smooth. If desired, dye portions of each design with fabric dyes (see photograph). Drill holes for cow's eye and tail; add yarn for tail.

SPATTERWARE WRAPPING PAPER
page 323

Materials: Acrylic latex paints (we used red and blue wall paints); unglazed shelf paper; toothbrush.

Instructions: Before you begin, spread newspapers on the floor to protect your work area. Then spread shelf paper across newspapers. Thin paint with water to the consistency of cream. Dip the toothbrush into the paint; tap off excess on the side of the can. Hold the brush 6 to 20 inches from the floor and flick paint onto the paper, making spatters as close or far apart as desired.

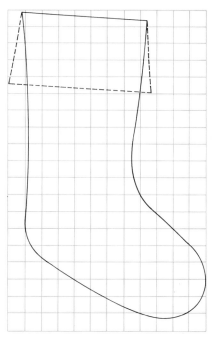

1 Square = 1 Inch

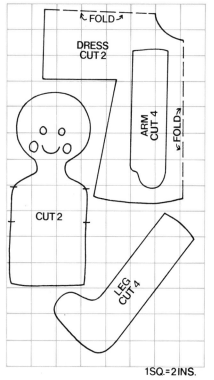

1 SQ. = 2 INS.

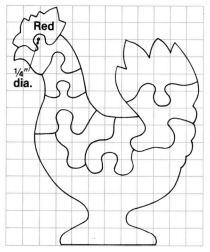

1 Square = 1 Inch

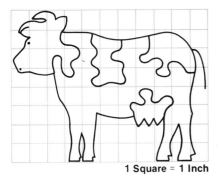

1 Square = 1 Inch

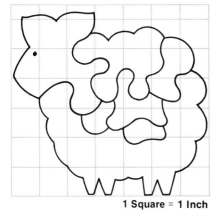

1 Square = 1 Inch

FABRIC CANDLE ORNAMENTS
page 323

Materials: ¼ yard muslin; assorted calico prints; yellow, orange, and red acrylic paints or embroidery floss; quilt batting; fiberfill; light-gauge wire; small paintbrush or needle; tissue paper.

Instructions: Enlarge pattern (below). Cut fabric pieces; cut one base from batting. Right sides facing and batting on top, sew base pieces (¼-inch seam). Leave opening. Turn; stitch.

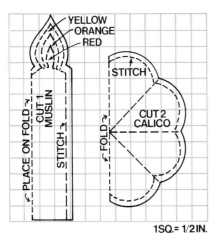

1SQ.= 1/2 IN.

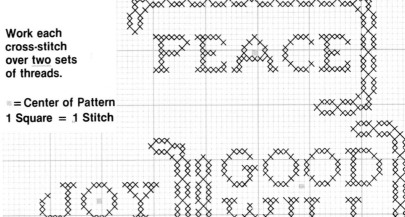

Work each cross-stitch over two sets of threads.

◼ = Center of Pattern
1 Square = 1 Stitch

Topstitch ⅛ inch from edge. Following dotted lines on pattern, sew ¼-inch tucks between each base scallop. Alternate stitching on both sides so tucks face front *and* back.

Fold candle, right sides together. Stitch, leaving end open. Turn; stitch two smaller flames inside large flame. Paint or embroider flame in red, orange, yellow. Wrap red embroidery floss below flame; tie.

Stuff candle; slip-stitch to base's center, turning raw edges under. Thread two 6-inch wires through bottom of base; twist ends around branch.

SAMPLER ORNAMENTS
page 323

Materials: 18-count ecru Aida cloth; #5 pearl cotton in red, blue, gold, and green; lace edging; calico scraps (backing); fiberfill; narrow satin ribbon.

Instructions: Following the charts (above), cross-stitch each pattern onto a 4x6-inch piece of Aida cloth. Begin in the center of the fabric and stitch toward the edges. When the embroidery is finished, trim the rectangle to within ⅝ inch of border. Baste lace ¼ inch inside raw edge of fabric.

Cut backing fabric to match the front. Sew to the front, right sides facing. Turn, stuff, and sew the opening closed. Add satin bow, ribbon loop.

SPOON DOLLS
page 323

Materials: Wooden spoons (5 inches long for ornaments, 6 inches long for treetop doll); black, red, and white acrylic paints; fabric and yarn scraps, trims; small gold pompons; gold paper; glue; fine-tip black felt pen; white felt; tissue; sandpaper.

Instructions: Enlarge patterns on page 330. Sand spoons. Paint faces with acrylics. Use pen for fine lines. From scrap fabrics, cut two sleeves. Sew side seam (¼-inch seam); turn. Turn under raw edge; insert doll's hand. Sew sleeve hems together, stitching through hand.

Cut dress pieces. Position sleeves between dress front and back, right sides together. Stitch sides, catching sleeve in seam. Turn. Hem skirt; add lace trim.

Turn neck under ¼ inch. Gather neckline and insert spoon. Pull thread tight. Glue neckline to wood.

Doll I with hat: Cut four 8-inch strands of yarn; glue along *edge* of spoon top for hair. For hat, cut 3½-inch fabric circle; gather. Slip spoon head into opening. Tighten to fit. Tuck raw edges inside. Knot thread; glue edge of hat front to spoon. Glue lace, bow to hat front. Trim hair as desired.

Doll II with book: Glue five pompons to edge of spoon head for hair. Cut gold paper book 1½x2½ inches. Fold; glue to hands. Glue lace to neck.

(Continued)

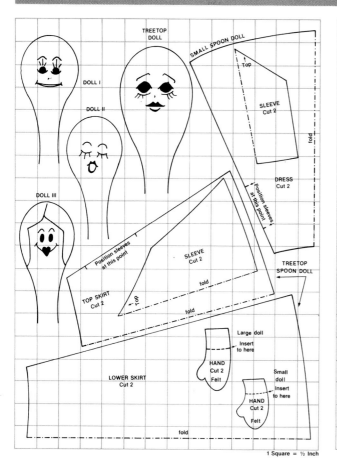

1 Square = ½ Inch

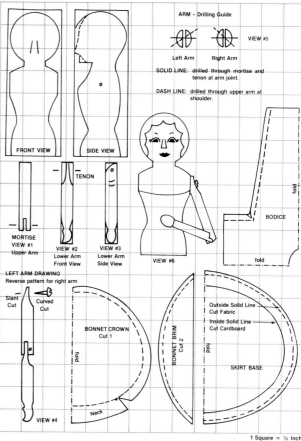

1 Square = ½ Inch

Doll III: Glue on trim for hat brim. Add bow to neck and rickrack to dress.

Treetop doll: Glue pompons to spoon head; gather lace around top edge of spoon to extend over pompons for halo.

See basic directions to add arms to top skirt. Sew seams; hem lower skirt. Slip top skirt over lower one; line up top edges. To gather, treat as one skirt.

WOODEN PINCUSHION DOLL
page 324

Materials: 1¼ x 1¼ x 3¼-inch piece pine or basswood; two 1½-inch pieces ¼-inch dowel (upper arms); two 1¾-inch pieces ¼-inch dowel (lower arms); $^{1}/_{16}$-inch dowel 1 inch long (or use round toothpick) for pegging arms; two ½-inch (No. 2) roundhead brass screws; satin varnish; paint; whittling knife; sandpaper; paintbrushes; jigsaw.

Instructions: Enlarge the patterns (above). Transfer patterns for front and side of doll to pine or basswood block;

drill holes ½-inch deep at shoulders using $^{1}/_{16}$-inch drill bit.

With jigsaw, cut away excess wood on front. Keep cuts outside pattern lines. Before cutting the curves, make straight cuts from edge of block to pattern line at neck and waist.

Redraw pattern on side of block. Cut away excess. Cut nose and chin last, following solid lines. See pattern for nose position. Lines are wider than necessary. As you shape face, carve and sand away excess.

With whittling knife, make slice cuts on nose lines to protect nose from chipping as the rest of the face is shaped.

Use knife to round corners, edges. Work from high to low places, turning doll often. As you shape cheeks, bridge of nose may look too high on forehead. Leave this until last, then curve bridge into forehead and round chin (see dashed line on pattern). Sand.

Cut ⅜-inch-deep mortise in upper arms as shown. Shape hands on lower

arms; whittle tenons as shown, reversing shaping for right arm.

Join upper and lower arm. Tenons must fit perfectly into mortise. Hold pieces with a vise. Drill a $^{1}/_{16}$-inch hole through both pieces. Insert a dowel or toothpick into hole. Trim ends of dowel or toothpick.

For arms to bend toward center front, slanted and curved cuts at top of arm must be on slight angle from mortise and tenon joint at elbow. (See views 4, 5, 6.) For correct placement of slant cut, hold arm along doll shoulder; slightly rotate arm and check direction of arm bend. Mark placement of slant cut. Make slanted, curved cuts. Drill hole with $^{3}/_{32}$-inch bit as shown in view 4. Sand arms. Varnish body, arms. Sand again. Paint doll's face, hair. Varnish when dry.

Clothing: Cut bodice front and back using the enlarged pattern. Cut open the center back of the bodice. Seal the raw edges of the fabric with a narrow bead of white glue. Trim neckline and sleeves with narrow lace. Sew under-

330

arm seams (¼-inch seam); clip corner; turn right side out.

For skirt, cut fabric 6x10½ inches. Gather one long side. Sew short sides together, leaving 1 inch open (placket). Gather to fit bodice waist; stitch. Fit dress onto doll; slip-stitch center back seam. Add buttons (small beads).

For base, cut fabric and cardboard to match pattern. Gather fabric; pull snug around cardboard. Turn up skirt hem ½ inch. Stuff skirt with fiberfill; whipstitch base to opening. Tie a ribbon around the doll's waist.

For sunbonnet, cut crown and brim. Gather the crown between small dots. Glue together raw edges between small dots at neck. Gather back neck of bonnet; fasten threads. Stitch curved edge of brim; turn. Gather crown between dots to fit straight edge of brim; stitch.

Make a tiny tote bag for doll's arm to hold thimble or needles.

MACRAME SNOWFLAKES
page 323

Note: Finished size of snowflake A (at left in photograph, above right), made with 3-ply waxed linen cord, is 3½ inches in diameter. Versions B (center) and C (at right) measure 4½ inches in diameter.

Materials: ½-inch diameter metal rings; twenty-four 24-inch lengths of 3-ply natural-colored waxed linen cord for each snowflake; round and oval natural-colored wooden beads; macrame board; T-pins.

Instructions: To work snowflakes, use lark's head knot, square knot, half hitch sennit, horizontal double half hitch, and diagonal double half hitch. For diagrams of the knots, consult a book on macrame.

Snowflake A: Fold 18 cords in half and mount in metal ring with lark's head knot. Insert pin in macrame board; place ring on it. Turn the ring as you work so the knotting is always in front of you.

With any four cords, tie a square knot. With the adjacent two cords, tie a half hitch sennit that is comprised of six knots. Repeat this sequence around.

Beneath any half hitch sennit, divide the two cords into one facing right and one facing left.

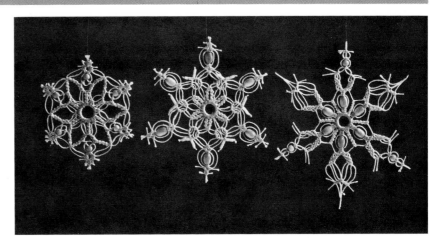

Using right sennit cord as bearer cord, and two closer cords from square knot on right as knotting cords, tie two diagonal double half hitch knots. (In a half hitch knot, cord that remains stationary is bearer cord; cords wrapped around it are knotting cords.)

Do not pull cords from square knots tight; doing so will destroy symmetry of snowflake and destroy lacy effect.

Repeat this procedure using the left sennit cords and the two closer cords from square knot on the left.

Repeat around ring until all sennit cords have been tied. This sequence of knots will form six inverted Y shapes around ring (see photo above). Each shape will have six cords falling from it.

From center of each Y, find the two center cords. Pull the left cord to the left and the right one to the right.

Tie two more rows of two diagonal double half hitch knots on these cords. Use the bearer cords from the previous row to complete this. All three rows of double half hitches should spread the Y outward. Repeat on each Y shape.

Using bearer cord and cord that tied the last half hitch knot, tie half hitch sennit composed of six knots on each "leg" of Y. Repeat on each Y shape around. This, in effect, will lengthen each Y shape. Two cords remain the center of each Y shape.

Pull together left leg of one Y and right leg of adjacent Y—there are four cords in your hand—and tie a square knot. Repeat around. The snowflake should have six "petals."

Securely pin the point of each petal to the macrame board, stretching the

points so the snowflake is symmetrical, but not so tightly that the snowflake warps when pins are removed. From now on turn the board as you work.

Attach six new cords between petals. Tie double half hitch knots; use cords remaining in Y shape as knotting cords and new cords as bearer cords. Hold the two knotting cords together and slide a wooden bead up them. Form a loose circle by bringing ends of new cord down around bead; anchor with square knot. Leave a little slack in new cord as you tie this knot so you won't crowd bead. Repeat until all six new cords and beads have been tied in.

Separate four cords beneath any bead into two groups. Gather together the left group with two closer cords from square knot at tip of petal to left. With these four cords, tie two square knots, one above the other, as close to bead as possible. Repeat with right group of cords beneath bead and two closer cords from square knot at tip of petal to the right. As you draw cords from petal tips, leave plenty of slack so snowflake will lie flat. Repeat this sequence beneath each bead. There are now eight cords beneath each bead.

Gather center four cords from eight-cord group under any bead. Tie two square knots, one above the other, with these cords. Repeat under each bead.

When all knots are completed, remove snowflake from macrame board. Trim cords so that they form a rough triangle as shown.

Snowflake B: Mount 18 cords in metal ring as for Snowflake A. Start with any two cords; tie a half hitch sennit comprised of six knots. Take the

(Continued)

331

adjacent two cords and repeat. Tie all four cords from both sennits together with a square knot. Skip next two cords; repeat sennit sequence over next four cords. Repeat around until there are six sennit "petals."

Pin all six points to macrame board. Then place one pin between the two cords between the petals. Tie in a new cord at these pins.

Using two cords between petals and two closer cords from square knots to right and left, tie row of double half hitch knots to new cord to form top of circle. Bring ends of new cord around and tie double half hitch knots for bottom half of circle. Inside the circle, the cords should fall straight down. Complete the circle by tying a double half hitch knot with one end to new cord to other end of same cord. Slide two seed beads (or more, depending on size) to ends of new cords. Secure with overhand knot; trim and add a drop of white glue. Repeat new cord addition until all six circles have been formed.

Between any two circles, join closer three cords from both circles on right and left. You have a total of six cords. At a point where snowflake will lie flat, tie a square knot with the four center cords. Divide six cords below this square knot into two groups of three cords. In each three-cord group, tie two square knots, one above the other, using only one cord as filler. Tie another square knot with center four cords. Repeat until you have tied this sequence between all six circles.

In any six-cord group, slide oval bead up two center cords. Bring two cords adjacent down and around in a loose oval shape; tie a square knot under bead. Bring two remaining cords around loosely (you have six cords in a group again). Divide cords into two groups of three cords; tie two square knots, one above other as before. Tie a square knot with four center cords as close to rest of knots as possible.

Remove snowflake from board and trim ends in a rough triangle shape as for snowflake A.

Snowflake C: Mount 18 cords in ring. From any two cords, tie a half hitch sennit comprised of 11 knots. With the adjacent four cords, tie two square knots, one above other. Alternating these knots, repeat around ring.

Beneath any two square knots, find the center two cords in the four-cord group. Slide an oval bead up to the square knots. Bring the two outer cords around loosely; anchor beneath bead with two square knots, one above the other. Repeat around. Pin snowflake out at six points.

*Attach a new cord by centering it under a group of square knots beneath any bead and pinning it straight out left and right.

Tie a row of horizontal double half hitch knots to new cord, using four cords from square knot as knotting cords. Draw closest cord from each of two adjacent half hitch sennits to new cord, pull taut to form even line, tie with double half hitch knots to new cord, forming hexagonal shape. There are now six cords knotted to new cord.

Divide all eight cords in half. Tie three rows of diagonal double half hitch knots, sloping out and downward from center of new cord.

Repeat previous steps (from asterisk) around. At this point, treat the six points of the snowflake alternately to completion.

At any point, find four center cords of an eight-cord group. Leaving about an inch of cord to fall free, tie a square knot with four cords. Draw over one cord from each adjacent sennit; tie two square knots (using three cords) below this square knot. Draw remaining two cords over; tie two more square knots beneath last two knots, using three cords per knot. These five knots will form a flattened, inverted V shape.

Trim four outer cords to ½ inch. Pull four center cords together, forming a point; trim, and secure point with white glue. Repeat this step on *every other* eight-cord group.

In skipped eight-cord group, bring bearer cords of last row of diagonal double half hitch knots toward center of eight-cord group; tie a row of diagonal double half hitch knots, sloping cords down and toward center of eight-cord group. Find center four cords of this group; tie a square knot at a point where snowflake will lie flat.

Slide small wooden bead up two center cords; draw two outer cords around loosely; anchor bead with square knot.

Tie another square knot ¼ inch below the first. Repeat until all points are formed. Trim ends, leaving ⅜ inch.

"LITTLE WOMEN" DOLLS TO DRESS
page 324

Materials: Doll kit; scraps of small-scale calicos and plaids; lace; ribbon.

Instructions: Follow instructions in kits for constructing dolls' bodies. Follow pattern instructions for clothes or design clothing using fabric cut into rectangles and squares. Gather and trim with laces and ribbons.

QUILT PATTERN CARDS
page 324

Materials: Blank greeting cards; calico scraps; spray adhesive.

Instructions: Size quilt patterns to fit cards. Cut pieces of designs from calico prints; glue to cards.

PINE TREE TABLECLOTH
page 325

Materials: #8 pearl cotton; 22-count hardanger cloth; tapestry needle.

Instructions: Buy enough fabric for your tablecloth to allow for a 10-inch drop plus an extra 3 inches all around.

Cross-stitch the tree motif (opposite) over 2 threads of fabric. Position the bottom row of the design 2 inches above the raw edge. Repeat tree motifs; sew ½-inch double hem.

WOVEN PATTERNS FOR EMBROIDERY
page 325

Materials: Even-weave fabric; pearl cotton; embroidery hoop (optional).

Instructions: Work these motifs (opposite) on any even-weave fabric with threads large enough to count. Or work them on fine fabrics over needlepoint waste canvas. Use the designs for borders on towels, tablecloths, place mats, curtains, sheets, or garments.

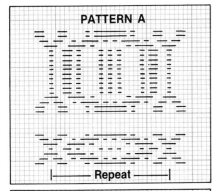
Work the designs from the center of the fabric toward the edges. Use darning stitches, making running stitches through the fabric.

CORN SHUCK FIGURES
pages 326, 327

These are general directions for corn shuck figures. Specific instructions follow for crèche, angel, dolls, and tree.

Materials: Corn shucks; glycerin; cotton balls; 1-inch foam balls; wire; light posterboard; straight pins; glue.

General instructions: Soak the corn shucks in warm water until they are flexible. Add a drop of glycerin if the shucks are thick or brittle.

Before the shucks dry, bend the figures into the desired positions. When they are dry, trim the bases of figures with sharp scissors so they stand easily.

For heads, wrap thread around middle of a 3-inch-wide shuck; place foam ball in center of shuck (thread will be at
(Continued)

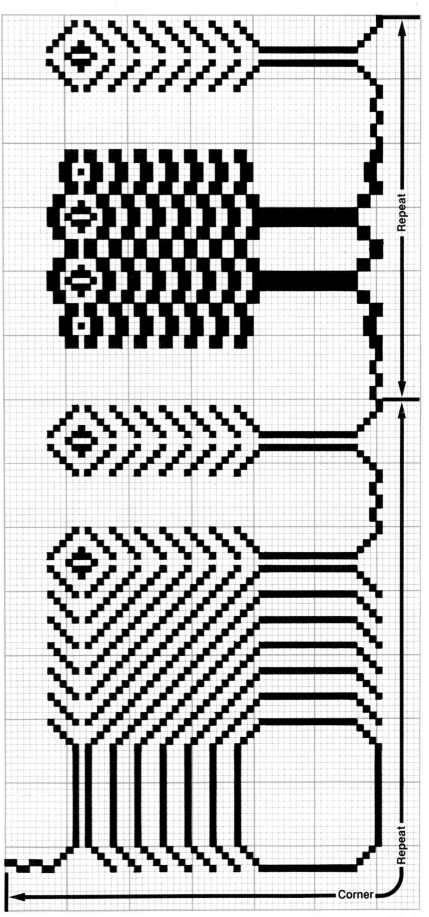

1 Square = 1 Stitch

top of head); cover ball. Wrap thread around bottom of ball for neck. Slide a 6-inch wire through neck and head.

For arms, cut a wire 11 inches long; bend ends inward ¾ inch to form loops (hands). Thread ¾-inch-wide strip of shuck through each hand; wrap around loops and to middle of wire; add strips as necessary. Wrap the sewing thread around hands and arms to secure. Remove thread when shucks are dry.

For sleeves, gather 6-inch-wide corn shucks around each wrist, extending shucks over hands; wrap shucks with thread. Pull shuck back over arm, shaping puffed sleeve; wrap near center of wire (shoulders). Push head wire through center of arms; wrap.

To form bust and waist, place two cotton balls side by side in center of a vertically positioned shuck. Fold long sides toward center; fold shuck in half across width. Wrap thread around the bottom for the waist. Position this section on front of neck wire ½ inch below neck. Secure with thread.

For dress bodice, center a 3-inch-wide shuck on each shoulder; cross shucks over bust front and back; gather at waist. Secure with thread, wrapping shucks below waist tightly to the wire. Repeat with two more shucks, pleating them across the shoulders.

For skirt, cut a cardboard half circle (15-inch diameter). Wrap edges of half circle into a cone approximately 5 inches in diameter across the bottom. Top opening will be about one inch wide.

For bottom skirt, cover half of cone with shucks; overlap each strip slightly; pin *only* at base of cone. Trim shucks toward top so they lie flat against cone. Wrap with thread. Repeat for remaining half of skirt. *For top skirt,* gather wide shucks around cone top, using thread; wrap shucks to cone until dry.

Insert bodice through opening in cone top. Secure bodice to skirt with a long needle, pushing it through skirt, bodice, and on through to other side of skirt. Glue waist area from inside the cone; remove needle when glue is dry.

For apron, cut a curved edge (hem) along the top of a wide shuck. Gather the straight edge of the shuck to the doll's waistline. Wrap a narrow strip around the waist, covering rough edges of the skirt and apron shucks. Tie in back. (*For doll with apron,* bend apron

as shown in photo and pin to hands until dry; glue.)

For shawl, drape a long shuck over shoulders; tie ends in front.

To form bonnet, fold under one inch on 3½-inch-wide shuck. With folded edge next to face, lay shuck across head; pin at top and sides (chin line). Gather shuck at back of head; wrap with thread. Tie shuck strip over the thread; end of shuck will look like ponytail. Trim ends just below shoulders; pin in place.

CORN SHUCK CRÈCHE
page 326

Materials: See general instructions above. You will also need small chunks of plastic foam; straw for the manger; ³⁄₁₆-inch-thick balsa wood for the manger; T-pins; lightweight cardboard; and yarn or cornsilk.

Instructions: Follow the general directions for the figures (above) except for the following:

For arms, cut 11-inch wire for Mary, 11½ inches for others (except infant). *For draped sleeves,* wrap shuck around middle of arm; secure. Fold arms into position; cut, pin cuff area into shape.

For men's chests, fold sides of wide shuck to center; pad center with paper towel folded into shape of chest. Wrap string around padding, then around figure to attach chest to wire that extends from neck. Pad in front and back.

To make men's garments (skirts), cut 15-inch square of heavy paper, wrap into cylindrical shape that flares slightly toward the bottom and has a 1- to 2-inch opening at top. Tape edges.

For lower part of robe, cover half of cylinder with shucks; overlap slightly, pin at base of paper. Trim shucks toward top so they lie flat against cone. Wrap with thread. For top skirt, gather wide corn shucks around top of cylinder with thread; secure until dry.

Insert chest through opening in cylinder; secure with long needle pushed through "skirt," chest, and other side of "skirt." Glue waist area inside cylinder; remove needle when glue is dry.

To make beards, sew a loop through chin area. Lay a bit of combed, natural-

color yarn or cornsilk through loop with bulk of the yarn or silk up over the head. Pull loop taut; fold "hair" back over chin and neck to form beard. Trim. Repeat along forehead for hair.

For men's hats, gift boxes, make small shapes of cardboard; cover with shucks. Position headdresses on heads; add flowing robes and drapery around heads by folding damp shucks and arranging them on figures. Pin or tie shucks in place until dry.

For Mary and the kneeling wiseman, make figures following the procedure above, except make skirts as follows:

Omit cylinder. Instead, gather and lay four shucks (two in front, two in back) around figure's waist so narrow edge is at waist and wide edge goes upward. Wrap string around waist, then flip shucks down and pin in place. Pin figures in sitting or kneeling position until dry (figures may be pinned to a box). For infant's blanket, drape shucks over edge of small box until dry.

For infant, use a ½-inch foam ball for head, 3½-inch wire for arms. For clothing, cut two 4x6-inch squares of shuck; taper one 4-inch side of each to 2 inches (top). Gather top of shuck; lay at neck with long end up over head. Wrap at neck. Bring shucks down over body; pin in place for dress. When dry, fold a damp shuck around baby like a hooded bunting; tie until dry.

For sheep, cut pieces of plastic foam into shapes of body, head. Pin head to body; wrap with shucks; secure. Add ears. For lamb's wool, wrap shuck around pencil; secure. When dry, tear shuck into ⅛-inch-wide curls; pin, glue on lambs. For legs, wrap pieces of wire with shucks; poke wire into foam.

For Mary's bench, cut and glue balsa wood into 2x5-inch seat with four 2-inch-high legs. For manger, cut two pieces balsa wood 2¾x6 inches; cut four legs, each 4x⅜ inches; assemble with glue as shown in photo.

CORN SHUCK ANGEL
page 326

Materials: See general instructions.
Instructions: Follow the general instructions that begin on page 333, except as noted below. Make wings before making the bodice.

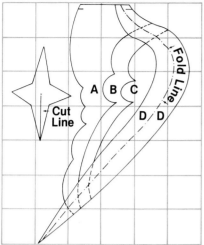

1 Square = 1 Inch

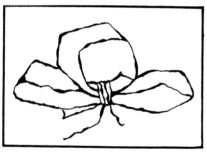

For wings, enlarge pattern above. Cut pieces for two wings from card stock; glue shucks to both sides of cardboard pieces. Weight wing sections when drying so pieces don't curl. Fold wing section D as shown while wet; cut to shape when dry. Glue sections together.

Make tab for attaching wings by cutting ¼-inch slits ¼ inch from straight edge of wing. At top and bottom, bend tab to back side of wing. Attach wings to angel after first layer of bodice is done. Wrap thread through slits and around doll until secure. Cover bodice

with last layer of shucks; complete angel except for hair and star.

For hair, tie three graduated loops in ½-inch-wide strips of shucks as shown in the diagram at left. Make ten clusters to encircle the head; dry. Glue; pin to the head. For the top of the head, make four loops as shown at left; dry; glue and pin to head.

Make star same as wings. When dry, cut both pieces on line to center. Slide cut portions together. Glue to hands.

MOTHER AND DAUGHTER DOLLS
page 327

Finished dolls measure 9½, 6½, and 5½ inches tall.

Materials: Corn shucks; glycerin; blue, red, yellow food coloring or dye; cotton balls; 1-inch foam ball; two ¾-inch foam balls; wire; lightweight posterboard or file folders (skirt supports); straight pins; white glue.

Instructions: Except for the following changes, follow general directions that begin on page 333. To color shucks, add food coloring or dye to water when you dampen shucks.

For heads of small dolls, slide 4- and 3-inch wires through neck and head.

For arms of small dolls, use 7½-inch and 6-inch wires.

For sleeves, use dyed shucks. Use 4- and 3-inch-wide shucks for daughters.

For bodices of small dolls, use 2- and 1-inch-wide strips on each shoulder.

For skirts, use dyed shucks. Cut cardboard half-circle 14 inches in diameter for mother, 8 and 6 inches in diameter for daughters. Wrap edges into a cone about 5 inches across the bottom for the mother, and 2½ and 2 inches across for the daughters. Top opening will be about 1 inch for mother, ¾ and ½ inches for daughters.

Follow general instructions above for the bottom and top skirts, except use dyed corn shucks.

For bonnets, use natural shucks. Use 3-inch-wide shuck for larger daughter. For smaller daughter, use end of dyed 1-inch-wide shuck. Place around neck back; wrap with string; cover string with shuck strip tied under chin. Cut,

then pin a corn shuck around the head for a bonnet. For the small daughter's hair, shape narrow (¼ inch wide) strips of dyed corn shucks into loops and pin them to the head.

Follow general instructions above for shaping, trimming, and finishing the dolls.

CORN SHUCK CHRISTMAS TREE
page 327

The finished tree measures approximately 11½ inches tall.

Materials: Corn shucks; glycerin; 9-inch-tall plastic foam cone; wire; green food coloring or liquid fabric dye; $^9/_{16}$-inch staples; crochet thread; assorted dried flowers.

Instructions: Soak corn shucks in green-tinted water. For loops at base of tree, cut shucks into 3¼x8-inch pieces with grain of shuck running lengthwise. Fold each piece in half, making a loop; tack to cone with staple. Repeat until first layer of loops surrounds base of cone. Secure loops in place with wire wrapped around top of shucks.

Position each layer of loops one inch above the preceding one. As you work toward the top of the tree, trim ¼ inch off the width of the loops, and shorten the strips as necessary.

For second-to-top layer of loops, cut shucks ¾x7½ inches. Make two loops in each strip by folding the first 4 inches into one loop and the remainder of the strip into the second (top) loop. Tie all layers together one inch below the fold on the top loop.

With larger loop facing cone, tack loops to foam with stem pointing *down* and both loops turned *up.* When all loops in this layer are in place, wrap stems with wire; *then turn the larger (outer) layer of loops down over stem ends to hide them.* Pin loops in position. When dry, glue in place.

For the topmost loops on the tree, cut a length of shuck ½ inch wide. Gather it into five or more loops; secure to cone with wire.

To decorate the tree, crochet long chains (garlands) using ecru crochet cotton. Carefully pin the garland to the tree, securing the thread in the foam base. Add tiny clusters of dried flowers.

335

COUNTRY FESTIVITIES
Our Christmas Heritage

enerations of Americans have grown up with at-home, country-style Christmas celebrations, those times when family and friends gather to share customs and traditions, food and fellowship. By crafting some of these handmade gifts and decorations, you can rekindle some of those memories of Christmas past. The patchwork accessories shown here are a traditionally American way to decorate your home at Christmas. These projects are inexpensive to make, especially if you use fabrics and trims from your sewing basket, the way our country ancestors did. Calico heart ornaments trim the tree and patchwork place mats adorn the dining table. You can give these projects as gifts, keep them for your own Christmas celebrations, or sell them at Christmas bazaars. Instructions for these projects begin on page 342.

Even if you're a city dweller, you probably dream of an old-fashioned country Christmas, complete with crackling fire, roasting chestnuts, the scent of pine, and the aroma of freshly baked goods from the kitchen. To bring that dream to life, craft these country-style projects for round-the-house personal touches at Christmas.

Duck decoys like these (right) are a delight for woodcarvers. If you'd like to carve your own, turn to the detailed instructions on pages 82 and 83. But if you want the same results without as much time and trouble, you can fashion decoys like these from kits.

Assemble the duck according to the kit directions. Then sand it well to bring out the natural grain of the wood. To finish, treat it to a splash of color by rubbing on liquid fabric dye that has been diluted in water. The dye will lightly tint the wood but still allow the grain to show through.

If you prefer a more natural look, stain your decoy, give it an antique finish, or treat it with several coats of polyurethane.

Consider using acrylic paints and woodburning if you want to embellish your woodworking projects. Acrylic paints on wooden fish decoys (above and right) lend old-time charm to these projects, which are so much like the antique originals. Woodburned flourishes on the wooden duck decoys, shoes, and plates (above and right) turn plain gifts into personal ones. To finish your woodburning projects and to help protect the designs, apply a light coat of linseed oil to the wood.

Instructions for these projects begin on page 342.

The fish decoys shown here are cut from ¾-inch-thick pine. After painting the designs and adding thin metal fins, the decoys are mounted on metal rods and secured to wooden bases for display.

Memories of Christmases long ago will always hold a special place in our hearts. To help recall those happy times, here are some holiday table accessories that are reminiscent of those fond moments.

The table runner (below) proclaims its message in colorful cross-stitches worked in pearl cotton floss on even-weave fabric. Both the greeting and the fanciful designs are well-suited to the season. The "Joy" design measures 14 inches wide, but you can vary that size to make banners, ornaments, or pillows. Use the small-scale border design to edge stockings, tree skirts, or a child's special Christmas-day outfit.

A stenciled Della Robbia wreath adorns the tablecloth, napkins, and chair cushions (right). The design, inspired by traditional fruit wreaths that graced many a country home, can be worked in appliqué or embroidery as well as with stencils and fabric paint.

Because the size of the motifs is the same for the cloth, napkins, and cushions, you only need to enlarge the design once, no matter how many of the projects you make.

Instructions for these projects begin on page 343.

By adjusting the length of the Christmas tree border, you can make this cross-stitch table runner (right) to fit your table. Just allow 12 inches for the drop on each end, then determine the border from the tabletop length. By adjusting the size of the designs, you can use them on other Christmas projects, too.

340

341

CHRISTMAS HEARTS
page 336

Materials: Tissue paper; small-scale cotton print fabrics in 4-inch squares; scraps of rickrack, braid, lace, and ribbon; gold cord, yarn, or pearl cotton; polyester fiberfill.

Instructions: Draw a heart pattern on a 4-inch square of tissue paper. Trace around the pattern on fabric. For each ornament, cut two fabric hearts, adding ¼-inch seam allowances.

Sew baby rickrack just inside the seam line of the heart front and back. Baste rickrack, braid, or lace edging along seam line of heart front. Sew two hearts together, right sides facing, leaving a 1½-inch opening. Clip curves, turn right side out, stuff, and slip-stitch the opening closed.

Thread gold cord, yarn, pearl cotton, or leftover trim through the top of the ornament, making a hanger. Add a small bow for accent, as shown.

REVERSIBLE PLACE MATS
page 337

Materials (for four place mats): ¾ yard each of three cotton prints in complementary colors; 16 small bells.

Instructions: From cotton prints, cut eight 13x18-inch pieces for place mats. Make tab pattern from 5x7-inch paper rectangle folded lengthwise. Measure up 3½ inches on outside edge. Cut along a line from this point to top of center fold on rectangle. Use opened pattern to make 32 tabs from cotton prints. (Do not add seam allowances.)

Pin together two contrasting print tabs, right sides facing. Stitch around the tabs (½-inch seams), leaving the end opposite the point open for turning. Turn and press. Repeat for all tabs.

Pin four tabs atop right side of large rectangle with raw edges even. Make sure end tabs are 1½ inches inside each end to allow for seams.

Baste. Place a contrasting rectangle facedown on top of rectangle with tabs inside. Stitch together (½-inch seams), leaving an 8-inch opening for turning. Turn and blindstitch opening.

If desired, attach a small bell to point of each place mat tab.

DYED DUCK DECOYS
page 338

Materials: Unfinished duck decoy kit; liquid fabric dyes; varnish.

Instructions: Assemble and sand the decoy according to kit directions. To add color to the assembled decoy, dilute fabric dye with hot water and apply sparingly. When completely dry, coat with varnish.

WOODBURNED PROJECTS
pages 338-339

The wooden shoes, ducks, plates, and cutting board are all simple wood projects to embellish with woodburning tools. However, before you begin, we suggest you practice woodburning on scraps of pine so you know what to expect from the tips on your woodburner and how much pressure to apply to achieve the result you want. Then use our patterns (below) and the photographs on pages 338 and 339 as guides to create your own designs.

For example, enlarge the designs for the shoes, transfer them to the tops of the shoes, and incise them into the wood with your woodburner. Then embellish the heels and edges of the shoes with stripes, a row of overlapping half circles, or designs of your own.

If you wish, enlarge and transfer the patterns for the heads of the ducks to unfinished wooden decoys. Work the designs with a woodburner, then add more motifs to the backs and sides of the ducks, referring to the photographs for design ideas.

Or, embellish wooden plates, cutting boards, boxes, and other wood projects with wheat, acorn, or ribbon motifs.

1 Square = 1 Inch

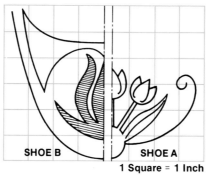

SHOE B | SHOE A

1 Square = 1 Inch

1 Square = 1 Inch

1 Square = ½ Inch

For example, using carbon paper, transfer the enlarged wheat or acorn pattern to the center of a wooden plate or serving tray. If necessary, adjust the size of the design to fit your project. Burn the design into the wood, then remove any carbon smudges by sanding with extra-fine sandpaper.

Another option is to trim the rim of a plate with the ribbon design, adjusting to fit as necessary. Add additional borders of your own design as desired.

FISH DECOYS
page 339

Materials: ¾x6x24 inches of pine; scraps of thin metal; ⅛-inch metal rods; glue; white, black, green, yellow, and red paint.

Instructions: Enlarge the patterns (below) and cut *two* of each fish shape, excluding the fins, from wood. (Duplicate fish shapes will be glued together with metal fins between.)

Round the outer edges of the wood shapes (that will not be next to fins) with a wood rasp and sandpaper.

Cut fins from a thin metal sheet, adding about 1 inch to the margin of the fins that will be sandwiched between the wooden fish sides.

Glue right and left sides of the fish together with the fins slipped between. Clamp until dry.

Paint each fish, using the photograph as a guide. Then drill a hole in the underside of the fish for the metal rod. Cut the rod 3 to 8 inches long; glue into fish.

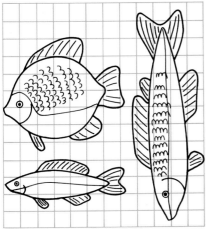

1 Square = 1 Inch

Cut a square or round base for each fish from scrap lumber; drill hole in center of each for the metal rod.

"JOYFUL" CROSS-STITCH RUNNER
page 340

Materials: 22-count white or ecru hardanger cloth 14½ inches wide and equal to table length plus 24 inches; lightweight white or ecru lining fabric equal in size to fabric for runner (optional); #8 D.M.C. pearl cotton floss in colors noted on chart (page 345); tapestry needle; graph paper and colored pencils (optional).

Instructions: Use the chart on page 345 for reference while embroidering the runner. If desired, transfer the design to graph paper using colored pencils, then work from the colored chart. For best results, mount the fabric in an embroidery hoop or frame before you begin.

Working each cross-stitch over two threads, embroider the tree-lined border the length of the table plus approximately 12 inches (overhang) at each end. Plan stitching carefully, so the center of the design (at the point) falls in the center of the fabric.

Stitch JOY at both ends of runner. Hem the runner, leaving a ¼-inch margin below border, or stitch lining to back if desired.

STENCILED FRUIT-WREATH DESIGN
page 341

Note: Finished cloth is 70 inches square.

Materials: 45x45 inches of muslin for cloth top; four 14x77-inch pieces of muslin for borders; 16x16 inches muslin for each napkin; 18x18 inches muslin for each chair cushion (or size to fit your chairs, plus 2 inches all around); 5¼ yards of ½-inch-wide red grosgrain ribbon for tablecloth; fiberboard or macrame board; staples or pins; pie tins; plastic wrap; turpentine; sharp craft knife; stencil brushes; stencil paper; fabric paints.

(We used Vogart ball-point paints in tubes in the following amounts and colors: 2 yellow, red, wine, and forest green; and 1 each of scarlet, violet, green, rust, brown, navy, and white.)

General instructions: Prewash your fabric to remove sizing. Enlarge the pattern on page 344. The size of individual motifs (such as the apple) is the same in all designs, so once you have enlarged the center wreath (which contains all the elements), you can enlarge the remaining drawings with ease. Cut stencils from glazed stencil paper, using a sharp knife.

Mix paint in pie tins, following color chart. To use ball-point paints, remove tip on tube with pliers; squeeze paint onto pie tins. When paint and brushes are not being used, cover them with plastic wrap. Clean up ball-point paints with turpentine.

Pin or staple fabric tautly to fiberboard, placing a piece of waxed paper behind fabric for absorption.

Line up or center stencil on fabric; pin in place. First stencil large fruit (apple, pear, and orange); then paint leaves and stems. Finally, stencil small units (boysenberries, holly berries, wheat, and nuts).

After stenciling, let the fabric dry overnight before pressing. Use a press cloth over the painted areas to absorb any damp paint.

Tablecloth: To make the square top, cut from brown paper a 24-inch wreath with a 12-inch inner circle. Center wreath on 45-inch muslin square; lightly draw around inner and outer circles with pencil.

Place stencil inside penciled circles; begin stenciling. Wreath stencil will fit four times around circle. Dry; press to set color. Sew grosgrain ribbon around all four edges of the tablecloth, using a ⅛-inch seam allowance.

To make the border, stencil the center 45 inches of each strip (see note, page 344). Match center of border repeat to center of muslin strip; stencil. Then stencil the repeat on each side of center section. Position lower edge of design about 2½ inches above raw edge of muslin strip. Do not stencil corners yet. Dry; press to set color.

Match stenciled portion of each strip to each side of the 45-inch square top.

(Continued)

With right sides together, sew strips to top, leaving ends of each strip loose for mitering. Press the seams toward the outside edge.

Lay cloth out flat. Carefully miter the corners, stitch, and trim the seam allowance on each miter to ¼ inch. Press the seam allowance to one side. Next, secure one corner of the cloth to fiberboard. Pin corner stencil in place, remembering to place it 2½ inches above the raw edge to allow room for the hem. Stencil the corner, dry, and press. Repeat for remaining corners.

Note: If your tablecloth is a different size from ours, add or subtract elements in the border to make the pattern fit your cloth.

To finish the cloth, line with a muslin sheet cut to fit, or turn up a double ¼-inch hem all around.

Napkins: Stencil holly leaves and berries in one corner, following directions for the cloth. Finish each napkin with a narrow hem.

Chair cushions: Stencil the design on muslin, following directions for cloth. Stitch stenciled tops into cushions and add grosgrain trim over the seam lines if desired.

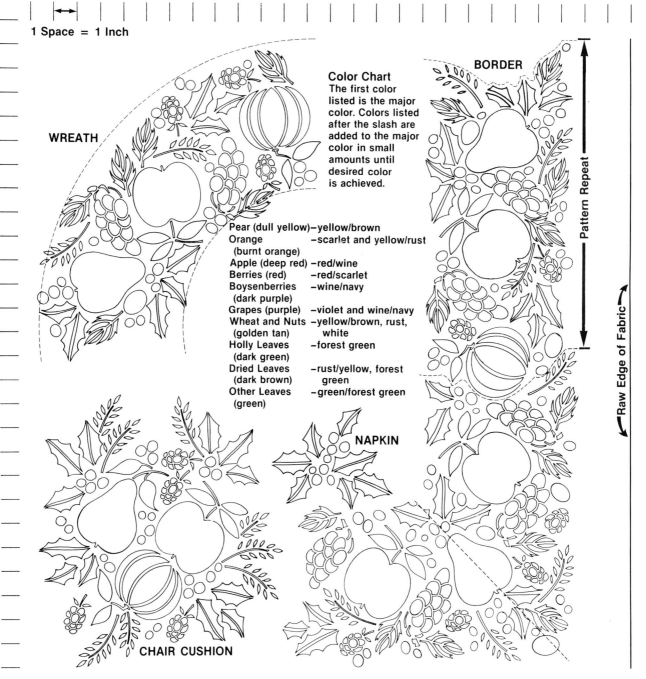

1 Space = 1 Inch

WREATH

BORDER

Color Chart
The first color listed is the major color. Colors listed after the slash are added to the major color in small amounts until desired color is achieved.

Pear (dull yellow)	–yellow/brown
Orange (burnt orange)	–scarlet and yellow/rust
Apple (deep red)	–red/wine
Berries (red)	–red/scarlet
Boysenberries (dark purple)	–wine/navy
Grapes (purple)	–violet and wine/navy
Wheat and Nuts (golden tan)	–yellow/brown, rust, white
Holly Leaves (dark green)	–forest green
Dried Leaves (dark brown)	–rust/yellow, forest green
Other Leaves (green)	–green/forest green

Pattern Repeat

Raw Edge of Fabric

NAPKIN

CHAIR CUSHION

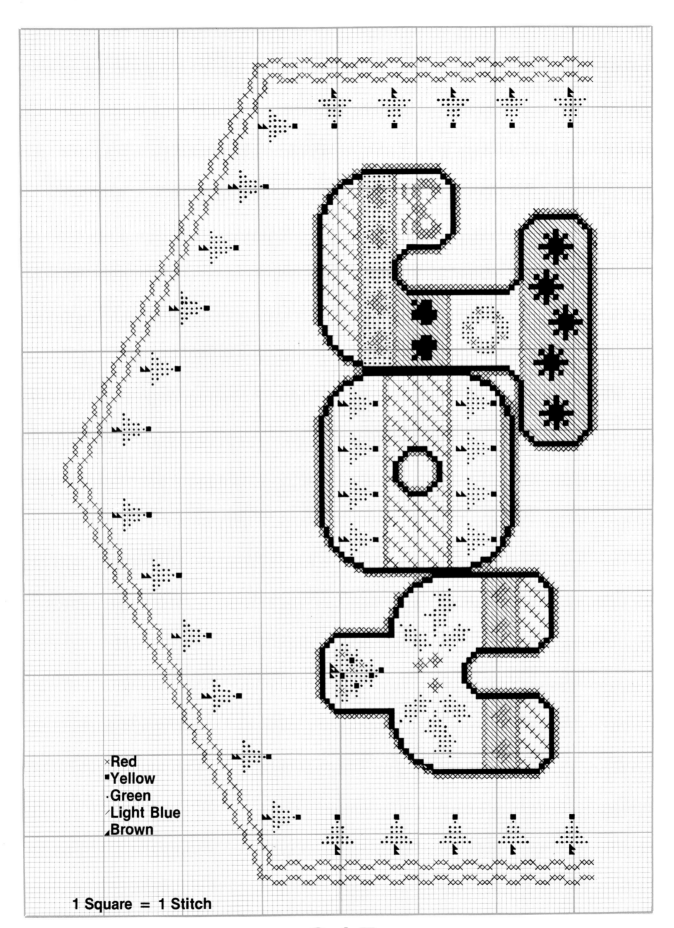

Red
Yellow
Green
Light Blue
Brown

1 Square = 1 Stitch

345

COUNTRY FESTIVITIES
Crafts for Year-Round Occasions

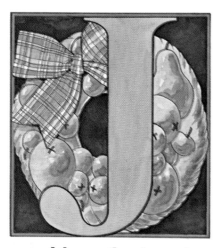

ust because Christmas usually gets top billing in the world of crafts doesn't mean you can't put your crafting skills to work during the rest of the year. There are lots of holidays and special occasions that are worth celebrating with some extra-special country-inspired crafts. Fashion the graceful wreaths shown here from bread dough and hang them on your mantel or door to celebrate anything from the coming of spring to the Thanksgiving harvest. After these wreaths dry slowly in a warm oven, coat them with butter and toast them for a golden hue. Then brush them with clear polyurethane for a shiny, protective finish. If you like, tie a big plaid bow to each wreath and use the wreaths as centerpieces. Another possibility is to place a candle in the center of one wreath for an unusual candlestick. Instructions begin on page 352.

Cheerful country-style greeting cards such as these can express your sentiments no matter what the occasion.

You can make a whole set of stenciled cards like those above with practically no painting experience. It's easy if you use clear stencil paper to cut your designs, acrylic paints in a wide range of colors, and an assortment of high-quality stencil brushes.

If you like, you can purchase commercial stencils at craft stores. But for a personalized card, design your own stencil using coloring books, wallpaper samples, or patterns for other craft projects as sources of inspiration. Keep the design simple, remembering that the cut-out portion of the stencil will be your printed design.

Practice your technique on scrap paper before you begin making the cards. For information on stenciling, refer to the section on stenciled cheese boxes, pages 72-73.

The paper doily cards (opposite, above), loaded with country charm, say a little bit about the person who made them. So next time you have a gift to give, dress it up with a handmade note card.

Make cards such as these from paper doilies, using your imagination to come up with a pleasing arrangement. For example, cut doilies apart and position them around the edges of the card as a frame for a picture or greeting.

Once you decide on the composition, use tiny drops of glue or a light application of spray adhesive to secure the doilies in place.

Print gift bags and tags like those shown at right by using linoleum block printing techniques. Draw the designs on linoleum blocks (you have to draw the pattern in reverse first) and cut away a relief pattern.

With the help of professional printer's tools (available at art supply stores), you can make consistently clear, even linoleum prints on brown paper bags, adhesive-backed labels, gift enclosure cards and tags, wrapping papers, or personalized stationery and envelopes.

Instructions for all of these projects begin on page 352.

To personalize the paper doily note cards (above), needlepoint perforated paper with special messages such as "I Love You," "Friend," or "Baby," using six strands of embroidery floss. (Perforated paper is available at craft and yarn shops.)

Say "country" with quilting anytime of year with these work-of-art wall hangings. No matter what the season or occasion, you can hang these beauties with pride, because they enable you to display a variety of your best quilting skills.

Always work the appliquéd designs first, then place the fabric in a frame to quilt. The designs are especially effective when appliquéd to plain white or muslin backgrounds.

An old-time country carol inspired the rollicking sleigh ride banner at right. Carefully appliqué the calico letters in place, then outline them with fine embroidery. The scroll-like designs help "frame" the piece, as if it were an old country painting or portrait. Mimic these scroll lines in your quilting to create the effect of swirling snow.

For the "Harvest Time" wall hanging (opposite), use calico fabrics in brilliant fall colors to stitch the basketful of fruits and vegetables. To achieve an entirely different look, we used the reverse side of some calico fabrics for the right side of the design.

To quilt, use a diamond pattern, spacing the rows about 1 inch apart. This creates a soft background that highlights the appliqués.

When your quilt is completed, hang it by hand-stitching a casing made of twill tape or muslin across the top edge of the quilt back. Insert a curtain rod through the casing and mount it on the wall. Or, sew strips of nylon fastening tape to the

top and bottom of the quilt back. Cut a plywood frame slightly smaller than the quilt and stretch a white sheet over it. Staple the corresponding pieces of fastening tape to the covered wood, carefully matching the position of the quilt's strips. Press the tape halves together to stretch the quilt, and mount the frame on the wall.

Complete instructions for these projects begin on page 353.

As with any pattern on a grid, you can resize these designs to make your finished projects larger or smaller. For example, if you'd like to stitch a pillow instead of a wall hanging, simply use a smaller scale when enlarging the pattern.

BREAD DOUGH WREATHS
page 346

Materials: 9 cups flour; 4½ cups salt; 4½ cups water (for small wreaths, see below); cloves; butter; round pizza pan; varnish.

Instructions: Mix flour, salt, and water in a bowl; knead dough until firm. Dough should not be too dry or moist.

Using a large pizza pan, make a doughnut-shaped ring of dough 3½ inches wide and ¾ inch thick for a 10- or 14-inch wreath (for small wreaths, see below). The hole in the center of the ring should be slightly larger than 4 or 5 inches, depending on the size candle you plan to use in the center. Because the dough expands slightly during baking, the diameter of the center hole will shrink. Be sure to allow for this when fitting the candle.

Roll out a portion of dough to ⅛-inch thickness. Cut leaves about 2½ inches wide and 3 inches long. Fringe the edges by slashing with a knife. Attach leaves with water to outer edges of wreath, overlapping leaves all around. Scatter leaves along top if desired.

Make fruit by forming dough balls into pears, apples, oranges, plums, and grape clusters. The shapes should be smooth and free of cracks. Attach the fruit to the wreath with water, placing the larger fruits on the inside and the smaller ones on the outside. Leave portions of the leaves exposed.

Press whole cloves into the fruit at angles to create stems. Remove the bead from the clove head to create stars at bottoms of the fruits.

Bake wreaths at 200 degrees for 18 hours. After 8 to 10 hours, or when the wreath seems hard, remove it from the pan and place it directly on oven rack to speed drying of bottom.

Note: Do not turn the oven to a temperature higher than 200 degrees. The wreaths should dry rather than cook.

For a toasted effect, place the wreath under the broiler (not too close); broil until it appears *lightly* toasted. If the wreath browns unevenly, use foil to cover areas that darken quickly so that the rest of the wreath can "catch up." When wreath is completely hard, remove from the oven and cool. Brush the top with ¼ cup melted butter.

Allow the wreath to cool, then coat with glossy polyurethane varnish.

For small wreaths (7 inches in diameter): use 2 cups flour, 1 cup salt, and 1 cup water. Shape wreath into a doughnut 2 inches wide and ¾ inch high. Cut leaves and shape fruit as for larger wreaths, but bake only 10 to 12 hours at 200 degrees.

STENCILED CARDS
page 348

Materials: Stencil paper and stencil brush; greeting card blanks and envelopes *or* railroad board and envelopes; acrylic paints in various colors; utility knife; masking tape.

Instructions: (*Note:* Stencil paper, brushes, and greeting card blanks are available at art supply stores.)

Gather several sizes and shapes of greeting card blanks, or cut the railroad board to sizes to fit the envelopes. Follow the procedure under Paper Doily Note Cards (right) for scoring and folding the railroad board into the desired card shapes.

Determine a design for the cards. If this is your first attempt at stenciling, choose simple shapes. You should be aware that the bridges between the shapes you cut out are important elements in the design. Experiment until you develop a design you like, then trace it onto the stencil paper.

When you cut out the design from the paper, remember that the cutaway portion of the stencil will end up as the painted portion of the card. To cut, hold the utility knife as if it were a pencil, and use your other hand to turn the stencil paper so that you are always cutting toward you.

Before beginning to paint on the cards, practice using your stencil brush. Pour a small amount of paint onto a shallow dish or pie pan. Dip a dry brush into the paint, then tamp it in an up-and-down motion on newspaper to remove excess paint.

Tape the stencil to a piece of paper. Then lightly dab paint onto the paper around the stencil, holding the brush perpendicular to the paper as you work. With large areas, begin painting at the outside of the design and work toward the center so the paint won't feather under the stencil edges.

As you practice, notice that it's always better to use too little paint on the brush than too much. Lightly stenciled areas can be touched up, but excess paint may seep under the edges of the stencil paper.

Paint light colors first, then progress to darker colors. Let one color dry before progressing to the next.

When you feel confident with the technique, stencil your cards using the same procedure.

If you tear a stencil, repair it by placing transparent tape over the tear; trim away the excess.

PAPER DOILY NOTE CARDS
page 349

Materials: Railroad board (available at art supply stores); perforated paper; wrapping paper; metallic, white, and colored paper doilies; Smart-Trim tassels, 18 inches long; embroidery floss; white glue; scissors; large paper clip.

Instructions: With a sharp craft or mat knife and using a metal-edged ruler as a guide, cut the mounting board (railroad board) into several 10x7-inch rectangles.

For a 5x7-inch card, place the ruler crosswise in the exact center of the board. Using the ruler as a guide, make a deep ridge in the board with the curved edge of the paper clip. (Do *not* cut through the board.) Holding the ruler firmly in place, bring the board up slowly so it folds but doesn't crack. Remove the ruler and bend the board completely to form the shape of a folded card.

Cut out designs from doilies, wrapping paper, and pieces of perforated paper, using sharp scissors. You can use undecorated perforated paper or, using six strands of floss, needlepoint it with special messages such as "I Love You," "Friend," or "Baby."

Before gluing the design elements in place on the cards, arrange them in different ways until you achieve a pleasing composition. (See the color photo on page 349 for ideas.) Then, using drops of glue, secure the pieces in place.

352

Fold a tassel cord in half, wrap it around the fold in the card, and tie it at the base of the folded edge of the greeting card. Then fold a piece of card-sized paper in half, slip it under the cord inside the card, and add your special greeting.

BLOCK-PRINTED ACCESSORIES
page 349

Materials: Linoleum blocks; block cutting blades and handle; inking plate; brayer; printmaker's baren (all of these materials are available at art supply stores); brown paper bags in various sizes; self-adhesive labels (available at office supply stores); tracing paper; carbon paper; masking tape.

Instructions: Refer to children's coloring books, wrapping paper, greeting cards, or other sources for design ideas. Experiment until you're satisfied with the design, then transfer it onto a sheet of tracing paper.

Turn tracing paper over and work with the reverse of the design. (Design will reverse as it is printed.) Place a piece of carbon paper, transfer side down, onto the linoleum block. Then put the tracing paper, wrong side up, on top. Tape the papers in place with masking tape.

With a ball-point pen, lightly trace design. Lift up a corner of the carbon paper to see whether design is transferring. When all of the design has been transferred to the linoleum block, remove the papers and tape.

Gouge out design (or the background of the design) according to manufacturer's directions. (*Note:* Carving out linoleum blocks involves using very sharp tools. This work is not suitable for young children, and older children should be supervised.) Remember that the portion of the block that is carved away will not print.

To save time, cut all the linoleum blocks at once. Then, when the carving is completed, brush away all loose linoleum particles.

Squeeze ink from the tube onto the inking plate. Roll ink evenly across the surface of the plate with the brayer so that brayer is well covered. Roll the brayer across the printing block from top to bottom and side to side so that the plate is well covered with ink.

Lay a test sheet atop block; press surfaces together with a baren. Peel testing paper away and re-ink block. The second inking should result in a clearer print. If more ink is needed, repeat steps of preceding paragraph. If corrections are needed, recarve block at this time. When all adjustments are made, begin to print bags and labels.

Let all projects dry thoroughly before using. If weather is humid, you may need to dry prints in a warm (250 degree) oven. Avoid stacking projects until after they are completely dry.

OVER-THE-RIVER WALL HANGING
page 350

Finished size is 42x36 inches.

Materials: (*Note:* All fabric requirements are based on 44/45-inch widths.) 2 yards white cotton; 4 yards medium blue for backing and oval border; 1 yard blue-on-white print for letters and border scrolls; ¼ yard white-on-blue companion print; various fabric scraps for appliqué motifs; 42½x36½-inch piece of polyester quilt batting; sewing thread; black embroidery floss; quilting thread in colors to match backgrounds; 3 yards narrow black bias tape.

Instructions: Enlarge pattern (page 354) and transfer to a sheet of brown paper to serve as the master pattern. Trace each pattern piece onto tissue paper; cut them out.

Trace all of the letters (except for the word, "grandmother's") and the border scrolls onto blue-on-white print fabric. Cut out each piece, allowing a ¼-inch seam allowance. Cut all the remaining letters from the white-on-blue companion print. Cut out punctuation marks from blue fabric. Cut out the remaining pieces for the horse, sleigh, and figures from fabric scraps.

From white cotton, cut a rectangle 42½x36½ inches; cut two rectangles to match from blue fabric. Cut out the oval from one of the blue rectangles. Center this border fabric piece over the white rectangle; baste in place. Stitch down black bias tape to frame the oval.

Position all letters and remaining pattern pieces on fabric. Turn under ¼ inch on the raw edges of the pattern pieces and whipstitch them to the fabric backing with matching colors of sewing thread.

To shape curves on appliqués, cut out the shape in its finished size from a sheet of typing paper. Lay the paper pattern on the wrong side of the appliqué, leaving an even seam allowance all around. Finger-press the raw edge of the fabric over the paper. Then baste the seam allowance through all thicknesses and press firmly with an iron. Gently remove the basting stitches and the paper pattern, leaving the curved, creased edge in place.

Outline each piece with embroidery, using three strands of floss. Add embroidered details to horse's tail and add a length of floss for the reins.

To assemble, layer the quilt batt and the top and backing pieces (right sides together). Stitch around three sides; trim seams. Pull the batt and one layer of fabric through the open side; slipstitch fourth side closed.

To quilt, lightly pencil (or use a water erasable pen to mark) decorative scrolls around the letters on the white background as shown in the photo on page 350. These lines should mimic the appliquéd scrolls in the border. Draw scallops under the sleigh and horse to look like mounds of snow, and add other curved lines to fill in the white cotton background.

When all the lines have been penciled onto the fabric, stretch the wall hanging in a large embroidery hoop or small quilting frame. With quilting thread in colors that match the backgrounds, use tiny running stitches to quilt over the lines and around each letter, figure, and border scroll.

HARVEST TIME WALL HANGING
page 351

Finished size is 40x48 inches.

Materials: (*Note:* All fabrics are medium-weight, 44/45 inches wide.) 3 yards of calico or print fabric for backing and border strips; 1⅓ yards of buff-colored fabric; 1⅓ yards of unbleached

(Continued)

muslin; ½ yard of gold fabric; ½ yard of brown fabric; various scraps for appliqué motifs; 40x48 inches of quilt batting; 6 yards of wide bias binding; sewing thread to match the appliqué pieces; embroidery floss in brown and black; quilting thread.

Instructions: Enlarge center motif pattern (opposite) and transfer it to a sheet of brown paper to serve as the master pattern. Trace all pattern pieces onto tissue paper; cut them out.

Refer to the photograph for colors and cut out the pattern pieces from medium-weight fabric. Allow ¼ inch for seam allowances. (Use a variety of fabric prints for the vegetable motifs. For example, select a yellow calico for an ear of corn or a green calico for leaves. In addition, try using the wrong side of a print as the right side of a pattern piece.)

For the background, cut a 33x41-inch piece of unbleached muslin. Center the motifs on the muslin panel; pin or baste them in place. Beginning at the bottom, secure the pattern pieces to the background by folding the raw edge under ¼ inch and whipstitching in place with sewing thread that matches the fabric.

When all pieces have been appliquéd, embroider around the outlines with three strands of brown and black embroidery floss. Embroider the corn silk and wheat details.

For borders, cut strips 1½ inches wide to fit along the sides of the muslin panel. For each side, cut two calico and one buff-colored strip. Stitch the three strips together (using ¼-inch seams) with the solid strip in the middle; stitch to muslin panel. For each corner, cut nine 1½-inch squares (five solid and four calico) and patch them together to form a 3½-inch square. Stitch each corner block into place.

Assemble the wall hanging by layering a 40x48-inch piece of calico backing, the quilt batt, and the completed quilt top. Baste together.

To quilt, lay the wall hanging flat. With a pencil or water erasable pen, draw in diagonal lines to form 1-inch

1 Square = 1 Inch

squares as shown in the photo on page 351. Draw lines on the muslin background only; skip over the appliques. Stretch the wall hanging in an embroidery hoop or quilting frame. Using tiny running stitches, quilt around each pattern piece, around each letter, and along the border strips. Then quilt over the diagonal lines penciled on the muslin background.

To finish, bind the raw edges with brown bias tape.

1 Square = 1 Inch

COUNTRY CELEBRATIONS

PARTIES FOR FRIENDS AND FAMILY

E ntertaining and warm, generous hospitality have long been hallmarks of country living. A vital part of most country shindigs, of course, is food, and lots of it. In this chapter you will find four savory menus for the typical down-home Thanksgiving, Christmas, Fourth of July, and family reunion dinners. Try some or all of the recipes from these menus for your next dinner party, family get-together, or special holiday meal. A nostalgic country Thanksgiving dinner is pictured at right. Clockwise from front left are: Turkey with Peanut Stuffing, Basic Yeast Bread, Cheese Soup, Harvey Wallbanger Pie, and Corn Relish. (See index for recipe pages.)

COUNTRY FOODS

THANKSGIVING

Roast Turkey

Peanut Dressing

Cheese Soup
or
Fish-Wine Bisque

Corn Relish

Basic Yeast Bread
or
Yankee Corn Sticks

Harvey Wallbanger Pie

CORN RELISH

See photo, pages 356-357—

Cook one 10-ounce package frozen *whole kernel corn* according to the package directions; drain. In saucepan combine ½ cup *sugar* and 1 tablespoon *cornstarch;* stir in ½ cup *vinegar* and ⅓ cup *cold water.* Add corn, ¼ cup chopped *green pepper,* 2 tablespoons chopped *pimiento,* 1 tablespoon finely chopped *onion,* 1 teaspoon ground *turmeric,* ½ teaspoon *dry mustard,* and ¼ teaspoon *celery seed.* Cook and stir till thickened and bubbly. Cook, stirring constantly, for 2 minutes. Cover; chill. Makes 2 cups.

CHEESE SOUP

See photo, pages 356-357—

> 2 **cups finely chopped carrot**
> ½ **cup finely chopped celery**
> ½ **cup finely chopped onion**
> 3½ **cups chicken broth**
> 4 **cups milk**
> ½ **cup all-purpose flour**
> 2 **cups shredded American cheese (8 ounces)**

In a saucepan mix the carrot, celery, and onion; add chicken broth. Heat to boiling; reduce heat. Cover; simmer for 15 minutes. Combine milk, flour, and ⅛ teaspoon *salt.* Stir into broth mixture. Cook and stir till thickened. Add the cheese, stirring till melted. Garnish with chopped peanuts if desired. Makes 12 servings.

YANKEE CORN STICKS

See photo, pages 20-21—

> 1 **cup yellow cornmeal**
> 1 **cup all-purpose flour**
> ¼ **cup sugar**
> 4 **teaspoons baking powder**
> 2 **eggs**
> 1 **cup milk**
> ¼ **cup cooking oil**

Mix cornmeal, flour, sugar, baking powder, and ¾ teaspoon *salt.* Add the eggs, milk, and oil. Beat just till smooth (do not overbeat). Spoon into greased corn stick pans; fill ⅔ full. Bake in a 425° oven 12 to 15 minutes. Makes 20.

FISH-WINE BISQUE

To serve 12, double the recipe. See photo, pages 20-21—

> 1 **pound fresh** *or* **frozen white fish fillets**
> 2 **slices bacon**
> ½ **cup chopped onion**
> 1 **cup chicken broth**
> ½ **cup dry white wine**
> ¼ **teaspoon dried basil, crushed**
> 1 **stalk celery, cut up**
> 2 **cloves garlic, halved**
> 4 **sprigs parsley**
> ½ **cup light cream**
> 3 **tablespoons all-purpose flour**
> **Parmesan Topper**

Thaw fish if frozen; cut into 1-inch pieces. In skillet cook bacon till crisp; drain, reserving 2 tablespoons drippings. Crumble the bacon; set aside. Cook onion in reserved drippings till tender. Add broth, wine, and basil. Tie celery, garlic, and parsley in a cheesecloth bag; add to pan. Bring to boiling. Reduce heat; cover. Simmer for 20 minutes. Remove cheesecloth bag. Add fish. Cover and cook 8 to 10 minutes. Combine light cream and flour. Add to fish mixture. Cook and stir till thickened. Cook and stir 1 minute more. Stir in bacon. Ladle soup into individual oven-proof casseroles. Sprinkle with the Parmesan Topper. Bake in a 400° oven for 10 minutes. Serves 6.

Parmesan Topper: In bowl mix ¾ cup *soft bread crumbs,* 1 tablespoon grated *Parmesan cheese,* and ½ teaspoon *paprika.* Stir in 2 tablespoons *butter or margarine,* melted.

TURKEY WITH PEANUT DRESSING

See photo, pages 356-357—

6 slices bacon
1 cup chopped celery
½ cup chopped onion
2 beaten eggs
1½ cups chicken broth
1 cup salted peanuts, chopped
2 tablespoons snipped parsley
1 teaspoon poultry seasoning
12 cups dry bread cubes
1 8-pound turkey
Cooking oil

Cook bacon till crisp; drain, reserving drippings in skillet. Crumble bacon; set aside. Cook celery and onion in drippings till tender. Mix eggs and chicken broth. Stir in peanuts, the parsley, poultry seasoning, crumbled bacon, and the cooked vegetables. Add the bread cubes; toss lightly. Rinse turkey and pat dry with paper toweling. Spoon some of the bread mixture into neck cavity; pull neck skin to back of turkey. Secure with a skewer. Lightly spoon some of the bread mixture into the body cavity. Tie legs to tail. Twist wing tips under back. Place turkey, breast side up, on a rack in shallow roasting pan. Brush with oil. Insert a meat thermometer in the center of the inside thigh muscle. Roast, uncovered, in a 325° oven for 4 to 4½ hours or till meat thermometer registers 185°. When bird is two-thirds done, cut string between legs. Form the remaining bread mixture into balls, using ⅓ to ½ cup mixture for each. During the last 25 to 30 minutes of roasting, bake the stuffing balls with turkey. Makes 12 to 16 servings.

HARVEY WALLBANGER PIE

To be sure you have enough pie for 12, make two pies. See photo, pages 356-357—

½ cup sugar
1 envelope unflavored gelatin
¼ teaspoon salt
½ cup orange juice
3 slightly beaten egg yolks
¼ cup water
2 teaspoons lemon juice
¼ cup Galliano
2 tablespoons vodka
3 egg whites
¼ cup sugar
1 cup whipping cream
1 *baked* 9-inch Pastry Shell (see recipe, page 318)
Whipped cream (optional)
Mandarin orange sections, drained (optional)

In a medium saucepan combine the ½ cup sugar, gelatin, and salt. Stir in orange juice, egg yolks, water, and lemon juice; mix well. Cook and stir over medium heat till gelatin dissolves and mixture is slightly thickened. Remove from heat; stir in Galliano and vodka. Chill till consistency of unbeaten egg whites (partially set). Beat egg whites to soft peaks (tips curl over); gradually add the ¼ cup sugar and beat to stiff peaks (tips stand straight). Fold egg white mixture into partially set gelatin mixture. Beat the 1 cup whipping cream to soft peaks; fold into gelatin mixture. Chill till the mixture mounds. Turn into Pastry Shell; chill 4 to 5 hours or till firm. Garnish the top of the pie with whipped cream and orange sections if desired. Makes 8 servings.

BANANA-NUT CAKE

See photo, page 360—

1½ cups sugar
¾ cup shortening
2 eggs
¾ cup mashed ripe banana
1 teaspoon vanilla
1¾ cups all-purpose flour
1 teaspoon baking soda
1 teaspoon baking powder
⅔ cup buttermilk *or* sour milk
½ cup chopped walnuts
Nut Filling
White Frosting

Beat sugar and shortening at high speed with an electric mixer till fluffy. Add eggs; beat 2 minutes at medium speed. Add banana and vanilla; beat 2 minutes. Mix flour, soda, baking powder, and ½ teaspoon *salt*; add dry ingredients and the buttermilk alternately to the creamed mixture; beat well after each addition. Stir in nuts. Pour into two greased and floured 9x1½-inch round cake pans. Bake in a 375° oven about 25 minutes or till cake tests done. Cool 10 minutes; remove pans. Cool on racks. Fill with Nut Filling; frost with White Frosting. Trim with walnuts if desired. Makes 12 servings.

Nut Filling: In saucepan mix ½ cup packed *brown sugar* and 2 tablespoons all-purpose *flour;* stir in ½ cup *evaporated milk.* Add 2 tablespoons *butter;* cook and stir till thickened. Stir in ⅓ cup chopped *walnuts,* ½ teaspoon *vanilla,* and dash *salt.* Chill 1 to 2 hours.

White Frosting: In bowl beat together 1 *egg white,* ½ cup *shortening,* ¼ cup *butter,* and 1 teaspoon *vanilla.* Gradually beat in 2 cups sifted *powdered sugar* till fluffy.

CHRISTMAS

Stuffed Veal

Deep-Dish Chicken Pie
or
Tourtière

Carrot and Potato Pudding
or
Buttered Green Beans

Whoopie Pies

Banana-Nut Cake
or
Regal Plum Pudding
or
Scotch Black Bun
or
Holiday Rice Pudding

Chocolate Candies

Clockwise from front: Stuffed Veal (see recipe, page 362), Carrot and Potato Pudding, Whoopie Pies (see recipe, page 362), Banana-Nut Cake (see recipe, page 359), Deep-Dish Chicken Pie, and chocolate candies.

DEEP-DISH CHICKEN PIE

1 3½- to 4-pound broiler-fryer chicken, cut up
Buttermilk Pastry
2 tablespoons butter
1 cup chicken broth
4 teaspoons cornstarch

Place chicken in large kettle; add 8 cups *water*. Add 2 teaspoons *salt* and ¼ teaspoon *pepper*. Cover and bring to boiling. Reduce heat and simmer, covered, about 1 hour or till chicken is tender. Cool slightly. Remove skin and bones from chicken; discard. Cut meat into 1-inch chunks. On lightly floured surface roll *three-fourths* of the Buttermilk Pastry into an ⅛-inch-thick circle; line a 1½-quart casserole with pastry. Trim 1 inch beyond edge. Add *half* of the chicken. Roll remainder of pastry dough into a 12x10-inch rectangle; cut *half* of the dough into ten 12x½-inch strips. Place the strips over chicken in crust. Top with remaining chicken. Cut remaining dough into five 12x1-inch strips. Place over pie in a lattice design. Seal and flute edge. Dot pie with butter. In a saucepan combine the broth and the cornstarch; cook and stir till thickened. Place pie on oven rack. Pour hot mixture atop. Bake in a 325° oven about 1 hour or till golden. Let stand 10 minutes before serving. Serves 6.

Buttermilk Pastry: Cut ½ cup *shortening* into 2 cups *self-rising flour* till mixture resembles small peas. Stir in enough *buttermilk* (about ½ cup) to make a soft dough. Cover; let stand 1 hour.

CARROT AND POTATO PUDDING

8 carrots, peeled and sliced
2 medium potatoes, peeled and cubed
1 egg
2 tablespoons dairy sour cream (optional)
2 tablespoons finely shredded onion
½ teaspoon salt
¼ teaspoon pepper
2 ounces cheddar cheese, cut into small cubes (½ cup)
1 tablespoon butter *or* margarine
Orange slices, halved (optional)

In a large covered saucepan cook sliced carrots in boiling salted water for 10 minutes. Add cubed potatoes; cook 10 to 15 minutes longer. Drain vegetables; mash.

Stir in egg, sour cream if desired, shredded onion, salt, and pepper. Beat till well blended. Stir in cheddar cheese.

Spoon carrot and potato mixture into a 1½-quart casserole; bake in a 350° oven for 30 minutes. Dot top of mixture with butter or margarine; place under broiler 5 inches from heat about 3 minutes or till top is golden brown.

Let stand 5 minutes before serving. If desired, garnish casserole with halved orange slices. Makes 6 to 8 servings.

STUFFED VEAL

See photo, page 360—

1 3- to 4-pound veal breast,
  boned
  Ground Beef Stuffing
3 tablespoons cooking oil
¾ cup beef broth
1 tablespoon cornstarch
¼ cup dairy sour cream
½ of a 6-ounce can sliced
  mushrooms, drained

With the wide end of the breast facing you, cut a deep slit in the long side. Spoon Ground Beef Stuffing into pocket. Close meat with skewers; tie with string. In a large Dutch oven brown meat in hot oil; drain. Transfer to a roasting pan; cover and roast in a 325° oven for 2 to 2½ hours, basting occasionally with the pan drippings. Transfer meat to platter; remove skewers. Cover and keep warm. Strain drippings; return to pan. Combine broth and cornstarch. Stir into sour cream; add to pan along with mushrooms. Cook and stir till thickened; cook and stir 1 minute more. Untie; slice meat. Garnish with cooked broccoli if desired. Pass gravy. Makes 10 to 15 servings.

Ground Beef Stuffing: Cook 3 strips *bacon* till crisp; drain and crumble. Cook ½ pound *ground beef* and ½ cup chopped *onion* till browned; drain. Stir in bacon; 1 cup *soft bread crumbs;* ½ of a 6-ounce can *sliced mushrooms,* drained; ⅓ cup *dairy sour cream;* 1 beaten *egg;* ¼ cup snipped *parsley;* 1 teaspoon dried *dillweed;* ½ teaspoon *salt;* ½ teaspoon dried *tarragon,* crushed; ½ teaspoon dried *basil,* crushed; and dash *pepper.*

HOLIDAY RICE PUDDING

See photo, pages 22-23—

4 cups milk
¾ cup long-grain rice
¼ cup sugar
¼ cup dry sherry
1½ teaspoons vanilla
¼ teaspoon almond extract
½ cup whipping cream
1 whole blanched almond
1 10-ounce package frozen
  raspberries, thawed
1 tablespoon cornstarch
½ cup currant jelly

In a heavy 2-quart saucepan combine milk, uncooked rice, and sugar. Bring the mixture to boiling. Reduce heat; cook, covered, 25 to 30 minutes or till rice is tender, stirring occasionally. Stir in sherry, vanilla, and almond extract; cool to room temperature.

In mixer bowl whip cream with electric mixer to soft peaks (tips curl over). Fold into rice mixture along with the blanched almond. Cover and chill thoroughly.

For sauce, in saucepan crush the raspberries. Stir in cornstarch. Add currant jelly. Cook and stir till mixture is thickened and bubbly; cook 1 minute more. Sieve sauce; discard seeds. Cover the surface with waxed paper; cool to room temperature.

To serve, spoon rice pudding into sherbet dishes. Drizzle some of the raspberry sauce over each serving. Makes 6 to 8 servings.

WHOOPIE PIES

See photo, page 360—

1 cup sugar
½ cup shortening
1 egg
1 egg yolk
2 cups all-purpose flour
⅔ cup unsweetened cocoa
  powder
¼ teaspoon salt
1 teaspoon baking soda
½ cup hot water
⅔ cup buttermilk
2 cups sifted powdered sugar
1 egg white
1 teaspoon vanilla
½ cup shortening
¼ cup butter *or* margarine,
  softened

In a mixer bowl beat together sugar and ½ cup shortening at high speed with an electric mixer till fluffy. Add the egg and egg yolk. Stir together the flour, cocoa powder, and salt; set aside. Dissolve baking soda in hot water; cool slightly. Add the flour mixture, the soda mixture, and the buttermilk alternately to the creamed mixture. Beat till well mixed. Drop batter by rounded tablespoonfuls 2 inches apart onto ungreased cookie sheets. Bake in a 350° oven for 8 to 10 minutes. Cool cookies on racks.

To make filling, in mixer bowl combine the powdered sugar, egg white, and vanilla. Beating with electric mixer at low speed, gradually add ½ cup shortening and the butter or margarine. Beat at high speed till fluffy. Spread some filling on the flat side of *half* of the cookies; top with remaining cookies, flat side down. Store in refrigerator. Makes 24.

SCOTCH BLACK BUN

See photo, pages 22-23—

- 1½ cups raisins
- 1½ cups currants
- ½ cup chopped mixed candied fruits and peels
  Double-Crust Pastry (see recipe, page 318)
- 1½ cups all-purpose flour
- ½ cup packed brown sugar
- 1 teaspoon baking soda
- 1 teaspoon cream of tartar
- 1 teaspoon ground cinnamon
- 1 teaspoon ground ginger
- ⅔ cup milk
- ½ cup Scotch whisky
- 1 slightly beaten egg
- 2 tablespoons butter, melted
  Milk

In a bowl mix raisins, currants, and fruits and peels; cover with *boiling water.* Let stand for 10 minutes. Drain. On floured surface roll *two-thirds* of the Double-Crust Pastry into a 12-inch circle. Line an 8x1½-inch round cake pan with pastry, adjusting fullness at sides. Combine flour, brown sugar, soda, cream of tartar, and spices; stir in the ⅔ cup milk, whisky, egg, and the butter till smooth. Fold in fruit mixture; spoon into crust. Fold edges of crust over filling. Roll remaining pastry into 9-inch circle. Place over filling. Turn the edges under and crimp. Prick top crust with fork; brush with milk. If desired, cut decorative pieces from the pastry trimmings. Place atop crust; brush with milk. Bake in a 300° oven about 1¾ hours. Cool completely; carefully remove from pan. Wrap; refrigerate for at least 1 week before serving. Serves 12 to 16.

REGAL PLUM PUDDING

See photo, pages 22-23—

- 4 slices white bread, torn
- 1 cup milk
- 1 cup packed brown sugar
- 6 ounces finely chopped beef suet
- 2 slightly beaten eggs
- ¼ cup orange juice
- 1 teaspoon vanilla
- 1 cup all-purpose flour
- 2 teaspoons ground cinnamon
- 1 teaspoon baking soda
- 1 teaspoon ground cloves
- 1 teaspoon ground mace
- ½ teaspoon salt
- 2 cups raisins
- 1 cup pitted dates, cut up
- ½ cup chopped mixed candied fruits and peels
- ½ cup broken pecans
  Fluffy Hard Sauce

Soak bread in milk; beat till combined. Stir in brown sugar, suet, eggs, orange juice, and vanilla. Stir together the flour, cinnamon, baking soda, cloves, mace, and salt; mix in raisins, dates, mixed fruits and peels, and nuts. Stir in bread mixture. Pour into a well-greased 2-quart mold. Cover with foil; tie with string. Place on rack in deep kettle; add *boiling water* to kettle to a depth of 1 inch. Cover; steam 3½ hours, adding more water if needed. Cool 10 minutes; unmold. Serve warm with the Fluffy Hard Sauce. Makes 12 servings.

Fluffy Hard Sauce: Cream together ½ cup softened *butter or margarine* with 2 cups sifted *powdered sugar.* Stir in 1 beaten *egg yolk* and 1 teaspoon *vanilla.* Fold in 1 stiff-beaten *egg white.* Chill.

TOURTIÈRE

See photo, pages 20-21—

- 2 large potatoes, peeled
- 1 pound ground pork
- ½ cup beef broth
- ½ cup finely chopped onion
- 1 clove garlic, minced
- 1 bay leaf
- ¼ teaspoon ground ginger
- ⅛ teaspoon ground cloves
  Tourtière Pastry

Cut up potatoes; cook in boiling salted water for 20 minutes. Drain; mash. In a Dutch oven brown pork; drain. Stir in broth, chopped onion, garlic, bay leaf, ginger, cloves, ½ teaspoon *salt,* and ¼ teaspoon *pepper.* Cover and simmer about 20 minutes, stirring often. Remove bay leaf. Mix in mashed potatoes; cool.

On floured surface roll *half* of the Tourtière Pastry into a 12-inch circle; line a 9-inch pie plate. Trim pastry to edge of plate. Fill with meat mixture. Roll out remaining pastry for top crust; cut slits for escape of steam. Place atop filling. Seal and flute edge. Bake in a 400° oven about 30 minutes. Cool 20 minutes before serving. Makes 6 servings.

Tourtière Pastry: Stir together 2 cups all-purpose *flour,* 2 teaspoons *baking powder*, and ½ teaspoon *salt.* Cut in ⅔ cup *shortening* till pieces are size of small peas. Mix 1 beaten *egg,* ¼ cup *cold water,* 1 teaspoon *lemon juice,* and ½ teaspoon dried *thyme,* crushed. Sprinkle *1 tablespoon* egg mixture over flour mixture; toss with fork. Push to side of bowl. Repeat till all is moistened. Form dough into two balls.

FOURTH OF JULY

Lemon Pepper Pinwheels

*Tossed Salad with
Coriander Dressing
or
Lemon-Frosted Plum Squares
or
Macaroni Salad*

Parmesan Beans

*Banana Split Dessert
or
Sunflower-Apricot Cookies*

PARMESAN BEANS

¼ cup salad oil
¼ cup tarragon vinegar
⅓ cup grated Parmesan cheese
½ teaspoon sugar
½ teaspoon salt
2 10-ounce packages frozen
     French-style green beans,
     cooked and drained

In a screw-top jar combine salad oil, vinegar, Parmesan cheese, sugar, and salt; cover and shake. Pour vinegar mixture over beans and toss. Cover; chill overnight, stirring occasionally. Serves 8.

TOSSED SALAD WITH CORIANDER DRESSING

½ cup olive oil *or* salad oil
½ cup red wine vinegar
1 cup chopped fresh coriander
     or ¼ teaspoon dried
     coriander, crushed
1 shallot, quartered
1 lemon slice, quartered
1 clove garlic, quartered
2 to 3 teaspoons sugar
1 teaspoon capers, drained
6 cups assorted torn greens
6 sorrel leaves, chopped
     (optional)
8 to 10 fresh asparagus spears,
     cut up, *or* one 10-ounce
     package frozen cut
     asparagus, thawed
10 cherry tomatoes, halved
3 shallots, chopped (¼ cup)
1 sweet red *or* green pepper,
     chopped (½ cup)
     Sliced radishes
     Few sprigs fresh coriander,
     chopped (optional)

For dressing, in a blender container or a food processor bowl combine olive oil or salad oil, vinegar, the 1 cup of chopped coriander or the dried coriander, the quartered shallot, lemon slice, garlic, sugar, and capers. Cover and blend or process till smooth. Add more sugar if desired. Cover and chill.

In a large serving bowl toss together the assorted torn greens, chopped sorrel if desired, asparagus, tomato halves, chopped shallots, chopped red or green pepper, radish slices, and the remaining chopped coriander if desired. Pass the dressing with salad. Makes 8 to 10 servings.

LEMON PEPPER PINWHEELS

2 beef flank steaks (1 pound
     each)
½ cup burgundy
¼ cup cooking oil
¼ cup soy sauce
1 tablespoon lemon pepper
1 tablespoon Worcestershire
     sauce
     Few drops bottled hot pepper
     sauce
8 cherry tomatoes *or*
     mushroom caps

Pound each flank steak into a 10x8-inch rectangle. Cut each of the rectangles into four 10x2-inch strips.

In a bowl combine the burgundy, cooking oil, soy sauce, lemon pepper, Worcestershire sauce, and bottled hot pepper sauce. Place the meat strips in a plastic bag; set in a deep bowl. Pour wine mixture over meat; close bag. Marinate 4 to 6 hours or overnight in refrigerator, turning twice.

Drain meat; reserve marinade. Loosely roll each strip around a cherry tomato or mushroom cap, starting with short side. Secure with wooden picks.

Grill the meat pinwheels over *medium* coals for 15 minutes. Turn pinwheels and grill to desired doneness. (Allow 10 minutes more for rare.) Baste with marinade often during the last 10 minutes of grilling. Remove wooden picks before serving. Makes 8 servings.

LEMON-FROSTED PLUM SQUARES

1 6-ounce package strawberry-flavored gelatin
Dash salt
2½ cups boiling water
1 cup lemon-lime carbonated beverage
2 tablespoons lemon juice
9 fresh plums, pitted and cut into wedges (2 cups)
1 4-serving-size package *instant* lemon pudding mix
1¼ cups cold milk
½ cup dairy sour cream
Leaf lettuce
Apple slices (optional)

In a bowl dissolve the strawberry-flavored gelatin and salt in boiling water. Cool to room temperature. Slowly pour in lemon-lime carbonated beverage and lemon juice; stir gently. Chill gelatin mixture till the consistency of unbeaten egg white (partially set).

Fold in fresh plums. Pour into an 8x8x2-inch pan. Chill till mixture is *almost* firm.

In a mixer bowl combine instant lemon pudding mix and milk; beat with electric mixer till smooth. Stir in dairy sour cream. Spread the pudding mixture atop gelatin. Chill till firm.

To serve, cut into squares and place on lettuce-lined salad plates. Garnish each gelatin square with a few apple slices if desired. Makes 8 or 9 servings.

MACARONI SALAD

8 ounces rotelle *or* ziti macaroni
¼ cup milk
1 teaspoon instant beef bouillon granules
1 tablespoon hot water
¾ cup mayonnaise *or* salad dressing
¼ cup dairy sour cream
¾ teaspoon salt
Several dashes freshly ground pepper
2 small tomatoes, seeded and chopped
⅓ cup finely chopped red onion
1 small green pepper, chopped
3 tablespoons chopped sweet pickle
1 to 2 large shallots, chopped
1 teaspoon dried dillweed

Cook rotelle or ziti in boiling salted water till tender; drain. If using ziti, cut up slightly. Toss with milk; cover and chill.

Dissolve beef bouillon granules in hot water. In a bowl stir together mayonnaise or salad dressing, dairy sour cream, salt, pepper, and the broth mixture. Stir into rotelle or ziti.

Fold chopped tomato, red onion, green pepper, chopped pickle, shallots, and dillweed into macaroni mixture. Turn into a large bowl. Chill until serving time. Makes 8 servings.

BANANA SPLIT DESSERT

½ cup butter *or* margarine, melted
2 cups crushed graham crackers (28 square crackers)
2 eggs
2 cups sifted powdered sugar
¾ cup butter *or* margarine, softened
1 teaspoon vanilla
1 20-ounce can crushed pineapple, well drained
4 medium bananas, sliced (about 3 cups)
1 9-ounce carton frozen whipped dessert topping, thawed
½ cup coarsely chopped pecans
1 4-ounce jar maraschino cherries, drained (⅓ cup)

In a mixing bowl combine the ½ cup melted butter or margarine and the crushed graham crackers. Pat into bottom of a 13x9x2-inch pan. Set aside.

In a large mixer bowl beat eggs at high speed with an electric mixer about 4 minutes or till light and lemon-colored. Add the sifted powdered sugar, ¾ cup softened butter or margarine, and vanilla. Beat 5 minutes more. Spread over crumb layer in pan. Chill 30 minutes.

Spread drained crushed pineapple over egg mixture. Arrange bananas over pineapple. Cover with whipped topping. Sprinkle with pecans. Cover; refrigerate 6 hours or overnight.

Before serving dessert, garnish with the drained maraschino cherries. Makes 12 servings.

FAMILY REUNION

Egg Basket Appetizers

Carrot-Potato Salad

Chicken Rolls

Coleslaw Salad Bowl

Spicy Bacon Bean Pot

Frozen Yogurt Sandwiches

Lemonade Watermelon Punch
or
Wine-Watermelon Punch

EGG BASKET APPETIZERS

20 hard-cooked eggs
 1 cup mayonnaise *or* salad
     dressing
 ½ cup finely shredded Swiss
     cheese (2 ounces)
 2 teaspoons lemon juice
 ½ teaspoon salt
 ½ teaspoon ground cumin
 ¼ teaspoon pepper

Shell eggs; cut in half. Remove yolk portion; set whites aside.

Mash egg yolks well in medium bowl. Beat in mayonnaise or salad dressing, cheese, lemon juice, salt, cumin, and pepper till fluffy.

Pile the yolk mixture back into whites, mounding the tops. Cover and chill. Just before serving, garnish each egg with strips of pimiento or a few pieces of green onion if desired. Makes 40.

CHICKEN ROLLS

 1 cup fine dry bread crumbs
 1 cup finely chopped dried
     apricots
 1 cup finely chopped walnuts
 1 cup light raisins
 2 tablespoons chopped onion
 1 teaspoon ground allspice
 1 teaspoon dried thyme,
     crushed
 ¾ to 1 cup chicken broth
 3 cups whole bran cereal,
     crushed
 ⅔ cup sunflower nuts, chopped
 ½ cup butter, melted
 3 tablespoons lemon juice
10 large chicken breasts, boned
     and halved lengthwise

In a bowl combine bread crumbs, apricots, walnuts, raisins, onion, allspice, and *half* of the thyme. Add enough of the chicken broth to moisten as desired. Set aside.

In a small bowl combine the cereal, sunflower nuts, and the remaining thyme. Set aside.

Combine butter, lemon juice, and ½ teaspoon *salt.* Place the chicken breasts, skin side down, between two pieces of clear plastic wrap. Pound chicken to ¼-inch thickness. Cover; chill.

Abour 1¼ hours before serving, place the chicken pieces, skin side down, on counter; sprinkle with salt. Place about ¼ *cup* of the apricot mixture on each breast; fold in the sides of meat and roll up from the short end. Secure with wooden picks. Brush each bundle with butter mixture; then roll in cereal mixture. Place the bundles, seam side down, in two 13x9x2-inch baking pans. Bake in a 375° oven 40 to 50 minutes. Serves 20.

COLESLAW SALAD BOWL

 ¾ cup red wine vinegar
 ½ cup salad oil
 ⅓ cup sugar
 2 teaspoons salt
 ½ teaspoon pepper
 2 14-ounce jars spiced apple
     rings, drained
 ½ large head red cabbage,
     shredded (8 cups)
 ½ large head green cabbage,
     shredded (6 cups)
 4 ounces fresh spinach, torn
     (4 cups)
 2 cups fresh mushrooms,
     sliced
   Red cabbage leaves

In a screw-top jar combine red wine vinegar, oil, sugar, salt, and pepper. Cover and shake; chill.

Reserve a few whole apple rings for garnish; quarter the remaining rings. In a bowl toss the shredded red and green cabbage, spinach, mushrooms, and quartered apple rings. Shake dressing; pour over the salad and toss to coat. Place in bowl lined with red cabbage leaves. Cover; chill several hours.

To serve, trim with reserved apple rings. Makes 20 servings.

Clockwise from front: Chicken Rolls, Frozen Yogurt Sandwiches (see recipe, page 368), Spicy Bacon Bean Pot (see recipe, page 368), Carrot-Potato Salad (see recipe, page 368), Coleslaw Salad Bowl, Lemonade-Watermelon Punch (see recipe, page 369) and Egg Basket Appetizers.

CARROT-POTATO SALAD

See photo, page 366—

1 cup mayonnaise *or* salad dressing
1 8-ounce carton dairy sour cream
3 tablespoons lemon juice
2 tablespoons snipped chives
1 tablespoon Worcestershire sauce
1 teaspoon salt
½ teaspoon dried dillweed
½ teaspoon dry mustard
⅛ teaspoon pepper
4 medium carrots, thinly bias-sliced (2 cups)
8 medium potatoes, cooked, peeled, and sliced (7 cups)
1 cup thinly bias-sliced celery
½ cup pitted ripe olives, sliced
    Leaf lettuce
    Carrot curls (optional)
    Pitted ripe olives (optional)

In a bowl mix mayonnaise *or* salad dressing, sour cream, lemon juice, chives, Worcestershire sauce, salt, dillweed, mustard, and pepper till well combined.

In a small saucepan heat a small amount of water to boiling; add sliced carrots and simmer, uncovered, for 2 minutes. Drain; rinse with cold water and drain again.

In a large bowl gently toss together the potatoes, celery, ½ cup olives, and carrots. Add sour cream mixture; gently toss to coat well. Place in lettuce-lined bowl. Cover and chill several hours.

To serve, garnish with carrot curls and pitted ripe olives if desired. Makes 20 servings.

SPICY BACON BEAN POT

See photo, page 366—

3 16-ounce cans baked beans in tomato sauce
2 15-ounce cans red kidney beans, drained
2 12-ounce cans whole kernel corn, drained
10 slices bacon, crisp-cooked, drained, and crumbled
1 cup chopped onion
1 cup chopped sweet red *or* green pepper
¼ cup smoke-flavored barbecue sauce
2 teaspoons chili powder
¼ teaspoon garlic powder
½ cup shredded sharp cheddar cheese (2 ounces)
    Sweet red or green pepper rings (optional)

In a large Dutch oven combine baked beans, kidney beans, corn, bacon, onion, 1 cup red or green pepper, barbecue sauce, chili powder, and garlic powder; stir to combine. Cover and cook over medium heat about 35 minutes, stirring occasionally. Just before serving, top with cheese and pepper rings if desired. Serves 20.

Crockery cooker method: In a 3½- to 4-quart electric slow crockery cooker place baked beans, kidney beans, corn, bacon, onion, 1 cup red or green pepper, barbecue sauce, chili powder, and garlic powder; stir to combine. Cover and cook on high-heat setting for 3½ to 4 hours, stirring once or twice. To serve, sprinkle with the cheese; garnish with pepper rings if desired.

FROZEN YOGURT SANDWICHES

See photo, page 366—

1 cup chocolate-flavored syrup
2 envelopes unflavored gelatin
1 7-ounce jar marshmallow creme
1 tablespoon vanilla
¼ teaspoon salt
2 8-ounce cartons plain yogurt
1 cup milk
48 large purchased cookies such as oatmeal-raisin *or* sugar

In a medium saucepan place chocolate-flavored syrup; sprinkle unflavored gelatin over syrup. Cook and stir constantly over low heat about 5 minutes or till gelatin is dissolved.

Thoroughly blend in the marshmallow creme; remove from heat. Cool slightly.

Stir in vanilla and salt. Stir in yogurt and milk till well combined. Chill thoroughly.

Turn yogurt mixture into a 2- to 4-quart ice cream freezer; freeze according to manufacturer's directions. Turn frozen yogurt into a 13x9x2-inch baking pan; freeze till mixture is firm.

To serve, cut frozen yogurt into squares slightly smaller than the cookies. Place each yogurt square between 2 cookies. Serve immediately or freeze. Makes about 1½ quarts frozen yogurt (enough for 24 sandwiches).

WINE-WATERMELON PUNCH

1 large watermelon (about 25 pounds)
2 750-milliliter bottles dry white wine
¾ cup kirsch *or* other cherry liqueur
  12- to 14-inch straws (optional)

Select a melon about 20 inches long with a flat base. The day before serving, cut an 8-inch oval section, making a sawtooth edge, out of the top of the melon. Remove cut portion and reserve.

Using long-handled spoon, scoop out pulp; remove seeds. Place *one-fourth* of the pulp at a time in blender container or food processor bowl; cover and blend or process till pureed. (Should have 12 cups puree.)

Place melon shell on tray. Return melon puree to melon shell; stir in the wine and kirsch. Replace cut portion of melon; refrigerate overnight.

To serve, remove cut portion of melon and ladle punch into cups. (*Or*, remove cut portion of melon; use a skewer to make ¼-inch holes for straws around the top half of the melon at just above the liquid level. Replace cut portion of melon. Insert straws; allow guests to help themselves.) Makes 20 (8-ounce) servings.

LEMONADE-WATERMELON PUNCH

See photo, page 366—

1 large watermelon (about 25 pounds)
2 cups water
1 12-ounce can frozen lemonade concentrate, thawed
¼ cup grenadine syrup
1 to 2 32-ounce bottles lemon-lime carbonated beverage, chilled
  12- to 14-inch straws (optional)

Select a melon about 20 inches long with a flat base. The day before serving, cut an 8-inch oval section, making a sawtooth edge, out of the top of the melon. Remove cut portion and reserve.

Using long-handled spoon, scoop out pulp; remove seeds. Place *one-fourth* of the pulp at a time in blender container or food processor bowl. Cover; blend or process till pureed. (Should have 12 cups.)

Place melon shell on tray. Return puree to melon shell; stir in water, lemonade concentrate, and grenadine. Replace cut portion of melon; refrigerate overnight.

Before serving, remove cut portion of melon; pour in lemon-lime beverage to fill three-fourths full. Stir with an up-and-down motion. Ladle punch into cups. (*Or*, use a skewer to make ¼-inch holes for straws around top half of melon at just above liquid level. Replace cut portion of melon. Insert straws; allow the guests to help themselves.) Makes 20 (8-ounce) servings.

SUNFLOWER-APRICOT COOKIES

See photo, page 180 and menu, page 364—

¾ cup whole wheat flour
¼ cup wheat germ
¼ cup nonfat dry milk powder
¾ teaspoon salt
¼ teaspoon baking powder
¼ teaspoon baking soda
¾ cup honey
½ cup butter *or* margarine
½ cup peanut butter
1 egg
1 teaspoon vanilla
1 cup raisins
1 cup dried apricots, snipped (5 ounces)
¾ cup quick-cooking rolled oats
½ cup chopped walnuts
⅓ cup unsalted sunflower nuts
⅓ cup shredded coconut

In a bowl stir together the whole wheat flour, wheat germ, milk powder, salt, baking powder, and baking soda. In large mixer bowl beat together honey, butter or margarine, and peanut butter. Add egg and vanilla; beat well. Add flour mixture, mixing well.

In bowl stir together raisins, apricots, rolled oats, walnuts, sunflower nuts, and coconut; add to honey mixture. Mix well.

Drop by rounded teaspoonfuls onto ungreased cookie sheet. Bake in a 350° oven 10 to 11 minutes. Let cool on cookie sheet 1 minute; remove to wire rack to cool completely. Makes 4½ to 5 dozen.

ENLARGING, REDUCING, AND TRANSFERRING DESIGNS

Here and on the following pages is a glossary of basic information to help you complete the projects in this book. You will find instructions for enlarging the scaled-down patterns in the book and transferring the designs to fabric; knitting and crochet abbreviations; and stitch diagrams for knitting, crocheting, embroidery, and needlepoint.

The first step toward the successful completion of a craft project is often the accurate enlargement (or reduction) of a pattern. Changing the size of a needlecraft pattern is easy when you use a grid.

Once you have mastered the grid technique, the design possibilities are endless. Besides enlarging scaled-down designs from crafts books and magazines, you can transfer designs from postcards, art books, posters, and many other sources and scale them up or down by using a grid. Here are tips for enlarging, reducing, and transferring designs with or without a grid.

Enlarging or Reducing Designs

Patterns with grids

Most of the patterns in this book appear on grids—small squares laid over the design. You can enlarge the patterns by drawing a grid of your own, using the scale indicated on the pattern. For example, if the scale is "one square equals 1 inch," draw a series of 1-inch squares on your paper.

Choose paper that can accommodate your finished pattern. Or, tape small pieces of paper together to get a piece large enough for the full-size pattern.

To avoid drawing a grid line by line, buy a supply of graph paper at an office supply or art store. It is available in sizes ranging from 1 square to 14 squares per inch. Mark off the paper in squares that correspond to the scale for your project.

Large graph paper is sold by the yard at many art stores and engineering supply companies. Some fabric shops carry pattern-enlarging tissue that has small dots at 1-inch intervals.

To form a working grid, first count the number of horizontal and vertical rows of squares on the original pattern. With a ruler, mark the same number of horizontal and vertical rows of squares on your graph paper. Number horizontal and vertical rows of squares in the margin of the original pattern. Then transfer these numbers to corresponding rows that appear on your paper.

Find a square on your grid that corresponds to a square on the original. Working one square at a time, mark your grid with a dot wherever a design line intersects a grid line.

After you mark several squares this way, connect the dots by lightly sketching in the contours of the original design. Always do this in pencil so you can erase errors.

Patterns without grids

If a pattern has no grid, it can be enlarged if you know the desired length of the enlarged pattern. First, draw a box around the original design. Then draw a diagonal line connecting two of the corners in the box.

On separate paper, draw a right angle, extending the bottom line to the desired length of the enlarged pattern. Lay the original in the corner. Using a ruler, extend the diagonal line drawn on the original. Then draw a perpendicular line between the diagonal and the end of the bottom line (see below).

Divide the original and new pattern into quarters; draw another diagonal

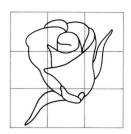

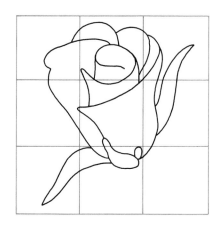

The original design

The enlarged design

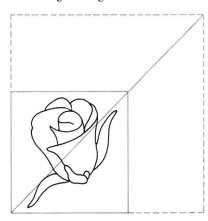

Enlarging without a grid

370

between the corners. Number the sections and transfer the design as explained above (see diagrams, right).

Another method for adapting a design without a grid is to sketch over the original on tracing paper and then pencil in a border and grid lines. On a sheet of paper with the same dimensions as you want the finished design to be, mark a series of 1- or 2-inch squares. Then follow the instructions for enlarging patterns with grids. Try to keep the design simple and uncluttered.

Designs also may be enlarged photographically at blueprint companies or photoengraving services.

Transferring Designs

Dressmaker's carbon paper

Use dressmaker's carbon in a color close to the color of the fabric (avoid extreme contrasts). Place it facedown between fabric and pattern. Trace the pattern with a tracing wheel or pencil.

Hot transfer pencil

This is used to trace pattern outlines onto paper. Then lay the paper facedown on fabric and press with a hot iron to transfer the pattern. Before you begin, make a test on scrap fabric to

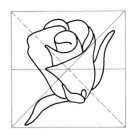

The original design

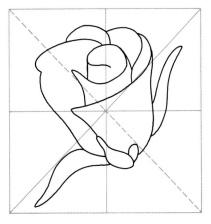

The enlarged design

make sure the transferred lines will fade when the article is washed or dry-cleaned. Vary the pressure on the pencil and the sharpness of its point until you mark a design line that is dark enough to see, but faint enough not to show on the completed project.

Blue lead pencil

Use this on light-colored, lightweight fabrics. Tape the pattern to a window, then tape the fabric over it (centering the design beneath the fabric). Trace the pattern with the pencil, making dotted lines.

Water erasable pen

This is a blue marker designed for crafts projects. Lightly draw or trace directly onto fabric. Work the design, then dampen the fabric, and blue lines will disappear. Look for this pen in needlework, fabric, and quilting shops.

Basting

For transferring design lines to dark, soft, highly textured, stretchy, or sheer fabrics, draw the pattern on tissue paper and pin it to fabric. Hand- or machine-baste around design lines. Tear away the tissue paper, proceed with the project, and remove the stitches.

Knitting and Crocheting Abbreviations

Abbreviations given here are for the knitted and crocheted projects shown in this book. For the stitch diagrams, please turn the page.

Knitting Abbreviations

beg	begin(ning)
dec	decrease
dp	double pointed
inc	increase
k	knit
MC	main color
p	purl
pat	pattern
psso	pass slip st over
rem	remaining
rep, rpt	repeat
rnd	round
sk	skip
sl st	slip stitch
sp	space
st(s)	stitch(es)
st st	stockinette stitch
tog	together
yo	yarn over
*	repeat from * as indicated

Crocheting Abbreviations

beg	begin(ning)
ch	chain
dc	double crochet
dec	decrease
dtr	double treble
hdc	half double crochet
inc	increase
lp(s)	loop(s)
pat	pattern
rnd	round
sc	single crochet
sl st	slip stitch
sp	space
st(s)	stitch(es)
tog	together
yo	yarn over

371

BASIC KNITTING STITCHES

Casting on

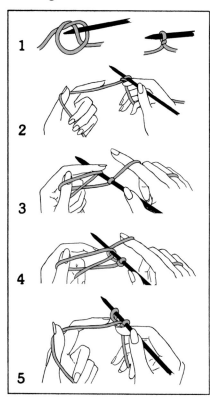

Make a slipknot around the needle at a distance from the yarn end that equals 1 inch for each stitch to be cast on (1). Hold the needle with the slipknot in your right hand; make a loop of the short length of yarn around your left thumb (2). Insert the point of the needle in your right hand under the loop on your left thumb (3). Loop yarn from the ball over the fingers of your right hand (4). Wind yarn from ball under and over the needle; draw it through the loop, leaving the stitch on the needle (5). Tighten stitches on the needle; bring the yarn end around your thumb. Repeat steps (2) through (5) for the desired number of stitches. Switch hands so stitches are on your left.

Knitting

Knitting (continued)

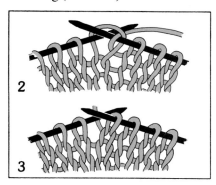

Hold the needle with the stitches on it in your left hand and the other needle in your right hand. Insert the right needle through the stitch on the left needle from the front to the back. Pass the yarn around the point of the right needle to form a loop (1, below left).

Pull this loop through the center of the stitch on the left needle; draw the loop onto the right needle (2, above).

Now, slip the stitch completely off the left needle (3).

Repeat these three steps until you have transferred all the stitches from the left needle to the right needle. This completes one row. When working the next row, move the needle holding the stitches to the left hand, and the other needle to the right hand.

Purling

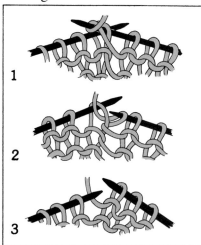

Hold the needle with the stitches in your left hand and the other needle in your right hand. Insert the right needle

through the stitch on the left needle from the back to the front. Wind the yarn around the point of the right needle to form a loop (1, below center). Draw a loop through the stitch on the needle in your left hand and transfer it to the needle in your right hand (2). Slip the stitch completely off the left needle (3). Repeat these steps until all loops are transferred to right needle.

Increasing & decreasing

In order to increase a stitch, knit or purl as usual, but do not slip the stitch off the left needle. Instead, insert the right needle into the back of the stitch and knit or purl into the stitch again as shown. Slip both onto the right needle, making two stitches.

To decrease, knit or purl two stitches together at the same time.

To slip a stitch, insert the right needle into the stitch on the left needle from the back, as if to purl (unless directions say as if to knit). Then slip the stitch onto the right needle without working or twisting it.

Binding off

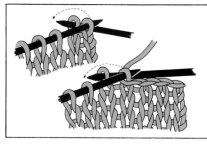

Work two stitches in pattern loosely. With left needle, lift first stitch over second stitch and off right needle. This binds off one stitch. Repeat this procedure for required number of stitches.

To bind off a row, continue until one stitch remains; break yarn and draw the end through the last stitch.

BASIC CROCHET STITCHES

Chain stitch

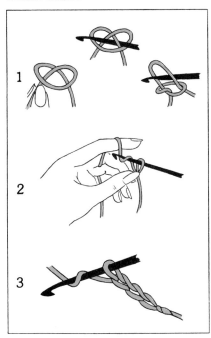

Make a slipknot on the crochet hook about 6 inches from end of yarn (1). Pull one end of yarn to tighten knot. Hold hook between right index finger and thumb, as you would a pencil. Wrap yarn over ring finger, under middle finger, and over index finger, holding short end between thumb and index finger. For more tension, wrap yarn around little finger. Insert hook under and over strand of yarn (2).

Make the foundation chain by catching the strand of yarn with the hook and drawing it through the loop (3). Make chain as long as pattern calls for.

Single crochet

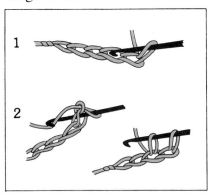

Single crochet (continued)

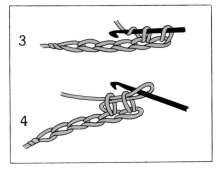

Insert hook into second chain from hook under two upper strands of yarn (l, below left). Draw up a loop (2). Draw yarn over hook (3). Pull yarn through two loops, completing a single crochet stitch (4). Insert hook into next stitch and repeat these four steps.

Half-double crochet

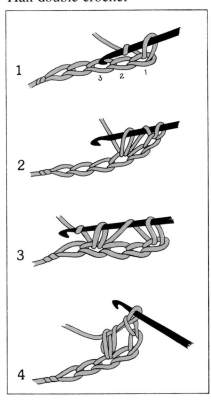

With yarn over hook, insert the hook into the third chain, under the two upper strands of yarn (1). Draw up a loop (2). Draw yarn over hook (3). Pull through three loops, completing half-double crochet (4).

Double crochet

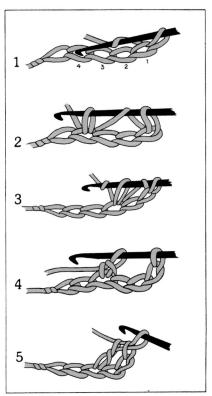

Holding yarn over hook, insert hook into fourth chain under two upper strands of yarn (1, above). Draw up a loop (2). Wrap yarn over hook (3). Draw yarn through two loops as shown (4). Yarn over again and draw through the last two loops on the hook (5) to complete the stitch.

Slip stitch

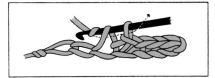

After you have made the foundation chain, insert crochet hook under top strand of second chain from hook; yarn over. With a single motion, pull yarn through stitch and loop on hook. Insert hook under top strand of next chain, then yarn over and draw yarn through stitch and loop on the hook. Repeat this procedure to end of chain. Use this stitch for decreasing.

GLOSSARY

BASIC EMBROIDERY STITCHES

Backstitch

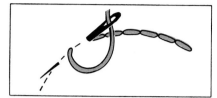

Buttonhole Stitch

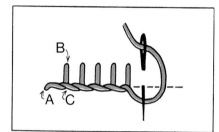

Chain Stitch

Couching Stitch

Laid Work

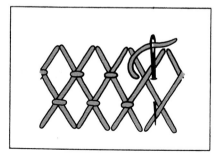

Feather Stitch

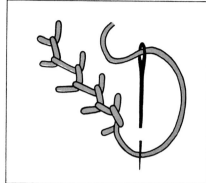

French Knot

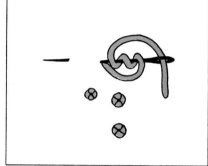

Outline (or Stem) Stitch

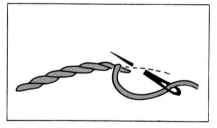

Long-and-Short Stitch

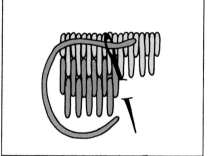

Running Stitch

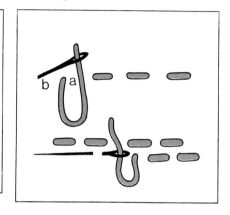

Satin Stitch

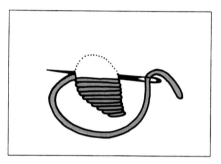

Seed Stitch

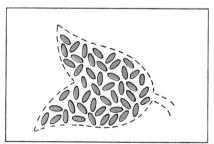

Straight Stitch

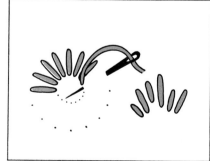

374

BASIC NEEDLEPOINT STITCHES

Bargello Stitch

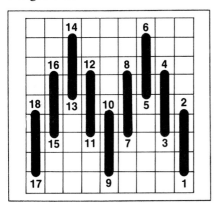

Basket-Weave Stitch

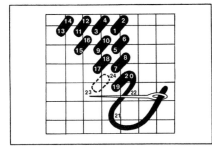

Continental Stitch

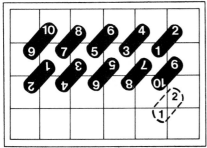

Cross-Stitch

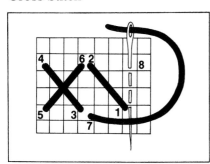

Diamond Eyelet Stitch

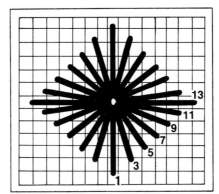

Mosaic Stitch

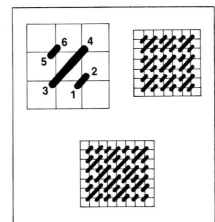

Smyrna Stitch

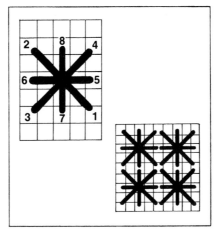

Slanting Gobelin Stitch

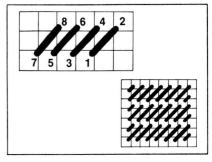

Straight Gobelin Stitch

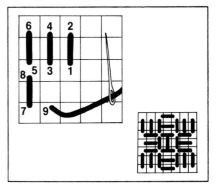

Upright Cross-Stitch

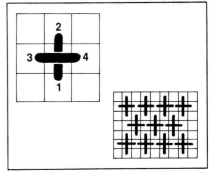

Waste Knot

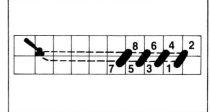

Design and Photography Credits

We are happy to acknowledge our indebtedness and extend our sincere thanks to all of the talented people who contributed craft designs and projects to this book.

David Ashe—furniture, 66-67; doll furniture, 228-229; barn puzzle, 246; duck decoys, plates, fish decoys, wooden shoes, 339.

Becky Baker—dishware, 28.

Margot Carter Blair—block print labels, 349.

Curt Boehringer—wall hangings, 346-347.

Gary Boling—needlepoint pillow, 6; granny square afghan, 196; afghans, 200-201; tabard, 222.

Charles Briarly—quilt, 89.

Judy Brown—country doll pincushions, 324.

Joan Cravens—patchwork stocking, 322; quilt pattern cards, 324; pine tree tablecloth, 325.

Phyllis Dunstan—bed coverlet, 27; table linens, 29; tea cozy, 56; spoon doll ornaments, 323.

Elizabeth Eakins—braided rug, 176.

Pat Gardner—dishware, 7.

Borghild Gillam—potpourri, 259.

Kay Gleason—dishware, 7.

Sara Gutierrez—cross-stitch sampler, 67; greeting cards, 348.

Laura Holtorf—embroidered tablecloth, 7; cross-stitch and needlepoint projects, 128-132; darning sampler, 159; table runner, 340.

Bernie Hopkins—duck decoys, 82.

Zuelia Ann Hurt—embroidered alphabet designs, 112-113.

Rebecca Jerdee—country curtains, 42; Amish quilt, 107; Amish star quilt, 108; Noah's ark, 247.

Tom Kamifugi—embroidered alphabet designs, 112-113.

We extend our thanks also to the following photographers whose creative talents and technical skills contributed much to this book.

Ross Chapple—82-83, 196-198, 210-211.

George de Gennaro—212-213.

Mike Dieter—8-9, 12-15, 28-29, 38-39, 42-43, 52-53, 55-56, 58-59, 66-68, 86-89, 92-93, 106-108, 201, 130-131, 133, 140-143, 148-149, 158-159, 162-163, 201, 246.

Harry Hartman—22-25, 27, 112-113.

Hedrich-Blessing—10-11, 57, 78, 117-119, 130, 176, 223, 247.

Tom Hooper—26, 40-41, 84-85, 90-91, 100-101, 108-109, 207-208.

RECIPE INDEX

A-B

C-E

379

CRAFT INDEX

Page numbers in heavy type refer to pictures with accompanying text. The remaining numbers refer to how-to instructions.

384